Association Brooklyn Ethical

Evolution in Science, Philosophy, And Art

Popular Lectures and Discussions Before the Brooklyn Ethical Association

Association Brooklyn Ethical

Evolution in Science, Philosophy, And Art
Popular Lectures and Discussions Before the Brooklyn Ethical Association

ISBN/EAN: 9783744675451

Printed in Europe, USA, Canada, Australia, Japan

Cover: Foto ©Andreas Hilbeck / pixelio.de

More available books at **www.hansebooks.com**

EVOLUTION

IN SCIENCE, PHILOSOPHY, AND ART

EVOLUTION

IN SCIENCE, PHILOSOPHY, AND ART

POPULAR LECTURES AND DISCUSSIONS
BEFORE THE
BROOKLYN ETHICAL ASSOCIATION

NEW YORK
D. APPLETON AND COMPANY
1891

PREFACE.

THE doctrine of Evolution, representing as it does Nature's uniform method whereby all progressive changes are accomplished, whether in Physics, Biology, Psychology, Sociology, or Ethics, is susceptible of an infinite variety of expository illustrations. The present volume, which is the natural successor of previous courses of lectures before the Brooklyn Ethical Association on Evolution and Sociology, exemplifies the workings of this universal law in some of the special departments of Science, Philosophy, and Art.

The seventeen lectures herewith presented may be naturally segregated under these several heads. To the department of Science belongs the able exposition and critique of the contributions of Alfred Russel Wallace, the co-discoverer with Charles Darwin of the law of Natural Selection, to the doctrine of Evolution, by our foremost American biologist, Prof. Edward D. Cope, together with the monographs on the evolution of Chemistry, Electric and Magnetic Physics, Botany, Zoölogy, and Optics, and Mr. Potts's interesting discussion of the development of Form and Color in Nature.

To the department of Philosophy may properly be assigned the exposition of the life, work, and philosophical system of Prof. Ernst Haeckel, the eminent German evolutionist, in the lecture of Mr. Wakeman and the appended discussion, Dr. Abbot's exposition of The Scientific Method, Mr. Underwood's able presentation of the principles of Herbert Spencer's Synthetic Philosophy, Dr. Janes's application of the philosophy of Evolution to the Art of Life, and the noteworthy discussion of The Doctrine of Evolution, its Scope and Influence, by Prof. John Fiske, our ablest American exponent of this doctrine in its ethical and philosophical aspects. The final outcome of these lectures constitutes, it is believed, a complete refutation of the charge of materialism sometimes unjustly made against Mr. Spencer and the whole modern school of evolutionists. This is a matter of great interest and profound significance, to which we commend the thoughtful attention of the reader and reviewer.

All lovers of art will be glad to read the lectures on The Evolution of Art, of Architecture, Sculpture, Painting, and Music, wherein the progress of art in general and of these special arts has been traced by able and sympathetic pens. Though aware of many gaps and imperfections in the discussion of themes so vast and various, it is believed that the average merit of these lectures as a whole is fully up to the standard of previous years; and it is confidently hoped that they will prove wisely educational, stimulating, and suggestive to thoughtful and inquiring minds.

The important bearing of many of the topics herein treated on human life has also been constantly borne in mind, with a view to giving to these discussions a value not merely speculative, but also practical and useful.

CONTENTS.

ALFRED RUSSEL WALLACE

BY

EDWARD D. COPE, Ph. D.

AUTHOR OF ORIGIN OF THE FITTEST, THE DESCENT OF MAN, ETC.

COLLATERAL READINGS RECOMMENDED:

Biographical sketches of *Alfred Russel Wallace*, in American Cyclopædia and Popular Science Monthly; Huxley's *Evolution*, in Encyclopædia Britannica, and article *Evolution*, in American Cyclopædia; Wallace's Contribution to the Theory of Natural Selection, Island Life, Tropical Nature, Malay Archipelago, Geographical Distribution of Plants and Animals, Bad Times, A Defense of Modern Spiritualism, and If a Man die shall he live again?; Wallace and Dyer's The Distribution of Life.

ALFRED RUSSEL WALLACE.

ALFRED RUSSEL WALLACE, LL. D.

By E. D. Cope.

Alfred Russel Wallace was born at Usk, Monmouthshire, in England, in the year 1822, and he is therefore at present in his sixty-ninth year. As I saw Mr. Wallace in London in 1863, and in America in 1889, I can speak of his appearance "from autopsy." He is above medium height, not of stout build, and with a slight stoop of the shoulders. His head is neither long nor short, and the face is rather round than long. The forehead is fuller at the base than at the summit, and prominent eyebrows overhang eyes which have a vivacious twinkle. The mouth is large and amiable, and is surrounded by a full beard. The complexion is pale, and the expression is a combination of *bonhommie* and open honesty of character.

Dr. Wallace's prominence as a teacher of biology is not due to original researches in paleontology or embryology, or extended papers in comparative anatomy; but it rests on his extensive investigation of living beings in their mutual relations in actual life. This science, which has been termed hexicology, owes its most important development to his labors, and to those of his contemporary, Charles Darwin. It is only possible to pursue it on an extended scale by the observation of Nature under many aspects in many regions, and it is therefore desirable that its cultivators shall be travelers. Such have been both Mr. Darwin and Mr. Wallace. Mr. Wallace's explorations have been principally in the tropics of both hemispheres. In 1848 he visited the Amazon and some of its tributaries, where he remained four years. He made extensive collections in zoölogy during this time, but they were most unfortunately burned in the vessel in which he was making the return voyage. He published an account of his observations in a popular book, which I read as a boy with great interest. He also published a brief account of the palms of the Amazons.

In 1854 Dr. Wallace visited the Malaysian Islands, where he remained eight years. The collections and observations which he made during this exploration gave him occupation for many years after his return. His collections were especially important in ornithology and entomology, and his observations brought to light many new facts in the life-history of animals of all branches. Among a multitude of new species discovered by him I only mention now the beautiful and chastely colored paradise-bird from New Guinea, the *Semioptera wallacei* Scl. When on the Amazon, Wallace had the opportunity of verifying and extending the observations of Bates on the remarkable phenomenon of mimetic analogy presented by the *Lepidoptera* of that region. In Malaysia he discovered many equally striking examples of the same thing. He observed not only cases of mimetism between living species of insects, but also wonderful mimicry of inanimate objects and plants by living animals. His studies of the variations of species by this time led him to formulate a theory to account for their origin and persistence identical with that given to the world by Mr. Darwin under the name of Natural Selection.

Dr. Wallace's first statement of this theory was contained in a letter to Mr. Darwin, written at Ternate in 1858. This letter was afterwards published in the Proceedings of the Linnæan Society of London for 1859 (read August, 1858), under the title On the Tendency of Varieties to depart indefinitely from the Original Type, in conjunction with two papers on the same subject by Mr. Darwin. The letter was shown to Sir Charles Lyell and to Dr. Joseph D. Hooker, who were familiar with the views of Mr. Darwin on the same subject. Mr. Darwin had written a paper as early as 1844, in which essentially the same views were propounded, which had been read to Dr. Hooker, but which had never been published. A letter containing the same general views had been also written by Mr. Darwin to Dr. Asa Gray in 1857. These two papers were published in connection with Mr Wallace's letter in the Proceedings of the Linnæan Society, as above mentioned, by Sir Charles Lyell and Dr. J. D. Hooker. Dr. Wallace's paper endeavors to demonstrate the evolution of species in ordinary descent by the action of two factors: First, that species tend naturally to produce varieties or variations of character; and, second, that if any of these variations or varieties present superior advantages in the struggle for existence over those possessed by its parent, it will separate or replace the latter, thus accomplishing the introduction of a new form or species in place of the old one. He cites among his various illustrations the following: "Even the peculiar colors of many animals, especially insects so closely resembling the soil or the leaves or trunks on which they habitually reside, are explained on the same principle, for though in the course of ages varieties of many tints may have occurred, yet those races having colors best adapted for concealment from their enemies would inevitably survive the longest."

The way in which Mr. Darwin reached the same result in his letter of 1844, above mentioned, is slightly different only in being a little more comprehensive, as it includes one more factor—viz., the necessarily enormous increase of animals and plants by reproduction and the consequent severity of the struggle for existence. He applies the Malthusian idea to the lower creation, and shows how that any one of the numerous species which exist would soon fill the earth were not checks present on every hand which only permit the survival of those individuals which possess exceptional facilities for success in the pursuit of subsistence. In this way profitable variations of structure have survived and been perpetuated; in other words, new species have originated and continued. The two papers by Drs. Darwin and Wallace embrace all the factors involved in the process of natural selection. Later elucidation of the doctrines of these two able expositors, and by others subsequently, have convinced thoughtful persons that it is an expression of a great fact of the evolution of life. Its acceptance has been general, and the impetus given to research and to thought has been great.

In the acceptance of the doctrine of natural selection the public has often confused it with the general doctrine of the evolution of animals by descent, of which natural selection is an explanation. The general doctrine of descent is as old as human thought, but it awaited the expositions of Darwin and Wallace before receiving general acceptance. Even the authority of Lamarck, who formulated it a half-century previously, was not sufficient to gain credence for it. Lamarck's principal explanation of the process, the change of structure through use and disuse, lacked the necessary evidence, and, although he taught the law of natural selection as a corollary, it did not compel assent as did the masterly presentation of Darwin and Wallace.

Dr. Wallace's first book on evolution was published in 1870, and was entitled Contributions to the Theory of Natural Selection. This work contains the germs of all of his

In 1878 Dr. Wallace published his two volumes On the Geographical Distribution of Animals. His original researches on the distribution of animals in the Malaysian Archipelago furnished the starting point of this work. It is an excellent general exposition of the subject, which has, however, from the nature of the case, become in some points superannuated. The systematic relations of many groups of animals are now better understood than they were then, and paleontology has made great advances beyond the state of knowledge recorded in this work. In 1878 the work of a popular character on Tropical Nature appeared. His book on Island Life was published in 1880. Here we have a discussion of the faunæ of islands, a very fertile subject in the evidence it contributes to questions of distribution in past and present time, and in the restricted, and therefore more comprehensible, fields which it offers for the solution of questions of subsistence, selection, etc. He here brings into final order the evidence as to the primitive separation of the Oriental and Australian faunæ which now approach each other so closely in the Malaysian Islands. He found during his residence in Malaysia that the islands of the respective groups were separated from each other by comparatively shallow seas, while a deep channel divides the two groups as a whole from each other. This channel, which passes between Celebes and Borneo at the northwest, and Lombok and Bally at the southwest, is known as Wallace's Channel. The fauna of Celebes is, however, somewhat intermediate in possessing some types of both faunæ.

In 1889 Dr. Wallace's last work, Darwinism, appeared. In this book he summarizes the facts and inferences which bear on evolution. As before, natural selection is regarded as the leading factor in structural evolution. The subjects treated of are arranged in the following order: Chapter I. What are Species, and what is meant by their Origin. II. The Struggle for Existence. III. The Variability of Species in a State of Nature. IV. Variations of Domestic Animals and Cultivated Plants. V. Natural Selection by Variation and Survival of the Fittest. VI. Difficulties and Objections. VII. Infertility of Crosses between Distinct Species, and the Usual Sterility of Hybrids. VIII. The Origin and Uses of Color in Animals. IX. Warning Coloration and Mimicry. X. Colors and Ornaments Characteristic of Sex. XI. Special Colors of Plants, their Origin and Purpose. XII. The Geographical Distribution of Organisms. XIII. The Geological Evidence of Evolution. XIV. Fundamental Problems in Relation to Variation and Heredity. XV. Darwinism as applied to Man. XVI. Criticisms. XVII. Forces other than Natural Selection.

The scope of Darwinism is wider than that of any of Wallace's previous books, and he gives attention to the voluminous literature which had grown up during the interval which had elapsed since his first general synopsis published in 1870. The most important part of the book is the large portion which is devoted to the nature and uses of colors in animals and plants. In this field Wallace's original contributions both to fact and theory are very interesting and valuable. His chapter on the geological (*i. e.*, paleontological) evidence of evolution was hardly up to the times, as the American work had not sufficiently attracted his attention at the time of his writing. In his criticisms of Spencer, Cope, Semper, and Geddes he denies the efficacy of the Lamarckian factors use and disuse, and the direct effect of the environment on organic structure, but accounts for all variations in the latter by natural selection. Thus Cope had endeavored to explain the origin of the divergence of the diplarthrous ungulate mammalia by supposing that the even-toed line (*Artiodactyla*) were produced by walking in muddy ground, which spreads the toes equally in all directions, while the odd-toed (*Perissodactyla*) have descended from forms that walked on dry ground, so that the stimulus of impact and strain was felt by the longest toe, which was accordingly developed at the expense of the others, thus producing the horse. Dr. Wallace says that such an explanation is not proved, and is unnecessary, since it is evident that it was only necessary for variation in these two directions to have appeared to have been at once taken advantage of by natural selection. The odd-toed type, being best adapted for progress on hard ground, would survive, and the even-toed be eliminated; while the reverse process would take place among the types that inhabited soft places. To the general proposition involved in this explanation I will return; but will only say now, in passing, that Dr. Wallace does not thus explain the origin of the two variations in question; nor is it certain that, having once originated, the even-toed is not quite as effective as the odd-toed for rapid progress on hard ground.

In his Chapter XV, Wallace again expresses his dissatisfaction with natural selection as an explanation of the origin of the human mind; and from this standpoint he takes a retrospect of the forces of creation in general. He says: "These three distinct stages (life, consciousness, and intellect) of progress from the inorganic world of matter and motion up to man point clearly to an unseen universe, to a world of spirit, to which the world of matter is altogether subordinate. To this spiritual world we may refer the marvelously complex forces which we know as gravitation, cohesion, chemical force, radiant force, and electricity, without which the material universe would not exist for a moment in its present form, and perhaps not at all, since without these forces, and perhaps others which may be termed atomic, it is doubtful whether matter itself could have any existence. And still more surely can we refer to it those progressive manifestations of life in the vegetable and the animal, and man, which we may classify as unconscious consciousness and intellectual life, and which probably depend upon different degrees of spiritual influx. I have shown that this involves no necessary infraction of the law of continuity in physical or mental evolution, whence it follows that any difficulty we may find in discriminating the organic from the inorganic, the lower vegetable from the lower animal organisms, or the higher animals from the lowest types of man, has no bearing on the question. This is to be decided by showing that a change in essential nature (due probably to causes of a higher order than those of the material universe) took place at the several stages of progress which I have indicated—a change which may be none the less real because absolutely imperceptible at its point of origin, as is the change which takes place in the curve in which a body is moving where the application of some new force causes the curve to be slightly altered."

Dr. Wallace, like other lovers of his kind, has interested himself in some questions of political economy, and has written on Land Nationalization (1882) and on Bad Times, an Essay on the Depression of Trade (1885). He also wrote a book in opposition to vaccination in 1885. He is known to be a believer in the verity of some of the phenomena of Spiritualism or Spiritism, and was a coadjutor of Prof. Crookes in the conduct of some of his experiments in this field. Without being a Swedenborgian, he is an adherent of one of the leading tenets of the founder of that body—viz., of the influx, upon man at least, of an influence from without him, from a personal spiritual source.

In reviewing the work of Dr. Wallace one can assert that it furnishes an admirable illustration of the intelligent spirit which is rife in the Indo-European of the nineteenth century. The desire and the determination to know is its actuating motive, and the good of mankind is its ostensible end. It is sustained by the faith that knowledge can not harm us, but that it is, on the other hand, necessary for our safe conduct through time, both as individuals and as a race. The labors undertaken with this end in view have been many and arduous, and Dr. Wallace's illustrate this aspect of the times as much as those of any other man. His work is a life labor conducted with persevering consistency to attain a definite result. His life is an excellent illustration of his own doctrine, that all force is will-force. The utility of his life is self-evident, and the effects of it on human thought, and therefore on human action, will remain as long as mankind thinks and acts.

As regards the position occupied by Dr. Wallace among the architects of our knowledge of the doctrine of evolution, I do not hesitate to say that, like that of his great coadjutor Darwin, he has occupied himself with a part only of the work. Like the builder engaged on one side of a building, he has been so attracted and impressed by the rich materials ready to his hand that he has not given heed to the other side of the edifice; and the higher he has builded, the less has he been able to see the hidden portions. This is natural, and perhaps beneficial, for had he seen the whole elevation in a mental *coup d'œil*, he might not have worked so well at his own nearest portion, and he might have been distracted by the multiplicity of his thoughts and ambitions. But it is certain that admirable powers of observation do not always coexist with the highest logical capacity. Whether this is because of the complementary relation of parts of the mental organism, or because constant occupation with the arrangement of sense impressions excludes the present activity of logical reflection, and *vice versa*, we do not know; but the two faculties are often dissociated in human minds.

It seems to have very rarely occurred to Mr. Darwin, and still more rarely to Dr. Wallace, to reflect on, or at least to discuss, the question of the origin of the variations concerning which they have said so much and so convincingly. In the writings of both we frequently meet with the expression that such and such a character has been "caused by natural selection." So habitual did this idea become that it is now the creed of a scientific school of the countrymen of Darwin and Wallace, and it has influenced the thought of English-speaking people everywhere. That natural selection is not the primary but a secondary factor in evolution it has been my aim to show in various publications since 1868, and an active school of evolutionists in America, England, and Germany occupies this position. In Germany, Nägeli and Eimer; in England, Spencer, Henslow, Turner, and Geddes; and in America, Hyatt, Jackson, Packard, Osborn, Ryder, Sharp, and Dall, have made important contributions to this doctrine; and as, in the case of most of these writers, their doctrine includes the essential of the position of Lamarck, the term Neolamarckian is appropriate to this school and to its opinions. To the opposite school the term Neodarwinian or Postdarwinian has been applied.

The failure of the Neodarwinian school to enter into a consideration of the origin of variation has precluded them from researches into the mechanical causes of modifications of structure, whether proceeding from the movements of the organism in relation to its environment, or whether due to the action of the environment on the organism. Yet they have occasionally slipped into Lamarckian explanations of the structures and colors of animals. Lankester has admitted that the spiral coil of the gastropod mollusca was due to an unsymmetrical position of the shell of the animal during growth. Wallace has suggested that the rotation of the eye of the flat-fish from one side of the head to the other was due to the effort of the animal to direct that eye upward, as the body gradually acquired the habit of lying and swimming on one side. Poulton ascribes the imitative colors of the pupæ of certain butterflies to the effect of the colors of the environment on the nervous organism of the caterpillar when about to change. But these explanations have been abandoned by Lankester and Wallace as implying the insufficiency of the action of natural selection to produce the observed results.

The opinions of Weissmann lend support to the Neodarwinians. This author declares that acquired characters can not be inherited, so that if use and disuse should produce modifications in the structure of adult animals, they could not be transmitted to their descendants. If this be true, the Lamarckian position is founded on error. This doctrine is accepted by Wallace in his last work (Darwinism).

Weissmann and the other Postdarwinians, however, admit the acquisition and inheritance of what they call "congenital" characters, which appear only in the reproductive elements, and which they distinguish broadly from the characters which may be acquired by the body in general through use and disuse, and which they call "somatic characters." They endeavor to prove their hypothesis that the latter are not inherited by endeavoring to reproduce mutilations, such as by the breeding of mice from which the tails have been amputated, etc. It is, however, evident that the distinction between "congenital" and "somatic" acquired characters does not exist, since evolution shows that all characters have been acquired at some period of time, and that the only difference in such characters is their greater or less antiquity. The non-inheritance of mutilations illustrates the principle that the general relations of the organism contribute to the production of a change of character, and that no isolated and sporadic, and therefore superficial, change affects the reproductive elements sufficiently to be transmitted. Paleontology shows that the causes which have been sufficient to produce inheritable changes of structure have been in daily or hourly operation for long ages; and that the results have been the gradual evolution of mechanisms especially adapted to the needs of their possessors in their relations to the environment.

We rise to another stage of the subject if, when we grant that the movements of the organism have produced the changes observed and which constitute progressive evolution (and *vice versa*), we seek for the causes that underlie animal motion. The inference on the part of those who observe living animals is that their conscious states influence their movements. To this two answers are made. One of these is by a school of physiologists who declare that a conscious (i. e., a mental) state can not influence (i. e., control or direct) the motion of a material body. The other objection is that animal movements are not nearly always consciously performed. To the latter objection it is replied that unconscious (automatic or reflex) acts are simply the product of education during conscious states, and that a designed act could not have originated in any other way. The first objection—that consciousness can not affect motion of material bodies—is a theoretical inference based on the supposed impossibility of violating the law of the conservation of energy. It is a special statement of a general principle—viz., that mind can not control matter. An equally necessary conclusion is that matter can not control mind. This is not the place to enter into a discussion of this broad question, so I will only refer to Dr. Wallace's position on this important subject.

Dr. Wallace has perceived the necessity of some agency other than mechanical energy to account for the intelligence displayed by animals and men. As he does not admit the Lamarckian idea of use and disuse, he finds no direct use for animal consciousness in the premises. He criticises the position of the writer of the present paper (Darwinism, Chapter XIV), that consciousness, and consequently intelligence, have been the determining causes of animal movements. He well remarks that since evolution has produced the vegetable kingdom and the lowest animals, intelligence can not well have been a factor, and that, this being the case, it is not necessary to suppose it to have been so in the case of the higher animals, as one rule must have governed all cases at the basis. Dr. Wallace does not appear to have taken into consideration the fact, however, that the simplest sensations belong to the department of mind, and that it is highly probable that the lowest animals and their almost indistinguishable vegetable allies give evidence of such rudimentary sense-perception; and sensation and memory are sufficient for the evolution of mind. The vegetable kingdom displays for the most part characters of degeneracy, its entire "efficient" cause being the reproductive function, which has speedily become automatic and unconscious.

The rational mind which has not surrendered to the idea of fortuity seeks some explanation of the ever-increasing intelligence found intimately associated with the evolution of animals. Prof. Haeckel conceived his theory of the "plastidule soul" to meet the difficulty; but the idea is indefinite, and would not probably have been entertained by its distinguished author if he had followed up the subject of animal psychology. It still remains in the limbo of unrealized fancies. But Dr. Wallace cuts the Gordian knot by the introduction of the idea of "influx" of a mind-energy from without. I can say of this proposition that it appears to be an unnecessary interjection into an otherwise continuous operation of known and visible causes. The presence of sensation and memory in very low animals is too well assured to render any external influence necessary except that of the environment; and the process of education is well known to produce types of energy which may run on in their unvarying automatic courses to eternity for aught that we know without betraying any indication of consciousness except that their nature can only be explained on the supposition that consciousness was present at their inception. It is also a self-evident proposition that the automatization of energy must be the cause of the *non-adaptability* of an organism to changes in the environment, and therefore the cause of the destruction or degeneracy of organisms. The opposite proposition is equally self-evident—viz., that consciousness or sensation is a guarantee of persistent life and *adaptability* to changed environment, and therefore of progressive evolution.

In conclusion, I present a table of the alternative positions held by opposite schools of evolutionists, which correspond in the main with the Neolamarckian and Neodarwinian. Although particular men may not hold all the affirmations of either side, they form two distinct and consistent bodies of doctrine.

NEOLAMARCKIAN.	NEODARWINIAN.
1. Variations are not promiscuous, but definite.	1. Variations are promiscuous or multifarious.
2. Variations are caused by the interaction of the organic being and its environment.	2. Variations are "congenital" and are not caused by the interaction with the environment.
3. Acquired variations may be inherited.	3. Acquired variations can not be inherited.
4. Variations survive directly as they are adapted to changing environments.	4. Variations survive directly as they are adapted to the environment.
5. Cause of inherited variation is physical and mechanical interaction of being and environment.	5. Cause of inherited variation is unknown or is the mingling of ♂ and ♀ characters in reproduction.
6. Movements of the organism are caused or directed by sensation and other conscious states.	6. Movements of organism are not caused by sensation or conscious states, but are a survival by natural selection from multifarious movements.
7. Conscious experience has developed habitual movements of the body.	7. Conscious experience has developed mental habits only.
8. The rational mind is developed by experience—i. e., memory and classification.	8. The rational mind is developed by natural selection from multifarious mental activities.

ABSTRACT OF THE DISCUSSION.

DR. MARTIN L. HOLBROOK:

In listening to the able and interesting lecture of Prof. Cope, I could not help wishing that he had given us more detailed information about the personal life of Mr. Wallace Knowledge of the personal characteristics of a writer often greatly helps us to an understanding of his thought and to a due appreciation of the value of his opinions. From a friend who knows Mr. Wallace well, I have obtained some facts concerning him which may be of interest. This friend describes him as a tall man, of distinguished appearance, and excellent balance of temperament. He is a good listener, but not gifted in conversation. When he speaks, however, his words carry conviction, on account of his evident sincerity and intelligence. Mr. Wallace became a spiritualist, as Dr. Cope has intimated, through the influence of a very intimate friend, who is possessed of mediumistic powers, so called, and he is now as firm as a rock in his belief in the general truth of the spiritualistic doctrine. As a scientific observer, he was as accurate and painstaking as Mr. Darwin, and, with him, is entitled to the honor of the discovery of the law of natural selection.

EX-SURROGATE ABRAM H. DAILEY:

I think I was invited here this evening under a misapprehension. I have no personal acquaintance with Mr. Wallace. I only know him through his writings. I have fallen on a similar line of investigation in the phenomena of spirit-communication with Dr. Wallace, and have come to similar conclusions. It is greatly to be regretted that a condition of society exists which deprecates such investigations, and that it requires moral heroism in a man like Mr. Wallace to proclaim his belief in the spiritualistic phenomena. I have no reason to doubt that he has exercised the same care in these investigations that he has in his biological studies.

MR. THADDEUS B. WAKEMAN:

The lecture of the evening is an able and valuable contribution to the literature of evolution. In his personal character Mr. Wallace stands as high as Darwin. Evolutionists have nothing to apologize for in the characters of the leading advocates of this doctrine. All men, however, have their limitations. Darwin was a great observer and discoverer, but not a theorist or philosopher. The development of a consistent philosophy based upon the facts of evolution was impossible to him. Mr. Wallace is more inclined to philosophical speculations, but he has never been trained in the scientific study of mind, and has therefore fallen a prey to the false theories and conclusions of spiritism. This is his limitation. For myself, I believe that Prof. Haeckel, about whom I am hereafter to speak to you, stands high and clear above all the other advocates of this doctrine as a philosophical evolutionist.

DR. LEWIS G. JANES:

It is interesting to note that the subject of this lecture has considered the doctrine of evolution in its higher aspects—as related to sociology and religion—as well as in its merely physical relations. In biology Dr. Wallace is more of a Darwinian than was Mr. Darwin himself. He attributes to natural selection alone many of those alterations in the structure and coloration of birds and animals which Darwin attributed to sexual selection. In reading his latest work, soon after its publication, under the influence of his cogent arguments —backed, as they were, by a strong array of facts, and charmed by his delightfully perspicuous style—it seemed to me that his conclusions in most of the cases cited by him were fully justified. At all events, his arguments must be squarely met by a fair appeal to the facts, in order to invalidate their conclusions. In regard to the question of heredity, however, and the effects of use and disuse in determining variations, I can not help thinking his judgment is at fault. He adopts the doctrine of Dr. Weissmann, that acquired characters are not inherited; but this doctrine has been recently and, as it appears to me, successfully combated by Prof. Theodor Eimer, and the facts with which I am familiar seem to be decidedly against it. Nevertheless, the judgment of so good an observer as Mr. Wallace is entitled to most respectful consideration.

PROF. COPE thanked the audience for their attention and briefly closed the discussion.

ERNST HAECKEL

BY

THADDEUS B. WAKEMAN

COLLATERAL READINGS RECOMMENDED:

Haeckel and Virchow, in Contemporary Review, vol. xxxiii, p. 540; *Darwin and Haeckel*, by Prof. Huxley, in Popular Science Monthly, vol. vi, p. 592; article *Haeckel*, in American Cyclopædia; Haeckel's History of Creation, Evolution of Man, General Morphology of Organisms, Freedom of Science and Teaching, and India and Ceylon.

Ernst Haeckel.

PROF. ERNST HAECKEL,

HIS LIFE, WORKS, CAREER, AND PROPHECY.

By Thaddeus B. Wakeman.

It has been wisely arranged that this course of lectures shall be enlivened from time to time by some account of the distinguished naturalists and philosophers whose discoveries and labors have given evolution its modern and scientific form. Thus, very appropriately, in the first course of this series in a former year, the pastor of this church gave an admirable discourse upon the personal career, discoveries, and influence of Charles Darwin. And equally appropriate was the most interesting account of the life, researches, and services of Alfred Russel Wallace, by our American scientist, Prof. Edward D. Cope, which opened the course of the present season. Next after these two co-discoverers of the great law of natural selection, no one has done more to sustain, explain, and defend evolution than Ernst Haeckel, the famous Professor of Zoölogy at the University of Jena. He is the leading exponent of evolution upon the continent of Europe, and has carried its conquests far beyond the concepts of Darwin or Wallace.

This evening is, therefore, properly devoted to an effort to get as near as possible to him, his discoveries, his philosophy or view of the world, and his religion. We can approach him best for this purpose if we consider his career first as a man and naturalist, then as the exponent of the monistic philosophy, and lastly as the prophet of "monism" as a religion—for he has brought into use this word "monism" to designate the final philosophy and religion of evolution and science.

First, then, we must regard him as a man and a naturalist, for these two, man and naturalist, in his case, have never been separated; and, as such, there are few personal characters in the world really more worthy of our acquaintance and study than this same German professor, now at the age of fifty-six, working busily as a bee at his pleasant villa, or in his lecture hall and museum, on the banks of the Saale River, or wandering over Europe, Asia, or Africa as the knight-errant of Science, or defending her latest acquisitions against retrogrades and Philistines in the scientific assemblies of Germany and Europe, and finally receiving their honors.

He was born at Potsdam, near Berlin, February 16, 1834, within a day of the anniversary of the martyrdom of Bruno (February 17, 1600) and two years after the death of Goethe, who is still remembered as the presiding genius of the Saale Valley—of Jena and the neighboring Weimar. Haeckel's chief characteristic—we may say inheritance—as a child seems to have been a love of nature, which justified his being called a German Linnæus. His love of flowers began in the cradle. When but twelve years of age, we are told, he was quite a botanist, and had collected two herbariums—one *official*, in which he had placed what were then called *typical* forms, all carefully labeled as separate and distinct species, while in the other, a secret one, were placed the "bad kinds," presenting a long series of specimens transitional from one good species to another. Such discoveries were at that time the forbidden fruits of knowledge, which, in leisure hours, were his secret delight—a delight which grew from year to year.

While at the Gymnasium, or high school, he prepared a botanical work for publication. At the university he determined to enter upon the medical profession as the open gateway to the secrets of nature. As a student he seems to have enjoyed rare advantages. Under the distinguished professors Kölliker and Leydig he studied physiology and anatomy at Würzburg, and then under Prof. Johannes Müller at Berlin, an instructor to whom he gives generous meed of praise as his great teacher—for in this tone he feelingly refers to him in his reply to, or rather duel with, the celebrated physiologist Rudolph Virchow in 1878. Whereof he then spoke he must have known well, for he was also the student and assistant of this same redoubtable Rudolph Virchow, and apparently a favorite of his, until his course of preparatory medical studies closed. At their conclusion we find him settling down as a practicing physician at Berlin in 1858.

But it was evident to his instructors and friends, and finally to himself, that he was called by nature to, let us say, a different rather than a higher work—for can there be a higher than the worthy practice of medicine? As early as 1854 he had been engaged with Professors Kölliker and Müller pursuing experiments and researches in animal tissues. In 1857 he published his first biological essay on the tissues of crabs. Two years after, in 1859, we find him withdrawing from his professional practice and spending fifteen months in Italy, engaged in special zoölogical researches. On his return, in 1861, he submitted the results of his studies and experiments to the University of Jena, especially in an essay on Rhizopods. This appears to have been the turning-point in his career, for in the next year (1862) he was appointed Professor Extraordinary at that university; and there he has ever since remained, and has been steadily advanced from one position of honor and usefulness to another, until it would seem that pretty much all that a naturalist, philosopher, and author could desire has fallen to his lot.

During the thirty years of his professorship he has had many calls to other and foreign institutions, but nothing could equal the attractions which bind him to this favored, we may say, to him, almost sacred locality; for, by singular good fortune, his "earthly days" are spent under the shadow of those Thuringian mountains where his great protagonist and inspirer, Goethe, dreamed and lived, and prophetically poetized the religion of evolution; and there he works, too, in that very same old independent University of Jena which Goethe directed for years with the expressed hope that it would some day open up this new science of evolution to the world. How deeply this landscape and these associations affect and inspire our professor is seen by his touching farewell to them on his departure to India and Ceylon in October, 1881. Take this page, for instance, which, as if a curtain were raised, opens our view at once into the very heart of the man (page 11):

"My arrangements at last completed, and the sixteen boxes sent in advance to Trieste, I was ready to take leave of dear quiet Jena on the morning of the 8th of October. When the last moment arrived, I found that a six months' absence from home would be no easy task for the father of a family who had already attained the age of forty-seven years. With what different emotions would I have taken my departure twenty-five years ago, when a tropical journey was the chief aim of my life! True, the experience of twenty-five years of teaching and zoölogical study would enable me to accomplish more than I could have done a quarter of a century ago. But I was twenty-five years older! Would the concrete wonders of tropical nature possess the same fascination for me, now that I had penetrated the abstract domains of natural philosophy?

"These and kindred thoughts, together with the most doleful impressions of my last farewells to home and friends, passed through my brain as the train bore me through the cold gray autumnal mist which enshrouded my beloved Saale Valley.

"Only the tallest peaks of our magnificent *Muschelkalk* mountains rose above the misty sea; on the right, Hausberg, with his 'rosy, radiant summit,' the proud pyramid of the Jenzig, and the romantic ruins of Kunitzberg. On the left stretched the wooded heights of Rauthal; and, further on, *Goethe's favorite retreat, charming Dornberg.* I waved an adieu to these dear old mountain friends, and promised to return to them in good health and richly laden with Indian treasures.

"As if to ratify the promise, they gave me their friendliest morning greeting; the dense mist suddenly fell from their shoulders, and the triumphant sun rose into a perfectly cloudless sky. Thousands of dew-drops blazed like jewels in the azure cups of the lovely gentians decorating the grassy slopes on either side of the iron road."

In these words we have recalled the exquisite landscape, with the mists and inspirations, of Goethe's Novelle, The Tale (*Mährchen*), and his final, noble, wisest Letter from Dornberg Castle, in those "saddest days" of 1828. Before this scene, and as its product largely, we see our heart-and-headful professor and his lovely family so clearly, lovingly depicted that ordinary details must not dim the picture.

At this university, Goethe's university, his scientific career began. Here his early enthusiasm was sheltered when, in 1861, he came from Italy with his love of nature kindled to a flame by his personal explorations, and not less, perhaps, by that wonderful epoch-making book, Darwin's Origin of Species, which had appeared during his absence in 1859. He saw at once that the simple but far-reaching discovery of the law of "natural selection" (implying "sexual selection" and so much more afterwards given to the world) contained in this work was the corner-stone upon which materials collected by others, and recently by himself, could finally be raised into a complete and noble science of biology; a solution of the problems of the whole organic world.

To this achievement he determined to devote himself as his lifework. Wonderful has been his success, because he has brought to bear upon it a rare genius sustained by a phenomenal industry

In order to gather some notion of what is meant by "phenomenal industry," we need but to glance over his works and explorations for a few years.

In 1862 he presented to his university a celebrated work on the *Radialaria*, for which a gold medal was awarded. In this work new genera and species were described and the whole subject newly classified in accordance with the new philosophy of the genealogical descent of organisms, by which he justified his adhesion to the new and then unpopular Darwinian doctrine of the origin of species.

In 1863, before the Convention of German Physicians at Stettin, he introduced and stood almost alone in advocating the new views and discoveries of Darwinism as the solving and renovating power in the biological sciences, and as tributary to medicine.

In 1864 he published in illustration of the descent of species, an important work on the *Crustacea*.

In 1865 appeared another work on the *Medusæ*. The result of these publications and of his teaching was such that the University of Jena began to be recognized as the unrivaled school of zoölogy, comparative anatomy, and Biology. A regular professorship was created for him. A museum was established with a lecture hall, and his friend and co-worker, Prof. Gegenbaur, was appointed his assistant.

The next year (1866) the first of his larger works appeared, The Organic Morphology, in two large volumes, with hundreds of charts and illustrations, which astonished the proverbially patient and industrious Germans by their extent, thoroughness, novelty, and general importance. Their main purpose was to prove that the whole domain of comparative physiology, anatomy, and embryology was scientifically reduced to successive order by the new views, which made correlative changes and functions the solution of the forms of all living organisms. By this law of evolution he proved that the changes in the development of the embryo epitomize the successive changes which the genus to which the animal belongs has undergone in its world-history. This law of comparative embryology at once gave to biologists an immense power of prevision and discovery; for the tribal history of every animal could be largely sketched out by indications and changes in the embryo, and then be verified by actual research and observation in nature. Thus the genesis of the tribe (*Phylogenesis*) and of the individual (*Ontogenesis*) were made to throw light upon and to reveal each other.

Another view of great interest was presented in this work, that the simpler organisms or microbes represented a primitive condition of life not only below the distinction of sex, but also below the distinction of animal and vegetable life, and were really such simple forms of protoplasm that they constitute *a kingdom* by themselves, which he calls *the Protista* and regards as the common foundation and source of both animals and plants. Prof. Huxley expressed the sentiment of those capable of judging when he pronounced this Morphology to be one of the greatest scientific works ever published. Its influence was largely instrumental in turning the tide of German thought in favor of the new biology.

Certainly after such a display of genius and labor the requirement of some rest would appear reasonable, but it seems that Prof.. Haeckel never rests. His vacations are spent in excursions for scientific research and verification. In the winter of 1866 he was at work among the Canary Islands, and upon his return he published an interesting report of his explorations there and on the Atlantic coasts.

In 1867–'68 he determined to give a popular exposition of the new philosophy—the new view of the world. A course of lectures was accordingly delivered, reported, and published, which are now known the world over as The Natural History of Creation. This work has gone on through revised editions from the first to the eighth, and has been translated into English (in two volumes, by the Appletons) and into every modern civilized language. Excepting, perhaps, some of Darwin's works, it has done more than any other to make evolution known as the fundamental law of the organic world. Of it, in the preface to his Descent of Man, Darwin uses these remarkable words:

"The conclusion that man is the co-descendant with other species of some ancient, lower, and extinct form is not in any degree new. Lamarck long ago came to this conclusion, which has lately been maintained by several eminent naturalists and philosophers—for instance, by Wallace, Huxley, Lyell, Vogt, Lubbock, Buchner, Rolle, and especially by Haeckel. This last naturalist, besides his great work, Generalle Morphologie (1866), has recently (1868, with a second edition, 1870) published his Natural History of Creation, in which he fully discusses the genealogy of man. If this work had appeared before my essay had been written, I should probably never have completed it. Almost all the conclusions at which I have arrived I find confirmed by this naturalist, whose knowledge on many points is much fuller than mine."

When we consider from whom these words come, they are the highest encomium a work of that kind could receive.

In 1869 Prof. Haeckel published an essay upon the evolution of the *Siphonophores*, which was awarded a gold medal at Utrecht.

In 1870 he published biological studies on the Monera and Protista of the Catallacts, a new group of *Protista.*

In 1871 he spent March and April on the Dalmatian coast near Trieste, and August and September on the coasts of Norway, in scientific researches.

In 1872 he visited the eastern coasts of the Mediterranean for similar purposes. During these three years he delivered courses of lectures at Jena and Berlin, and published articles on the division of labor in nature and in human life; also on life at great sea depths, on the genealogical tree of the human race, and on the relationship of the sponges and corals.

In 1872 appeared another of his great works—viz., The Calcareous Sponges, in three volumes, with sixty plates. This, like his Morphology, is an epoch-making work. It answered the demand of those who insisted upon "actual facts" as the only proofs of evolution by showing the history, connection, and descent of the species of sponges in such masterly detail that ignorance of the work was the only escape from conviction. With its publication evolution was generally admitted to have passed from the stage of hypothesis and to stand forever as a verified law of biology—its fundamental law.

In 1874 he published essays upon the Gastræa, or stomach, theory; The Phylogenic Classification of Animals; and the Homology of Germ-layers of Animals. All these were preparatory to the great work which followed.

In 1874–'75 appeared his celebrated Anthropogenie, or Evolution of Man. This is a popular exposition of the origin and evolution of man as a race (phylogenic), and of man as an individual (ontogenic), with all his organs, compared together step by step. It is the true Book of Genesis in the Bible of Nature, and proves how much more strange, wonderful, and interesting truth can be than miracle, fiction, tradition, and mythology. It is going through as many editions as the Natural History of Creation, and should be read directly after it, as its counterpart and conclusion. (Published by D. Appleton & Co.)

In 1877, before the Association of German Naturalists and Physicians (the leading scientific body of Germany), our knight-errant of evolution was called upon to enter the lists with the celebrated pathologist, Rudolph Virchow, his former instructor, and the leading spirit of the university and scientific coterie of Berlin. In this duel, as Mr. Gladstone would call it, our knight bore himself right gallantly and well, as all may see in his work which resulted from it, which appeared in 1878 as the Liberty in Science and Teaching (published also in English by the Appletons), with a noble and useful introduction by Prof. Huxley. Of this work and its bearing upon philosophic thought more must be said when we touch his philosophy.

We have noticed enough of his publications from year to year to show what an indomitable man, naturalist, and worker this Ernst Haeckel must be. His past assures us that he will go on learning, teaching, and publishing to the end of his days, and that he will never touch any topic that he will not enlighten and adorn.

In a letter to an American friend, written by his own hand, he classifies his important works to date as follows:

I. *General Biology and Philosophical Works.*
   1. General Morphology, 1866.
   2. Natural History of Creation, 1868, etc. (8 editions, 12 translations).
   3. Collected Popular Essays, 1878. (Bonn, 2 vols.)

II. *General Zoölogical and Phylogenetic Works.*
   1. Gastræa Theory, 1873.
   2. Studies of the Monera and other Protista, 1870.
   3. Anthropogenie, 1877 (3 editions).

III. *Zoölogical Monographs.*
   1. Radialaria (35 plates), 1862.
   2. Calcarspongiæ (60 plates), 1872.
   3. Medusæ (72 plates), 1877.
   4. Siphonophoræ (64 plates), 1869, 1888.

IV. *Reports on the Zoölogy of H. M. S. Challenger.*
1. Deep-sea Medusæ (32 plates), 1880.
2. Deep-sea Keratoræ (8 plates), 1889.
3. Siphonophoræ (50 plates), 1888.
4. Radialaria (740 plates), 1887.

V. *Vogages and Travels.*
1. Articles on Corfu, Brussa, Teneriffe, Norway, etc., from the Deutsche Rundschau, 1866 to 1878.
2. India and Ceylon, and Egypt (published in German, English, etc.), 1882.

To those who wish to be introduced to our author personally, we say read his India and Ceylon, and he will live with you as a delightful friend and companion ever after. No book of travels is superior to it—not even Darwin's Voyage of the Beagle, said to be the best of all. In it we learn to admire the physical courage and dexterity which served him so well in the moving incidents of flood and field. We see in him a good physical type of the German, a little over six feet tall, body well proportioned, firm but not gross, with brainy head, straight face, auburn hair, grayish-blue eyes, and sanguine temperament of the true knight; ready for the contest with Virchow at Munich, the elephant hunt on the Ceylon mountain, or the dangers of the coral grove in the depths of the Indian Ocean. To appreciate these physical and mental qualities, think of a German professor naked and *open-eyed* in such a water-world as this! We quote from his experience at Punta Gallia:

"The entire attraction of a coral bank can not be seen from above, even though you float immediately over it at ebb-tide, and the water is so shallow your boat scrapes against the points. A descent into the fluid element is therefore necessary. Not possessing a diving-bell, I attempted to swim to the bottom, keeping my eyes open, and after considerable practice accomplished this feat. Quite wonderful, then, is the mystical green glimmer that illumines the whole of this submarine world. The fascinated eye is continually surprised by the most remarkable light-effects, quite different from those of the familiar upper world with its 'rosy radiance'; and doubly curious and interesting are the forms and movements of all the thousand different creatures swarming in the coral gardens. The diver is in a new world. Here are multitudes of remarkable fishes, crabs, snails, mussels, star-creatures, worms, etc., whose nourishment consists exclusively of the flesh of the coral animals on which their habitations are fixed; and these coral-devourers—one may appropriately term them 'parasites'—have, through adaptation to their peculiar mode of life, acquired the most astonishing forms, and have been furnished with weapons of defense and of offense of the most singular shapes.

"But, if the naturalist may not ramble free from danger among palms, neither may he swim unmolested among coral banks. The *Oceanidæ*, who jealously guard these cool fairy regions of the sea, threaten the intruder with a thousand dangers. The fire-corals (*Millepora*), as well as the medusæ swimming among their branches, sting, when touched, like the most resentful nettles. The floating cilia of many of the mailed fishes (*Synanceia*) inflict wounds that are as painful and dangerous as those of a scorpion. Many crabs nip in the severest manner with their powerful claws. Black sea-urchins (*Diadema*) bore their barbed spines, a foot long, into the flesh, where they break off and cause annoying sores. But the worst damage to the venturesome diver is inflicted by the corals themselves. The thousands of sharp points on their calcareous structures cut and abrade the skin in various ways. In all my life I never had such an excoriated and lacerated body as when coral-fishing at Punta Gallia, and I suffered from the wounds for several weeks. But what are these transitory sufferings to the naturalist whose whole life has been enriched by the marvelous experience and natural enjoyments of his visit to the wonderful banks of coral!"

Nature may well be willing to reveal her secrets to those who woo her in this courageous way. Nor is it less the delight of such lovers of nature to make the treasures they acquire the common possession of their kind, and such a treasure he is now preparing. The work of the professor now passing through the press is upon the organic world beneath the sea.*

In this blessed work of acquiring and imparting knowledge our author-hero spends his days, and we may almost say his nights too, surrounded by a happy family and a circle of friends to whom he is the most loveable and therefore

* It appeared in January, 1891, entitled Plankton-Studien—that is, Sea-Drift Studies—and is a remarkable contribution to the wonder-world of protoplasm, which has its real home in the sea-world hidden from our eyes. We hope soon to see a translation in English.

the most beloved of men—a circle that bids fair to include the enlightened world; and some parts not so enlightened, if we may judge from his difficulty in tearing himself from the embraces of his dusky Ceylonese attendants when he had to bid them a sad farewell! So also we must part from our consideration of him as a man, to greet him as a philosopher. But, in so doing, let us say: Fortunate it is for "the new thought" that he is not alone or singular among evolutionists and scientists, in being worthy of a new order of sainthood, in which devotion to truth and humanity is a saving grace to them, and to themselves for others. So was it with Darwin and Lyell, and so is it with their living co-workers and followers generally. There is no discount to be taken from their personal or general worth. When these pure nature-worshipers enter the Heaven where the whole human race appears in the Pantheon of memory, how soon will they rise above those ancient, mediæval, abnormal, sickly fanatics who have been canonized as "saints"!

And now, *secondly*, let us turn to the philosophy of these men, and especially of Prof. Haeckel, to find, if we can, the life motive, or *religion*, which inspires such noble results. They are all, indeed, scientific evolutionists; but, of them all, Haeckel appears to be the persistent, consistent, and complete evolutionist, and as such he is entitled to name this new philosophy and religion. The name which he has bestowed upon it is *Monism*. The only complete evolutionist? Darwin, Lyell, Huxley, Hooker, Gray, and others never went far beyond their special sciences—never assumed to be general philosophers, much less prophets and teachers of religion. Of those who have expressed "religious" views, we notice that Alfred R. Wallace, who shares with Darwin the discovery of natural selection, has become fatally involved in spiritualism and the ghost world, so that he believes that we can not reach the human Ego by natural selection. That assumption is, of course, fatal to his consistency and usefulness as far as general science and complete evolution are concerned. We follow him gladly until his appeal to our rational nature vanishes in the shadowy realms where superstition defies science. Then, like Newton, before the "Prophecies," his observing intellect is powerless. In a similar way Herbert Spencer starts out grandly, in his scheme of universal evolution, but develops his doctrine of the "Unknowable" before he reaches the human Ego, and thus his system becomes a duality which denies that the Ego is a correlate of the known or knowable world. His philosophy, therefore, leaves the backbone of the world of causal-sequence broken at the vital point where the objective and subjective unite in Humanity, but *not* in any Unknowable. The human head is thus fatally dissevered from its world-body. That is to say, he assumes that everything is only a symbol of reality; that every phenomenon is related to a "noumenon"; and that the consciousness of man is not a correlate of nerve and world changes; and so between the world *and* man lies an unaccountable gulf, which is an open gateway through which Fiske and Wallace and the clerical and spiritual "mediums" have (doubtless contrary to his intention) brought back the whole ghostly tribe of entities and spirits, gods and devils, to torture and rob the human race again. The trouble is, that Mr. Spencer, in assuming an "infinite and eternal energy" back of "all things," an absolutely unknowable, inscrutable, *unhuman* noumenon, has lost his grip on the infinite and eternal causal concatenation of things. He has run science ashore on the old sand and fog bank of superstition. There is nothing to do but to pull off, and to change our course under the true lights and verifiable methods of the correlation of "all things." *

Let us be thankful, then, that there is one complete evolutionist who knows that there is "a causal sequence of *phenomena*" from the farthest star up to and including the mind of man; and that *phenomena* are not metaphysical appearances or "symbols," but facts, events, changes, processes, realities! This avowal of the universality of the law of equivalence and correlation in the works of Prof. Haeckel renders them epoch-making books in philosophy and religion as well as in science. According to that law, which has no limit, no exception (not even of the human consciousness or Ego), THE WORLD is ONE; this doctrine is MONISM. All of the world's changes are held together by this one fundamental law of causal correlation, from our mind that thinks (the true noumenon), ever on in boundless space and time. Others had said the same thing partially, or in whispers. Haeckel said it boldly, and with an evident de-

* It may seem ungracious to refer thus to the "Prophecies" of Newton, the "Papacy" of Comte, the "Spiritism" of Wallace, and the "Unknowable" of Spencer and Fiske. But the errors of great men do great harm. Gratitude to them for their pre-eminent services, and protection from the harm of their errors, both require a fearless appeal to science, evolution, and their practical results. Sufficient time has passed to show, in the opinion of the writer, that none of the ideas above quoted can stand such an appeal.

termination to endure the consequences. The religious and political leaders of Germany were therefore not a little agitated when he came forward at the Association of German Naturalists and Physicians at Munich, in the autumn of 1877, with a paper that actually favored the practical teaching of evolutionary science and philosophy instead of the old-time theories. Thereupon, before the same assembly, as we have stated, Virchow was put to the front to defend the conservative, or *status in quo* position, against the incoming tide of evolution and monism. Haeckel replied, in a discourse known to the world as the book on Freedom in Science and Teaching. Together with Prof. Huxley's careful introduction, it should be familiar to all our readers. By this discussion the thinking world was brought face to face with monism as a philosophy, and thoughtful men everywhere are trying to answer the question, Can it stand?

Prof. Haeckel has chosen this term monism, so, as he says, to break away from the errors of the past, as indicated by the terms theism, materialism, spiritualism, etc., and also from complications *pro* or *con* with other modern philosophies, such as the positivism of Comte, the synthetism of Spencer, and the cosmism of Fiske, with whose systems any evolutionary philosophy must be nearly allied. But he prefers a new name and a fresh start, and takes it accordingly.

Both in Europe and in America monism has already a considerable and an influential following. The weekly paper and quarterly review, The Open Court and The Monist, under the very able editorship of Dr. Paul Carus, of Chicago, are devoted to the new philosophy, and may be taken as illustrations of the hold and ground which this new phase of scientific thought is gaining in America and elsewhere. We can no longer ignore it or be indifferent to it. We must squarely meet the question, Can it stand? *

Monism claims to be the last and most consistent word of science in philosophy. As above noted, it grows out of the extended application of the fundamental law of science—that of the equivalence and correlation of all knowable phenomena or changes possible to the whole world—thus binding it all together *ad infinitum* as a unity. The advocates

* Fundamental Problems, by Dr. Paul Carus, published by The Open Court Company, Chicago (price, $1), is the important opening work on monism in America.

of this philosophy are waiting for some one to bring forward good reasons for not assenting to this completed philosophy of science.

Let us see how it stands: The world is divided, as Aristotle of old said it, into matter, *not* living, and living. How does this doctrine apply to each? In the inorganic or material world, or world of *not* living matter, this law of the equivalence and correlation of changes or phenomena is universally accepted. The volume of essays by Grove and others, on The Correlation and Conservation of Forces, collected years ago by our friend Prof. E. L. Youmans (published by D. Appleton & Co.), swept the field and prepared the way for monism in this country. That is the substance of the story of our science, both of the least and of the greatest world-changes; they are all "correlates." The pull or push and the consequent motions, revolutions, and changes of our sun and of the solar system—are they not the correlates of other far-off celestial changes? Our earth and its surface, and all that takes place upon it—are these phenomena not correlates of the solar heat? Those mechanical and other changes as to the masses of matter of which we read in physics, as to its elements, of which chemistry informs us, and its modes of motion or processes, called heat, light, electricity, etc.—are they not correlates all? As to non-living matter, the question, therefore, is settled.

Next, as to living matter, or protoplasm, known only on the surface of our little earth, yet the most wonderful of all substances, "the physical basis of life"—can there be a different verdict? Its chemistry shows it to be a nitro-carbon in unstable chemical equilibrium (C, O, H, N, P, and S). Its changes are not only those chemical and physical changes attending other colloid or jelly forms of matter, but they include that wonderful process called life, which is the constant adjustment, reaction, and interaction of the organic mass, with its environment, including the processes of assimilation, growth, and division into cells and special organs. But these vital processes are manifest correlations of the changes occurring in the body of the organism and in the course of its ancestral development, or in the environment. Protoplasm is the material upon which the impinging world environment plays the music of life and ultimately the symphony of consciousness. That life-music is the correlate of the two series of changes—viz., the protoplasmic changes and the world changes. Life is not an entity, a substance, or spirit, or ghost, or spook; still less is consciousness such an entity. The latter as a correlate is *sui generis*. But if it must be compared to anything, let it be not to any gas or material substance, however impalpable, but to the imponderable agencies or forces—electricity, heat, light, etc. The life of man is a process resembling electric phenomena more than a rarefied gas, but it is distinctly correlated with certain physical conditions, and neither a gas, ether, nor electricity, nor anything but itself; and we must get rid of such gross materialism in dealing with the subject as that involved in the conception that life is a substantial entity. A state of consciousness is not a property or quality, or even a process of matter, but a *sui generis* correlate of such processes, and in no sense one of them or like them else it could not be their correlate.*

We must also thoroughly recover from the crude idea that correlates are mechanical mixtures, or we shall be materialists or spiritualists and not understand monism. The law is, that no correlate *ever* resembles its antecedent correlates, but is entirely distinct from them. For instance, water is the result of the chemical combination of oxygen and hydrogen gases, but is entirely different from them, and so it is with every other chemical, vital, or mental process and product.

In regard to vital and social phenomena, they are in a still higher degree disparate and entirely different from, and wholly incomparable with, the materials and changes from which they result. There is no "music" in the player or the piano, nor in the vibration of the air caused by the playing; but the correlate of that vibration, as it affects our nervous system, is the state of consciousness which we call music; and it resembles nothing whatever which has produced it, not even the changes in the nerve-cells immediately preceding or attending the consciousness. The passage from the physiological change to its psychical correlate, as Prof. Tyndall says in his Belfast address, is "unthinkable," but yet, as he says, it is a correlate; it "has its correlative in the physics of the brain"—and that is the all-important fact.† All correlations are in the same sense

* "My final conclusion, then, about the substantial soul is that it explains nothing and guarantees nothing. Its successive thoughts are the only intelligible and verifiable things about it, and definitely to ascertain the correlations of these with brain-processes is as much as psychology can empirically do." (Principles of Psychology, Chap. X, by Prof. William James, of Harvard University.)

† See his Fragments of Science, fifth edition (Appleton's), pp. 419, 420, 463, 524, and to the end of the volume.

"unthinkable." The music sensation is the resultant, the unthinkable correlate, of just such a concomitant nerve-change, and no other; and that nerve-change depends upon the correlation of the whole world, which stands behind and accompanies it. The consciousnesses of man, and the co-operation by which they become the Ego, may be called the *felt* music which the world constantly plays on our nervous systems, sensitive and quivering with their own unstable and assimilative life processes. Or, to say it again, like the *color* music, when the apparently *solid* rainbow springs from the falling drops as the sunlight plays upon them. That the psychical changes are "co-related" to the physical changes in the nerves, Mr. Spencer would doubtless admit, but the *correlation* is only complete when we take into account the generally omitted factor, the world environment, which really plays the music. Speculations on this subject are generally vitiated by the omission of or failure to realize this factor.

Thus it is in the organic world of nerve-action, and the mental world of consciousness, correlation is the bond of unlikes. Nor less is it true in sociology. The "body corporate and political," the Leviathan, as Hobbes calls it, exists as the co-operation of all the individuals and sub-organizations which compose it and influence its action. But the city, county, state, and nation is not to be found by any analysis of those parts. There is no city or quality of a city in any one citizen—no "teaminess" in one ox. Yet we have anarchists constantly reminding us that the whole can not be greater than all its parts! Just as though it could be anything like them, or they greater than it or like it?

It is necessary to bear in mind this law of the unlikeness of inseparable correlates, or monism can never be understood. When it is understood, the ever-varying world is made one, and is at the same time unlocked by it. Haeckel has beautifully illustrated this law in biology, where he has frequently made discoveries that would make the fortune and fame of ordinary naturalists. Take, for instance, his Evolution of Man, and follow the relations of the race in history and of the individual in embryo through the twenty-two stages. (On pages 44 and 189, vol. ii, of the Evolution of Man.) The formation of cells is correlated to their past and to their environment in the four simpler states. Then the inner and outer skins change forms, and develop into four other and higher stages. Then come the vertebrates in six grand divisions; then the mammals in eight higher classes, ending in man. Then every organ of the human system—the eye, ear, heart, lungs, etc.—is traced back to its original formation, and its changes are given till it evolves into its present form. The masterly way in which this is done we can hardly appreciate until we see it restated by other competent naturalists; for instance, in a pamphlet which I hold in my hand, by Prof. Lester F. Ward, of the Smithsonian Institution of Washington, entitled Haeckel's Genesis of Man, which I hope you may see, and which you may doubtless obtain from him on application.

But still more wonderful than this physical correlation is the constant increase of the *mental* correlation in proportion to the rise and complexity of the physical organization of animals until, finally, the highest individual manhood and socially the highest civilization is reached. Each of the twenty-two steps which lead from protoplasm to man has its "soul," the psychical correlate of its own physical state, its conditions, and its world environment. In all this Haeckel follows the plain intimation and conclusion of Darwin, and leaves the world of matter, life, and mind a unity and not a duality. He traces mental evolution back to the *protozoa*, and thence, step by step, up to the highest "creations" of Shakespeare or Goethe. There is no break, no duality in this world, and no limit to its correlated phenomena. The *is* is ever the child of the *was*. There is no creation other than causal, efficient, inevitable correlation. In nature every transaction is a reality—a complete effect and cause. *Phenomena* are not *appearances* in the sense of being symbols of an unknowable reality, as Herbert Spencer and his agnostic disciples would make us believe, but they are actual *events* of which our sensation is a direct correlate. There can be, therefore, no "unknowable," for everything, including the mind of man, being a correlate of every other thing, may be brought into correlation with it and with our consciousness. The unknown may be practically affirmed to be infinite, but there is no break in or duality between the mind of man and the world of which it is a correlative part.

To the agnosticism of Huxley and Dr. Carus as a confession of intellectual modesty, monism would answer, Yes. To that of Spencer (or Huxley) as an assertion of an unknowable "entity," "energy" or "power," back of phenomena, "from whence *all* things proceed," and beyond *possible* correlation and knowledge—decidedly, *No!* *

By the same law, the spiritism of Wallace and the supernatural beings and entities of theologians and metaphysicians are simply impossible. They are all illusions, or the results of illusions or delusions, which have been explained or are to be explained by science. The verdict of the law of scientific correlation remands them at once to the limbo of all spooks—the world of the imagination. You might as well argue in favor of the astronomy of Ptolemy because the sun rises in the east, as to argue in favor of the existence of disembodied ghosts because of the common illusions of our senses. There are illusions, delusions, and frauds, naturally enough and in abundance, but there can be no genuine "spiritual phenomena." There is no chance of a possibility for such a thing as a spirit, a ghost, or Spencer's unknowable "entity" to exist, for there is nothing left over, and no chance-work possible between correlations under this law of correlation. Existence and correlation are one and the same thing. There can be no life to come, except as it may be a correlate of this life. There can be no duality in the universe. Belief in duality is a sin against science. Everything, *ad infinitum*, is conceivable as correlation, and therefore it is reality or nothing. There is no possible room for an extra-mundane God, a ghost, or a spook any way or anywhere The true God is the totality of the correlated universe—the divine reality. The monistic conception is not of a "first cause," "power," or "energy" outside of all things, "from whence all things flow," but that the *only* cause and causes are *in* things—all things. Every change is effect *and* cause in never-ending correlation, of which no exception or limit is conceivable. The *phenomenal* world is a reality having its *noumenon* in the human intellect, its correlate and its interpreter.

Such is the philosophy of monism. In it we have the philosophy of Bruno, Spinoza, and Goethe extended and made exact by the discoveries of modern science—the indestructibility of matter and the equivalence and correlation of all knowable world-changes or "forces," as they are sometimes dangerously called, for some people are in danger of thinking of force as an entity and not a change.

* See Fundamental Problems, by Dr. Paul Carus, especially the chapter on Agnosticism and Phenomenalism. The Stronghold of Mysticism, pp. 137-154-162, and *passim*. See, also, Discussion on the Nature and Reality of Religion, between Herbert Spencer and Frederick Harrison, pp. 35, 166, 172, and *passim*.

But if this philosophy must stand, where are we? What is left for human consolation? Well, things may not be so very bad, after all. "There is no wisdom save in truth." We used to be frightened by ghost stories, but now people seem to be frightened when science tells them that they are realities and not spooks. They seem to think that life becomes too terrifically earnest when we consider it so, and a flight back into some "unknowable" mystery is sought as a relief—much as we seek shade from the glare of the sun. When each Ego sees itself as the *burning* point where the infinite world correlates into consciousness, it naturally at first looks around for a more modest and less responsible position. But, again, correlation is our refuge and defense. The freedom of the will is the grateful illusion which gives us a little world of our own, by which we relieve our fatality and bring *our* light to bear upon the great objective world, and weave our existence into it as a satisfying immortal creative power. Thus, life is worth living, and insures immortality by its beneficence; thus, religion and morals receive a solid, scientific foundation. For the will, scientifically explained, becomes the basis of the world of human effort—our subjective world.

The freedom of the will results as a practical fact from the law that correlations are distinct from each other. The will, as a faculty of the life, mind, or soul, has, and can have, no *consciousness* of its own origin, and so is, as to itself, *free.* As such, it acts *apparently* independently in the order of affairs, and counts for much (in Prof. Huxley's phrase) "in the order of events." In this way it becomes the foundation of morals and discipline and practical life. In a similar way, the rising of the sun in the east founds our practical almanacs and daily duties; but objectively the sun does not rise at all; so our will is disclosed by science to be a result of our own life and mind and the world about us. Thus will, free as a correlate, becomes the base of moral relations; but all those relations are shown by science to be subject to objective law, which underlies the human will just as it does the "rising sun." The illusions are explained, the lights remain!

The objections to this monistic philosophy generally come from those who fail to comprehend or to realize the free-will and moral results of its fundamental laws of correlation, and especially the fact that no correlate resembles its antecedent correlates. Prof. Haeckel is by no means clear of confusing expressions. For instance, he speaks of "*mechanical* life phenomena," "atom soul," all matter being considered "equally living," "molecule soul," "carbon soul," etc., which enable objectors like Virchow and others to obtain the only advantage they have ever obtained in their discussions with him. But until life and mind are found to be the correlate of non-living matter, and not of the organic action of protoplasm *only*, such expressions by Prof. Haeckel and other monists are to be limited to the protoplasmic matter—the brains of animals, where only sentiency and thought do exist. Otherwise they are simply poetical expressions as though they were used by the poets Goethe or Wordsworth, or by Comte, "subjectively," as when, for "worship" purposes, he styles the earth "Le grand fétich." So the word "mechanical" is often used by Haeckel to mean natural, causal, correlative. Objectors who have nothing better than criticisms of such verbal errors of expression have need to remember logician Mill's rule of safety in such discussions, viz.: "Unless you refute your opponent at his best, you are refuted by him." Haeckel is a German and a specialist, and thus, as a monist, may have sometimes hazy or limited modes of expression and exposition, but, at his best, he stands on the verified, irrefragable, invincible, inexpugnable law which makes realities of and unifies the facts and processes of the whole world, and compels us to conceive the world as an objective unity, and not as a duality. Therefore, until this law of correlation can be shown to have a *limit* or an *exception*, the philosophy of monism stands impregnable; and Haeckel, who gave it this name and recognized its scientific completeness, is rightfully regarded as its latest leading champion.

For, *thirdly*, Prof. Haeckel is prominent as a religionist and a reformer-prophet.

The position of Prof. Haeckel as a leading naturalist and philosopher would doubtless be gracefully acknowledged by the conservative and even the retrograde influences if he would not, as he does on every fitting occasion, lift up the voice of a *prophet* and insist that this "monism" is also a religion. In a word, that it is *the* future Religion of Science and Humanity, now in its nascent state. This fact makes him a sort of terror to the spiritual, political, and temporal "powers that be," and a subject of greater interest to us. For if the philosophy of monism is scientifically sound there is no escape from monism as the religion of scientific people

—that is, of people really intelligent on this subject. All religion has been very well defined as some philosophy of the world applied in practice and warmed by the consequent emotions. Our morality we may then call our individual practice of such religion in social life and intercourse. Back of every religion, therefore, lies some view and theory of the world, a cosmology or philosophy, by which each people or sect ciphers out, as best it can, some tolerable relation to the mighty world and the social organism and all their fellow human beings. We find the religious history of our race to consist, therefore, of a gradual evolution of its leading peoples from a broad base of general animism and fetichism, thence to astrology, thence to polytheism, thence to monotheism, and thence to *scientism*, expressed chiefly to us in the pantheism of Goethe, the positivism of Comte, the synthetism of Spencer, the cosmism of Fiske, and finally by the *monism* of Haeckel. He proposed this word monism as expressive of the world-unifying law of science, as the summary of all that was true and good in the other philosophic names proposed by the philosophers just named, while it excluded what he regards as the crude and vulgar notions of materialism, spiritualism, and dualism.

Our professor is very brave, like many Germans, in inventing new words instead of adding new meanings or shades of meaning to old ones. If scientific people would take *religiously* to this name, monism, it would certainly help to clear up things wonderfully, for it excludes at once a mass of old errors and misconceptions which will hang around the old words; but to many it is just this protective twilight of uncertainty in philosophy and religion—half concealing and half revealing—which makes old names, symbols, and ideas alternately repelling and attractive, tantalizing and comforting. Our monist prophet has brought us well out of this twilight, and the situation looks better the clearer it is seen. Every clear view of the world is followed by a sincere conviction, and such conviction becomes a "faith" and an enduring well-spring of energy and consolation. Monism in that view rises above all religions as the culmination of all. If anything can be, it is the *universal faith.* Because it is based upon verified science, it is *positive* monism; because it depends upon the objective unity of the world, it is *monistic* positivism. By one name or another the highest scientific solution of the world, society, and man, when scientific methods are carried to their final results over every known domain, must result in a scientific faith.

This scientific faith, or faith according to knowledge, is certainly the rising faith of mankind. It received its solid, everlasting foundation when Copernicus, Bruno, and Galileo gave us the true solar system, which revealed to us a new earth and a new heaven, and consequently a new philosophy, finally to lead to this new religion. From Descartes, Spinoza, Bacon, and Diderot, Goethe received this new world of science, barren and forlorn, as it rose out of the chaos of the French revolution. He was the first great creative and furnishing soul that fully moved into it to stay. He peopled it with enduring and even human characters, sowed the seed to cover the naked landscape with use and beauty, and made the very clouds glow with a light that foretold a higher heaven than humanity had ever dreamed.

Haeckel is fond of quoting Goethe; and well he may be. As we recede in time, the distance brings out, mountain-like, the true height of this poet-prophet of the new faith of the new era. We begin to see how he, in science, had a sure prevision of the results of our evolution; in politics, he discounted the French revolution and the metaphysical anarchy of his and even of our time; in religion, he rightly estimated all the theologies, and sung the emancipation of erring man (Faust), from the very devil to whom he had sold himself, and the conquest of a heaven of ever-increasing progress and blessedness by his *own* victorious striving to accomplish the good. In a wonderful poem called Inheritance (*Vermächtniss*) Goethe expressly dates the new era from "the sage who showed the earth to circle around the sun and taught her sister orbs their paths."

These triumphs of astronomy, followed by similar progress in physics and chemistry, made sure the *material* foundation of the scientific faith at the close of the last century. Our century opened with the great triumphs in biology, or the organic world, led by Oken, Goethe, and especially the unappreciated Lamarck. They laid the foundation of the new faith in the *vital* world, upon which Darwin and Haeckel have well-nigh completed the structure. From Lamarck's Philosophie Zoologique (1809) Haeckel quotes this biological foundation in a useful summary, as follows (History of Creation, vol. i, p. 112):

"The systematic division of classes, orders, families, genera, and species, as well as their designations, are the arbitrary and artificial productions of man. The kinds or species of organisms are of unequal age, developed one after another, and show only a relative and temporary persistence. Species arise out of varieties. The differences in the conditions of life have a modifying influence on the organization, the general form, and the parts of animals, and so has the use or disuse of organs. In the first beginning only the very simplest and lowest animals and plants came into existence; those of a more complex organization only at a later period. The course of the earth's development, and that of its organic inhabitants, was continuous, not interrupted by violent revolutions. Life is purely a physical phenomenon. All the phenomena of life depend on mechanical, physical, and chemical causes, which are inherent in the nature of matter itself. The simplest animals and the simplest plants, which stand at the lowest point in the scale of organization, have originated and still originate by spontaneous generation. All animate natural bodies or organisms are subject to the same laws as inanimate natural bodies or organs. The ideas and actions of the understanding are the emotional phenomena of the central nerve system. The will is in truth never free. Reason is only a higher degree of development and combination of judgments." Thus was the truth spoken, but none then had ears to hear.

Next as to the sociological foundation:

In 1857 Auguste Comte, another unappreciated Frenchman, had done for sociology what Copernicus did for astronomy and Lamarck had done for biology. He had named and outlined and *misapplied* that science. He discovered that man was not the product of Nature only, but of society and its continuity and solidarity; that there was no solution of man without society: "*Entre l'homme et le monde il faut l'humanité.*" Between man and the world, he said, there lies, and there is need of, humanity, as the solution of the world and the saviour of man. Comte, if he did not originate, brought into order *the* first positive philosophy, and on it founded *his* "positive" religion. We have from him some indispensable things lying at the very base of monism, which, because of his papistic notions, are fatally overlooked, but without which monism can not be understood or appreciated, viz.:

1. A truer view of the relativity of knowledge; that it relates to man and not to any objective "noumenon."

2. A true correlative classification of the special sciences, viz., astronomy, physics, chemistry, biology, sociology, ethics, psychology; that is, from the greater and general to the smaller and more complex—i. e., from the star-world down to the mind of man.

3. The law of the "three states," or of "deanthropomorphization," as John Fiske states it with his peculiar brevity. That is, that man's philosophical conceptions develop from theology to metaphysics, and finally to science.

4. The supremacy of humanity; as the solution, guarantor, and chief factor of human life and human affairs.

5. The general law of interdependence; that the higher rests upon the lower, but that both are for each other.

6. That rights and duties are the two sides of the same relation under the love, order, and progress of scientific sociology.

The French people are slow to discover their great men. Lamarck and Comte have never been understood by theological and metaphysical France; and the France of science, aside from narrow-minded specialism, has yet chiefly to come.

The works of Herbert Spencer and of our own John Fiske are also able approaches to monism, and are too well known in this country to require lengthy exposition here. They have added materially to the better understanding of the new philosophy and religion of science, and, as commentaries upon and contributions toward it, are invaluable. We have noted the error that seems to many common to them both, so plainly pointed out and dwelt upon by Frederic Harrison, the English positivist, in his celebrated religious discussions with Mr. Spencer—viz., the unwarranted assumption of an unknowable "entity" or "energy" back of *phenomena* and back of human consciousness. This seems to be plainly irreconcilable with the doctrine of universal correlation. And that it is as plainly "unreligious" in its practical consequences, I think Mr. Harrison has made equally manifest in the Discussion referred to.

The cosmic emotion, with its wonder, awe, and veneration, is excited and best sustained by *The All*—the world of correlation—and not by any "energy" outside of it: "from whence *all* things flow," as Mr. Spencer tells us. The "*all* things" which does not include all possible "energy" is an incomplete schedule. "Energy" is a correlated part of "*all* things" or it is nothing. It is this uncorrelated nothing which is the nest-egg of all superstition and which breeds uncertainty and terror instead of true, healthy world-worship, the cosmic emotion of Goethe, Shelley, Byron, Wordsworth, and of the modern school of natural poetry and painting—the proper emotional side of modern science.

Fortunately, Prof. Haeckel is not bothered by the "unknowable noumenon," nor was Comte or Goethe. All expressions from their works that seem to imply that they placed a "noumenon" outside of the world, mankind or the Ego, are, in religion, as in philosophy, to be reconciled with science or read as poetry. As scientists and religionists they held no parley with "unknowable" energies, entities, or spooks of any kind, following strictly Faust's last advice to man:

> "Wenn Geister spucken, geh' er seinen Gang."
> When ghosts spook, let him go straight on his way.

Or, again:

> "Willst du in Unendliches schreiten?
> Geh' nur in endlichen nach allen Seiten!"
>
> In the Infinite wilt thou stray?
> Through the Finite take thy way!

The astonishing thing about Goethe, Comte, and Haeckel is that they in religion so thoroughly emancipated themselves from theology and metaphysics; and two of them were Germans! The result is, that they and their school of *general* scientists and reformers are, as we enter the new era, the chief sources of any true enlightenment or guidance, especially in religious, social, or political affairs. Of course these men are in no sense to be regarded individually as models, but they had reached the scientific, historical spirit, which is always integrative, saving, and yet progressive. Take, for example, Comte's view of sociology and politics. These, like the conception of God and every other subject, according to Comte's law, evolve through the three stages of theology, metaphysics, and science. The old theologic phase or method in sociology and politics is that of divine command or authority. "Thus saith the Lord," etc. Then comes the metaphysical stage and phase, which is one of defiance, rights, revolutions, "administrative nihilism," refusal to co-operate or do anything but to agitate, fume, and grumble. This spirit of anarchy, now rampant among our reformers, is in many respects more destructive and unprogressive than the old principle of authority. It can never agree upon any proposition for social reform but not to do it. Rights are fatally divorced from duties.

But there is a third view and spirit in regard to social and political affairs—a spirit of science, which breathes from the works of the great men we have named. That spirit is evolutionary. It is integrative and yet differentiative, conservative and yet progressive—laying the sure foundation of the real liberty and welfare of the individual in the social, integrative order, which, no matter what the form of government, can alone make such liberty and welfare possible. Take, for instance, Goethe's remarkable letter from the Dornberg Castle in 1828, to which we have referred, on the death of the Duke, upon the administration of the little world of the Duchy of Weimar, and compare its far-reaching wisdom, resting upon the continuity and solidarity of society, with the shallowness of the French social philosophy of that day or of our current metaphysical anarchism. Or do the same with the sociology of Comte—excepting, of course, his papistic Utopia, which belongs only to the past polity of the Latin races, as to which he was misled, largely by De Maistre's work on the Pope.

Then turn to the latter part of Haeckel's Freedom of Science and Teaching, and see how under the scientific spirit he, too, preserves the integrative and the differentiative sides of social progress, and refuses to be driven into anarchy by the taunts of Virchow, who evidently sought in that way to compass his destruction. Haeckel had never the time to study deeply history, law, statesmanship, or politics, yet his scientific instinct and spirit enabled him to apply in sociology the law of biology; that true progress in the social, as in the animal, world must be an ever-increasing integration of the functions of organs ever increasing in their freedom of individual action. This law, stated by Goethe fifty years ago and quoted from him by our Carey as the basis of his great work on Social Science, is just as true of a jelly-fish as of an elephant—of a Roman Empire as of a man; it is true of every social organism; of the Republic of the United States, or of the Republic of the World! If some intimation of this law could reach our anarchistic reformers, how soon their metaphysical bubbles would collapse!

Finally.—If we turn to the treatment of the religious progress of mankind under this scientific spirit of evolution, we find the wisdom and influence of the same great men a source of real health and strength. They *only* give us *religion* without the superstition of theology or the anarchy of metaphysics. It seems clear that from them and their spirit we must learn or go on from bad to worse. The religion which is the social, integrative, co-operative, and saving element of human nature can no longer be fed and sustained by ghostly gods, spooky devils, categorical imperatives, or inscrutable unknowables. Voltaire (as quoted on the title-page of his Biography by James Parton) asks the pertinent question which he could not answer:

> "'Tis a pity to spend half of our life in destroying enchanted castles. Far better to establish truths than to examine lies—but where are the truths?"

Thanks to evolution, the truths have come and are coming in their good time. Up to Voltaire's day the known world had been little more than an enchanted, or rather ghost-haunted, castle of existence. His German successor, Goethe, used the true to realize the good and beautiful. He accepted this life in the monistic spirit as the real fact, and the whole world and God as *one—The All.* The conceptions of God from the Hebrew prophets down, when freed from limitations and anthropomorphisms, end in this objective conception of God as *The All;* not as a ghost, spirit, or spook, outside of the universe, but as reality itself, infinite and eternal. We have thus the scientifically revised definition: God is the world, infinite, eternal, and unchangeable in its being and in its laws, but ever varying in its correlations.

Goethe, by true and grand expressions of divine and cosmic emotion, raised aloft as the true revelation of God the monistic concept which has been worked out by the modern objective sciences still in their glorious career of progress.

The next great fruitful religious development of our time seems to come from the Latin race through the word of Comte, that the true Christ is Humanity itself.

"Between man and the world there lies, and there is need of, humanity"; this can not be repeated too often. The organic action of society is the foundation of all social and individual progress.

Only by this mediator and saviour, Humanity, is there any real hope or salvation for the individual. Only by this Son of Man and of God can we come unto the Father—the divine universe. Herbert Spencer, though often dissenting from M. Comte's ideas, bases his own best work upon his sociological principles. Notice, for instance, his splendid demonstration of the organic nature of society and history in his Sociology, and his often-repeated proof that the "innate ideas" are the results of *race*-inheritance instead of individual experience. In all such cases he is following the line of the great inspirations of our day, which are based upon the continuity and solidarity of mankind. Our great American patriots and orators from the Revolution to Lincoln, and especially in the grander orations of Daniel Webster, have these fundamental ideas and sentiments as their inspiration. The generations past and to come underlie, sustain, and consecrate every appeal to duty and patriotism.

Thus, as the conception of the Christ as a man, under evolutional criticism, vanishes from history, the *ideal Messiah*, which gave rise to the belief that there was once such a man, has become incarnated in the history and fact of the evolution of the race itself, revealing it as our ever-living Saviour.

The next *person* of the old religious Trinity is no longer the Holy Ghost, but the holy life of man, in which we all partake, and which is the most precious thing in the world —human life! Its co-operative altruistic power is our true sustainer and "comforter."

The "Holy Mother" of the Roman faith is enlarged, as in the concluding line of Faust, into the "Eternal-womanly" that leads humanity ever upward and on. In a word, she is Womanhood—continuous, replacing, sustaining, glorified as "Maiden, Mother, Queen, and Goddess."

The true Bible is no longer those old Hebrew and Greek documents, strangely bound together as one book; but the books, good and true, of the whole world and of all time.

The Creed is not any number of Church Articles, but the conclusions of science, ever being revised, and expressed in a positive philosophy as the best description of the knowable world.

Of the *Heavens and Hells*, "the places that knew them once now know them no more." But in the misery and joy, the remorse and blessedness of the human hearts they have their new location; and between them stands every day as the *Day of Judgment.*

There is scarcely a name, symbol, or line of the old faiths which can not be thus found to be replaced and enlarged by the new and true view of the world and of human life and destiny.

There is no time nor need to continue further here these old religious names, once believed in as facts, and which now are of value only as symbols of the grander truths since evolved, but which they, if still used, may express. How to thus translate them, these hints only must suffice. The illusions depart, the truths remain!

When the old religions fall, what will you give in their place? We answer, *Religion!* Look around! The enchanted castle of existence of the past was but a half-seen, discolored prophecy of the truth which is replacing it, with a grandeur and a reality that terrifies the soul at first. People are frightened when science tells them that this world is the real one, and "the other" its shadow. But this true world includes all—is The All! It brings with it a new philosophy, religion, morality, life, and motive, which is an enduring well-spring of energy, consolation, and hope—not of pessimism nor optimism, but of ever-victorious meliorism.

Do not as an ethical society fear that the old moral lights will be blown out and darkness result. The true scientific foundation will replace the old, as in our cities the scientific electric light has come to take the place of the old smoky lamps. To secure such replacement, throughout the whole individual and social domain of human affairs, is the motive and inspiration of those scientists who, in Europe and America, put their conclusions before the people in the simplest language, yet ever eloquent with these new purposes and hopes. Of the noblest of such teachers and prophets none stands forth more prominently than Ernst Haeckel. From his concluding words at that Munich contest rings out the motto which, in a word, expresses the impulse of his own life, and of the creative era of the new faith of Monism: *Impavidi progrediamur!* "Undaunted we press ever on!" But in this motto we can not escape the echo of a verse of Goethe's magnificent "Symbol" of the progress of man—progress between "the great silences" of the stars and the grave—a poem which Carlyle has called, and made immortal to us as, the deepest, grandest word of our time:

Die Zukunft decket	The future hides
Schmerzen und Glücke.	Sorrows and gladness.
Schrittweis dem Blicke,	Stepwise to the sight,
Doch ungeschrecket,	Yet undaunted,
Dringen wir vorwärts!	We press ever on!

ABSTRACT OF THE DISCUSSION.

Mr. Nelson J. Gates:

The intelligent world owes a debt of gratitude to Prof. Haeckel. It is due to his labors, mainly, that the doctrine of evolution is now as well established as Kepler's laws of the motions of the planetary bodies, or Newton's law of gravitation. No careful student of modern scientific thought now doubts that the law of cause and effect prevails throughout all phenomena, whether physical or mental. Every effect is the exact product of antecedent causes. Thought is as much the product of the conditions under which it arises as is the formation of a crystal or the growth of a tree. There is no room for supernatural interference anywhere. Though the natural evolution of living forms out of non-living matter has not been demonstrated as a fact of present occurrence, there is no doubt in the mind of consistent evolutionists that the most primitive organisms were originally produced by spontaneous generation. Prof. Haeckel's investigations in embryology constitute a most important confirmation of the Darwinian theory, and entitle him to be placed in the front rank of experimental scientists.

Prof. P. H. Van der Weyde:

Dr. Vander Weyde exhibited a series of drawings enlarged from plates contained in the works of Prof. Haeckel, illustrative of human evolution. The lowest form of mankind was shown to be scarcely as intelligent in appearance as the higher apes, and the brain capacity of the lowest races was but little superior to that of the highest non-human mammals. He also explained, by the aid of a map, Prof. Haeckel's theory as to the geographical distribution of the human race. Dr. Van der Weyde saw no difficulty in conceiving that all living things, including man, were developed from eternally existing matter—only the matter itself must have been living matter, not dead and inert, as was formerly believed.

Dr. Robert G. Eccles:

Mr. Wakeman wholly misunderstands Mr. Spencer's position as to the nature of mind or consciousness. Mr. Spencer does not regard consciousness as an entity, but as a phenomenal process. Mr. Wakeman's position respecting consciousness as a temporary phase of being, causally correlated with brain changes, positively implies the miracle of creation and opposes the doctrine of natural evolution. The physical facts of extension, motion, and time involved in the molecular or functional activities of the brain can by no possible conjuring be conceived of in terms of consciousness. Between the two series of processes there is an impassable gulf in thought. No thinkable arrangements of the former can enable us to conceive the latter as being caused thereby. An unthinkable proposition is a false proposition, if we can place any reliance on reason. He wants us to believe that when matter and motion are properly arranged together in the brain, and played upon by the changes of the external world, by some "presto, change" process, we get mind; and yet he holds that neither matter nor motion contains any distinctly psychic elements when apart or combined in any other manner than in the brain. His statement is exactly equivalent to saying that by certain arrangements of the particles of two mountains they could be set side by side without a valley between. We know that Nature changes her form incessantly, but we have no evidence that she ever creates anything new. The substance, time, space, motion, and consciousness of things may assume endless guises, but we have no reason for supposing an increase or diminution in quantity of either. Modes of consciousness, like modes of motion, may change, but both, so far as we know, persist everlastingly in some form; at least, such is the logical conclusion of the evolutionist. When Mr. Wakeman tells us that there is no room anywhere in the universe for a god or a spook, he arrogantly assumes knowledge which man neither does nor ever can possess. What can a finite creature with finite knowledge ever know about the possibilities of the infinite? Has he grasped every fact of nature to enable him to tell whether his stupendous assumption does or does not agree with them? A more modest man might make his statement as a mere unverified belief, for which he alone is responsible, but to put it forward as established truth is preposterous. We know nothing of the universe as it exists apart from our own consciousness, which is finite and limited in its modes of activity. Our knowledge is necessarily limited to the narrow range of our experience. What we know, therefore, is in ourselves. We can know the external universe only symbolically. As well might the eyeless worm try to picture the world as we see it, as we to picture the actual totality of conditions of the Universal Being in which we are incessantly enveloped.

DR. LEWIS G. JANES:

Evolution has a very broad back. It can carry all sorts of theories of the universe, and not break down under the load. Our biographical lectures have at least been successful in demonstrating that the doctrine of evolution can be held in connection with a great variety of theological and anti-theological speculations. Yet, when any complete philosophical statement of the doctrine is attempted, we find, I think, substantial agreement in fundamental principles. Darwin, as has been said, did not assume to have any consistent, well-ordered explanation of the general philosophy of evolution. He appeared to incline at one time to theistic, at another to materialistic views of the world, yet he named Herbert Spencer "our greatest philosopher," and did not expressly dissent from his main doctrines. Asa Gray was a pronounced theist, who did not regard the doctrine of evolution as inconsistent with his Presbyterian profession of faith. Wallace is a spiritualist, and Prof. Haeckel a monist, but not more of one, as I understand it, than Darwin or Spencer. The doctrine of evolution is unquestionably indebted to Prof. Haeckel more than to any living biological investigator for an immense and orderly array of facts in its support. He has also contributed something of value to its broader field of philosophical thought. Mr. Wakeman's interpretation of Haeckel's monistic philosophy, however, to my mind, is not entirely correct or adequate. It is not, as I understand it from his writings, inconsistent with the recognition of the psychological principle of the relativity of our knowledge, on which rests Herbert Spencer's doctrine of the unknowable. On the contrary, it expressly recognizes this principle. Prof. Haeckel clearly states the doctrine of relativity in numerous passages in his writings. In his History of Creation he says: "We nowhere arrive at a knowledge of first causes. . . . In explaining the most simple physical or chemical phenomena, as the falling of a stone, or the formation of chemical combinations, we arrive . . . at other remoter phenomena which are in themselves mysterious. This arises from the limitation or relativity of our powers of understanding. We must not forget that human knowledge is absolutely limited, and possesses only a relative extension. It is, in its essence, limited by the very nature of our senses and of our brains." He also evidently believes that life is no mere by-play of nature, as Mr. Wakeman has represented it to be, but a constant and eternal ingredient in the universe. He speaks of "the animating of all matter, the inseparability of mental power and corporeal substance." He quotes approvingly Goethe's assertion that "matter can never exist and be active without mind, nor can mind without matter." With Mr. Spencer he recognizes mind and matter as the eternally related but opposing sides of one substantial reality. He calls his philosophy a "mechanical" philosophy, it is true—using this term, as I understand him, in common with a school of European thinkers, to indicate the universality of the principle of causation—of what we term "law," as opposed to chance, caprice, or miracle. In this respect, too, he is in entire agreement with Mr. Spencer. The doctrine of the unknowable does not imply any interference with the causal correlation of phenomena. It does not open the door, as Mr. Wakeman has implied, to the primitive ghost or "spook" idea. Prof. Haeckel's views are not, in the old-fashioned "metaphysical" terminology, materialistic, any more than are Mr. Spencer's. In his reply to Prof. Virchow he says: "All human knowledge as such is subjective." He declares gravitation a mere hypothesis, and says: "All the conceptions which we possess of the chemical structure and affinities of matter are subjective hypotheses, mere conceptions as to the positions and changes of position of the various atoms, whose very existence is incapable of proof." It would be easier to construct a system of idealism on such foundation principles than a materialistic system. Both Herbert Spencer and John Fiske, the ablest exponents of the philosophy of evolution in England and America, have expressly disclaimed the alleged materialistic implications of this philosophy. Neither mind nor matter, according to Mr. Spencer, is a substance or "thing in itself"; both are phenomenal, symbolically representative of one unknowable reality. The Spencerian philosophy is a monistic system, based upon this unknowable reality. The proof that this reality is unknowable, in its essential nature, is not metaphysical, but purely scientific, depending as it does upon the scientific demonstration of the nature and limitations of our modes of sense-perception. The pictures which we form of the external world are simply synthetized symbols of the psycho-physiological sensations which we derive from contact with it. As the symbols are constant, however, we recognize the order of nature as steadfast, we accept it as a real, objective fact, which corresponds with our symbolical conceptions. The world, therefore, is not an illusion; our knowledge is a real, though representative and symbolical, knowledge of real objective relations.

Mr. Wakeman, in reply:

My thanks are due to Mr. Gates for his very concise, clear, and able statement of the general conclusion set forth in my lecture, and which, I believe, will in time become the conviction of all who carefully think and investigate.

I am also under deep obligations to Prof. Vander Weyde for his kind and sustaining words, as often I have been during many years of pleasant and helpful intercourse with him in matters of science and reform. We all recognize in him a worthy representative—may we not almost say, in view of his advanced years, survivor?—successor, certainly, of Huygens and the great physicists and discoverers, who have made his native Holland glorious as the nursery and home of science and liberty. His remarks this evening have not only been in the line of my lecture, but his charts and drawings have made evolution visible to the eye and mind at once, and so have done what no lecture otherwise could.

But what shall I say of my two opposing critics, Dr. Eccles and Dr. Janes? Fortunately, by taking the last first, they help to explain the lecture, and to extinguish each other.

Dr. Janes, for instance, well confirms all I said about the great variety of limited and incomplete evolutionists; and he joins with me in placing Prof. Haeckel in the front rank as a naturalist and philosopher. That the lecture was "inadequate" may be true, for the whole of a new system of philosophy and religion could hardly be adequately presented in one lecture, and I claim to deserve well of you that I did not further try to insert in it the "whole world and the rest of mankind."

Whether what I did insert is "correct" or not must not be left to critics prepossessed by opposite views, but to an impartial view of the whole field. I was trying to see how the science, philosophy, and religion of positive monism, or monistic positivism—either will do—could be held in its extreme and most thorough statement, and without regard to captious and verbal objections which could be picked out of Haeckel or any master. I am familiar with all these clauses the doctor has cited, and think they amount to nothing but the using of Haeckel's words in an anti-monistic sense. For instance, he invokes "The Relativity of Knowledge." Yes, certainly; but relative to what? Why, as the rest of the sentence shows, "to our senses and brains," the human mind; as all monists say: but not at all to any "unknowable entity." Then the doctor mistakenly makes me say that life or consciousness is a "by-play of nature." No expression could be more anti-monistic. Nature, as Goethe and Haeckel teach, has no by-plays nor inside nor out. Life, mind, and the Ego are the outflowering correlate and glory of all nature, and no by-play at all! But for that very reason they can not be a constant, universal, eternal "ingredient" in nature—any more than the flower and fragrance of the plant are ingredients in its roots, or the earth out of which it grows. Of course, we also say: "Mental power and corporeal substance are inseparable." But this substance is no unknowable entity or spook, but the *prior* correlations from which mental action is the caused and causal sequence.

The doctor then makes a fog by confounding what Goethe, Haeckel, and other poets and philosophers have said about matter being "alive." This he does by overlooking the distinction between the spontaneous motion, or "life," of inorganic matter, and the vital and psychic life found only in organized matter—i. e., *protoplasm.* Goethe, Haeckel, Carus, and the rest of them are constantly comparing these very disparate processes; but no one now, with a bit of sense left, ever really confounds them. They are compared for poetic purposes, as Goethe does artistically and avowedly, or for pseudo-religious purposes, as some modern theological "apologists" do. Dr. Carus (Fundamental Problems, pp. 111, 114, 128, 130, etc.) thus states the proper distinction, made by common sense every time: "We must well distinguish this kind of life in a broader sense (which is an inherent quality of matter) from the vegetable and animal organisms. The former is elementary and eternal; the latter is complex and unstable, because produced by a combination of the former. Spontaneity is an inherent quality in all matter, and if spontaneously moving bodies have to be called 'alive,' we must acknowledge that nature throughout is alive. . . . The word life, however, as commonly understood, is applied to organized life only. . . . The essential difference is the *absence* of organic growth and psychic life in one, and its presence in the other." Then he speaks of "all organized and psychic life as evolved from the general life of the universe," and he adds that a "psychic life, considered as foreign to our world," is the "corner-stone of dualism."

This is the monistic view, and Dr. Carus expressly states in The Open Court of March 13, 1890, after a personal interview with Prof. Haeckel at Jena, that this professor agrees with this version of monism, and not with agnosticism at all.*

Now, all this is stated by monists to refute and rule out "the unknowable, substantial, inscrutable reality" which Dr. Janes gives us from Mr. Spencer, and which on one side, Spencer and he say, gives us matter, and, on the other side, mind. But as correlation does the whole business, whence comes this fifth wheel, "inscrutable," and what for? And being *inscrutable*, how do we know that it has sides and gives us matter or mind or anything else? It can not be the correlate

* Dr. Paul Carus, in The Open Court of March 13, 1890, says: "Prof. Ernst Haeckel is again and again erroneously quoted as an authority in support of agnosticism. When I visited him in Jena last summer he very warmly expressed his sympathy with the attitude of The Open Court for taking such a decided and unmistakable stand against the *ignorabimus* (we can not know) of agnosticism. He called my attention in this connection to his own controversies with Virchow and Du Bois-Reymond (especially Freie Wissenschaft und Freie Lehre)."

The first number of The Open Court, page 17, contains the following quotation from Haeckel without reference:

"I believe that my monistic convictions agree in all essential points with that natural philosophy which in England is represented as agnosticism. . . . "

Prof. Haeckel declared that he did not remember ever having written a sentence to that purport, and I come to the conclusion that there is something wrong about the quotation.

of anything; for then it would be, as such, knowable. Can we not see that "unknowability" is not a thing, but an adjective word, simply descriptive of our ignorance, and exists nowhere but in our minds; when, therefore, it is applied to the objective world it is a misty anthropomorphism; and as the basis of a philosophy an intellectual fog plainly derived from theology?

Therefore the positivists—as, for instance, Mr. Frederic Harrison in the Religious Discussions with Mr. Spencer—cleared Comte from this fog, and all the monists and clear objective scientists have done the same. That was "the parting of the ways" between them and the Spencerians, and there is no danger of those ways ever uniting again, for they all see that the Spencerian philosophy as "a monistic system, *based* upon this unknowable reality," as Dr. Janes repeats it, is a hopeless duality. The limitations of our faculties are modestly acknowledged, but they in no wise prove that the law of correlation has an exception or a limit, much less that it ends in an *entical* "Unknowable," or leaves room for that, or for any one of the countless varieties of spooks which have led up to that pseudo-idea. But those limitations do prove that all our knowledge is "relative" to ourselves, and "subjective and hypothetical," as the doctor states, and that "atoms" are not only "hypothetical," but extremely dubious, as he quotes from Prof. Haeckel, doubtless for the enlightenment of our atomic friend, Dr. Eccles, who often in these lectures trots out those submicroscopic spooks, as though they were realities.

These remarks clear up Dr. Janes's quotations, and do much also to relieve the terror which the thunder of Dr. Eccles's adjectives, so formidable, but unnecessary, might otherwise inspire. Certainly, I have not (as he says) misunderstood Mr. Spencer. I have used the very words quoted and used by Dr. Janes, and which are taken from the close of Mr. Spencer's First Principles, his Psychology (pp. 206, 504, 627, and 469, 475, 487, third English edition), and his own articles printed in his Discussion with Mr. Harrison. Certainly Spencer says mind is a "phenomenal process," is "co-related with nerve changes," but not *causally* correlated with them *and* the world, but "flows," as do "all things," from the "infinite eternal unknowable energy." Not a friend or opponent of Mr. Spencer fails to understand this position. As a friend, Mr. Fiske gives us from it The Unseen World and The Idea of God, and Mr. Harrison, as an opponent, makes this whole unknowable energy, power, substance, and entity religiously absurd; but neither misunderstand him nor it; nor do I, or you, or Dr. Eccles. We all take what Mr. Spencer says in this regard for what we think it is worth. There is no misunderstanding, but a difference as to facts, judgment, and conclusions. Whether the mind is merely attendantly co-related, or *causally* correlated, or how related to or with this Unknowable, must, according to Mr. Spencer, be forever unknown, because it by this explanation becomes an unknowable "portion" of this unknowable. Therefrom Mr. Spencer informs us that it "flows," but Mr. Fiske says it "wells up." We give it up! Science, philosophy, religion, have no refuge before this *entical* explanation except the old awe, terror, or horror of the old superstition and devil worship. The theologs, mediums, and "medicine men" very naturally resume their ghost dance before this unknowable spook back of *their* knowable world, which is always their god. How different are all such feelings from the healthy, rational, sustaining, scientific, cosmic-emotion excited by Goethe and the monistic theory of The All, the world, as a possibly knowable, an ever-correlated and an ever-causal cosmos of law and order! Read, for instance, Goethe's poem Inheritance, to which I have referred.

The doctor next tries to misappropriate the law of correlation so as to exclude mind, because we can not "think" *how* its previous conditions and correlates actually make it, and so he thinks that as an independent entity it "may persist everlastingly in some form." Well! what correlations are thinkable? We have answered, None! I have pointed out, for instance, how the *will* can not think how it comes, and so it is seemingly free. We learn by science to gradually think out and know correlations, like the rainbow, music, or our thoughts, until we can oversee, but probably never can *exactly* grasp, each detail of the wonderful complexity. To grasp the law is the triumph of science! But how can a scientist, a correlationist, like Dr. Eccles, talk of mind as not a correlate of the correlated world, and yet as "persisting everlastingly," and so consequently flitting about forever as persisting and yet in "Erehwon" (Nowhere), and not see the absurdity of the situation? In a universe of solid correlation, where is the "needless point" left for his uncorrelated spook?

If, as he says, I am "arrogant" and "preposterous" because I can not appreciate this position except as an absurdity, remember that I am not alone. The whole school of scientific psychologists from Bain and Mill and Maudsley down to the last work of Prof. James,* of Har-

* In justice to Prof. James, as he has been twice quoted by Mr. Wakeman in support of his views, he should be briefly heard in explanation of his own position. In a note to Dr. Janes he says: "Empirically, everything points to brain-activities as being conditions of our thoughts. There is thus a 'correlation' in the sense of invariable antecedence or concomitance, which must be written down as a scientific law. Such a law of concomitance says nothing of deeper relations of causation, identity, etc.; nor, in scientific exactness, can we say anything rational about the relation of brain to thought. If we remain positivistic, we will write down the correlation and pretend to no further knowledge. We can't help postulating, however, that there is further matter *to be known*. . . . Everything points to some sort of idealism. But the question of immortality doesn't seem to be soluble either by science or philosophy; it is a teleological

vard University, to say nothing of the distinguished positivists, scientists, and monists I have already named—all deserve the same "preposterous" epithets. But why are such epithets used? Evidently they are iuspired in our otherwise gracious friend by his unfortunate belief in "the unknowable"—the very same unscientific faith which placed more than burning words around Bruno and Servetus. Does not this lapse and the tendency of that faith also show that Mr. Harrison was right in his contention that the friends of science and humanity have no more pressing duty than the exorcism of this last of the unknowable spooks from a haunted world?

hope, which, if the world have a teleological constitution, may have prophetic value."

THE SCIENTIFIC METHOD

BY

FRANCIS ELLINGWOOD ABBOT, Ph. D.

AUTHOR OF SCIENTIFIC THEISM, THE WAY OUT OF AGNOSTICISM, ETC.

COLLATERAL READINGS SUGGESTED:

Spencer's *First Principles* and *Essay on the Classification of the Sciences*, in Recent Discussions; Abbot's Scientific Theism, and The Way out of Agnosticism; Fiske's Cosmic Philosophy; Jevons's The Principles of Science; Clifford's The Teachings of Science; Picton's The Mystery of Matter; Hinton's Life in Nature; Mill's System of Logic; Bacon's Novum Organum.

THE SCIENTIFIC METHOD.

By Francis Ellingwood Abbot, Ph. D.

Is there any such thing as ignorance?
Is there any such thing as knowledge?
Is there any real difference between the two?
Is there any possibility of learning—that is, of passing gradually from ignorance to knowledge?

Surely these are strange questions to put, especially to an intelligent audience; but they go deep and mean a great deal. Perhaps it is not so easy to answer them as it appears to be, or at least to give adequate, conclusive, and satisfactory reasons for the answers. In order to bring out the significance of the questions, allow me to take a concrete instance.

Several years ago a negro preacher of Richmond, Rev. Mr. Jasper, created amusement throughout the country by stoutly maintaining that "the sun do move"—that the sun revolves around the earth, not the earth around the sun. What created the amusement was Mr. Jasper's unconscious and courageous ignorance. Everybody laughed to see a public man defend astronomical notions of his own which every school-boy knew to be untrue, and laughed all the harder the more vigorously he defended them, for knowledge, unlike religion, has never yet persecuted any one; it subjects ignorance to no worse persecution than the ordeal of laughter.

Now, Mr. Jasper was a preacher, not a philosopher. If he had been a modern idealist or individualist we can easily imagine him turning upon his hilarious opponents and addressing to them arguments to which merriment would be no reply.

"You call me ignorant," he might have said, "but you do not know yourselves what ignorance is. Each of you fancies himself to be the standard of knowledge, and dubs me ignorant simply because I differ from himself. Now, knowledge is nothing in the world but thought, and your knowledge is nothing but your individual thought. There is nothing whatever above individual thought; there is no criterion of knowledge above it or beyond it, no authority to appeal to, no tribunal to decide betwixt you and me. The right of private judgment is absolute, and there exists no objective standard of truth to limit or control it. If there does exist any such standard, tell me, if you can, what it is. But you can not. When two individuals differ, it is simply absurd for either to claim for his own thought any higher authority than itself. It is simply absurd for any one to say 'I know' in any higher sense than 'I think,' or to assert that his neighbor is ignorant merely because they two think differently. Now, I think that the sun revolves around the earth; you think that the earth revolves around the sun. Very well, we think differently; that is all. Who has any right to decide between us? Nobody. You have no more right to call me ignorant because I think differently from you than I have to call you ignorant because you think differently from me. There is and can be no ignorance at all unless there is a standard of knowledge over and above all individual thought. Yet what standard of knowledge do you confess to be superior to your own thought? None whatever! Then you can not prove me to be ignorant; you can only assert it without a shadow of proof. The plain truth is that, except as mere individual opinion, mere assertion by the individual on the sole warrant of his own individual thought, there is no such thing as either ignorance or knowledge. So long as you have no standard of knowledge higher than yourselves, you have no right to call me ignorant. I deny the jurisdiction of the court which has rashly undertaken to try me. I, too, am an individual, and all individuals are equal before the laws of thought."

If Mr. Jasper had defended himself at the time in this fashion, he might not have convinced his critics, but he would certainly have puzzled them and abated their complacent merriment. How many of them could have refuted his idealistic individualism? Suppose that they had tried to reply to him as follows:

"You declare that all individuals are equal before the laws of thought. Granted. But no individual is equal to all individuals. You are in a minority of one against the civilized world. Therefore we laugh at you as ignorant just because you fancy yourself wiser than all mankind."

Would this reply have silenced our imaginary philosophical Jasper? Not at all.

"You now assert," he would coolly have retorted, "that mankind, a mere multitude of individuals, are wiser than any one individual. But no crowd is so tall as its tallest man; no army on the march can keep up with its stoutest pedestrian; no multitude of individuals is so wise as the wisest man in it. But, waiving this point and conceding your argument to be sound, you now refute yourselves and prove me to be in the right, for your own boasted Copernicus, when he first broached his nonsensical notion that the earth revolves around the sun, was himself in a minority of one against the civilized world. By your own argument, then, Copernicus was ignorant; and the civilized world of his time, whose verdict of condemnation I do but echo, was wiser than he, and alone understood the matter. It is time for you to laugh at yourselves, not me, as ignorant. A mere majority of individual votes may elect a member of Congress, but never yet established a truth."

Biting as this retort appears, the critics of Mr. Jasper, who were undoubtedly in the right, would not quite yet have surrendered their case. We may conceive them as making some such rejoinder as this:

"Very well, then; we give up our argument on that point. We appeal now, not to the verdict of a mere majority of individuals, but to the verdict of the facts of the universe. These facts prove that the sun does not revolve about the earth, but the earth about the sun. When you maintain the contrary, you fly in the face of the facts themselves; and the facts themselves prove you to be ignorant. In those facts the universe speaks for itself, and you are in a minority of one against it. Therefore we now laugh at you because you fancy yourself to be wiser than the whole universe."

Would our idealist Jasper be silenced by this argument? Not in the least. His counter-argument would be ready thus:

"How do you know these 'facts of the universe' of which you talk so glibly? It is a very pretty figure of speech to say that the universe speaks for itself; but the figure is just as empty as any other 'iridescent dream.' I know nothing about the facts of the universe except what I myself observe; you know nothing of them except what you observe; no individual either does or can know anything about them except what he himself observes; and one individual's observation is just as good as any other's. Now, my own observation of the universe convinces me that the sun revolves about the earth; I see it rise in the east, traverse the sky, and set in the west. The inference of my own thought from my own observation is that 'the sun do move.' Against this thought of mine you have nothing whatever to oppose except your own thought; but one individual's thought is just as much knowledge as another's. You may multiply your mere thought by a thousand million, but that does not make it either ignorance or knowledge. Individuals differ just as much in their observations as in their inferences; and there is no judge, no criterion of knowledge, to appeal to in either case. Hence your 'facts of the universe' exist only as my own observations and inferences—in a word, as my own thoughts; and it is inane for you to appeal from my thoughts to my thoughts, as if you could array me against myself.

"But this is not all; I go still further. What do you mean by your 'universe' anyhow? You mean a real external world, wholly outside of your own consciousness, and wholly independent of it. It is absurd to postulate any such world as that. If there is any truth whatever in the doctrine of the relativity of knowledge (which you will not venture to call in question), you can not possibly know anything whatever of an external world. You can only know certain changes or affections of your own consciousness, caused you can not tell how. The individual mind can know nothing but its own changing states of consciousness. It can never know anything external to those states. All its observations, all its inferences, all its knowledge, all its ignorance, lie solely within the sphere of that consciousness, and have no meaning at all with reference to any external world lying beyond that sphere. In fact, to be perfectly candid, I am bound to deny, and I do deny, the very possibility of any external world beyond my own individual mind; for, if I admit that an external world may possibly exist and that I may yet be ignorant of it, I thereby contradict my fundamental principle that knowledge and ignorance have no possible reference to anything outside of individual consciousness. If knowledge is nothing but thought (and who disputes that?), then ignorance, the absence of knowledge, can only be thoughtlessness, the absence of thought—can only be unconsciousness, the absence of consciousness. If knowledge were *thinking rightly*, then ignorance would be *thinking wrongly;* but this would imply a standard of truth above mere thought as such, and this, as we all agree, is absurd. Hence I conclude that those 'facts of the universe' to which you so confidently appeal do not exist at all except as my own thoughts; and, since I know my own thoughts better than you do or can, I maintain that the 'facts of the universe' are all on my side and sustain my astronomical theory. Wherefore, O laughing philosophers, I am not ignorant; and your laughter, like the laughter of fools, is the crackling of thorns under the pot."

And would this pæan of triumph end the controversy? Far from it. The critics of our imaginary Jasper, however checked in their mirth by that last unkindest cut of all, could hardly fail to perceive their advantage and close in upon the doughty idealist in some such terms as these:

"You now explicitly concede that you know no real world external to your own thought—in fact, that no such world can possibly exist without upsetting your whole philosophy. In this confession you are either more candid or else more clear-headed than some other philosophers of your tribe. But we now put your candor or your clear-headedness, whichever it may be, to a still severer test. Do you claim that we, too, your critics, have no existence except as your own thoughts or conscious states? Are we real beings like yourself, or are we mere phantoms of your thought, mere creatures of your imagination, mere things in your dream? Answer this question frankly, and give a reason for your answer; for we are only a part of your external world, and, if your philosophy has any coherence with itself, it must treat the question of our reality just as it treats that of the reality of a material world."

To this crucial question let us imagine that Mr. Jasper gives a bold, logical, and unequivocal reply. If so, he can reply only in these terms:

"Your challenge, I admit, is a perfectly fair one. It would be unspeakably absurd, because self-evidently contradictory, to say that the whole external world, as I know it, is only my own conscious thoughts or states, and yet to say that you, as I know you, are real beings independent of my conscious states. Other idealists are all guilty of this absurdity and self-contradiction, but I scorn to be guilty of it myself. Therefore I tell you unflinchingly that you are in no sense real beings outside of my thought. You are only phenomena of my individual consciousness, mere creatures of my own imagination mere things in my own dream. If I argue with you, and thereby seem to treat you as real beings, it is only to amuse myself with a conversation which is, in fact, only a soliloquy, just as in dreams I seem to talk with persons who seem to be real, yet are nothing but myself in disguise. However harsh this conclusion may be, it is the only logical consequence of the fundamental principles of idealism—namely, that my knowledge is only my thought, and my ignorance is only my ceasing to think. These principles I apply rigorously to every problem without exception, and therefore I do not hesitate to declare myself a solipsist—that is, one who denies all real existence except his own. So long as these principles stand unshaken, it is absurd to call me ignorant merely because I assert that 'the sun do move'; for this assertion, being my expressed thought, is a part of my knowledge, not of my ignorance. And you, gentlemen phantoms, whom I indulge in this pleasant pastime of calling me ignorant, only betray your own phantasmal and untrustworthy character when you utter that very amusing bit of nonsense. Laugh as you may, you can never begin with the principle that knowledge is nothing but thought, and yet end with any other logical conclusion than mine."

The last word in this instructive controversy, however, lies not with the idealist Jasper, but with his realist critics. The idealist has been at last driven to a frank avowal of solipsism or absolute individualism—to a frank confession that he knows nothing but himself and denies the existence of anything but himself. But this is the reduction of idealism itself to glaring absurdity; for thus idealism denies all universal science, the surest fact of human life, the knowledge by all men of a real universe in which the individual is only a part, and a very small part at that. Hence the controversy comes to a necessary close in this final response of the critics:

"We admit your candor, your courage, and your logical consistency, in starting with the principle that knowledge is nothing but your own thought, and ending with the conclusion that the universe is nothing but yourself. There stands the whole philosophy of idealism, carried out heroically to its only logical completion. But now we join issue on your original first principle. We deny that your knowledge is nothing but your individual thought, and your ignorance nothing but your ceasing to think. Knowledge is thinking rightly, and ignorance is thinking wrongly; and the objective standard of knowledge high above all individual thought, the objective criterion of truth by which right thinking and wrong thinking are accurately distinguishable, is the *Scientific Method*, the universal learning process by which every individual acquires whatever knowledge he possesses, and by which science itself has become a vast body of solidly established truth, over and above all individual acquirements. Through the scientific method, the private thought which is active in innumerable individuals becomes vitally organized into public thought; and the supreme organism of universal human reason gives authoritative law to all individual thinking. Do you fancy you can think like a fool and not be found out? Science is universally verified knowledge of a real universe which includes countless individuals; and the very definition of a fool is one who conceives himself wiser than science. The scientific method of observation, hypothesis, and verification, by which alone truth has ever been or can ever be learned, and the validity of which is itself the most certain of all facts known to man, is the organic life-principle of universal human reason. You are an ignorant man because you despise this universal reason—because you reject this universal law of all truth-seeking and truth-finding; and the fit reward of your ignorant self-conceit is the inextinguishable laughter of gods and men."

Here, then, if you please, we will drop the curtain upon the stage and put an end to our little philosophical drama. It has well served its purpose if it has brought clearly before you the irrepressible conflict between modern philosophical idealism and modern scientific realism, and emphasized the importance, so far as sound thinking is concerned, of a sound intellectual method in the pursuit of truth. The question of method in this issue between science and idealism is, at bottom, a question of fundamental principles respecting the nature of ignorance and of knowledge.

The fundamental principle of idealism underlying all its forms—subjective, objective, absolute, or what not—is that knowledge is nothing but thought and ignorance nothing but ceasing to think—in other words, that the individual mind knows only its own conscious states, and, from the very nature of knowledge, can never know any reality external to itself. Hence no living or thinking man can be ignorant—the only ignorant man is the corpse. But idealism, as we find it, always professes to *believe* in external reality, at least in the form of other human consciousnesses or of an infinite consciousness, on the sole warrant of some alleged inference, postulate, assumption, deduction of reason, or act of faith. All these, however, it holds to fall far short of knowledge; and knowledge, the supreme ground of certitude, it finds exclusively in self-knowledge—in that immediate self-consciousness which can never know anything beyond itself.

Now, since no form of philosophy has ever maintained that the individual does *not* know his own conscious states, it is clear as day that the only distinctive principle of idealism is a merely negative one, and lies nowhere but in its absolute assertion that *the individual can never know an external world.* Further, since all self-consciousness or self-knowledge is simply self-observation, and since, therefore, *observation alone is knowledge*, as distinguished from inference, assumption, postulation, deduction, or faith, it follows that the whole essence of idealism is summed up in this short and perfectly intelligible statement—*the individual can never observe an external world.* The whole activity of idealism has been an attempt, forever hopeless as it is, to reconcile this statement with the fact of universal human knowledge.

For it is precisely at this point that idealism comes into deadly collision with science and the scientific method. The whole essence of science is summed up in this equally short and intelligible statement—*man, both individual and generic, can and does observe an external world.* Idealism declares that such observation is impossible, and therefore can not be actual; science declares that such observation is actual, and therefore must be possible. Idealism, culminating in the Kantian theory of knowledge, declares that man has no faculty by which he can observe an external world, and therefore knows none; science, culminating in the scientific method, declares that man already knows an external world, and therefore must have some faculty by which he can observe it. This is the exact issue between the two, and it turns on the essential nature of knowledge and ignorance. Is knowledge nothing but thought, consciousness, self-observation? Or is it at once both self-observation and world-observion? Is ignorance nothing but mere ceasing to think? Or is it ceasing to think according to the known facts and laws of a known real universe?

Now, if knowledge is nothing but self-observation, idealism is right; but, if knowledge is both self-observation and world-observation, science is right. Since they directly contradict each other, both can not be right. The issue is simply one of fact; for, if science plants itself upon world-observation as a fact, idealism plants itself upon self-observation, not only as a fact, but also as the only possible fact. Despite its lofty claims and its affected contempt for science as founded on a "mere brute fact" or a "mere physical fact," idealism, just as much as science, rests on a fact of precisely the same nature; for how is the individual ever to prove that he knows his own conscious states? If he does not know his own consciousness without proof by reason, proof by reason will not help him in the least. To attempt to prove consciousness by reason is merely to beg the question, for reason presupposes consciousness. Hence it is an amusing affectation for idealism to claim an ultimate ground in reason; its ultimate ground, just like that of science, is a mere fact and nothing but a fact.

The real question, therefore, is simply whether self-observation, which nobody disputes, is the whole fact or only half the fact. This question can not be settled by argument directly. But we have at least one direct and decisive test to apply to all possible answers to it—namely, *the true answer, whatever it may be, must be consistent with itself, and not self-contradictory.* This is the test of logic, of reason, of all thought; and this test idealism, which professes to build upon thought alone, can not reject.

Now, it is the application of the logical test which proves absolutely fatal to idealism, for it shows that idealism, when (as it always does) it rejects absolute individualism or solipsism, commits logical suicide. Plainly, if I say that I know nothing whatever except my own thoughts or conscious states, I do but say in other words that whatever I know, whether Nature, Man, or God, is *nothing more* than my own thoughts or conscious states—can exist only in myself—can not exist outside of myself; I do but say in other words that I myself, in my poor little individuality, am the whole real universe. Idealism and solipsism can not be separated logically, for they are one and the same thought. Yet idealism as it is presented by all idealists undertakes to separate them, and rejects solipsism. It thus says *yes* and *no* in one breath, and, to the question whether self-observation is the whole fact of knowledge or only half that fact, it has no answer except one which contradicts and destroys itself.

This amazing internal self-contradiction in the answer which idealism gives to the fundamental question of all philosophy—namely, "What can I know?"—is, of itself, the unanswerable refutation of its claim to be philosophy at all. Yet let us look further, since idealism and its offspring are the only dangerous opponents of the scientific method outside of the circle of theological dogmatism.

The scientific method is essentially summed up in the three words observation, hypothesis, verification. The data of observation, including both self-observation and world-observation, comprise the whole materials of knowledge. These materials idealism arbitrarily cuts down by half, and its declaration that the individual can not observe a real external world is the distinctive idealistic principle. Since, however, this principle, if logically carried out, asserts the absolutely solitary existence of the individual thinker, and therefore denies the existence of all other individuals, idealism, in order to rescue itself from patent and ridiculous absurdity, supplements its idealistic principle by the realistic inference—that is, it allows itself to concede the existence of a real external world so far as other individuals are concerned, as a mere inference, postulate, or hypothesis, which can never be converted into knowledge by any possible observation. We have seen that the idealistic principle destroys itself by self-contradiction unless it is rigorously carried out into positive denial of the existence of all individuals except the solitary thinker; or, in other words, that solipsism is the only self-consistent form of idealism. But now let us ask, What is the value of its alleged realistic inference?

I answer that this practical concession of the existence of other individuals is no inference at all, has no logical value whatever, and is at bottom nothing but a mere common-sense belief, precisely similar to that "naïve realism" which idealists themselves are never tired of satirizing. The actual existence of other individuals is not a question of inference at all, but a question of fact; and no fact can be logically inferred from another fact. Inference remains mere hypothesis until it has been converted into knowledge by verification; and all verification is fresh observation. That is, mere unverified inference does not and can not infer a fact, except as a merely possible fact; it takes the verification of positive observation to convert a possible fact into a known fact. The scientific method never infers one fact from another fact, except as a simple hypothesis. If it suspects the existence of a hitherto undiscovered fact, it devises and makes a new observation, and accepts or rejects the new fact according as it is verified or not verified by the new observation. The logic of knowledge permits no other course. Now, idealism professes to infer an external world, spiritual if not material, from merely internal conscious states, while yet it denies that this new fact can ever be verified by observation. It is this acceptance of an unverified inference as a satisfactory proof, this treatment of a mere hypothesis as an established fact, this rejection of every observation which could prove, establish, or verify, that renders idealism hopelessly illogical and unscientific, and its method thoroughly irrational in the eyes of all who value either logic or science. In truth, this professed inference of outside consciousnesses is as clear a case as was ever seen of a thoroughly naïve and uncritical realism. Strip it of its borrowed peacock plumes of idealistic phraseology, and we see at once that familiar old bird, the jackdaw of common sense. In short, the idealistic principle is suicidally self-contradictory, unless carried out boldly into solipsism, while the realistic inference is no rational ground of belief, unless supplemented and verified by that world-observation which idealism groundlessly declares impossible. The scientific method, which no more begins with a "mere fact" than idealism itself does, but which is wise enough to take the whole of the fact instead of mistaking, as idealism does, the half for the whole, begins with the primal fact of world-observation, and uses inference, hypothesis, all free intellectual activity, as a mere means to fresh world-observation in the final fact of verification. Such, and such alone, is the method by which all knowledge of the world, including our own knowledge of ourselves as part of the world, has ever been or ever will be won. Idealism garbles the great world-fact, throws away all knowledge of it that comes to us from without, and limits us strictly to that which we originate by our own thought-activity within; but, instead of adhering to the logic of this idealistic principle and declaring that the individual is himself the whole universe which he thus actively creates within his own being, it falters, fears, and, contrary to its own testimony, admits that, after all, we are in vital relation with at least a spiritual world outside of us, and that our whole morality and religion consist in somehow putting ourselves into right relation with it. Science, however, accepts unmutilated the great world-fact, studies it unhampered by this confused and halting theory, and gives us that knowledge of it without which we never could put ourselves into right relation with it. Which of the two better subserves the cause of truth, morality, and religion? Verily, it demands only a clear head and a sound conscience for truth to answer that question in favor of science and its matchless method.

Idealism and science both rest ultimately upon a mere fact—one and the same fact—the fact of observation or direct knowledge. But, while idealism curtails this fact by half and arbitrarily limits it to self-observation, or direct knowledge by the individual of his own consciousness or thought, science takes it in its fullness, comprehensiveness, and unity, as world-observation, or direct knowledge by the human race of the world itself, including the individual and his self-consciousness.

With this difference in starting-point corresponds necessarily a difference in method. Immured hopelessly in his own consciousness, as inclusive of all that he can observe or directly know, the idealistic individual struggles in vain to arrive at knowledge of a real universe by the method of *inference alone*—that is, by the method of *hypothesis without verification.* Denying all direct observation of a real world, he can neither begin with observation nor end with observation, except within the limits of his own individual consciousness; and this gives him no other individual, no Nature, no God. Unable, however, to remain content with himself as a substitute for universal being, and eager to arrive at some solid ground for ethics and religion, he forgets his logic, and tries to make faith do the work of knowledge. But, as the whole history of thought proves, this attempt eternally fails; hypothesis without verification can be converted into knowledge by no device of inference, postulate, deduction, or faith, and the idealistic method of pure individualism breaks down in utter failure, theoretically and practically alike.

But science is fettered by no such arbitrary and ruinous curtailment of its method. The scientific individual begins with direct observation as knowledge in the first instance, and he proceeds to enlarge this original knowledge by the scientific method of *hypothesis with verification*—that is, he subjects every inference to the test of verification by fresh observation. No scientific individual ever aspires, as the idealist invariably does, to begin with himself alone and merely infer his way to real knowledge of a real universe; the first step he takes is to recognize the existence of a vast accumulation of universal human knowledge, acquired before he was born, and now to be enlarged a little by him, if he can only add a little new knowledge to the world's great stock of it. He observes, he hypothesizes, he verifies by observing once more how far his hypothesis agrees with the real world; and then he is ready to offer his modest contribution of discovery to his fellow-men.

Now begins a process, a most important process, of which no idealist can conceive even the possibility; for, denying that the individual can acquire one iota of knowledge of an external world, he, of course, denies that the individual can contribute one iota of it to any general treasury of world-knowledge. But the scientific man, when he has made a real discovery and verified it carefully and conscientiously, knows well that *verification for himself* is by no means *verification for mankind.* Convinced as he may be of the truth of his new observation, he nevertheless knows well that it can not yet be declared or treated as a part of universal human knowledge. The new discovery must be flung into the arena of the world, and battle for its life against the wild beasts of ignorance, indifference, incredulity, prejudice, jealousy, envy, hatred, malice, and all uncharitableness. Before the new truth, no matter how well verified to the discoverer's own mind, can become verified to the world's mind, it must run the gantlet of universal criticism; it must be doubted, denied, assailed, maligned, and hustled about unmercifully; it must be subjected to fresh verification by every trained investigator who suspects that it may be indeed a truth; it must thereby conquer here and there a new adherent, and prove itself to be a truth indeed by conquering at last the adhesion of all who are competent to be its judge.

This process by which a new discovery, after meeting successfully the severest tests of fresh examination, and after being confirmed by the independent investigations of all whose judgment is entitled to weight, passes gradually into the category of established truths—this process by which *verification for the individual* is slowly deepened and extended into *verification for the race,* through the slowly formed opinion of all whose proved acquirement has made them lawful judges in that special department of investigation—this process, I say, is an integral part of the scientific method, and constitutes its irrefutable superiority to the method of idealism or pure individualism. Idealism conceives no higher authority, criterion, or test of truth than the *private reason of the individual;* but science, developed into philosophy, conceives the organization of innumerable private reasons into the one *universal reason of the race,* and, in this organized reason of mankind, which is infinitely removed from a mere multitude of individual reasons as such, discerns that supreme authority, test, or criterion of truth from which dissent is ignorance, in its only intelligible sense. In the unanimous agreement of all who, by actual achievement or by admirable work done, have compelled universal recognition of their right to pass a weighty judgment in any branch of science—that is, in the *unanimous consensus of the competent*—lies the supreme tribunal which alone can decide authoritatively what is known and what is not known. All questions remain open questions in science until absolute unanimity is reached; no judgment can be claimed to have been authoritatively given until dissent has already died down into silence among the judges themselves. But their unanimous voice is the highest authority or test of truth to which man, for whom there is no infallibility anywhere, can possibly appeal. It is in virtue of this authority alone that schools and universities exist; for how could they exist if there were no solidly established truth to teach? On the wall of Science Hall, at Smith College, I read, a few weeks since, this simple and impressive inscription:

"*The Gift of Alfred Theodore Lilly, to teach the Truth in Nature.*"

Yes, to teach the truth in Nature, not, as idealism confusedly claims, on the warrant of any individual's deduction, inference, assumption, postulate, or faith, but on the warrant of the consensus of the competent alone, on the authority of that organic reason of humanity which the consensus of the competent alone has any shadow of right to represent, to interpret, and to expound—*to teach the truth in Nature;* for that, and nothing else, every school and every university exists, even when ignorant and incompetent professors deny all knowledge of that truth, and teach their own empty vagaries in its stead. It is not an open question whether such truth exists; it is not an open question whether such truth is known and can be taught; every university in the civilized world is demonstration that it exists, is known, can be taught. Strange indeed it is, strange beyond belief, that the existence of the knowledge of Nature should be denied in the name of "philosophy, falsely so called." The time is fast approaching when all such philosophy will melt away like mist before the sun. The next age will be the age of the scientific method, and not much longer will the philosophy of the scientific method tarry beneath the horizon; for nothing save the scientific method, the work of no individual man, but the grand self-affirmation of the living and organic reason of the universal human race, can declare authoritatively what is that truth in Nature which is the solid ground of all true ethics and religion; for nothing else can ever emancipate man from the delusive idealisms, individualisms, agnosticisms, positivisms, and mysticisms which now tyrannize over his half-taught mind. It will take more than idealistic sophistry to put down the scientific method, or the philosophy which it is destined to create. This is not the place or time to tell my dream of what its teachings will be, nor is it needed that I should do so; enough to know that they will be more beautiful than any or all of our dreams, and bring out of the universal soul of man the sublimest thoughts about God and Nature, about man the individual and man the society, about freedom, courage, and hope, and duty, and about destiny, which can spring out of the concentrated wisdom of the universal reason of the race. And best of all is it to know that the sublimest thoughts of man, wrought out by his sublimest instrument, the scientific method, fall infinitely short of the *truth as it is in Nature.*

ABSTRACT OF THE DISCUSSION.

MR. GEORGE ILES:

Among the recent decisions by that supreme court of reason which Dr. Abbot has so impressively described to us is the one which this society exists to teach and to enlarge—evolution. As that truth has dawned upon the world, the atmosphere of controversy has undergone a notable change. Old elements of irritation have melted away, and the clearing air gives inquiry a keener edge than it ever had. Before the latter half of this century, when, for example, a man of science argued with a theologian about miracles, the debate was apt to turn upon the direct issue of truth or error. The man of science would adduce grounds for holding that miracles never did or could happen, and very probably add to his case the innuendo that belief in miracles was based on fraud and sustained by willful ignorance. To-day claims continue to be made by powerful institutions around us of access to higher sources of knowledge than mere observation, hypothesis, and verification. We are pointed to revelations of supernatural descent as the only sources of light regarding man's relation to the all and the highest. Here the method of science departs from the old controversial practice. The leaves of human history are turned, and from such of them as may be deciphered we read how the supernatural came to be believed in. And as the time and place of birth of that belief are gradually restored to us, then, incidentally, the question of truth or error is settled. To disprove an error is much, to explain how it came to be deemed truth is more, to rightly appraise inheritances of mingled truth and error is most of all.

When our fathers in the long ago beheld lightning and tempest, were awed by the starry heavens, felt the suggestions of the closing grave, knew that good men were often miserable, and the wicked often prosperous, they interpreted the facts as they saw them. Their eyes may have been dim, their reasoning capacity defective, yet their method, if by stretch of courtesy we can call it such, was the scientific method in the making. The claim of unalterableness, of infallibility, marks the earliness of the age which proclaimed it. Men of old thought of truth as of a thing they might grasp as fully and perfectly as a child's hand holds a pebble. They had no conception of the infinity and complexity of the universe as we see it, its every thread interlaced with every other, so that we think of truth as of the shimmering face of a star, discerned through difficulties of distance, distortions of media, defects of the seeing eye. It is as if the tree of knowledge had been uprooted as a sapling, labeled Ultimate, and now were made to do duty for the thing of life and infinite expansion which knowledge really is. The conflict we hear so much about is really, then, a conflict between new science and old, or rather between new science and old guesses. Yet, after all, too much must not be made of the war so strenuously waged against theology; it is but a particular case of the antagonism between belated thought and new thought, which we can see just as plainly in the exchanges, the courts, the legislatures, as in the churches; views essentially transient become crystallized into institutions and remain long after their usefulness has departed.

Of derivative alliance with the claims we have been glancing at is the intuitional philosophy once counting many disciples in America, but now a philosophy we hear comparatively little about. It ceased to thrive when evolution explained intuitions as due to experiences, not always either profound or clear which had coalesced in consciousness so long as to have forgotten their age, and at last come to deny ever having been born at all. To the objections of the intuitionalists were often joined those of other critics; it was said man has other modes of apprehension than by his intellect, and therefore the scientific method, intellectual as it is, can not have sway in more than a province of human experience. For man feels no less than reasons; indeed, he feels more than he reasons. To this the answer is modern psychology, so fast becoming an ordered, coherent, and luminous body of truth. Emotion, sentiment, will, may count for the larger part of man, yet is intellect their observer, examiner, and judge. The scales may balance many things weightier than themselves. Science acknowledges no limits to its jurisdiction, sets no bound to its future conquests. Dr. Abbot has effectively gainsaid the position that knowledge can be phenomenal only. We know a thing *in* its appearances, and if there be no unknowable, then every problem of nature and life offers itself for solution to faithful inquiry and patient thinking.

In this connection let me say that an important educational advance in the scientific method is taking shape in the neighboring city. For some time past Prof. Felix Adler, leader of the Society for Ethical Culture, has been advocating the establishment of a School of Philosophy and Applied Ethics. In this school it is proposed that the leading phases of philosophy shall be taught by men who are disciples of the thinkers they expound. Religion is to be studied from the historical standpoint, and the comparative method will be applied to the study of the evolution of religious doctrines, institutions, and ceremonies.

The department of Applied Ethics is intended to embrace education, economics, and practical reforms. The method of artificially protecting the truth, or what is supposed to be the truth, from contact with error is to be abandoned for the better plan of inviting the different systems of thought to enter into free competition with one another, in the expectation that that which is intrinsically the strongest will prevail, and that a higher and larger form of truth will be the outcome of the conflict of ideas. No student is to be pledged beforehand to arrive at certain conclusions. No professor or instructor shall be appointed or excluded because of any opinions he may or may not hold. Intellectual and moral fitness are to be the only tests applied. Toward the realization of these plans progress is being made. On December 5th the convention of ethical societies will meet in New York, and then it is expected that definite steps will be taken to give America its first free college.

Rev. John W. Chadwick:

I am extremely glad that we have had the privilege and pleasure of hearing Dr. Abbot speak. I have heard him many times, and never without satisfaction and delight, though sometimes when he has said "Come right along," and has gone through the philosophical stream without wetting his feet, I have found the waters over my head. I have watched the growth of his philosophic system with the greatest interest and perhaps with a too lively confidence, it has tallied so agreeably with the predilections of my own mind and heart. We have had many essays *about* philosophers read to the association from the first, and they have been very fine and good, but I must say that it is particularly good to have a real live philosopher expounding to us his own system. And yet I must make bold to say that if Dr. Abbot's system were something quite peculiar to himself I should distrust it as I do not now. I should fear it might be his idiosyncrasy come in the line of the world's growing thought. I do not know a truer judgment than that of my friend Joseph Henry Allen when he says: "The only intellectual scheme that history respects is that which grows by its own slow irresistible process from the contributions of millions of honest, intelligent, thinking men who do each his best to shape his own thought to the demand of his own time." Now, while Dr. Abbot's thought impresses me by its originality and by the force and clearness of his exposition, what I value it most for is for that element it has in common with the philosophy of many other thinkers in our time, that element in which science and philosophy, psychology and metaphysics, are finding the adjustment of their long-standing differences and dislikes—the idea of organic evolution which resolves matter and spirit ultimately into one substance which is more than either and includes them both, for which we have no better name than God.

If I have any criticism to make on Dr. Abbot—and this may be more of his two noble books than of the lecture of to-night—it is with reference to his seeming implication that the world must wait for science to give it assurance of a God, and that the world's belief in God has been heretofore without any real legitimacy. I do not believe this. I believe that the world has experienced religion, that it has experienced God, that the unscientific man has a belief in him which is perfectly legitimate—a belief which science may clarify and confirm, but which it has not given and which it can never take away. I speak under correction, and if there is not the implication I have mentioned I am very glad. Perhaps Dr. Abbot would say that as there is much unconscious cerebration, so is there much unconscious science which in the past has anticipated rudely what scientific realism or relationism has made wholly clear and bright.

Rev. Theodore C. Williams: *

The lecture of Dr. Abbot, while it illustrates to my mind the saying that "the knowledge of God is full of difficulties," also encourages me to believe that we can finally work through the difficulties and not be compelled to rest content in the negative attitude of agnosticism. I believe that a reconciliation is coming between philosophy and science, though I am not able to believe that it will be brought about in the way set forth by Dr. Abbot. My criticism upon his essay would be that he has spent too much time in knocking down a man of straw, which exists only in his own hypersensitive imagination. I came here to-night hoping to be enlightened by a clear presentation of the lecturer's own theory of knowledge, and have been somewhat disappointed that he has spent so much effort in exposing the fallacy of "solipsism," in which no sensible idealist believes.

A *résumé* of the history of philosophy shows that all the great metaphysicians have been working at this problem. Dr. Abbot has not done justice to their work, nor has he, as far as I can see, given us any new idea. I suppose modern psychology has hardly advanced in its theory of knowledge beyond the statement of Ferrier, which I learned in my school days—that the ultimate psychic act makes known to us both subject and object. Beyond this we can hardly go; and in

* No complete report of Mr. Williams's remarks was made at the time of their delivery. The accompanying abstract, much condensed, is made up from very insufficient data, but has been submitted to Mr. Williams and is recognized by him as substantially correct, though necessarily incomplete. Mr. Williams gave a very interesting *résumé* of the history of philosophy in the course of his remarks.

the recognition of this fundamental principle we find a corrective of the tendency to solipsism which Dr. Abbot has endeavored to combat, as well as a justification for a rational idealism, which, I think, is the accepted philosophy of the present day.

Dr. Robert G. Eccles:

I agree almost perfectly with the last speaker, though I am no idealist. It seems to me that the principles which he has laid down and indorsed are those which must underlie all scientific conceptions of the nature of knowledge, but that their logical outcome is not solipsism or any extreme form of idealism, but the "transfigured realism" of Mr. Herbert Spencer. I can not agree with Dr. Abbot that the true test of scientific knowledge is the "consensus of the competent." Who are "the competent"? Those whom the world has recognized as "the competent" in past ages have been the persecutors of science; they have condemned the men who were actually in the right to the dungeon and the stake. The criterion set up by the lecturer seems to me to be no true test of knowledge because it is itself in need of a test whereby to establish its claims. Who shall decide who "the competent" are in any given instance? We need another "consensus of the competent" to decide who the competent are, and so on *ad infinitum.* Dr. Abbot's test actually relegates the criterion of truth to the bar of individual opinion, and is therefore not a scientific test at all. Each man will decide for himself who are the competent according to his own individual bias. The true test of the scientific value of opinions is the agreement thereof with objective facts. That theory is true and has scientific justification which agrees with all the facts to which it relates, no matter if the promulgator be in a minority of one. Bruno and Galileo are thus justified, though the theories they promulgated were new to the world and were rejected by "the competent," or those recognized as such, in their own time.

Dr. Lewis G. Janes:

To me, I must confess, Dr. Abbot's doctrine of the "consensus of the competent" as the ultimate criterion of knowledge has always seemed the strongest part of his system. Dr. Eccles's remarks appear to me somewhat hypercritical. Dr. Abbot's rejection of the Spencerian "unknowable" seems to me to be based on an imperfect comprehension of that doctrine, and of the psycho-physiological principles and facts upon which it is based. Admitting the arbitrary limitations of the human faculties of sense-perception, whereby we have contact with an external reality, this doctrine follows as a logical and inevitable deduction. I sympathize strongly with Dr. Abbot, however, in his affirmation of the competence of the human reason to deal with these great problems of thought.

MR. RAYMOND S. PERRIN:

Mr. Perrin complimented Dr. Abbot on his able and interesting lecture and briefly commented thereon, in the main agreeing with the lecturer.

HERBERT SPENCER'S SYNTHETIC PHILOSOPHY

BY

BENJAMIN F. UNDERWOOD

COLLATERAL READINGS SUGGESTED:

Spencer's First Principles, Principles of Biology, Principles of Psychology, Principles of Sociology, Data of Ethics, and Chapters on *Justice*, in Popular Science Monthly; Fiske's Cosmic Philosophy; Thompson's A System of Psychology; Cazelles's Evolution Philosophy; E. L. Youmans's Lecture on *Herbert Spencer and the Doctrine of Evolution*, in Cazelles.

HERBERT SPENCER'S SYNTHETIC PHILOSOPHY.*

By B. F. Underwood.

The movement imparted to philosophy by the application of the "Newtonian method" to philosophical problems gave rise to that form of sensationalism which originated with Locke and culminated with Hume. Its motto was: *Nihil est in intellectu quod non fuerit in sensu.*

Before this movement was started philosophical tenets were principally deduced from "innate ideas." Descartes had appealed to the innate idea of God as *ens realissimum*, as supreme truth, with which all philosophy had to conform; and to Leibnitz innate ideas afforded the main premises for philosophical deductions. But, of course, if there is nothing in mind but what enters into it through the senses, there can not be any innate ideas, such, for instance, as an innate idea of "God" or of "immortal soul." All knowledge must, then, be derived from sensorial experience.

The negative or destructive phase of the sensation philosophy resulted consistently in the annihilation of all ideas not sense-derived. Its positive or constructive phase consisted in the attempt to build up knowledge out of sensorial data alone.

Berkeley dissipated the idea of the "extended substance," or matter as externally subsisting, by showing that the sensorial elements entering into the idea of matter—its primary qualities, such as extension, form, etc., as well as its secondary qualities, such as hardness, color, etc.—that all these elements, without exception, are subjective, mere modes of feeling; that the belief that there exists an extended, formed, hard, and colored substance outside the perceiving mind is an illusion. Berkeley made use of this way of reasoning to combat materialism, and to glorify the idea of God and of the immortality of man. With him it was God who awakened the sensorial perceptions in us, and our immortal soul that perceived them.

* This lecture is intended not merely as an exposition of the Synthetic Philosophy, but also as a history of its origin, and its relation to other systems, especially to those of Hume and Kant.

Hume, following Berkeley's manner of reasoning, aimed to show that our belief in the "thinking substance" or soul is just as much an illusion as our belief in the extended substance or matter; and that no sensorial experience can bring us any knowledge of supreme being awakening perceptions in us. The sensation philosophy had thus run out in complete nihilism—a godless, soulless, matterless world, consisting of nothing but sensorial elements more or less closely connected by mental links, so as to form a somewhat consistent experience.

Amid these nihilistic implications of the sensation philosophy it remained clear beyond doctrinal cavil that the sensorial particulars leave faint copies behind them in memory; and that these faint copies, called ideas, enter into manifold combinations among themselves, and also with the direct or vivid sensorial feelings. The question concerning the nature of the bond of connection between experiential data became from now on the principal question in philosophy. Hume had rendered it evident that the connection between the direct, vivid, matter-of-fact data is of an essentially different kind from that between the faint remembered copies of them—different, above all, from mere logical connection.

In modern philosophy, through the influence of Descartes and Leibnitz, the method of acquiring knowledge was held to be exclusively that of deduction, as taught by formal logic; the ancient and current method of syllogistic reasoning from universals to particulars.

Hume's argumentation left no doubt that direct matter-of-fact knowledge is derived in an opposite manner—namely, by beginning with particular sensorial feelings, whose connection is not ascertained by a process of thought, but is entirely given in direct sensorial experience. Not because I originally have the general idea that fire burns do I know that this particular fire will burn when I touch it: but because I have numbers of times experienced that particular fires burn, have I formed the general idea that all fires burn. This means that the logical connection found to exist in the realm of ideas is secondary to the real connection found to exist in the realm of sensorial experience. The connection between natural events or matter-of-fact occurrences can be derived solely through sensorial experience, and can not be arrived at by purely logical or mental processes. Causal connection differs *toto genere* from logical connection.

The relation of cause and effect consists merely in the succession of our impressions and ideas. The sequence is ideal and its order has become established by a habit of expectation derived from many and frequent experiences of a definite succession of impressions. Thus the sight of a flame having been uniformly followed by the feeling of heat, this feeling will always in the future arise vividly whenever and wherever a flame is seen. The connection of cause and effect is therefore only ideal, having no relation to an invariable permanent objective order, being only a subjective bond between the transitory particulars of sense and their reflected remembrance.

Besides the fundamental distinction between causal connection and logical connection implied in Hume's argumentation, the derivation of all ideas from sensorial experience—purely experiential links forming the connection between these data of knowledge—gave rise to what is known as English experientialism, or the association philosophy. The aim of this philosophical method is to discover the general laws that govern the association of ideas experientially derived, and to show that all our complex ideas are formed by association of experienced particulars, in accordance with those general laws.

It was Hume's elucidation of the process of matter-of-fact experience that awakened Kant from the "dogmatic slumber" into which he had been rocked by the purely logical or deductive philosophy of the Leibnitz-Wolffian school, "leading him," as Dr. Edmund Montgomery says, "to discover the enchanted path traveled by so many since, on which the charmed wanderer is carried, far away from real nature, to the mystic realm of transcendental idealism." By this school of thought it has been taken for granted incontestably that the general ideas or so-called concepts, found ready-made in our mind when we begin to philosophize, are eternal and universal verities implanted in us independently of all external experience, and that our understanding of truth is arrived at solely by deriving it from these pre-existing concepts by means of syllogistic reasoning.

Kant was the first fully to appreciate the important implications involved in Hume's experiential derivation of all knowledge; for if there is really no other way of arriving at the knowledge of truth than that of accepting it as it comes to us in sensorial experience, and if the knowledge of such truth consists simply in an experienced connection of sensorial and therefore wholly natural data, then all metaphysical conceptions out of which philosophy had been hitherto constructed could be nothing but idle illusions, and all existing metaphysics nothing but a baseless dream, a mere castle in the air.

Kant's life-long and most earnest endeavor was to extricate philosophy from these God and soul eliminating implications of sensorial experientialism. With him the problem assumed the following form: Is our mind endowed or not endowed with a faculty of forming *a priori* synthetical propositions? Or, in other words, is it or is it not capable of forming knowledge of some kind without the existence of sensorial experience? If not, then the cause of metaphysical philosophy is hopeless.

Kant believed that in pure mathematics he had discovered a kind of knowledge constructed wholly from *a priori* data by the mind without the aid of sensorial experience. That the truths of pure mathematics consist of such *a priori* synthetical propositions is the fundamental assertion upon which the entire Kantian philosophy is grounded. To make good his case, he had first to show that space and time, in which all mathematical constructions take form, are themselves *a priori* possessions of the mind, and he had furthermore to show that the synthetic power—the power which combines particular data into systematic knowledge—is likewise an *a priori* possession of the mind.

Philosophers in Germany before Kant had looked upon perception, or the manifold of experience which appears in time and space, as merely an indistinct kind of apprehension, whose clear and distinct knowledge they held to consist exclusively in concepts. Kant now declared perceptual sensibility to be a fundamental faculty of the mind altogether distinct from its conceptual apprehension. According to him, this original or pure perceptual sensibility of the mind consists in the empty forms of space and time, which he calls the outer and the inner sense, respectively. Into these *a priori* forms of our sensibility all sense-derived material, all *a posteriori* or externally imparted sensorial data, are received. This occurs in a purely receptive manner without the active part of our nature coming into play. The active part of our nature Kant declares to be intelligence exclusively. In his view sensibility is an entirely passive faculty, all activity being exclusively a matter of intellect.

It is this lodging of all activity, of all combining and apprehending power in nature, in a special faculty called intelligence, and believed to constitute mind proper, that inevitably leads to pure transcendental idealism, such as was taught by the late Thomas Hill Green, and is taught at present in many of the universities; for, if our knowledge is in fact out and out, and through and through, a synthetized compound, it follows that—intelligence being declared the only synthetical power extant—our knowledge must be out and out, and through and through, a product of intelligence. And this means that thought and being are identical, that the world consists of nothing but thought.

Kant himself abhorred pure idealism. He firmly believed that sense-material is given to sensibility from outside; that there exists actually a realm of things in themselves, of the true nature of which, however, he was positive that we can know nothing, and this because space and time, the forms in which the sense-given material appears to us, and the different modes of combination, the so-called categories, through which this raw material is elaborated into systematic knowledge, are faculties belonging to our own mental nature.

Moreover, though Kant believed that pure mathematics is constructed *a priori* by force of our sensorially unaided mental endowments, he came to the final conclusion that our combining faculty, in order to constitute real knowledge, requires imperatively sense-given material to work upon; that constructions formed of any other material are baseless. It is, however, important to notice that Kant believed the combining categories or synthetical functions of the intellect to inhere in an intelligible Ego, belonging to a supernatural sphere of existence. In spite of his complete overthrow of the old metaphysical idols by force of his theoretical speculations, Kant had in reserve a loop-hole through which he was convinced he could more effectively than ever establish connection with the intelligible world, the real existence of which he had never doubted. God and the immortal soul of man, as intelligible or supernatural existences, were to him primordial verities, attested beyond contention by the moral law, in obedience to which our own intelligible nature has power to determine the course of nature by means of free volitional causation.

Leibnitz, having become acquainted with Locke's sensationalism, modified considerably his view of innate ideas. He changed, however, the motto of the sensation philosophy by adding a clause to it, which made it read: *Nihil est in intellectu quod non fuerit in sensu, nisi ipse intellectus.* Thus changed, it became the motto of Kant's transcendental idealism, and this view of innate *faculties*, instead of innate *ideas*, distinguishes the Kantian view, on the one hand, from the old Leibnitz-Wolffian philosophy that rested entirely on innate ideas, and on the other hand from Hume's sensorial experientialism, which denies the existence of any sort of innate possession, whether in the form of ready-made ideas or of mere potential faculties. Kant undertakes to show that the mind brings with it certain elements of *a priori* knowledge in which no empirical influence, personal or ancestral, is traceable. "Experience," he says, "consists of intuitions which are entirely the work of the understanding." "Experience consists in the synthetical connections of phenomena (perceptions) in consciousness, so far as the connection is necessary" (Prolegomena 1, sec. 22, 23). "The reader had probably been long accustomed to consider experience a mere empirical synthesis of perception, and hence not to reflect that it goes much further than these extend, as it gives empirical judgments universal validity, and for that presupposes pure unity of the understanding which precedes *a priori*" (ibid., sec. 26, Mahaffy's translation). "It is the matter of all phenomena that is given to us *a posteriori;* the form must be ready *a priori* for them in the mind."

"Before objects are given to me, that is *a priori*, I must presuppose in myself laws of the understanding which are expressed in conceptions *a priori*. To these conceptions all objects of experience must necessarily conform" (Preface to second edition of Kritik). We are affected by objects, he argued, only by intuition, which is always sensuous. The faculty of thinking the object of sensuous intuition is the understanding. "Understanding can not intuit, the sensibility can not think. In no other way than from the united operation of both can knowledge arise."

Thus Kant maintains that before sensuous impressions can be changed into experience they must be molded by the mutual forms of sensible intuition and logical conception. It is universally admitted among thinkers that Kant tried to hold positions that are contradictory; but on this point I can not dwell here.

The post-Kantian philosophers aimed to overcome the new dualism implied by Kant's contention that not only sensations as such, but also space and time, the very media in which they appeared, and their whole synthesis in consciousness, are products of the feeling and thinking individual, and by his insisting on the existence of an outside realm of things-in-themselves affecting the individual's sensibility. Fichte tried to prove the synthetical power of the individual to create the objective world; Hegel, by identifying thought with being, and subjective thought with universal thought (transcendental idealism); Schelling, by making the subjective and objective both inhere in one and the same all-comprising hyper-subjective and hyper-objective substance or subject-object (transcendental realism). Fichte, Hegel, Schelling, Schopenhauer, all founded their systems on Kant's *a priori* elements in knowledge. The main line of descent from Hume in England was represented by Hartley, James Mill, and John Stuart Mill; and none of them were able to reconcile with their experiential philosophy the fact of *a priori* forms of intuition on which Kant had rightly insisted.

It remained for Herbert Spencer to apply the principle of evolution to mind and to show that Kant's "forms of thought," although *a priori* in the individual, are experiential in the race—in other words, were acquired in the evolutionary process. Long before Spencer, instincts were regarded as acquired mental habitudes that had become organically fixed. Conscious experience and conscious memory of it were thus held to pass, by means of organic fixation and subsequent transmission of the modified structure, into organized experience and memory. This conception forms the nucleus of Spencer's mental philosophy. Thus Herbert Spencer, "our great philosopher"—as Darwin called him—in his Principles of Psychology, published before Darwin's Origin of Species had appeared, assuming the truth of organic evolution, endeavored to show how man's mental constitution was acquired. Spencer, recognizing the existence of the subjective forms, with a grasp of thought and philosophic insight never surpassed, shows that while in the individual they are *a priori*, in the race they are experiential, since they are constant, universal experiences organized as tendencies and transmitted, like any of the physical organs, as a heritage; that thus such *a priori* forms as those of space, time, causality, etc., must have had their origin in experience. Says Dr. Carpenter: "No physiologist can deem it improbable that the intuitions which we recognize in our mental constitution have been acquired by a process of gradual development in the race corresponding to that which we trace by observation in the individual. . . . The doctrine that the intellectual and moral intuitions of any one generation are the embodiment in its mental constitution of the experience of the race was first explicitly put forth by Mr. Herbert Spencer, in whose philosophical treatises it will be found most ably developed."

Lewes remarks: "Such is one of the many profound conceptions with which this great thinker has enriched philosophy, and it ought to have finally closed the debate between the *a priori* and the experiential schools, in so far as both admit a common ground of biological interpretation, though, of course, it leaves the metempirical hypothesis untouched."

Spencer saw that this conception affords a solution of the problems of sensorial experience and innate faculties, and is a compromise between Locke's and Kant's school of thought; between the sensation philosophy and transcendental idealism. With Hume, and against Kant, this view maintains that all knowledge is derived from sensorial experience. But with Kant, and against Hume, it asserts that we are, nevertheless, born with predisposed faculties of thought, which necessarily constitute a preformed recipient and norm for all new experience.

As regards the inseparable bond of connection between experiential particulars, it holds that it is, indeed, established through habit, but by means of generical inheritance, and not merely during individual life; that it is, however, certainly not established through the functional play of faculties inherent in mind prior to all experience, individual or ancestral.

Hume ignored completely the existence of anything beyond consciousness. He does not assume powers outside of us awakening our sensations. He takes account of nothing but vivid and faint ideas and their combinations. Spencer, on the contrary, assumes with Kant the existence of a realm external to us that has power to affect our sensibility. But, unlike Kant, who allows these affections to fall chaotically into empty space and time, and to receive all their significance solely from the combining, systematizing, and apprehending power of the intellect, Spencer teaches that the order found obtaining among conscious states has been established by vital and organic adjustment to a corresponding order obtaining among the forces that constitute existence outside of consciousness. Life, with all its mental as well as vital manifestations, consists with him in the adjustment of internal or subjective relations to external or objective relations.

The psychological fact is that the forms are connate, therefore *a priori;* the psychogenetical fact is that the forms are products of ancestral experience, and therefore *a posteriori.* Locke was right in claiming that all knowledge is ultimately derived from experience, from intercourse between organism and its medium. Kant was right in recognizing the fact that there are definite tendencies or predispositions in the individual at birth. Locke was wrong in denying that there is any element in mind *a priori* to the individual. Kant was wrong in ignoring the results in the individual mind of ancestral experiences.

Says Mr. John Fiske: "Though Kant was one of the chief pioneers of the doctrine of evolution, having been the first to propose and to elaborate in detail the theory of the nebular origin of planetary systems, yet the conception of a continuous development of life in all its modes, physical and psychical, was not sufficiently advanced in Kant's day to be adopted into philosophy. Hence, in his treatment of mind, as regards both intelligence and emotion, Kant took what may be called a statical view of the subject; and finding in the adult, civilized mind, upon the study of which his systems of psychology and ethics were founded, a number of organized moral intuitions and an organized moral sense, which urges men to seek the right and shun the wrong, irrespective of utilitarian considerations of pleasure and pain, he proceeded to deal with these moral intuitions and this moral sense as if they were ultimate facts, incapable of being analyzed into simpler emotional elements. . . . So long as the subject is contemplated from a statical point of view, so long as individual experience is studied without reference to ancestral experience, the follower of Kant can always hold his ground against the followers of Locke in ethics as well as in psychology. When the Kantian asserts that the intuitions of right and wrong, as well as the intuitions of time and space, are independent of experience, he occupies a position which is impregnable so long as the organization of experiences through successive generations is left out of the discussion. . . . Admitting the truth of the Kantian position that there exists in us a moral sense for analyzing which our individual experience does not afford the requisite data, and which must therefore be regarded as ultimate for each individual, it is, nevertheless, open to us to inquire into the emotional antecedents of this organized moral sense as indicated in ancestral types of physical life. The inquiry will result in the conviction that the moral sense is not ultimate, but derivative, and that it has been built up out of slowly organized experiences of pleasures and pains."

Says Dr. Edmund Montgomery, learned in all the schools of philosophic thought: "Philosophy, after twenty-four centuries of most diversified trials, had failed to discover the ways of knowledge. In no manner could it be adequately extracted from reason, and just as little could it be fully derived from the senses. Nor had any compromise at all succeeded. Nativism and empiricism remained fundamentally irreconcilable. Suddenly, however, light began to pierce the hitherto immovable darkness. It was Mr. Herbert Spencer who caught one of those rare revealing glimpses that initiate a new epoch in the history of thought. He saw that the evolution hypothesis furnishes a solution of the controversy between the disciples of Locke and Kant. To us younger thinkers, into whose serious meditations Darwinism entered from the beginning as a potent solvent of many an ancient mystery, this reconciliation of transcendentalism and experientialism may have consistently presented itself as an evident corollary from the laws of heredity. But what an achievement for a solitary thinker, aided by no other light than the penetration of his own genius, before Darwinism was current, to discover this deeply hidden secret of nature, which with one stroke disclosed the true relation of innate and acquired faculties, an enigma over which so many generations of philosophers had pondered in vain!"

Du Bois-Reymond disputes the priority of this foreshadowing insight. In his lecture on The Physiology of Exercise he says: "With Mr. Herbert Spencer meeting me in the same thought, which I believe, however, I have more sharply grasped, I deduced on a former occasion how, in such transmissibility of educationally derived aptitude, possibly lies the reconciliation of the great antithesis of the theory of knowledge—of the empirical and the innate views."

I am not able to judge as to the justice of Du Bois-Reymond's claim, but evidently he had no clear conception of the subject such as alone could have enabled him to make the discovery a consistent part of a scientific theory or a philosophical system.

As regards the intimate nature of the ultimate reality represented in consciousness, Spencer, like Kant, professes complete ignorance. He holds it to be wholly unknowable. Yet, unlike Kant, who derives his God from the existence of the moral law, he concludes that the noumenal power behind phenomena, though unknowable, is an all-efficient Absolute, a First Cause or Supreme Power, from which all natural phenomena proceed, they being manifestations of the same.

Spencer maintains, with Kant substantially, that external things are known to us only *as states of consciousness*, alike in their so-called primary and secondary qualities. What things are in themselves can not be represented by feeling. Matter, space, motion, force, all our fundamental ideas are derived from generalizing and abstracting our experiences of resistance—the ultimate material of knowledge—"the primordial, universal, ever-present constituent of consciousness." To us, matter is a congeries of qualities—weight, resistance, extension, etc.; and these are names for different ways in which our consciousness is affected. If we were destitute of sight, touch, smell, taste, and hearing, these qualities would cease to exist, although the external reality which causes these groups of sensations would still exist. To beings organized differently from ourselves—so differently that their mode of being could not be conceived by us—the objective reality might give rise to states of which the word "matter" would to our minds convey no idea. Nevertheless, the fact that we have sensations that come and go independently of our volitions is evidence of *something* that determines them. The doctrine of the *relativity of knowledge* necessitates the postulation of an unknowable existence beyond consciousness.

Aërial vibrations communicated to the acoustic nerve give rise to the sensation known as sound. Without a nerve of hearing there can be no sound; for sound is a sensible phenomenon and not something external to the hearer. Color is also a subjective affection; and particular colors depend upon the particular velocities of the waves of attenuated matter gathered together by the optical apparatus of the eye, and which impinge upon the retina, affecting the optic nerve and giving rise to what appear objectively as colors—blue, green, violet, etc.—but which are known to be sensations or conscious states. In some persons, vibrations as different in velocity as those which commonly cause redness and greenness awaken identical sensations. Luminousness is a sensation produced by the action of waves of ether upon the retina and fibers of the optic nerve. This sensation may also be produced by a blow or by electricity, which, singularly enough, while it causes luminous phenomena through the eye, brought in contact with other parts gives rise to quite different sensations—sounds in the ear, taste in the mouth, ticklings in the tactile nerves. That tastes and odors are not intrinsic in things with which we associate them is very evident. The sweetness of sugar and the fragrance of the rose are sensations in us caused by these objects, the one appreciated by the sense of taste, the other by the sense of smell. Heat, too, is a sensation, and is conceivable objectively only as a mode of motion.

Another quality which we ascribe to things is hardness; but hardness can not be intelligently conceived except as a feeling. When we say that a stone is hard we mean that, if we press against it, we experience a sensation of touch, a feeling of resistance, which is designated by the word "hardness." To illustrate that both hardness and form belong to the groups of our conscious states which we call sensations of sight and touch Huxley observes: "If the surface of the cornea were cylindrical we should have a very different notion of a round body from that which we possess now; and if the strength of the fabric and the force of the muscles of the body were increased a hundredfold, our marble would seem to be as soft as a pellet of bread crumbs." What we call impenetrability is the consciousness of extension and the consciousness of resistance constantly accompanying one another. What we call extension is a consciousness of relation between two or more coexistent states produced through the sense of sight or the sense of touch. Even the conception of vibrations among particles of matter, mentioned above as objective factors in the production of sound and color, is but an inference from states of consciousness caused in us by vibrations which have been appreciated by the optic or tactile nerves; in other words, by subjective experiences produced in us by some unknown cause.

Thus, what are popularly believed to be qualities and states of matter—sound, color, odor, taste, hardness, extension, and motion—are names for different ways in which our consciousness is affected; and, were we destitute of hearing, sight, smell, taste, and touch, the supposed qualities of matter would not, so far as we can know or conceive, have any existence whatever, for by psychological analysis they are reducible to states of consciousness.

As to space and time, whether we regard them with Kant as forms of sensibility belonging to the subject and not to the object, or adopt Spencer's theory that space is the abstract of all relations of position among coexistent states of consciousness or the blank form of all these relations, and that time is the abstract of all relations of position among successive states of consciousness or the blank form in which they are presented and represented, and that both classes of relations are predetermined in the individual, so far as the inherited organization is developed, when it comes into activity, while both have been developed in the race and are resolvable into relations, coexistent and sequent, between subject and object as disclosed by the act of touch—whichever of these theories we adopt or whatever theory be affirmed, still we know space and time only as subjective forms, not as external realities. Both space relations and time relations vary with structural organization, position, vital activity, mental development, and condition.

How great in childhood seemed the height and mass of buildings which now seem small or of but moderate size! How long the days seemed when we were young! How short now! How rapidly time passes in agreeable company, how slowly in waiting for a delayed train! That there is equality or likeness between our differently estimated lengths of distance or duration—but so many variations of subjective relations—and any nexus of external things there is no reason to believe.

Inability to banish from the mind the idea of space illustrates Spencer's prime test of truth—viz., the inconceivability of the negation of a proposition. "If space be an universal form of the *non-ego*, it must produce some corresponding universal form of the *ego*—a form which, as being the constant element of all impressions presented in experience, and therefore of *all* impressions represented in thought, is independent of every *particular* impression; and consequently remains when every particular impression is as far as possible banished." Space intuitions are "the fixed functions of fixed structures that have become molded into correspondence with fixed outer relations" pre-established so far as the inherited organization is developed at the time it comes into activity. Thus the consciousness of space is reached through a process of evolution.

But does not the mind possess a synthetic power by which it can put together the materials furnished by the senses, and thus enable us to realize and understand the objective world as it actually exists? Is there not in the mind a faculty by which we can discover relations as they are beyond consciousness? If we do not know the nature of noumenal existence, we can not know anything about its relations. Kant dwelt upon this subject for years; and, although he believed in an existence transcending sense and understanding, the conclusion of his years of laborious thought was that we can only put together the materials furnished by the senses, and that we can know nothing of the world as it exists, unmodified by and independent of consciousness. To the same conclusion, after years of profound thought, came Herbert Spencer.

Mr. Spencer holds that things in themselves are not perceived, yet that they correspond with perceptions, and are known symbolically only; that "there exist beyond consciousness conditions of objective manifestation which are symbolized by relations as we conceive them." The objective existences and conditions which remain as the final necessity of thought are the correlatives of our feelings and the relations between them. There is no valid reason for the belief that the objective existence is what it appears to be, nor for the belief that the connections among its modes are what they seem in consciousness. There is congruity, but not resemblance, between the external and the internal order.

"Inner thoughts," says Spencer, "answer to outer things in such wise that cohesions in the one correspond to persistences in the other," but this correspondence is only symbolical. Such, briefly stated, is the view which, in distinction to crude realism and idealism, is called Transfigured Realism. "It recognizes," to quote again from the great thinker, "an external, independent existence which is the cause of changes in consciousness, while the effects it works in consciousness constitute the perception of it; and the inference is that the knowledge constituted by these effects can not be a knowledge of that which causes them, but can only imply its existence. May it not be said that in thus interpreting itself subjective existence makes definite that differentiation from objective existence which has been going on from the beginning of evolution?" (Spencer's Principles of Psychology, vol. ii, p. 555.)

What may be called, with propriety, Relationism, the doctrine that we know objective relations as they actually exist, belongs to crude realism, and it has no philosophical basis whatever. The theory that the intellect alone constitutes relations, that we intellectually reconstitute and therefore understand the relations making up the noumenal constitution of things, is an old conception, sometimes put forward in these later days as original, in a phraseology which at first makes difficult the immediate discovery of its identity with a system that has been weighed in the balance and found wanting. One of these relational philosophers maintains that space relations belong to the noumenal world. But these are relations constituted by the facts of sensibility, and the theorist referred to does not allow sensibility to contribute to knowledge. He can not, therefore, consistently maintain that space relations are knowingly apperceived by us.

Although there seems to be almost a complete unanimity among the great thinkers of the world that we can form no conception of the objective world apart from the conditions imposed upon it by our intelligence, and that changes of consciousness are the materials out of which our knowledge is entirely built, let no one hastily conclude that there is anything in this position inimical to, or inconsistent with, what is called "objective science." Prof. Huxley, one of the greatest of living scientists and a philosophic thinker of no mean ability, pursuing the "scientific method" with which he is supposed to be well acquainted, comes to the conclusion "that all the phenomena are, in their ultimate analysis, known to us only as facts of consciousness."

George Henry Lewes, eminent as a physiologist and psychologist, as well as a remarkably acute analytical thinker, declares, in his Problems of Life and Mind: "Whether we affirm the objective existence of something distinct from the affections of consciousness or affirm that this object is simply a reflection from consciousness, in either case we declare that the objective world is to each man the sum of his visionary experience—an existence bounded on all sides by what he feels and thinks—a form shaped by the reaction of his organism. The world is the sum total of phenomena, and phenomena are affections of consciousness with external signs" (vol. i, p. 183).

Dr. Maudsley, the distinguished physiologist, who is no more than Spencer or Lewes a subjectivist or idealist—who, indeed, is commonly regarded as a materialist—says: "After all, the world which we apprehend when we are awake may have as little resemblance or relation to the external world, of which we can have no manner of apprehension through our senses, as the dream-world has to the world with which our senses make us acquainted; nay, perhaps less, since there is some resemblance in the latter case, and there may be none whatever in the former. . . . The external world as it is in itself may not be in the least what we conceive it through our forms of perception and modes of thought. No prior experience of it has ever been so much as possible; and therefore the analogy of the dreamer is altogether defective in that respect" (Body and Will, p. 51).

Now Mr. Spencer's conclusions from relativity are in order. He says: "If, after finding that the same tepid water may feel warm to one hand and cold to another, it is inferred that warmth is relative to our nature and our own state, the inference is valid, only supposing the activity to which these different sensations are referred is an activity out of ourselves, which has not been modified by our own activities.

"When we are taught that a piece of matter, regarded by us as existing externally, can not be really known, but that we can know only certain impressions produced on us, we are yet, by the relativity of our thought, compelled to think of a positive cause. The notion of a real existence which generated these impressions becomes nascent. The momentum of thought inevitably carries us beyond conditioned existence to unconditioned existence; and this ever persists in us as the body of a thought to which we can give no shape. . . . At the same time that, by the laws of thought, we are rigorously prevented from forming a conception of absolute existence, we are, by the laws of thought, prevented from ridding ourselves of the consciousness of absolute existence, this unconsciousness being, as we see, the obverse of absolute existence" (First Principles, p. 396).

The absolute existence, then, can be known only as it is manifested in consciousness, only as it is colored and modified, so to speak, by the conditions of the organism. It can not be identified with what we call matter, for that we know only as a series of phenomenal manifestations, or, psychologically speaking, only as the coexistent states of consciousness, which we call resistance, extension, color, sound, or odor. It can not be identified with mind, for that we know only as the series of our own states of consciousness.

Says Spencer: "If I am asked to frame a notion of mind, divested of all those structural traits under which alone I am conscious of mind in myself, I can not do it. . . . If, then, I have to conceive evolution as caused by an 'originating mind,' I must conceive this mind as having attributes akin to those of the only mind I know, and without which I can not conceive mind at all. . . . I can not think of a single series of states of consciousness as causing even the relatively small groups of action going on over the earth's surface. . . . How, then, is it possible for me to conceive an 'original mind,' which I must represent to myself as a single series of states of consciousness, working the infinitely multiplied sets of changes simultaneously going on in worlds too numerous to count, dispersed throughout a space that baffles imagination? If to account for this infinitude of changes everywhere going on 'mind' must be conceived as there under the guise of simple dynamics, then the reply is that, to be so conceived, mind must be divested of all attributes by which it is distinguished, and that when thus divested of its distinguishing attributes the conception disappears, the word 'mind' stands for a blank."

According to Spencer, force, matter, space, time, motion, are but forms which the indeterminate substance assumes in consciousness. But matter and movement he reduces—as is sufficiently evident from the foregoing—to manifestations of force; and space and time are cohesions—one of coexistence, the other of succession—in the manifestations of force. Force then remains the primary datum, but that we know only as states of consciousness—in other words, as the changes in us produced by an absolute reality of which in itself we know nothing.

It may be well to illustrate a little more fully that, according to Spencer, we know matter only as co-existent states of consciousness: "A whiff of ammonia coming in contact with the eyes produces a smart, getting into the nostrils excites the consciousness we described as an intolerably strong odor, being condensed on the tongue generates an acrid taste, while ammonia applied in solution to a tender part of the skin makes it burn, as we say." This illustration from Spencer's Principles of Psychology shows that one and the same external agency produces in us different sensations, according to the avenues through which it affects our consciousness. Which of these feelings, so widely different, does the external cause resemble? Probably none of them. What it is, independently of consciousness, we never can know, owing to limitations imposed by the very constitution of the human mind.

The effects produced on our consciousness—different feelings—can be compared and classified; but how can we compare and classify that of which nothing can be known?

Knowledge consists in the classification of experiences. We observe distinctions existing between phenomena, and group together those that are similar. Anything newly discovered is known only when it can be classed with some other thing which is known; in other words, only when the impressions it produces can be recognized as belonging to an existing group of impressions. "Whence it is manifest that a thing is perfectly known when it is in all respects like certain things previously observed; that in proportion to the number of respects in which it is unlike them is the extent to which it is unknown; and that hence, when it has absolutely no attribute in common with anything else, it must be absolutely beyond the bounds of knowledge." Without distinction, which implies limitation, of course, knowledge would be impossible. All that we can compare and classify are phenomena, between which are distinguishable various degrees of likeness and unlikeness. These phenomena are effects produced in us by that which is manifested objectively as matter and force, and subjectively as feeling and thought. We can think of matter only in terms of mind, as, indeed, we can think of mind only in terms of matter. That of which both are manifestations can not be known. "The antithesis of subject and object," says Spencer, "never to be transcended while consciousness lasts, renders impossible all knowledge of that ultimate reality in which subject and object are united."

There are those who, after making use of the doctrine of the relativity of knowledge to prove that we know only our conscious states, deny or question the existence of any objective reality that produces these states. But relativity implies object as well as subject, and it would have no meaning unless there were existence, known only as it affects us and unknown as pure object. The statement that a house of a certain size, form, color, etc., is what it is conceived to be only in relation to consciousness, implies that there is something beyond consciousness that exists *per se*, and that, as such, it is unknown. The statement that knowledge is relative involves the statement that there is absolute existence—existence that does not depend upon our consciousness, and of which we know only its effects upon us. If, in asserting the relativity of knowledge, we do not postulate absolute existence, the relative itself becomes absolute; and that involves a contradiction of the doctrine of relativity—the very indisputable doctrine by which the so-called qualities of matter are shown to be sensible phenomena.

An oyster is conceived as having some vague sort of consciousness of its environment. In this consciousness man is not included. If we conceive the oyster as a creature out of whose consciousness we exist, is it not a trifle absurd to say that there is no objective reality; that our conception of the oyster, instead of being the product of the co-operation of the mind with an external something, is only one of the modifications of ourselves, uncaused by anything existing objectively; and that, therefore, the oyster exists only in our own minds? And other human beings than ourselves can only be regarded as but so many modifications of our own consciousness. The truth is that, while we know directly only our own conscious states—the material out of which is woven all thought—we know by inference other human beings, although, of course, relatively only; and that which is not known is the reality which awakens in us all similarly perceptive activity.

The conviction "that human intelligence is incapable of absolute knowledge," says Spencer, "is one that has been slowly gaining ground as civilization has advanced. . . . All possible conceptions have been, one by one, tried and found wanting; and so the entire field of speculation has been gradually exhausted without positive result, the only one arrived at being the negative one above stated—that the reality existing behind all appearances is, and must ever be, unknown. To this conclusion almost every thinker of note has subscribed. 'With the exception,' says Sir William Hamilton, 'of a few late absolutist theorizers in Germany, this is, perhaps, the truth of all others most harmoniously re-echoed by every philosopher of every school.'"

To Herbert Spencer belongs the great credit of having formulated the principles of universal evolution and shown that what von Baer demonstrated to be true in the development of an animal is true of worlds, of all life, of society, of all thought, of language, religion, literature, government, art, science, philosophy, etc.—viz., that progress is from a homogeneous, indefinite, incoherent condition to the heterogeneous, definite, and coherent condition. The rhythm of evolution and dissolution, completing itself during short periods in small aggregates, and in the vast aggregate distributed through space completing itself in periods which are immeasurable by human thought, is, so far as we can see, universal and eternal, each alternating phase of the process predominating, now in this region of space, and now in that, as local conditions determine.

Von Baer, and doubtless others before Spencer, had glimpses of this law beyond its application to organic development, but it required the cyclopædiac knowledge, philosophic genius, and synthetical powers of a Spencer to illustrate and prove the law of universal evolution, as it required a Darwin to establish the principle of natural selection. Von Baer, as a writer in the Encyclopædia Britannica says, "prepared the way for Mr Spencer's generalization of the law of organic evolution as the law of all evolution." But this fact no more lessens the credit due Spencer for his great contributions to thought than the fact that many investigators prepared the way for Darwin's researches diminishes the credit to which the great naturalist is fairly entitled.

"A great method is always within the perception of many," says De Morgan, "before it is within the grasp of one." Prof. Owen, the paleontologist, expressed himself, in correspondence with the editor of the London Review, so as to convey the impression—which he afterward said was not intended—that he claimed to have promulgated the theory of natural selection before Darwin had done so. This led Darwin to say: "As far as the mere enunciation of the principle of natural selection is concerned, it is quite immaterial whether or not Prof. Owen preceded me, for both of us, as shown in this historical sketch, were long ago preceded by Dr. Wells and Mr. Mathew." Darwin quotes even from Aristotle's Physical Auscultations, and adds: "We here see the principle of natural selection shadowed forth," etc. Doubtless many had thought of the principle of natural selection, but they lacked the knowledge to understand it with its many implications, the wonderful powers of patient observation and laborious experimental investigation necessary to the study of details, and the verification of what was conjectured or but dimly perceived, as well as the wonderful powers of generalization required to classify the multitude of facts and bring them together in a comprehensive unity so as to make clear and certain the principle underlying them. These qualifications were possessed in an eminent degree by Darwin, and they enabled him to prove what others had but imagined—to show that natural selection was a great factor in evolution, and to put organic evolution upon an impregnable foundation. But Darwin's work would not have been possible if the labors of others had not led up to them, and the acceptance of evolution would have remained confined to but a few if the scientific mind had not been, through the work of others, prepared for the change. Buffon, Lamarck, Geoffroy Saint-Hilaire, Goethe, Erasmus Darwin, the author of the Vestiges, with others, are entitled to the credit of having helped to prepare the way for Darwin's work and for the adoption, with comparatively little opposition, of the doctrine of development in the place of belief in special creations. Yet Darwin's name will be forever identified with natural selection.

And as Prof. Youmans says: "The same ethical canons of research . . . which gave to Copernicus the glory of the heliocentric astronomy, to Newton that of the law of gravitation, to Harvey that of the circulation of the blood, to Priestley that of the discovery of oxygen, and to Darwin that of natural selection, will also give to Herbert Spencer the honor of having first elucidated and established the law of universal evolution."

Prof. Huxley, in his Survey of Fifty Years of Progress, says: "Evolution as a philosophical doctrine applicable to all phenomena, whether physical or mental, whether manifested by material atoms or by men in society, has been dealt with systematically in the Synthetic Philosophy of Mr. Herbert Spencer. Comment on that great undertaking would not be in place here. I mention it because, so far as I know, it is the first attempt to deal on scientific principles with modern scientific facts and speculations. For the Philosophie Positive of M. Comte, with which Mr. Spencer's system of philosophy is sometimes compared, although it professes a similar object, is unfortunately permeated by a thoroughly unscientific spirit, and its author had no adequate acquaintance with the physical science even of his own time."

I will now endeavor to give a brief synopsis of Mr. Spencer's doctrine of evolution.

1. Under the appearances which the universe presents to our senses, there persists, unchanging in quantity but ever changing in form and ever transcending human knowledge and conception, an unknown and unknowable power or reality, which we are obliged to recognize as without limit in space and without beginning or end in time.

Matter, motion, space, and time are forms which the unknowable reality assumes in consciousness. Matter and motion are manifestations of force, and space and time are cohesions—one of coexistence, the other of succession—in the manifestation of force. Force, then, is the primary datum, but that we only know as states of consciousness; in other words, as the changes in us produced by an unknowable reality, of which our conceptions of matter and motion are symbols. That which appears to be, outside of consciousness, as matter and force, is the same as that which appears in consciousness as thought and feeling. In Spencer's own language: "A power of which the nature remains forever inconceivable, and to which no limit in time and space can be imagined, works in us certain effects. These effects have certain likenesses of kind, the most general of which we class under the names of matter and force, and between these effects there are likenesses of kind, the most constant of which we class as laws of the highest certainty."

2. The field of science and philosophy is in the phenomenal world. It is the function of philosophy to give to knowledge a unity that shall comprehend the fundamental truths of all the sciences, as the general definitions and propositions of each include all the diversified phenomena of its recognized province. The sciences deal with different orders of phenomena, and their formulæ are those which express the changes and relations of these orders respectively. Philosophy is a synthesis of all these sciences into a universal system.

3. Force is persistent, and is revealed to us under the two opposite modes of attraction and expansion—in the ceaseless redistribution of matter and motion, which extends throughout the universe, involving, on the one hand, the integration of matter and the dissipation of motion, and on the other a disintegration of matter and absorption of motion.

4. Where the integration of matter and the dissipation

of motion predominate, there is evolution. Where there is a predominant disintegration of matter and absorption of motion, there is dissolution. In that portion of the universe observable by us attraction predominates now, as seen in the integration of matter and the evolution of forms. In other regions expansion may exceed attraction, dissolution may predominate over evolution. In ages inconceivably remote, the elements of our system, now undergoing evolution, were doubtless subject to the opposite process. Every condition grows out of pre-existent conditions.

5. Of beginning there is no indication. The evolution of a world from the "chaos" of star-dust involves a "beginning" only as the formation of a crystal from the "chaos" of a solution implies a beginning. There is, according to Spencer's philosophy, as little need of a "supernatural factor" to explain evolution as there is to explain the opposite process, dissolution; and one is as little indication of a "beginning" as the other, except the word "beginning" be applied to certain rhythms of motion, certain manifestations of force, certain forms of matter, which, nevertheless, were preceded by and sprang from other rhythms, manifestations, and forms, all due to and dependent upon self-existent, inscrutable power. As Spencer said, in reply to a critic: "The affirmation of a universal evolution is in itself the negation of an 'absolute commencement' of anything. Construed in terms of evolution, every kind of being is conceived as a product of modifications, wrought by insensible gradations on a pre-existing kind of being; and this holds as fully of the supposed 'commencement of organic life' as of all subsequent development of organic life."

6. When the formation of an aggregate proceeds uncomplicated by secondary processes, as in the crystallization of carbon into a diamond, evolution is simple.

7. When, in the process of evolution, there are secondary rearrangements of matter, and sufficient retained motion to admit a redistribution among the parts of the body—as, for instance, in the growth of an animal—there is exemplified not only the integration of matter and the dissipation of motion, the primary law of evolution, but also an increase of complexity. When this is accompanied with increased coherence, definiteness, and mutual dependence of parts, and the subordination of the parts to the movements of the whole structure, there is progress. Thus we have evolution

as a double process—a movement toward unity as well as diversity.

The following is from an article which appeared in The Index (Boston), in 1880, in which I reviewed at considerable length Prof. Van Buren Denslow's essay on Herbert Spencer, contained in his work entitled Modern Thinkers:

Prof. Denslow says: "Given space, matter, force, motion, and time as the factors, would all progress be found to consist in evolution of forms, organisms, motions, and activities from the homogeneous or simple into the heterogeneous? It must be conceded that the array of instances in which this is true dazzles and almost bewilders the imagination by its variety and beauty. . . . But if it shall appear that each instance he (Spencer) adduces as an illustration of differentiation of the simple into the complex also illustrates a unification of previously differentiated and diverse elements into one simple and homogeneous entity or substance, is it quite clear that we have made any advance in our knowledge of the principles of universal science?" (pp. 218, 222).

To strengthen his objection, the author selects one of Spencer's own illustrations, furnished by the differentiation of the bean seed "into vine, leaf, blossom, and ultimately the new fruit," and calls attention to what he declares is a fact—that this process equally illustrates the unification of diverse elements into one homogeneous substance.

That in the growth of the bean plant diverse elements are united in one structure is very evident; but the correctness of characterizing as a "homogeneous entity" a complex production, in which several elements united in different proportions have produced all the variety afforded by the root, vine, leaf, blossom, and fruit of a bean plant, is by no means apparent. On the contrary, a bean plant is, in substance, as well as in form and activity, a very heterogeneous structure. The chemical differentiations produced in plants generally by rearrangements of the chemical elements and by modification of tissues and organs are well described by Spencer.

"In plants," he observes, "the albuminous and amylaceous matters which form the substance of the embryo give origin here to a preponderance of chlorophyll and there to a preponderance of cellulose. Over the parts that are becoming leaf-surfaces, certain of the materials are metamorphosed into wax. In this place, starch passes into one of its isomeric equivalents, sugar, and in that place into another of its isomeric equivalents, gum. By secondary changes, some of the cellulose is modified into wood, while some of it is modified into the allied substance, which in large masses we distinguish as cork. And the more numerous compounds thus gradually arising initiate further unlikenesses by mingling in unlike ratios." (First Principles.)

In the inorganic world there are compound substances, like water, produced by the union of different elements, which to all appearances are homogeneous as to substance; but we must not expect to find such homogeneity in highly evolved organisms like the bean plant. And how the integration of a number of diverse elements into one structure diminishes the weight of Spencer's claims it is not easy to see. Spencer's primary law of evolution is not, as Prof. Denslow seems to think, change from the homogeneous to the heterogeneous, but *the integration of matter and concomitant dissipation of motion*, which we see exemplified in the concentration of units that form a crystal as well as in the combination of elements that compose the structure of a complex organism. And consider a moment how the integration of matter, the combinations of several elements into one body, gives rise to heterogeneity and differentiation in the inorganic as well as in the organic world. Think of the different combinations and transpositions of which the elements admit, and the multitude of substances thus produced. Add a molecule of carbon to a hundred molecules of iron, and a peculiar hardness is produced by the conversion of the iron into steel. Carbon in variously proportioned combinations with oxygen and nitrogen develops the several properties of wood, fruits, grain, grasses, tobacco, and opium. Carbon united with oxygen as carbonic-acid gas combines with molecules of the metal calcium in forming lime-rocks and marbles, the bones of animals, and beautiful translucent pearls. A triple alliance of molecules of hydrogen, oxygen, and carbon imparts a wonderful diversity of proportion to a multitude of organic substances, as wood, vegetable oil, animal flesh, and fat. Hydrogen molecules united with oxygen are converted into acids, and, combined with nitrogen, are converted into alkaloids, as in the formation of ammonia. If the proportion of molecules of nitrogen and oxygen in the atmosphere, composed by weight of nitrogen seventy-seven and of oxygen twenty-three, be reversed to oxygen seventy-seven and nitrogen twenty-three, *nitric acid* is developed. Vinegar, burnt sugar, butter, animal fat, nutmeg oil, are all composed of carbon, hydrogen, and oxygen in different proportions. Opium and quinine contain the same elements in different proportions. It is unnecessary to multiply illustrations to show that the union of diverse elements in different proportions gives us compounds more or less homogeneous in substance, but all differentiated from one another as to substance as well as in form and motion. The number of such substances is limited only by the inconceivably immense number of combinations and varying proportions in which between sixty and seventy elements may unite. So the combination of heterogeneous elements in substances less heterogeneous is a process by which variety, differentiation, and heterogeneity, in substance as well as in form, have been produced. By this process has grown, from a nebulous mass, a planet with all its variety of water, land, and sky, fitted for the habitation of living creatures, themselves an exemplification of the same process. It is the primary law of evolution.

8. In the process of evolution, increase of heterogeneity results from "the multiplication of effects," for in "actions and reaction of force and matter an unlikeness of either of the factors necessitates an unlikeness of the effects." All parts of a body can not be conditioned precisely alike with reference to the environment, since the parts must be subject to unlike forces and to different intensities of the same force. Exemplifications of the instability of the homogeneous are afforded by the rusting of iron, the uneven cooling

of molten lead or sulphur, and the impossibility of keeping a body of water free from currents. The more heterogeneous a body becomes, the more rapid the multiplication of effects. Every event which involves the decomposition of force into several forces produces greater complication and increased heterogeneity; and, when this process of differentiation combines with the process of integration to make the change from the homogeneous to the heterogeneous at the same time as that from the indefinite to the definite, we have compound evolution. Mere increase of heterogeneity and multiformity of parts does not constitute progress. A cancer introduces into an organism changes that make it more heterogeneous, yet it may cause death. The anarchy resulting from a revolution makes a state more heterogeneous, yet it may be the precursor of its dissolution. The law of passage from the homogeneous to the heterogeneous is a law of progress, but not *the* law of progress. The *primary* law of progress (or evolution, which in his later works Spencer substitutes for the word "progress") is the integration of matter and the concomitant dissipation of motion, which is alike exhibited in the crystallization of carbon into a diamond and the growth of an animal from a germ; but when, as in the field of biology, there is with continual integration of matter increasing heterogeneity of form, progress is possible only when there is also increasing coherence, definiteness, and mutual dependence of parts and a subordination of the various parts and manifold functions to the movements of the whole structure. Cancers produce differentiation; but, as they can not be integrated in harmony with the rest of the body, they result not in progress but in death. Thus it is seen that evolution is a *double* process—a movement toward unity as well as diversity. Integration, the primary process, under certain conditions the most completely realized by organic bodies, is accompanied by a complementary process from indefinite, incoherent homogeneity to definite coherent heterogeneity. Variety increases with the unity it accomplishes. The evolution of an animal from an egg or a tree from a seed occurs by the integration of various elements into a complex structure, in which at the same time go on continual differentiations and local integrations, making the whole a compact aggregate that presents great heterogeneity in itself and at the same time a wide differentiation from all other aggregates.

9. The field of this compound evolution is among bodies

of differing densities, between gases wherein the molecular motion is too rapid to admit of a structural arrangement, and solids in which the amount of retained motion is too small to admit of molecular rearrangement. Spencer observes: "A large amount of secondary redistribution is possible only where there is a great quantity of retained motion; and, on the other hand, these distributions can have prominence only when the contained motion has become small, opposing conditions that seem to negative any large amount of secondary redistribution." It is in organic bodies "that these apparently contradictory conditions are reconciled," for their peculiarity consists in the concentration of matter in a high degree with a far larger amount of molecular motion than is found in other bodies of the same degree of concentration.

10. All living forms have been evolved in accordance with the above-mentioned laws. The most complex are the product of modifications wrought on pre-existent animals. The evolution of species goes on, not in ascending lineal series, but by continual divergence and redivergence. Complexity of life and intelligence is correlated with complexity of structure. The highest form of intelligence, the human, has been reached by modifications wrought through ages upon pre-existing intelligences.

11. The mental faculties of man, not less than his brain and nervous system, are the product of innumerable modifications in the evolution of the highest creatures from the lowest.

Experiences registered in the nervous system produce structural changes and are accompanied by mental modifications. The aptitudes and intuitions of the human mind are the product of accumulated human experiences, transmitted and organized in the race. Even the "*a priori* forms of thought" have been slowly acquired. Whatever in the mind transcends the experience of the individual is nevertheless the product of ancestral experiences.

12. Not only is it true that our highest conceptions of morality have been evolved in accordance with these laws, but even the moral sense has been formed by accumulated and multiplied experiences, registered in the slowly evolving organism and transmitted as intuition, as sensitive in some persons to a moral wrong as the tactile sense is to the sting of a bee. The ultimate basis of morality is the source of all phenomena, "an inscrutable power," as John Fiske well

says, "of which the properties of matter and motion necessitating the process of evolution, with pain and wrong as its concomitants, are the phenomenal manifestations."

13. The religious sentiment, equally with the moral sense, has been evolved through psychical conditions represented by all the stages of life below man. The object of religious sentiment is the unknowable reality. The essential truth of religion is involved in a recognition of an absolute upon which all phenomena depend, while its fundamental error begins with investing this reality with anthropomorphic qualities.

14. All conceptions and systems, philosophical, ethical, and religious; language, government, poetry, art, science, philosophy, and industrial pursuits; all human activities, equally with animal and vegetable forms, plants, solar and stellar systems—have been evolved from a homogeneous, indefinite, and incoherent condition to a heterogeneous, definite, and coherent state.

Such is the merest abstract, and a very imperfect one, of the doctrine of evolution as maintained by Herbert Spencer.

The doctrine of the unknowable is unwelcome to theologians generally and to those theologically inclined, because it is opposed to all systems and theories based upon the assumption of the knowledge of God—his nature, attributes, purpose, etc. It is opposed by others of anti-theological views, because they think, especially when they see Unknowable printed with the initial letter a capital, that it implies the existence of a God more or less like the theological conception which they have renounced. Both classes may, when they come to appreciate fully the reasoning by which the conclusion has been reached by men like Kant and Spencer, reconsider more carefully their objections, and adopt the view in which are united all that is tenable in the affirmation of the theist with all that is warranted in the criticism of the atheist.

One anti-theological writer characterizes Spencer's thought as a "spook" philosophy; on the other hand, an idealist, a disciple of the late Prof. Thomas Hill Green, in the latest number of the Journal of Speculative Philosophy (date, January, 1888), speaks of "the philosophy of scientific materialism and agnosticism, of which Mr. Herbert Spencer is the most distinguished exponent," of the "full-fledged scientific materialistic philosophy of Lewes and Spencer and their adjutants," ignoring the fact that in Spencer's philosophy conceptions of matter and motion are treated merely as symbols of an ultimate reality which is manifested beyond consciousness as matter and motion and in consciousness as feeling and thought. Some writers have characterized Spencer's philosophy by the word dualism, to make it appear to be in opposition to what they call "monism," whereas Mr. Spencer is thoroughly monistic, since, as he says: "I recognize no forces within the organism or without the organism but the variously conditional modes of the universal immanent force; and the whole process of organic evolution is everywhere attributed by me to the co-operation of its variously conditioned modes, internal and external."

Quite a common impression is that the doctrine that all knowledge is relative, that we can not know the absolute, carries with it the implication somehow that there is no possibility of any plane of intelligent existence except that known.

There is nothing in the doctrine of the "absolute" or the "unknowable," as expounded either by Kant or Spencer, that is inconsistent with the continuance of life under other conditions than those of the present state of being. There is nothing in this doctrine which implies that man does not survive physical death or that there are not higher planes of existence than are known here. The philosophy of the absolute or the unknowable merely teaches that all knowledge is relative, that in perception there are two factors—the mind and the objective reality—and that, instead of actually perceiving the objective reality as it absolutely is, the mind perceives a phenomenon, an appearance, a representation symbolical of and corresponding with, but not a likeness of, the objective thing. The "substratum" of mental phenomena is no more known than is that of physical phenomena. As Daniel Greenleaf Thompson says: "The truth is, we are forced by the laws of cognition to postulate an unknown reality behind the known reality, both of matter and mind, a dark side of the material world and of intelligence, an imperceptible substantive being, out of which somehow comes the perceptible, and into which it disappears, a source of both material and mental phenomena, a cause of their effects, a permanent in which alone change is possible, a possibility for all actualities and a power which transcends knowledge but which is presupposed in all knowledge. This is the meaning of the paradox."

This philosophy does not make conceivability, much less sensibility, the test of possibility. On the contrary, it recognizes the fact that there are many motions of the universe to which the dull senses of man make no response whatever. There are a great number and variety of movements of which sense-bound beings can take no cognizance. With superior sensorial perceptions man would be able to discern many of these movements which are now incognizable.

"Indeed," says Tyndall in the Reade Lectures on Radiant Heat, "the domain of the senses in Nature is almost infinitely small in comparison with the vast region accessible to thought which lies beyond them. From a few observations of a comet when it comes within the range of his telescope, an astronomer can calculate its path in regions which no telescope can reach; and in like manner, by means of data furnished in the narrow world of the senses, we make ourselves at home in other and wider worlds, which can be traversed by the intellect alone."

And Lewes remarks to the same purport: "We do not actually experience through feeling a tithe of what we firmly believe and can demonstrate to intuition. The invisible is like the snow at the North Pole; no human eye has beheld it, but the mind is assured of its existence; and is, moreover, convinced that if the snow exists there, it has the properties found elsewhere. Nor is the invisible confined to objects which have never been presented to sense, although they may be presented on some future occasion; it also comprises objects beyond even this possible range, beyond all practicable extension of sense."

But however extended is man's knowledge, it is always knowledge possessed under the conditions of knowing, which include a relation between the me and the not-me, and perception and thought according to the mental constitution.

As Mr. E. D. Fawcet says, Kant, who denied that the mind could know things in themselves, "expressed himself favorable to the view that a world of supersensuous beings environs this planet, and that the establishment of communication with such beings is only a matter of time. Kant indeed was far too acute not to see that a speculative agnosticism (shutting out the possibility of absolute knowledge of realities) can not possibly assert that there is no plane of relative or phenomenal experience except that called the physical world. Contrariwise, there may be innumerable strata of materiality all alike relative to the consciousness of their 'percipients.'"

The doctrine of the relativity of knowledge and of the inscrutableness of the ultimate nature of things has been held by nearly all the great thinkers of ancient and modern times, including men of firm faith in immortality. To confound this doctrine with the doctrine of materialism is to betray ignorance of philosophic thought. With the question whether there is or is not a future life for man I am not here concerned. Spencer neither affirms belief in such a life nor denies its possibility. There is nothing in his system of philosophy that involves necessarily, so far as I can see, either the acceptance or rejection of the doctrine of the continuance of conscious existence after bodily dissolution. If it could be disproved, his philosophy would not be affected thereby; if it could be demonstrated beyond doubt to be true, the philosophy would be in no need of modification, for the phenomenal world would only be extended and the domain of science enlarged. One may hold to Spencer's philosophy and yet believe with Shadworth Hodgson in "an ethereal body built up during our lifetime within our grosser body, destined to preserve our individuality after death." The only question is, Is there proof of this theory of an ethereal body? Our American psychologist and philosopher, Mr. D. G. Thompson, who accepts Mr. Spencer's philosophy in all its essential doctrines and implications, is "inclined to the opinion that the ground for the assertion of post-mortem personal self-consciousness in identity with ante-mortem self-consciousness is firmer than for the contrary belief." He thinks it is "no harder to understand the continued existence of personal existence after death than to comprehend its occultation in sleep and restoration afterward." Mr. Thompson adds: "The same arguments that support the belief in continued personal existence after death tend also to prove an existence before birth. Is it possible that we must return to the pre-existence doctrines of the ancient philosophers? Is it possible that we must each say, I am; therefore I always was and always shall be? *Dios sabe!*" Others think that the implications of Spencer's philosophy point to physical dissolution as the end of consciousness.

A few years ago Mr. Richard A. Proctor, in conversation, gave me his estimate of Herbert Spencer, which subsequently, by my request, he put in a form for publication, and it appeared as a contribution in a journal which I then conducted. From that paper the following is an extract: "If we compare Herbert Spencer, in any department of science, with some chief master in that department, we find him at once less and greater; less in knowledge of details and in mastery of facts and methods; greater in that he sees outside and beyond the mere details of that special subject and recognizes the relation of its region of inquiry to the much wider domain over which his own philosophy extends. . . .

"Yet one can not but pause, when contemplating Herbert Spencer's work in departments of research, to note with wonder how he has been enabled, by mere clearness of insight, to discern truths which escaped the notice of the very leaders in those special subjects of inquiry. To take astronomy, for example, a subject which, more, perhaps, than any other, requires long and special study before the facts with which it deals can be rightly interpreted, Spencer reasoned justly respecting the most difficult as well as the highest of all subjects of astronomical research, the architecture of the stellar system, when the Herschels, Arago, and Humboldt adopted or accepted erroneous views. In this particular matter I had a noteworthy illustration of the justice of a remark made (either by Youmans or Fiske, I forget which) at the Spencer banquet in New York a few years ago: 'In every department of inquiry even the most zealous specialists must take the ideas of Herbert Spencer into consideration.' After long and careful study specially directed to that subject, I advanced in 1869 opinions which I supposed to be new respecting the architecture of the heavens—opinions which Spencer himself, in his Study of Sociology, has described as 'going far to help us in conceiving the constitution of our own galaxy.' Yet I found that twelve years before, dealing with that part of science in his specially planned survey of the whole domain, he had seen clearly many of the points on which I insisted later, and had found in such points sufficient evidence to lead him to correct views respecting the complexity and variety of the sidereal system."

In conclusion, The Synthetic Philosophy, as at present constituted, is not, of course, to be regarded as a finality. While man continues to advance in knowledge, all systems, to be of current value, will have to be subjected to much revision and supplementation; but I am, I think, warranted in saying that the leading principles of the synthetic philosophy are likely to remain a solid and permanent contribution to scientific and philosophic thought. Herbert Spencer's discovery and elucidation of the experiential origin of intuition and his consequent reconciliation of the sensation philosophy and the intuitional school, together with his formulation and establishment of the principles of universal evolution, entitle him to rank among the most original thinkers of modern times. He will easily hold his place as the most profound and comprehensive philosophic mind of the nineteenth century.

ABSTRACT OF THE DISCUSSION.

MR. RAYMOND S. PERRIN:

As I have listened to the lecture of the evening, I have experienced, in common, I have no doubt, with a great many in this audience, an impression of being overwhelmed with an avalanche of philosophic terms. The speaker has impressed us with the store of knowledge which he has acquired, but he has left us confused and unhappy. A few simple truths clearly and properly presented would have resulted in something more practical in the way of information than this abstruse philosophical discussion. I am a great admirer of Herbert Spencer, who has undoubtedly given us the most remarkable philosophical system of the present century. On its objective side its mode of procedure has been scientific, and it is in effect a synthesis of all the special sciences. But I am no admirer of Kant; and in so far as Spencer has borrowed from Kant, I can not accept his conclusions as rational and valid. To one who is familiar with the philosophy of Plato, Kant's Critique of Pure Reason is a roaring farce. Mr. Spencer has apparently accepted his conclusion that there is a *Ding an sich* behind phenomena—an absolute Being which is to us unknowable. But if it is unknowable, how do we know that there is any such absolute Being? This conclusion is not the result of scientific analysis, but of metaphysical speculation. The truly scientific procedure in philosophy would be, instead of resolving all things into an unknowable substance, to discover analytically what is the common content of all phenomena—those which are called mental as well as those which are called physical. The only quality or principle common to all known modes of being is motion. Motion is a principle of life and mind as well as of material things. Absence of motion would be absolute death or nonentity. In the ultimate analysis we reach this principle of motion or life everywhere, and we are therefore justified in positing it as the supreme reality in the place of the unknowable of Mr. Spencer.

MR. WILLIAM H. BOUGHTON:

The comprehensive, just, judicious, and judicial paper to which we have listened to-night has yielded to us all the pleasure which a model review can give, and leaves nothing for criticism of matter or method.

But it may be of interest to call attention to some conclusions of Mr. Spencer which he may not have established upon as firm a foundation as that upon which he has reared his doctrine of evolution. I refer to his theory of an unknowable power, or ultimate force or final first cause, from which all things proceed.

This conclusion can not be drawn from such unassailable premises as Mr. Spencer's definition of space—viz., the abstract of all coexistences; nor from the character of such existences to be found in his definition of matter—viz., coexistent positions which offer resistance—implying, as he must imply, all of motion in that word "positions," and excluding, as he must exclude therefrom, all ideas of fixity. Finality can not be ascribed to cause; and with the fall of finality comes the fall of its illogical conclusion—viz., that creative power which is implied in Mr. Spencer's words, "from which all things proceed."

All we know or can imagine of cause is antecedence—that one thing precedes another and a different thing in time.

There is no question of a series here. The last thing is not the end of cause, and the first thing does not begin it. The one is as unthinkable as the other. With the demolition of finality, what becomes of its creative power? There is no question here of quantity nor of quality. If matter is indestructible, power could not have caused it; and, if power is imperishable, it can not in that respect be distinguished from matter. If power has any existence, it falls under the definition of matter; if space is all existence, it can have no other meaning than indefinitely extended matter, and their coexistence prevents procession and throws out all ideas of final cause and final antecedence.

It seems to me that Mr. Spencer's error flows from a misapplication of the fact that we think in relations and can not think of a knowable power except as related to an unknowable power.

This relation has nothing to do with the subject, for the reason that it is not a question of the relation of a knowable whole or a knowable part to an unknowable whole, for space is not a limited whole, and an unlimited whole is a contradiction in terms. Space has no opposite, no antithesis. Form is not its opposite. The constantly changing forms which indefinitely extended matter assumes are included in space, as the shape of the apple is included in the apple.

Of course there is no time to-night to amplify the views which I have expressed, nor to state them except dogmatically, and I will therefore close by thanking the lecturer for his paper and the audience for its attention.

Dr. Robert G. Eccles:

Mr. Underwood's lecture is a very able and satisfactory exposition of the synthetic philosophy. He had a big subject to deal with, and, of course, could only be expected to present the merest outline in an hour's talk. He dwelt chiefly on the psychological side rather than the physical. This was almost inevitable under existing circumstances, and no doubt the best, since Mr. Spencer's contributions have been more notable and original here than in the physical domain. In the latter he relied more on the work of eminent biologists like Darwin and Huxley. All he has done is but a continuation of the work of preceding philosophers. The doctrine of evolution is itself an evolution, and was only synthetized by Mr. Spencer. It is in the direct line of descent of the work of the best reasoners of all ages, and only became possible in its present form after the advent of modern science. It is really a growth of the ages and not the work of a day or even a century. It owes much to Kant, Berkeley, Reid, Hume, and other great thinkers who have been mentioned to-night. It has found allied truths in contending schools of thought, brought them together and fused them into a harmonic whole. To understand it correctly requires breadth of thought, abundance of data, and persistent, hard mental work. Without these it remains as incomprehensible as the higher mathematics to the non-educated.

It is quite evident from Mr. Perrin's remarks that he has failed completely to grasp the basic principles of its psychology. There is a *pons asinorum* here that he has not crossed. This surprises me very much. Himself a writer on philosophical subjects of acknowledged ability, one would have expected better things from him here. What he has said reveals the fact that the doctrine of the "unknowable" is unknown to him except in name. He neither has grasped what Spencer and his disciples mean by it, nor the significance of the facts upon which it rests. Its basis is wholly physiological, and as an implication it is imperative. All that it involves is a correct comprehension of the nature and limitations of human sense and perception. To know what we know, and how we know it, is to demonstrate what Mr. Perrin denies. For him to characterize Kant's Critique of Pure Reason as a "farce" is only to reveal the sad limitations of his own mental grasp. However much we may dissent from some of this great German's conclusions, we all must admit him to be one of the very ablest and most profound reasoners the world has ever seen. Whoever attempts to ignore or underestimate his work only discountenances his own prowess. That he believed in "things in themselves" was but evidence that he held the universe to be real instead of illusory. The pictures in our brains have as causes substantial verities. Mr. Perrin holds that real being is motion. "Things in themselves," he contends, are mere motions. But motions of what? Of nothing, he maintains. How many of you can picture to your minds motions of nothings? Reason rebels against being forced to accept such a thought. Are not such motions unknowable? This apotheosis of motion does not help philosophy in the least. It is practically telling us that the world rests on the shoulders of Atlas, but fails to say what that worthy stands upon for his support.

MR. JOHN A. TAYLOR:

The essay to which we have listened this evening must be regarded, I think, by all competent to judge, as one of the most candid and able expositions of philosophical truth to which this association has ever listened. It is indeed a large subject, and can hardly be treated in the form of a popular lecture. I think, however, that Mr. Underwood has been remarkably successful in presenting to us a clear and correct exposition of Mr. Spencer's philosophy. If Mr. Perrin had given a little more thought to the matter, he would hardly have complained, I think, of the abstruse character of the essay. Surely the lecturer has used no terms so technical that a philosophical student can not readily grasp and understand them. It should have been left to us who make no claims to philosophical distinction to make this criticism—if it is to be made. But, unfamiliar as I am with Kant—whose works I have tried in vain to read—and the abstruse discussions of other metaphysicians, I found no difficulty in comprehending the lecturer's exposition. I regard Mr. Spencer as the foremost philosopher of our time, and think the association is to be congratulated on the opportunity of listening to such an able presentation of his views. I would move, sir, as an expression of our appreciation of the ability of the lecturer as a foremost advocate of evolution views, that Mr. Underwood be elected a corresponding member of the Brooklyn Ethical Association.

(The motion being duly seconded and put to vote by the president, Mr. Underwood was unanimously elected).

MR. UNDERWOOD:

Recognizing the excellent work which this association has done, with which I have long been familiar, I regard your election of myself as corresponding member as a high honor, and accept it in the spirit in which it has been tendered. I also thank you for the general character of your criticisms. The task imposed upon me was a great one—one which required a course of lectures rather than an hour's discussion for its accomplishment. No one can be better aware than myself of the imperfections of my lecture. The subject is one which necessitates the use of philosophical terms, but I have endeavored to present it as clearly and concisely as possible. The animadversions on Mr. Spencer's views have been so fully answered by other speakers that I will not occupy your time by a further reply.

THE EVOLUTION OF CHEMISTRY

BY

ROBERT G. ECCLES, M. D.

AUTHOR OF EVOLUTION OF MIND, THE RELATIVITY OF KNOWLEDGE, EVOLUTION OF MEDICAL SCIENCE, ETC.

COLLATERAL READINGS SUGGESTED:

Article *Chemistry* in American Cyclopædia and Encyclopædia Britannica; Cooke's New Chemistry; Johnston's The Chemistry of Common Life; Meyer's Modern Theories of Chemistry; Galloway's The Fundamental Principles of Chemistry; Rodwell's On the Birth of Chemistry; Whewell's History of the Inductive Sciences.

THE EVOLUTION OF CHEMISTRY.

By R. G. Eccles, M. D.

Chemistry has been defined as the science of matter. Though but recently organized as a compact body of related facts, its roots run back into the depths of the prehistoric past. The first fire kindled, the first food cooked, and the first metal extracted from its ore, constitute the earliest chemical experiments consciously performed by man. The facts accumulated since then are practically numberless, and the explanations advanced as to their meaning have in no wise been meager. By guessing every possible way, men could not help occasionally guessing the right way. However whimsical the reasons given by the ancients for their theories of matter, the fact stands prominently forth that sometimes they struck what we now believe to be truth. How could they help it? One of the ways must be right if every way is tried. Time may vanquish error, but can not demolish truth. From their narrow standpoints of limited data they no doubt reasoned as soundly as we do, so that what to us seems very absurd, to them was not in the least incongruous. When their earliest fetichism gave way to polytheism and monotheism their speculations about matter met a corresponding revision. The Parsee, who saw in fire his god, naturally supposed all things were made by or of fire. The Hindoo looked beyond fire to a hypothetic ether for his gods, and so deemed that the primal substance. Homer's Okeanus, or god of the ocean, was the source of all other gods, and so we find Thales of Miletus teaching the early Greeks that water was the first matter. Aneximenes at a later date reasoned that as clouds form water and invisible air clouds, air, not water, is the beginning of things. Pherecides evidently had no other theological cosmogony than his fetich-worshiping predecessors when he called earth primal. Like Topsy, he believed that things "just grew." The building of the Pantheon diffused a spirit of eclecticism. Acceptance of all the gods meant acknowledgment of all their elements. Aristotle presents five. These are ether, fire, air, water, and earth. At a little later date the first of these was dropped and thenceforward, for some fifteen hundred years, the doctrine of the four elements dominated philosophy. When we critically examine Aristotelianism on its chemical side, we discover that abstract principles or supposed qualities, and not things, were by its advocates deemed the actual elements. They took all extended bodies to be continuous in structure, and thought them capable of becoming anything or everything. We see this in the language of the founder of the system when he tells us that "fire is hot and dry, air is hot and moist, water is cold and moist, and earth is cold and dry." When ordinary water is boiled away to dryness an earthy residue is found. This was explained as the heat of fire vanquishing the moist of water and leaving the dry of fire combined with the cold of water. Dry and cold being to them earth, of course a residue must, by their logic, be expected. The establishment of alchemy among such thinkers was inevitable. If the opposing qualities of substances demolish each other and the residual ones form new substances, transmutation is a necessity.

The word *Chemeia* (Chemistry) first occurs in a Greek lexicon of the eleventh century. The definition given is "the preparation of gold and silver." Such indeed we know to have been the aim of early chemists. Later on attention was directed to the preparation of medicines. The prefix "al" before chemist simply means "the"—i. e., the chemist. It is the Arabic definite article. Alchemy was a natural outgrowth of the four-element theory, but the necessity of experiments engendered by it was fatal to such a metaphysical structure. Where abstractions take the place of facts the laboratory should be excluded as dangerous. For their unique way of reasoning about how gold could be made, the old elements failed to give expected results. Not suspecting that their reasoning might be at fault, they proceeded to hunt for new elements better able to match their logic. Sulphur was found by combustion to produce fire and a gas which they took to be air. Besides, it had a yellow color, a quality of gold which the old elements lacked. Mercury had the fluidity of water and likewise possessed the quality "metal," a condition very much needed in gold-making. Salt contained all the qualities not found in sulphur and mercury, but necessary to form a world. Thenceforth sulphur, mercury, and salt took the places of air, fire, earth, and water. The introduction of this innovation changed somewhat their mental attitude, leading them to perceive that, instead of mere qualities flitting from thing to thing, material transfers had some part in the matter. About this time chemistry was known as the spagyric art, or art of synthesis and analysis. The chemical behavior of sour bodies or acids to acrid bodies or alkalies was shown by Sylvius early in the seventeenth century. This at once awakened the idea of chemical attraction, and at a little later date that of elective affinities. Geoffroy tells us that "in all cases where two substances that have any disposition to combine are united, if there approaches them a third, which has more affinity with one of the two, this one unites with the third and lets go the other."

Here it is to be noted that abstract qualities are not referred to, and only the behavior of substances considered. About this time Boyle severely criticised the three-element theory, and Beckner and Stahl introduced a substitute for sulphur that dethroned it. They taught that all inflammable substances contained within them an element the escape of which was the cause of fire. This hypothetic element was called phlogiston. Bodies that would not burn were thought to be dephlogisticated. In this theory we hear the last echo of metaphysical chemistry as a dominant system. Phlogiston was the logical and lineal descendant of the god of fire. To destroy this was to subvert all ancient processes of reasoning and compel men to gather their facts together and begin again to build *de novo*. Being the masterpiece of centuries of thought, it was not to be expected that it would die easily. The best minds were wedded to it, and the very men who forged the weapons for its destruction refused to accept the results of their own work. In 1755 a young man named Black, then twenty-four years of age, startled the scientific world by a graduation thesis, the topic of which was something he called "fixed air." At a little later date this gas was known as carbonic acid. When writing this thesis it occurred to him that it would not be a bad idea to weigh the materials with which he was dealing experimentally to gain his data. No chemist had ever thought of doing such a thing before. It had invariably been taken for granted that as qualities, not substances, were altered, it made little or no difference whether creation and annihilation were incessantly going on or not. He at once proceeded to act by the suggestion. In the pivot of that pair of Scotch scales we find the turning point between scholastic dogma and modern verification. The first turn under that young man's control let into this world most of the blessings and comforts of our modern civilization. Little did he dream of the momentous issues that hung on his work. His was the first quantitative estimate ever known to have been made in our planet—the first telling proof of the utter worthlessness of purely abstract reasoning. He followed fixed air into and out of magnesia, limestone, and the alkalies. He noted the changes caused by its presence and absence. He saw plainly that these changes in no way agreed with current notions about the unions and vanquishments of qualities. He started other able men to work in the same field, who not only verified what he had done, but extended our knowledge in the same direction. Priestley soon after discovered what he supposed was "dephlogisticated air." We now know it as oxygen. Cavendish found that Black's fixed air was a union of charcoal and Priestley's new gas, and that water was a union of this same gas and another combustible—one then called "phlogisticated air." We now know it as hydrogen. Lavoisier thought he saw in Priestley's "dephlogisticated air" the cause of sourness in bodies, and so he called it oxygen or "acid producer." Sir Humphry Davy at a later date demonstrated that muriatic acid contains no oxygen, although it is one of our most powerful mineral acids, and that Lavoisier was therefore in error. While the French savant was evidently mistaken in this, he was certainly right in his solution of the phenomena of combustion. He pointed out the fact that in all ordinary combustion we have the union of oxygen with some body having an affinity therefor. An appreciation of this fact put an end to the phlogiston theory, and established a center around which chemical facts could readily crystallize. And yet how strange it even now seems! That the burning of wood or coal and the rusting of iron should be phenomena of the same kind seems scarcely credible. That water is the rust of hydrogen, and choke-damp that of carbon, is wonderful. The heat of our bodies, the thoughts of our brains, the movements we make, hardly look, to the uninitiated, as if they were all due to changes in us identical in kind with those producing iron rust. Yet such is the fact, and the knowledge thereof came like bright sunshine into the chemical world, making clear everything where before was darkness and ignorant groping. The human race might hunt long before it could find two men who ever were greater benefactors than Priestley and Lavoisier. What was their meed for the good they did? Did they form a Bell-Berliner-Edison combine and mount into fortunes therefrom? Did their respective Governments shower favors on their heads? No! Priestley's theology being distasteful to his neighbors, they made a bonfire of his home, his library, and his laboratory, and compelled him to seek peace by leaving England and fleeing to America. Lavoisier was unlucky enough to have been born rich, and the freethinking, communistic cranks who rode into power by the French Revolution could not stand a crime so hideous, and so they cut his head off with the guillotine.

With the advent of Lavoisier's theory came a revolution in chemical nomenclature. Up to this time names were given to substances in the most arbitrary manner. Erratic, fanciful, and unsystematic titles were the rule. After this an effort was made to make the title tell something about the structure of the substance bearing it. Bodies that defied the chemist's power of decomposition usually retained the old names, but such as were found to be compound had their names made to fit their structures. Direct unions with oxygen, chlorine, iodine, and the like were called oxides, chlorides, or iodides of the substance thus uniting. Acids bore suffixes that indicated the relative quantities of oxygen in each, as sulphurous and sulphuric acids. Salts from these acids were called, respectively, sulphites and sulphates. Improvement has gone on in this direction ever since, and will probably keep going on for a long time to come.

A new world for the chemist was opened up, and the close of the eighteenth century was as fruitful of discovery in this department of knowledge as had been the sixteenth century in geography. Cavendish introduced the pneumatic trough, Bergman the blowpipe, and Davy the electric battery, as instruments of investigation. Wenzel, Richter, and Cavendish showed that in every chemical union a definite weight of one substance is necessary to saturate a given weight of another. You may mix substances in all conceivable proportions, but they never chemically unite except in certain definite proportions. Any excess beyond the weight Nature fixes is simply left over unchanged. Dalton, however, found that if sixteen ounces of one of the ingredients made perfect saturation and there happened to be two compounds with the same ingredients, the second compound would be apt to require thirty-two ounces to complete the second form of saturation. The amount of the substance to be saturated would be the same in both cases. Where there were three such, the third would require three times sixteen, or forty-eight ounces. The unions in every chemical bond were found to be in definite and multiple proportions. On looking around for an explanation of this curious fact, he found himself compelled to adopt the idea that every body is composed of a great number of like discrete parts, and that all these parts in the same substance have the same size and weight. A solid body is thus conceived to be like an army of soldiers, where weight and height are regulated by statute. Supposing the army contains two thousand, and an army of amazons comes along of the same number. If every soldier marries an amazon we are thus able to see why a given weight of male army always matches a corresponding, though perhaps lower, weight of the female one. The weight of the army is the sum of the weight of its individual units. If every amazon has a mother with her or every soldier a father with him, then every one of one side will take two of the other. In such a case, double the weight of one side would be needed and multiple proportions shown. If every soldier took into the union a father and a brother, then three times the weight of male army would be needed to supply one weight of amazon. Dalton's explanation is called the atomic theory, and the ultimate parts of a substance bear the name "atom." Two thousand five hundred years ago Leucippos undertook to explain facts then known by a somewhat similar theory. In 450 B. C. Democritus renewed the same, while still later Epicurus gave it a fuller development. The Epicurean philosophy was set forth by Lucretius in a poem written a little over half a century before Christ. The Epicureans were bitterly opposed to the school of Aristotle, but during the dark ages they were practically annihilated by the followers of the latter. In 1592 Gassendi undertook to rehabilitate the atomic theory, but failed to gain a following. Sir Isaac Newton saw in the atomic theory a possible explanation of gravity. From Newton to Dalton nothing was done to advance this hypothesis.

Either matter is continuous, as it seems to be to carnal sense, or else it is discrete and therefore atomic. There is no third alternative. The followers of Aristotle chose one side and those of Epicurus the other. One must be right.

Dalton shows us that Aristotle is wrong, so Epicurus must be right. The crucial test lay in the law of definite and multiple proportions which the ancients knew nothing about. Every discovery since made has confirmed the idea. No one has been able to advance an alternative hypothesis that could face the facts. Occasionally we hear of some chemical Rev. Mr. Jasper who tells his class that although he teaches the atomic theory, he does not believe it. Some far-reaching teleological speculation that he is ashamed to publish dominates his thoughts. Some spook of the imagination answering to no facts of experience, but maintaining the continuity of his heritage of superstition, prompts the utterance. For modern chemistry the atomic theory is the only satisfactory one. Of course the atoms are not believed to be the "uncuttable" things of Democritus. They are minute, organized bodies of some kind, having as real an existence in the world of fact as ourselves. In the working out of Dalton's idea Berzelius took an active part, but, as both confined themselves to gravimetric estimations, confirmation from a new standpoint was reserved for Gay-Lussac. His volumetric study of gases revealed the fact that they invariably unite in definite and multiple volumes. A cubic foot of chlorine unites with a cubic foot of hydrogen only. A cubic foot of oxygen unites with two cubic feet of hydrogen. Sir Humphry Davy assisted him in this investigation.

In 1811 Avogadro declared that equal volumes of any two or more gases under the same temperature and pressure contain the same number of molecules. All gases were found by him to contract or expand in the same degree for the same subtractions or additions of pressure or temperature. No other hypothesis than this one of Avogadro's has been advanced to explain why gases behave as they do. No other is needed, as this matches the facts accurately. That gases are discrete is proved by the fact that a volume of a heavy and light gas when mixed does not make two volumes. The one occupies the interspaces of the other, which it could not do if they were continuous. This discovery of Avogadro's came before chemists were prepared to receive it. The distinction which he made between an atom and a molecule sorely puzzled his contemporaries. They did not see that his molecule was a family of atoms. It is a moving, compound unit capable of chemical decomposition into several atoms. His law was only true of molecules and not of atoms; yet they persistently confounded the two and tried to show him and his followers how ridiculous it was as applied to atoms. Even Berzelius made fun of it, saying that it undertook to split atoms. One volume of chlorine and one of hydrogen forms two volumes of muriatic acid. If the chlorine or hydrogen exists as free atoms (and they thought they did), then to form two volumes the atoms must be split. Later facts supported Avogadro and showed that both hydrogen and chlorine as found free went in pairs, or molecules of two atoms. After nearly fifty years of idleness the law was accepted, and our latest new chemistry is founded thereon. Since its acceptance progress has been marvelous. Discoveries by the million have jostled each other for public recognition, not one of which would probably ever have been made but for it. It has enabled us to weigh the atoms, to follow them through their complex blendings in organic bodies, and to understand something of the magic of biology. It has even given us some cues as to the possible inner structure of these so-called atoms of ours, and points out their probable evolutionary derivation. In this way it has been the indirect means of showing us that absolutely elementary bodies are unknown to us. We have over sixty substances which we call elements, but it is doubtful whether a single chemist can be found who believes any one of them to be primordial. We take sugar and pull its molecules asunder. It ceases to be sugar and becomes charcoal, oxygen, and hydrogen. We try to pull these three apart in a similar manner, but fail. Because we fail, and for no other reason, we call them elements. To-morrow some one may find a way of decomposing charcoal, and for ever after it will cease to be classed as an element. These three substances—carbon (charcoal), oxygen, and hydrogen —are known to make bodies of the most unlike qualities. They assume all the colors of the rainbow, all the tastes imaginable, and odors without end. Vinegar and sugar, whisky and pepper, aloes and butter, are only a few of their protean forms. The ancients classed gold and silver as compounds, but with us they are elements. They called water an element, and we know it to be a compound. Sulphur and mercury we still call elements, but our reason for applying this name to them is totally different from theirs.

With the advent of the atomic theory of Dalton came an effort to discover the relative weights of the ultimate particles of all undecomposable bodies. Of course they had to take one element as a standard of reference for the rest. Oxygen was chosen by some and hydrogen by others, while some scattering chemists tried plans of their own. It was finally seen that the lightest element of all should be chosen for a standard, while the rest were adjusted in relation to it. Hydrogen, being the lightest, became the standard of reference. When oxygen is said to weigh sixteen, the meaning is that it is sixteen times as heavy as hydrogen. When sulphur is placed at thirty-two, we are to understand that that substance has an atom thirty-two times the weight of an atom of hydrogen. In early determinations only rough approximations were made toward the true figures and, before the acceptance of Avogadro's law, figures, were often chosen that were not true atomic weights but only ratios thereof. In water they found eight times more weight of oxygen than hydrogen, and so the heavier element was put down as "eight." Avogadro showed that since it took two volumes of hydrogen to saturate one of oxygen in forming water, therefore there must be two atoms of hydrogen to one of oxygen. This lowered the comparative weight of hydrogen one half, so that oxygen had to be called sixteen instead of eight. Many changes of this kind had to be introduced. The old formula for water was HO, but the new one is H_2O. In the first the relationship was as one to eight, but in the second it is two to sixteen. In writing chemical formulæ the letters stand for atoms of the elements. H means one atom of hydrogen. H_2 means two atoms of hydrogen. H_2O means one molecule of water containing two atoms of hydrogen and one of oxygen. $5H_2O$ would mean five molecules of water. The study of the laws of heat that was going on *pari passu* with the development of chemistry led Dulong and Petit in 1819 to make a very remarkable discovery. When bodies are warmed it is found that the amount of heat required to raise them one degree varies very materially among them. Taking water as unity and calculating the relation for other substances, we get what is called their specific heat. These physicists found that for thirteen elements which they had tried, the specific heats were inversely proportional to their atomic weights. This meant directly proportional to the number of atoms present. Here then was a new means of determining atomic weights confirmatory and supplementary to the law of Avogadro. Although later investigations showed limiting conditions to the law, it has been successfully used in settling disputed points between various ratios as to which is the true atomic weight, and in determining atomic weights not otherwise ascertainable. In 1821 Mitscherlich pointed out a law of crystallography that has been used as a third method of determining atomic weights. It has been found that, as a rule, the similar combination of atoms without regard to their chemical natures gives crystals of similar forms. When crystals isomeric in form but different in composition occur, they are pretty certain to be built up of molecules in which the atoms are grouped alike. Knowing this fact, we can know the number of atoms in an unknown group by comparing it with a known, and if all the atoms in the group but one have had their weights determined, that one is easily calculated. Therefore we have in this method a means of confirming results gained by other methods. A fourth method has lately been devised, and is known as the periodic law. It was first presented a few years ago by a Russian chemist called Mendelejeff. According to this law, all the leading properties of an element are functions of its atomic weight. Given the atomic weight of any element and its place upon a spirally ascending expanding curve, distance being arranged proportional to weight, and its chief properties may at once be predicted. Of course it follows that the reverse is true. Given the properties of the element, and the atomic weight can be approximated from the place where it belongs on the spiral. If the whole series is bisected from top to bottom, paramagnetic elements will all be found in one half and diamagnetic in the other. All related groups like chlorine, bromine, and iodine will be found almost directly one above the other. In this way every element takes a place by its weight that answers to its leading properties. On such a spiral a number of gaps are found where undiscovered elements are believed to belong. Soon after enunciating the law, Mendelejeff called attention to two of the lower gaps then existing, and described the properties of the elements that should belong there. He called the hypothetic elements eka-aluminium and eka-boron. Since then two elements possessing properties similar to those described by Mendelejeff have been found and named, by their respective discoverers, gallium and scandium.

In atomic weights, ease of reduction, melting points, specific gravities, power of oxidation, ability to decompose water, methods of being attacked by acids or alkalies, methods of crystallization of salts, oxides and chlorides formed, etc., the hypothetic and real elements agree exactly. The predicted atomic weight of gallium was 69 and the found weight was 69. The predicted atomic weight of scandium was 44 and the found weight was 44. In the presence of such facts is it not strange that there are intelligent men who pretend to believe that atoms are as unreal and intangible as hobgoblins and fairies? So really physical, indeed, are the molecules made up from these atoms that Sir William Thomson and others have been able to calculate their approximate weights in terms of fractions of a grain.

No one can carefully study the periodic law of Mendelejeff, comparing it at the same time with a homologous series and its heterologous derivatives, without being struck with the idea that the atoms are products of evolution. If all the properties of matter are simply due to the weight of the little pieces from which it is built (and so the law declares), then at bottom every element must be the same. This implication is confirmed by spectrum analysis.

Within the present generation Prof. Bunsen and Prof. Kirchhoff, of Heidelberg, Germany, devised a plan by which the composition of sun and stars might be accurately determined from their light. The instrument used is made of prisms that separate the different colors found in the beam to be examined. Certain lines of colored light are given forth by every element, and a knowledge of the appearance and places of these lines enables one to tell just what element is coloring a flame. If such light passes through a vapor of the same element before reaching the prism, dark bars appear just where the colored lines should have been that belonged to that element. By the initiated the bars are as easily read as the colored lines. In ordinary chemical analysis one one-hundred-and-twentieth of a grain approaches very nearly the lowest limit of practical determination. The spectroscope, however, is so sensitive that it can tell the presence of a substance when the quantity is nearly two million times less than this, or one two-hundred-and-forty-millionth of a grain.

Very soon after the spectroscope was sufficiently perfected for practical work the four elements cæsium, rubidium, thallium, and indium were discovered by its aid. The workers knew they were there from the lines they gave, although they had never been isolated. The use of this instrument by astronomers has revealed the strange fact that the number of elements increases with the progress of a nebula toward stardom. Another remarkable fact is that as the numbers do increase it is from those with light atomic weights to those with heavy ones. Who would have thought a century ago that man would ever be able to analyze the matter stars are made of? To-day it is an accomplished fact, and the revelation given teaches us that what we call matter is a product of something unknown and indescribable by us. That from which matter grew must have been wholly unlike matter as we know it.

Many facts seem to indicate that the successive steps of integration among the atoms while forming followed well-known chemical laws. Lately, however, an English chemist named Crookes has shown that it is possible to take a large mass of the molecules of a single element, and by successive siftings separate them into two classes with slight shades of difference in qualities. Minute fractional differences of this kind go to show that while known methods of chemical grouping may have been used in their development, yet there is some different law at work from any as yet discovered. The fact, too, that Prout's supposed law has not been confirmed by the most careful determinations of atomic weights, points the same way.

While many of the heavier elements are multiples by whole numbers of hydrogen, most of them do not seem to be so. The spectroscope points to the existence in the sun of an element lighter than hydrogen, and that has been called helium. If this or a lighter element still has been the starting point, Prout's law may yet prove to be true for all elements, as it is now for a goodly number. It would give us a fractional part of a hydrogen atom as point of comparison.

To understand the bearings of this hypothesis of Prout's on evolution it is necessary to know something about how atoms link themselves together to form molecules and what compound radicals are. During the development of the science of chemistry this branch of the tree has borne more fruit than any other, and yet it is the one that pronounces most emphatically in favor of the physical existence of atoms and molecules as real beings. We have already seen that all the elements bear names, and that one letter (or sometimes two) of the Latin name is used as a symbol. The chemist undertakes to group on paper these symbols in some such way as the atoms themselves are grouped within their molecules. He is thus able to foresee possible compounds not yet discovered or made, and gains cues concerning the proper method whereby to discover them. In constructing such pictures, or "graphic formulæ," as they are designated, what has been called by Hoffman quantivalence is of great importance. Molecules do not, like the deacon's one-horse chaise, go to pieces all at once. Their bonds of union are of such a character that what breaks one does not break all. By studying the way they break, and how certain elements or groups of elements may be substituted for each other within them, valuable information concerning their structures can be obtained.

In no chemical change has hydrogen ever been known to fill the place of another atom with more than a single atom of itself. There are, on the other hand, innumerable cases of other elements filling the place of two, three, and four atoms of hydrogen with one atom of itself. If hydrogen be figured as having but one bond of attraction, then such elements as can only saturate that one bond are with hydrogen itself called monads. An element that can saturate two bonds of hydrogen or replace two atoms of hydrogen in a compound is called a dyad. One that represents three hydrogen bonds, a triad. Beyond these we have tetrads, pentads, and hexads. Chlorine saturates but one bond of hydrogen, and is therefore a monad. One volume of chlorine gas unites with an equal volume of hydrogen gas to form a volume of muriatic acid. The saturating powers of chlorine and hydrogen atoms are seen to be equal. Using some of the muriatic acid to precipitate a solution of nitrate of silver as chloride, we will find our hydrogen replace the silver as its equivalent, and our chlorine saturate it. Chlorine, hydrogen, and silver are thus shown to be monads. In water we find that it takes two volumes of hydrogen to saturate one of oxygen. When the oxygen is replaced by chlorine, we find that two volumes of chlorine are required to take the place of one of oxygen. This proves oxygen to be a dyad. If we take oxide of zinc and act upon it with muriatic acid, we will discover that two equivalents of the chlorine from the acid are needed to replace the one of oxygen, and two of hydrogen to replace the one of zinc. The quantivalence of oxygen and zinc is therefore the same. They are dyads. In this way all the elements are found to arrange themselves in separate groups, according to their attractive powers. Hydrogen and the other monads are like little magnets having a single pole of attraction. Oxygen and the other dyads are like magnets with two poles. Nitrogen and the other triads are like triple-poled magnets. Carbon and the other tetrads are like crossed magnets with four poles. To represent these facts we can write the symbols with strokes drawn from them representing the number of bonds, thus:

Cl–
–O–
N
C
H–

Saturating these bonds with hydrogen, we have the following symbols of common substances:

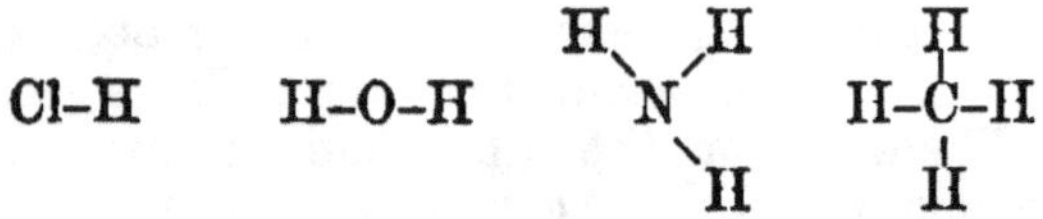
Cl–H
H–O–H
H H N H
H H–C–H H

Muriatic acid. Water. Ammonia. Marsh gas.

As oxygen has two bonds and carbon four, we can take two of oxygen and they will satisfy one of carbon. Because of these bonds the elements named are unable to exist as single, free atoms. Chlorine is not found as Cl– except during the brief instant of a change. As known to us in its elemental condition it is Cl–Cl, or Cl_2. The same is true of most elements. Hydrogen is H–H, or H_2, and oxygen O–O, or O_2. The last named exists sometimes as ozone, and then it is

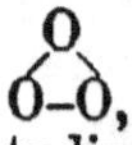

, or O_3. Many groups of atoms cohere through multitudinous changes, and in such group form they simulate more or less perfectly the atoms themselves. Sulphuric acid is always written by chemists as H_2SO_4, and never as SH_2O_4. The $-SO_4-$ part is known to maintain itself intact through many changes, and to act like a dyad element. The two hydrogen atoms leave it together to let a dyad metal take their places. One of them will go at a time to make room for a monad metal. The group NH_4- acts in a similar manner by non-metals. Two such groups will satisfy the vacant bonds of $-SO_4-$ just as readily as two monad metals or one dyad. NH_4- differs from a metal in that we know its composition, can pull it asunder, and have not yet been able to make two such groups intermarry. $-SO_4-$ differs from a non-metallic element in the same manner. In their chemical behavior both act like elements. There are radicals, however, that intermarry just as the elements do. If we were as ignorant of their structures as we are of the structures of the elements we would certainly take them to be elements. The hydroxyl group, so common in acids, alcohols, and metallic hydrates, weds with its own counterpart in peroxide of hydrogen. The cyanogen group does the same in cyanogen gas. The methyl group doubles itself in ethane and the methyenyl in acetylene. There is not a solitary feature about the behavior of an element that is not exactly repeated in these compound radicals. This coherence in groups of more or less permanence is what makes the evolution of chemistry along its lines of present greatest discovery possible.

If complex molecules did not break down in a systematic manner it would be impossible to tell how they were put together. If neither atoms nor molecules exist, as metaphysical speculators would have us believe, it is pretty nearly time for them to tell us what it is that acts so much as if they did. In Dalton's days they should have given their theory when the facts were few, and therefore susceptible to many explanations. If they had no explanation, then how can they ever hope to have one now, when the data are a millionfold what they were then? When we further perceive that very few of these millions of facts could ever have been dreamed of or known without picturing Dalton's atoms as their cause, we see how wild and silly their statements are. The whole field of organic chemistry has been opened up and developed because of our belief in atoms. Our facts were discovered and are now held together by this hypothesis. Remove it, and they drop apart like a rope of sand, with not even an explanation of how we ever discovered them. At the beginning of this century everybody held to the vital-principle theory of organic substances. It was counted absurd to imagine for a moment that organic materials could ever be synthetically produced. Wohler, sixty years ago, began the work of discovery in this field. From the synthesis of urea to the synthesis of cocaine is a long stretch through a mazy labyrinth manifoldly more complex and obscure than that in which Ariadne's thread was supposed to have been used. Dalton's thread has guided chemistry.

In 1827 Gmelin was writing a book on organic chemistry. This was only at the beginning—the first shower, so to speak—of the deluge of facts that is now pouring in upon us. He begged the chemists to stay their researches for a little while that he might get a chance to complete his book. But they did not stop; and now if Leopold Gmelin were alive he would find it not only impossible to finish such a book, but almost impossible to write down the facts as rapidly as discovered. No mortal now lives who can master all the minute particulars of organic chemistry. The only way to keep abreast of the times is to learn the principles of these facts. They are all principles of the actions and interactions of atoms. The way the carbon compounds are chained together enables the forgetful chemist with a minimum of effort to recall forgotten formulæ. For instance, having forgotten the formula of alcohol, he can readily reconstruct it thus: To four-bonded carbon ($-\overset{|}{\underset{|}{\mathrm{C}}}-$) he adds four hydrogen atoms, forming methane ($\mathrm{H-\overset{H}{\underset{H}{C}}-H}$), two molecules of which being united, after releasing a bond in each, gives ethane ($\mathrm{H-\overset{H}{\underset{H}{C}}-\overset{H}{\underset{H}{C}}-H}$), and finally adding hydroxyl ($\mathrm{H-O-}$), after removing a terminal hydrogen, we get ethyl hydrate or alcohol ($\mathrm{H-\overset{H}{\underset{H}{C}}-\overset{H}{\underset{H}{C}}-O-H}$). The points to remember are that it is a hydrate and the second of the series. Let an atom of oxygen replace two hydrogens in alcohol, and we have acetic acid ($\mathrm{H-\overset{H}{\underset{H}{C}}-\overset{O}{C}-O-H}$). From marsh gas through kerosene oil and vaseline to paraffin or mineral wax we have hundreds of substances that only differ from each other in an additional $=\mathrm{CH_2}$ group to ethane ($\mathrm{H-\overset{H}{\underset{H}{C}}-\overset{H}{\underset{H}{C}}-H}$, then $\mathrm{H-\overset{H}{\underset{H}{C}}-\overset{H}{\underset{H}{C}}-\overset{H}{\underset{H}{C}}-H}$, then $\mathrm{H-\overset{H}{\underset{H}{C}}-\overset{H}{\underset{H}{C}}-\overset{H}{\underset{H}{C}}-\overset{H}{\underset{H}{C}}-H}$, etc.). Their hydrates give many alcohols, and the acids, as well as other substances that can be formed along the same line, are multitudinous. Recalling how far up the line any one of them may happen to be enables the chemist to at once reconstruct the formula.

The groupings are not all so simple as in this series. Some are bound in complex rings instead of chains. These are the most promising for progress and most interesting for science of any. In 1865 Kekulé discovered that benzine had its atoms so connected. This was the first known to have such a structure. Just before this, coal-tar had become an object of intense interest. The brilliant anilines had begun to be made, and the search for more had led to Kekulé's investigations. What a triumph of chemistry this was! From dirty, black coal-tar came the many hues and shades now deemed so necessary for the adornment of our ladies. The gaudy array of colors in every dry-goods and millinery display window attests the commercial worth of such studies. Those ribbons, threads, silks, flowers, and feathers constitute a much more substantial iridescence than that of any dream.

About forty years ago a Scotch chemist, called Anderson, with most commendable heroism began the study of sludge oil. A more obnoxious task can scarcely be conceived. No financial considerations inspired him. He wrought for science, pure and simple, little dreaming of the rich lead he was opening up for coming generations. He distilled two hundred and fifty gallons, the sickening stench from which cost him many a meal. The outcome of that task for several years seemed totally valueless, and might have remained so if a countryman of his own had not taken up the same investigation where he left off. This resulted in the synthesis of pyridine, the basic group of many, and probably all, of the alkaloids. It placed us on the route to quinine, morphine, atropine, and cocaine, with most other active medicinal agents of plants, as well as the ptomaines and leucomaines of animals. It seems, too, to be the direct line to protoplasm itself. While Anderson and his immediate successors in the work gained scarcely honor for what they did, others have since reaped their harvest and made millions of dollars. Still others, yet to come, are bound to make millions more. The gain to the race of such work is incalculable.

A list of all the valuable additions made by synthetic chemistry within a score of years would occupy more time to read than could possibly be given in this lecture. To afford some idea of the subject let us scan rapidly a few of the most important. Thousands of acres of land at one time were occupied in the growth of madder and indigo. This is nearly all relieved now for grain and other crops. These dye-stuffs no longer come from their respective plants, but are produced by the chemist in his laboratory, adding materially to the world's wealth. Cocaine, the alkaloid that enables surgeons to painlessly cut into the most sensitive parts of the body, is now built up from what might be waste products in its extraction from *Erythroxylon coca.* Oil of wintergreen, so useful for flavoring candies and soda-water, as well as for relieving rheumatism, is no longer produced from either wintergreen or sweet birch to the extent it once was, but is synthetically prepared by the chemist. Musk, the well-known costly perfume and flavoring ingredient of candies, is likewise being made at lower rates by the chemist. Bitter oil of almonds, another flavoring substance and constituent of perfumery, the chemist makes. Cumarine, the flavoring ingredient of Tonka beans, which is so often used as a substitute for vanilla, is likewise synthetically prepared. Vanilline, the rich flavoring ingredient of vanilla and constituent of some perfumes, is now made in the temperate zone independent of the family *Orchidaceæ.* Saccharine, a substance two hundred and eighty times sweeter than sugar, and saccharine amide, a related compound said to be sweeter still, are products of the laboratory that beat those of unassisted Nature. Antipyrine, phenacetine, exalgine, acetanilide, and resorcin are products of the laboratory pure and simple that in many ways excel as curative agents any product of the vegetable world, in spite of the Scripture statement that "the leaves of the trees are for the healing of the nations." These relieve the most excruciating pains, check profuse hæmorrhages, reduce fevers, quiet unrest, relieve nausea, and stop the nervous, irritating cough of pertussis (whooping-cough). Paraldehyde, somnal, hypnal, hypnone, chloral-amide, and many other new substances are produced in the laboratory to bring sweet, refreshing sleep to delirious and fever-excited brains.

The number of antiseptics for external and internal use is large and constantly being multiplied by the busy chemist. One of them, called salol, can pass the stomach unchanged and arrest inflammatory processes below the duodenum. Fluoresceine has no rival in the vegetable world, as it alone is able to stain diseased tissue in the eye and leave the healthy tissue untouched. But why give more? Their name is almost legion, and more are coming.

Within this same time new processes have been devised for producing on a larger scale and at cheaper rates such common substances as soda, chloroform, salicylic acid, oxygen, nickel, aluminium, etc. The last-named metal is now marketed at an exceedingly low price as compared with that of a quarter of a century ago. The claim has lately been put forward that a newer process has been devised by which it can be produced as cheaply as iron. If this proves true, then the present generation is about to see the most wonderful industrial revolution that has occurred since man came on this planet. Such a discovery would be apt to produce greater changes than did railways, telegraphs, and electric lights combined. It is probably too good news to be true, and chemists generally are skeptical upon the matter. Such a discovery would solve the problem of fire-proof, rust-proof, and almost cyclone-proof homes. It would give us finer, cheaper, and swifter railway-cars, steam and other ships, and machinery. It would probably solve the problem of aërial navigation. In fact, it would require pages to give the changes it would introduce. But if we have not this, we have one chemical discovery that is destined to do great things for us in the not distant future as it becomes more perfect in its development.

It is said that Sir William Thomson was asked not long ago to state what he believed to be the discovery of greatest promise to the race that has been made within the present generation. Pausing long enough to duly weigh the question, he replied that in his judgment it was the storage battery. Here we have bottled lightning that can run trains and all forms of machinery without fire or smoke, furnace or boiler, and not even a conducting wire to disfigure the landscape or endanger life. It can be used for heating or illuminating as well. Its invention let new light into philosophical chemistry and showed us that the attractions of our atoms are probably but a reversed condition of what we call electrolysis. Here we have a discovery that belongs equally to chemistry and physics, as it lies on the boundary line of both. There is another of the same kind that should be mentioned here.

For a long time chemists have believed that the permanent gases might by a sufficient increase of pressure and reduction of temperature be brought into the conditions of liquid or solid. About thirteen years ago the most stubborn gave way and the belief was verified. The air we breathe has been made into a water-like liquid that boils at 337° F. below zero. At a somewhat lower temperature two liquids with different specific gravities are plainly seen. The one floats upon the surface of the other. Nitrogen, one of these two, has been frozen into crystals like snow The lowest temperature that has yet been reached in experiments of this kind is 373° F. below zero, and the highest pressure used was upward of 3,000 pounds to the square inch. Between this very low temperature and the high ones used in volatilizing metals a wide range exists within which some rather startling chemical facts have appeared. Bodies having very powerful affinities for each other at one temperature may have none at another higher one, while at a still higher the original affinity is restored. Here, as elsewhere in nature, the rhythm of motion exerts its sway. This is particularly apparent in chlorine and its behavior toward platinum. Every one knows how sulphuric acid and ammonia boil and splutter the instant they touch each other, yet pure liquefied ammonia at a low temperature will rest on the surface of the same acid as peacefully as a sleeping babe. Chlorine and oxygen in the liquid state can not be made to unite with bodies that at normal temperatures they seize upon with avidity. Every chemist is familiar with reactions that are only possible within not only certain temperature limits, but also certain degrees of dilution. At one time it was supposed that most chemical changes were immediate and direct. Now we know that the majority, and possibly all, are mediate and indirect. It is coming to be the belief of chemists that no two bodies can unite with each other without the aid of a third. So common a reaction as the burning of wood, that was long supposed to be merely a direct union of oxygen and carbon, is now found to involve a number of hitherto unsuspected intermediate changes in which water and peroxide of hydrogen take a part. Pure water can not be decomposed by electrolysis. An acid is needed in the matter. The action of this acid and that of all such go-between chemical bodies used to be called catalysis. We now speak of it as contact action. As electricity was once considered a rare and remarkable phenomenon when exhibited after the rubbing of a piece of amber, so contact action was long believed to be an exceptional process in nature. But electricity is now well-nigh claiming universal domain as the force of forces, and so old-fashioned catalysis seems almost bound to swallow up all chemical activity. The number of substances that unite with each other rapidly when third bodies are present as impurities or otherwise, but that refuse to unite in a state of absolute purity, is multiplying daily. As to how such third bodies act in aiding the change is still in grave doubt for the majority of such cases, but has been pretty clearly traced in a few. In the manufacture of sulphuric acid from sulphurous anhydride, nitric acid, though acting as a go-between, is very far from a mere passive agent in the change. During the molecular dance it suffers successive decompositions and recompositions, always ending up in its original state. If we had not discovered the part it really plays in the matter it would be registered in the list of catalytic bodies.

When we turn to the organic world and undertake the study of physiological chemistry and botany we find contact action at every turn. Numerous ferments have been isolated and studied by organic chemists, and with some of them there can be little doubt that they act by successive decompositions and recompositions of themselves. Much of their apparently magical power depends upon their ability to decompose water at normal temperatures.

Let us but learn how to isolate such substances in paying quantities and in such a form that they can accomplish the same task as in the plant, and the growth in knowledge will be marvelous for rapidity. We have known several organic ferments for a good many years. Pepsin and trypsin are probably the two with which we are most familiar. To solve the secret of their composition would be to gain a key to the situation. For nearly thirty years chemist after chemist has been baffled in attempting to do so. Not a single ray of light has been thrown upon the problem. Until we succeed in getting them in a pure state for analysis, or in securing some decomposition product of them in such a state, nothing can be done. A very faint glimmer was for the first time discovered during the present year by your essayist. A substance was isolated from pepsin that bears a constant relationship in quantity to its proteolytic power. This is a very small result for thirty years of trial by scores of chemists, but it must not be forgotten that the problem is a big one, and the first gleam is always followed before very long by the dawn. A complete solution of this problem will tell us in terms of chemistry the cause and cure of disease and the conditions of life and health.

So simple-looking a substance as the white of an egg is yet a most stupendous mystery to our science. It and all the albuminoids are awaiting this very light. The fever and pain, discomfort and delirium of disease are now known to be due, in many cases, to ptomaines manufactured by bacteria. They are believed to break down albuminous substances by aid of the ferments they secrete. We want to know the nature of these ferments. Until such knowledge is acquired we can not really say that we know how nitric or acetic acids, and all the nitrates and acetates, are made as common and cheap as they are. Micro-organisms produce them. The bread problem of the future is believed to carry its solution in this same question.

From cellulose to starch is a very short step, but we can not take it in the proper way. By a crude process long known, sawdust can be converted into an exceedingly coarse article of bread, the catalytic body being sulphuric acid. We await the discovery of the proper organic contact action body to do perfectly what can now be roughly done. The world may yet see deal boards transmuted into the whitest kind of starch. We can and do now change starch into that kind of sugar called glucose. Let us next find how to make it into levulose, and then discover how to unite these two, and we will have cane sugar. Hundreds of chemists have worked at this problem. The man lucky enough to solve it has an enormous fortune awaiting him. We have lately found how to give cane sugar the flavor of maple sugar, so that, should the maple forests give out, the supply of that sweet morsel can still be maintained.

Among the many problems that still await solution, but that lie along the line we have been considering, is the synthetic production of such valuable substances as India rubber, cotton, silk, and wool. The possibilities of organic chemistry are numberless, and many of them may never be realized; but we have already the sweet consciousness of having mastered more than enough to pay for the disappointment of our alchemical predecessors who hoped to be able to convert iron into gold. But their dream, wild as it really was at that time, may yet become an established fact. No chemist would to-day risk his professional reputation by asserting it an impossible feat. Let some reliable man of good repute in this department of science assert that he had made such a discovery, and it would doubtlessly raise considerable skepticism, but that would be all. No one knowing the present status of the science would use the word "impossible." Reasoning *a priori* on the subject, we would expect that the cost of production would always exceed the value of the product. This is poor encouragement for this line of investigation. In the fields hitherto invaded and conquered the reverse has been true. Substances worth less than nothing—actually having a negative value because of being incumbrances that it cost cash to remove—have been and are being made into goods worth many millions of dollars. The actual facts, when stated in simple language, are more wonderful than the tales of the Arabian Nights. "Yes!" some one answers, "and the names found in the story are perhaps quite as remarkable as any in that volume." This is very true. To read of a substance that has been christened methyl-ethyl-hydroxyl-tetra-hydro-pyridinetropate sounds anything but musical to the ears of nonchemists, especially when they learn that it is the dangerous medical poison atropine. Every syllable of this name has a meaning, and the whole tells just how the molecule is constructed. To say that rheumatic pains can be relieved by oil of wintergreen is a plain statement to ordinary mortals. Tell him such relief can be had by the use of methyl-orthomono-hydroxyl-benzoate, and you will puzzle him sorely, though the things are the same.

In this hasty and necessarily imperfect review of the development of modern chemistry from the absurd notions of the ancients, it will be observed that our knowledge has in almost every particular imitated the habits of the atoms themselves. When Lavoisier gave us a true theory of combustion, all the facts had up to that time been subsisting as isolated units. After that they were clustered together like a molecule. When Dalton explained definite and multiple proportions, another set of independent facts immediately cohered. Next came the generalizations of Mitscherlich, Hoffman, Mendelejeff, and others, each gathering into united groups its own special data. A central nucleus for the total was found in the law of Avogadro. As the atom facts clustered together by the laws of lesser scope, so the clusters themselves, like so many compound radicals, gained bonds of mental union by this far-reaching generalization. Our chemical knowledge, therefore, like matter itself, began indefinite and incoherent. Illy understood facts were without bonds of union. Growth began as they grouped together into a definite, coherent whole. With such growth came complexity, the minor laws each taking the part of branches to a common tree. Each new hypothesis by confirmation brought new integrations, and dissipated the looseness of thought that characterized the carlier stages. The growth of chemistry is thus seen to be a typical illustration of the law of evolution.

ABSTRACT OF THE DISCUSSION.

Dr. E. H. Bartley:

I have certainly no adverse criticism to make upon the lecture of the evening. Dr. Eccles has, it seems to me, been remarkably successful in crowding a great deal of accurate information into a very little space. In the brief time allotted to me, I can only call attention to one or two points in connection with the evolution of chemistry which have not been elaborated by the lecturer. If we examine the earliest records of chemical investigation, we shall note the lack of definiteness in the language with which they are described, as compared with the clear, accurate form of our modern scientific terminology. The development of language itself has gone on hand in hand with development in science, and has been aided and stimulated by it. Modern language begins and ends in a point: is terse, lucid, and accurate. It shows the same tendency toward increased coherency and integration that appears in all other processes of evolution. This is particularly true of the language of science. And this accuracy of descriptive terminology is an essential condition of the progress of science. By means thereof, new discoveries and investigations are made known to other investigators, the world over, almost as rapidly as they are accomplished—thus furnishing the clews in other minds for yet further advancement in scientific knowledge. In the same direction is seen the effect of the admirable work of artisans, at the present day, in the manufacture of chemical apparatus. Formerly each investigator had to make his own apparatus, often in a very rude and clumsy way. Now it is prepared for him, and most perfectly adapted to its uses, thereby greatly assisting discoveries in scientific research, and constituting a most important element in the evolution of science. This is true of all the practical sciences, and specially true of chemistry. Thus we see illustrated the universal law of evolution: the tendency to differentiation, to the creation of separate and distinct divisions of labor, accompanied by a greater coherence—a more perfect co-operation of all in the advancement of knowledge and the improvement and unification of the race.

Dr. P. H. Van der Weyde:

I have been astonished at the amount of material which has been crowded into the lecture this evening. As an historical paper, and a general statement of present tendencies and results in chemical investigation, it leaves nothing to be desired. I can only call attention to the remarkable character of recent laboratory discoveries, which seem to indicate that in time all our food products may be produced directly, by chemical combinations, from the inorganic world, instead of compelling us to rely, as at present, on vegetable and animal products for the sustenance of life. There has also been great progress of late in the field of biology. The old notion of a vital force has given way before the results of scientific investigation. That which was formerly known as vital force and supposed to indicate a direct, creative action in the production of organic life is now known to be merely the result of chemical change.

Dr. Eccles replied briefly, saying that vital force is no longer believed in by chemists. The field of chemistry is so vast that no one mind can grasp it all, and it is impossible to describe its conquests in a single lecture.

THE EVOLUTION OF ELECTRIC AND MAGNETIC PHYSICS

BY

ARTHUR E. KENNELLY

CHIEF ELECTRICIAN OF THE EDISON LABORATORY

COLLATERAL READINGS SUGGESTED:

Benjamin Franklin's Experiments and Observations on Electricity; J. J. Fahie's A History of Electric Telegraphy; Park Benjamin's The Age of Electricity; Marvels of Electricity and Magnetism; Brennan's A Popular Exposition of Electricity; Lodge's Modern Views of Electricity; Tyndall's Lectures on Electric Phenomena, Light and Electricity, and Lessons in Electricity; Sir William Thomson's Electro-Statics and Magnetism; Balfour Stewart's Electricity and Magnetism; Reid's The Telegraph in America; Prescott's History, Theory, and Practice of the Electric Telegraph; Molloy's The Electric Light and the Storing of Electric Energy.

THE EVOLUTION OF ELECTRIC AND MAGNETIC PHYSICS.

By Arthur E. Kennelly.

The subject for your consideration this evening is one of the most interesting and important of all the topics which have attracted the attention of the modern scientific thinker.

In the earliest recorded observations of electric force it appears to have been regarded as a phase or mode of vitality. Thales of Miletus, the Greek mathematician whose home was on the woody Asiatic shore of the Ægean Sea, twenty-five hundred years ago, noticing that amber after being rubbed attracted or repelled light objects, such as down or lint, is said to have attributed the property to some condition of life resident in the substance.

The centuries that have intervened have smiled upon so superstitious a belief, but perhaps when futurity shall judge, the thought, under a different interpretation, may not seem so far astray; for to us of to-day vitality is still incomprehensible, and the very nature of electricity is enveloped in mystery; yet we know that whatever nerve force may be, it must at least be closely associated with electric force. Nerve-fibers strangely resemble insulated wires; electricity can stimulate them into an involuntary performance of their functions, while not a muscle contracts without electrical manifestations, if care only be taken to observe them. Even light, it would seem, falling on the retina, excites electrical disturbances through the optic nerve, and it is possible, if it is not at present demonstrated, that electricity may be the active principle in the processes of animal vitality. The relation between electricity and vitality may be so close as to amount to identity.

For twenty-two centuries after this first announcement, electricity, one ever-present phase of the universal activity, remained not absolutely unnoticed, but unknown. In the saying of the Greeks, "There were brave men before Agamemnon," but not even the violence of thunder nor the vivid lightning-flash can announce the facts of an all-enveloping environment to human intelligence of the highest order we can boast until the progress of evolution shall have prepared the human mind to usher and reveal the mysteries of Nature.

The renascent dawn of the scientific era, or the age of objective investigation—a method of study that had almost become extinguished with the ruin of Alexandria—threw open the pathways of physical research and brought the first recognition of electricity to light. The commencement of the seventeenth century was noted for its discoveries in electric and magnetic science. Thales lived about six hundred years before Christ, and Dr. Gilbert, of Colchester, christened and presented the new science to the world in his celebrated book De Magnete, published in 1600.

The early history of magnetism tells a similar tale. The attracting power of the loadstone was known to the Greeks, and the knowledge of the directive property of the suspended needle or mariner's compass is said to have been possessed by the Chinese long before the Christian era; but the first published researches in the subject were by Norman and Boroughs, of London, in 1580. Just at this time Francis Bacon, the champion of experimental science and inductive philosophy, was preparing those works that have made his name immortal. The time was ripe for the new thought, for human intelligence at length stood ready to burst through the trammels that inthralled it, and to vindicate its prerogative to judge according to evidence.

Slowly, and against much opposition, experimental physics developed the sciences of magnetism and electricity. For two hundred years the two sciences stood entirely apart; their intimate relationship was perhaps only suggested in the poet's fancy, nor was it scientifically demonstrated till 1820. Even at the present moment, intimate though we recognize that relationship to be, the line that separates and the tie that unites them are still matters of speculation that the future must resolve.

The earlier progress was shown by electricity. Von Guericke, in 1672, made the first electrical machine out of a globe of sulphur rotated by hand, and produced with it the first artificial electric spark. The sound accompanying the spark was also noticed by von Guericke. Newton three years later improved upon this machine by substituting a glass sphere for the globe in place of sulphur. Now that a simple generator of electricity was capable of being made, experiments became more common and facts accumulated. Gray and Wheeler in particular, between 1720 and 1736, gave a great impetus to the science by the discovery of conduction. They showed that glass, resin, silk, and other substances were insulators, or impervious to electricity, but that metals and liquids conducted it. They succeeded in transmitting electric force to a distance of several hundred feet, and by these experiments laid the foundation for telegraphy. This classification of substances into conductors and nonconductors since their time has not altered in fact, but its principle is better understood. More delicate measurements have since shown that no known solid or liquid body insulates perfectly. On the other hand, the best conductors obstruct to a certain degree the flow of electricity, so that conduction and insulation are only the limiting attributes of one property common in varying degrees to every description of matter. No conducting power has yet been detected in dry gases, but it is possible that if an electrified body could be maintained suspended in a gas without any solid or liquid support, such conducting power might be discovered. The best solid insulator yet found is dry, spun quartz, glass following next. The best measurements of the conducting power of glass at the temperature of melting ice show that it is inferior to that of silver—the best conductor—in the ratio of one to three followed by twenty-two zeros.

From the time of Gray and Wheeler a very extraordinary advance was made in electrical science; the world of science now gave out myriads of electric sparks. Nearly every year brought to light some fresh discovery in electricity. A gentleman in Leyden, Holland, tried to see if he could store up electricity in a bottle, and succeeded. The Leyden jar, the properties of which were thus discovered, was first introduced in 1745, and this not only drew much attention to the subject, but enabled the experimenter to collect and suddenly discharge a greater store of electrical energy than had been previously possible.

The researches on electricity that made Franklin so famous came next, and were made between 1747 and 1760. In that time he added greatly to the knowledge of the subject. He proved at Philadelphia that lightning was an electric spark. Lightning had been going on since the world began, but it needed the brightest human intelligence to discover that lightning was electricity. It needed even more than that—it needed evolution. Franklin erected the first lightning conductor for the protection of buildings, and thus appears to have been the first to apply electrical science to utilitarian purposes; for up to this time there was no electric art. In every other branch of study, even astronomy not excepted, as evidenced in astrology, art had long preceded science, that vainly toiled to keep pace in theory with the steps of practice. To this day the race is still all uneven; for the capabilities of skill and mechanism often transcend calculation and set analytical pursuit at defiance; but here a new order was celebrated; for perhaps the first time in the history of the world Science preceded and created an art.

To Franklin and Canton jointly we owe the discovery, dimly foreshadowed by Stephen Gray, that electrical force develops electrification in surrounding bodies, at a distance, or by induction. This made another example of forces acting at a distance, such as gravitation and radiant energy. This then was a great mystery. Later investigations have partly explained these phenomena, though the matter is still only dimly understood. Newton had always confessed himself unable to comprehend the *modus operandi* of definite forces acting through indefinitely extended vacancy. He suggested as an explanation the corpuscular theory of light —that light consisted of solid particles of matter emanating from a luminous body. This theory has since given way to the undulatory theory of vibratory and progressive disturbances in an elastic ether. The electrical phenomena of action at a distance have also been proved to be produced by elastic stress, and possibly even deformation of the same invisible but ubiquitous element. We know now what Franklin and Canton did not—that induction is due to pushing the electric force through the surrounding air or ether. It is not improbable that similar solutions may ultimately be found for the other problems of radiant energy. Gravitation yet remains unexplained, but remains, it is believed, only to succumb to a similar and equally simple hypothesis. We seem to know for a certainty, at least, that so-called action at a distance is caused by stress through the intervening medium.

Now that sufficient facts had been collected, generalization became possible, and the first mathematical theory of electricity was propounded by Æpinus in 1759. This, however, was succeeded and eclipsed by the researches and results of Coulomb and Cavendish, who first applied definite measurements to the study of the science. It has been aptly said that all physical science is measurement. It is measurement that distinguishes science from vague theorizing. Just as Franklin founded the art, Coulomb and Cavendish founded the quantitative science of electricity, as distinguished from purely experimental or qualitative knowledge. This branch of the subject next received special cultivation at the hands of the French savants in the Napoleonic period.

The task of developing electrical knowledge had hitherto been one of acquiring facts by direct experiment, but at this time it naturally divided between two different sets of workers. There now sprang up a set of electrical philosophers who theorized upon the facts already known. One of these classes continued as before to seek for new facts and new discoveries by direct experiment, continually varying their cross-examination of Nature; the other party took the facts already gleaned, submitted them to analysis, and determined mathematically the laws those facts uttered. By a continuation of the same process, they endeavored to determine new facts and more recondite laws by mathematical reasoning from the existing premises. As leaders of these parties, Faraday might be cited for the first, Clerk-Maxwell of the second. Much futile controversy has been waged as to the power, advantage, and rank of these two schools. Both are necessary; the one supplements and corrects the work of the other, for it is impossible to apply intelligent labor to the vanguard of science in any direction without gaining ground. The danger of the method of the experimental school, when carried to extremes, is loss of labor by groping without definite object in the dark, lacking competent leadership; the danger of over-impetuous activity in the analytical camp is in missing truth, through the assumption that all the necessary premises are already known, or else in terminating research with mere symbols—pure mathematics, instead of physics written in mathematical language—forgetting the significance of the symbols and losing the grasp they hold on facts. The best successes are generally made by the co-operation of both parties, for all observation must stand the test of analytical trial, and all calculations must be confirmed under the ordeal of experiment.

Many improvements in methods and apparatus were made after the date of Franklin's discoveries, but the next great epoch was the discovery of galvanic electricity by Galvani, of Bologna, in 1786. An electrical machine was being worked in a room where some frogs were being dissected.

When their bodies were brought into the vicinity of the machine it was noticed that their legs twitched. The operator commenced to reflect upon this phenomenon, and the result of his reflection and further investigation was the discovery of galvanism, as it was called from his name. The subject afterward received much attention. The results of that discovery were developed and followed up with greater success by Volta, who published in 1800 his first account of the voltaic pile, the lineal ancestor of all the different batteries with which we are to-day familiar, from which they have been differentiated by a natural process of evolution. Volta made use of Galvani's experiments, but he arrived independently at new and important results, and so is entitled to equal credit with Galvani. Galvani had supposed that the electricity came from the frog. Volta showed that it resulted from the contact of dissimilar substances.

Much dispute arose at the time as to the source of the electrical activity in the generator, and up to this date the question is yet open; but it appears safe to conclude that electrical activity is capable of being developed whenever two dissimilar substances, or even dissimilar parts of the same substance, are brought into contact. If the two substances are non-conductors, as, for example, glass and silk, the electrical force indicates a high tension or pressure, especially when the substances are rubbed together. It would burst through the air in sparks, across a considerable space. This was the condition of the electricity generated before the time of Galvani. On the other hand, when the substances in contact are conductors, such as metals, no accumulative effect is obtained by the mutual friction of their surfaces, and the electricity produced, while it may be abundant in quantity, is of low pressure, and can not burst through the air in sparks, or evince powerful attraction for surrounding objects. The electricity in each case is supposed to be identical in nature, but to differ in behavior, through differences in the pressure under which it acts.

Many years were passed in establishing this relationship between statical or frictional and dynamic or galvanic electricity, but now galvanic effects can be obtained from frictionally produced electricity, and all the phenomena peculiar to so-called static electricity can be produced by increasing sufficiently the number of galvanic cells, and thus accumulating their pressure. This property of pressure, or its electrical analogue, is quantitatively expressed in terms of a unit named the "volt," after Volta. The various galvanic cells have singly a pressure of from half a volt to two volts and a half. The lowest pressure that will cause a spark to burst through a thin film of air is about six hundred volts. Lightning flashes indicate enormous pressures, whose magnitude is only guessed at, perhaps, in millions of volts. The higher the pressure, the greater the distance over which the electric spark will jump.

The discovery of Volta's pile was no sooner published than Sir Humphry Davy commenced experimenting with it in London, and his example was followed in every direction. In 1807 he announced the decomposition by the galvanic current of the alkalies hitherto supposed to be elements, or simple, undecomposable forms of matter. Galvanism now opened a wide field for investigation, and attention for the time almost deserted frictional electricity. The search was not long in danger of subsiding, for the next great epoch was Oersted's discovery of the influence of a current upon a suspended magnetic needle. This was in 1820. He discovered that a needle so suspended stands at right angles to an electric current passing near it. Up to this date electricity and magnetism had been studied apart, and had held aloof; now they met and were linked into one branch of physics. Magnetism alone had not made great advances, but, associated with electricity, it has since developed, practically as well as theoretically, in a manner that has almost outstripped fancy. Oersted's discovery roused the whole scientific world. A few weeks after its publication, Ampère issued the first of those analytical investigations on the subject that have made his name so familiar. While the French school chiefly developed the mathematical consequences of the new facts, the experimental study was actively pushed by Davy and Faraday in England, and Seebeck and Berzelius in Germany. The first electro-magnets were produced by Arago and Sturgeon about 1825, and these laid the foundation of the modern telegraph. The electro-magnet also received special development in the hands of Joseph Henry at Princeton about 1829. This was the period at which the electric telegraph was first inaugurated. Electricity had been suggested for this application as far back as 1753, and Ronalds had made a working model telegraph in 1816, but frictional high-pressure electricity had always been the agent, and the difficulty of insulating it had invariably interfered with its practical application. The low-pressure galvanic current, however, was much more amenable to control in this respect, and telegraphy, with the aid of the magnetic needle, in 1833 became a successful experiment. Morse succeeded in making his electro-magnetic system practicable in 1837.

The stimulus that electricity gave to the study of magnetism, immediately following Oersted's discovery, reacted by reflection upon electrical progress also, and an electro-magnetic era was entered that has gone on with ever-increasing impetus since that time. The telegraph, fairly in operation by 1840, spread from city to city, and in 1850 first crossed the sea. Electroplating as an art sprang into existence about the same time, the first practical experiment being performed about the year 1832. The debt that commerce and civilization owed to science for these arts has since been richly repaid by the aid that commerce has given in the direction of pure science; for, in order to foster and invigorate these arts, commerce has defrayed the expense of many scientific investigations intermediately necessary, and this community of object is continually strengthening and enriching each at the present time.

From 1830 to 1859 Faraday made his masterly researches. He discovered among other things the electro-chemical law that now bears his name, and the influence of magnetism upon light; but his crowning discovery was that of electro-magnetic induction, which has paved the way for the dynamo-electric machinery of the present time.

The scientific development of the subject was also active during this period. In 1840 Ohm published his well-known law that reduced the elements of the galvanic circuit to simplicity. There was still, however, a difficulty in measuring electricity quantitatively, owing to the absence of any common system of units. Each observer measured and recorded his results in arbitrary units of his own selection, and great confusion existed when attempts were made to compare the results so obtained. Nor was the deficiency confined to science only, for practical telegraphy sorely labored under the same disadvantages. To meet the growing need for a universal system of measurements, the British Association for the Advancement of Science appointed a committee to consider the matter in 1861, and this committee succeeded in establishing within four years the celebrated centimetre, gramme, and second system that is now the basis of all international measurements, electrical as well as scientific. This system is like a universal language, which enables observers in one part of the world to make their discoveries intelligible in other countries. This is now the base for all international scientific measurements. The advantage that science has gained by this co-operative effort has been very great, and engineering has been similarly benefited.

The great utilitarian progress made since that time has been in the invention of the telephone, the electric light, and machinery for the transmission of electric power—all the outcome of electro-magnetic induction. The first electric telephone was made by Reis in 1868, but it was only applicable to the reproduction of musical sounds at a distance, its articulation being too restricted to convey speech successfully. The first practical speaking telephone was made by Alexander Graham Bell in 1876. It is now in use all over the civilized world, and many pages could be written upon its development alone.

The carbon arc light of Davy, while very useful for many purposes calling for intense illumination, was very costly while sustained by galvanic batteries. To produce it more conveniently and cheaply, the dynamo machine was slowly improved. The dynamo as it existed in the year of Faraday's discovery was little more than a scientific toy; at the present time dynamos are in operation that singly transform the mechanical power of a steam-engine into electrical energy to the working value of five thousand horses.

The study of the arc light and its capabilities led to the search for an incandescent lamp. In the hands of Edison the incandescent lamp became not only a possibility, but a practical success.

The most important phases of the subject at the present time may thus be summed up:

1. In electro-magnetic science the great achievement since Faraday's time has been the determination of the fact that all electricity flows, or tends to flow, in closed curves or circuits, so that we have the electrostatic circuit, the galvanic circuit, and the magnetic circuit, each resembling, as it were, an endless chain or a bundle of endless chains; and the laws which control these three different types of circuit show wonderful analogies.

2. The due appreciation of the influence of the ether and

its importance in all electro-magnetic phenomena. While originally the electrical activity seemed to be confined to the battery or conducting wires of a galvanic circuit, it is now believed that the ether surrounding these conductors plays fully as active a part in the process of conduction; and the mind sees free space no longer void, but filled with an active and responsive substance—the ether. It looks almost as if matter were inert in comparison with the ether which surrounds it. Once more in the evolution of thought the tide of unbelief has turned, and we hold, under somewhat altered premises, the dictum that Torricelli refuted—namely, that "Nature abhors a vacuum." The properties of the ether almost threaten to surpass in interest and importance the properties of the matter it environs and pervades.

3. The evidence in favor of the proposition that light is a vibratory disturbance in the ether of an electro-magnetic nature is such as almost to amount to demonstration. When this shall be generally accepted, the whole domain of optics and radiant energy will be enrolled as one department and property of electro-magnetic physics.

Difficult as it is to clearly apprehend the course of evolution in the near past, where events press upon us in a narrow bounding throng, and the workers at the great loom of history yet stand by the mesh their hands have helped to weave, how still more difficult it is to guess the future! The prospect that opens is, however, a brilliant one. We may well believe that in science the same evolutionary process which has united electricity and magnetism, and welded both with radiation, will continue to magnify, simplify, and unify. Contrary to the course of evolution in the organic world, "from the homogeneous to the heterogeneous, the simple to the complex," the development of science is from the heterogeneous to the homogeneous, from the complex to the simple, and just as the evolutionary course of religious belief was from polytheism to monotheism, so with every fresh acquisition science becomes greater and grander and more succinct.

In the arts, electricity is destined, even apart from future discoveries, to take into its own hands the distribution of power. The telegraph has conquered time, and the electric motor is born to triumph over space; but whether we watch the vibration of the telegraphic recorder that spells its message across the sea, or watch the electric car, urged by invisible hands, pursuing its stealthy way, the rhythmic words of Ruskin rise into recollection's sight, "Not in a week, or a month, or a year, but by the lives of many souls, a beautiful thing must be done."

ABSTRACT OF THE DISCUSSION.

Mr. George M. Phelps:

Mr. Phelps suggested that the nexus between the purpose of the Ethical Association as implied in its title, and the present course of lectures and discussions upon evolution as manifested in the physical sciences, might be found in the closing words of Emerson's Cambridge Divinity School Address of 1838. That seer looked for the "new teacher that shall follow so far those shining laws that he shall see them come full circle; shall see their rounding, complete grace; shall see the world to be the mirror of the soul; shall see the identity of the law of gravitation with purity of heart; and shall show that the Ought, that Duty, is one thing with Science, with Beauty, and with Joy."

Mr. Kennelly had shown, in his comprehensive address, that from the inception of electric science and the useful arts dependent upon it, up to the present development, there had gone forward a course of evolution, analogous to that traced in previous lectures in the domain of nature; a slight and crude beginning in a remote past, followed, however slowly or rapidly, by successive modifications of theory and practice with advancing knowledge, accompanied by an ever-increasing elaboration and complexity, and attended by the elimination, from time to time, of outworn or unsound views and methods, all tending steadily to enhanced use and benefit.

The expansion of use and benefit during the ten years just passed was a most striking feature of electrical evolution; an expansion requiring the employment of an amount of electrical energy still more striking as compared with the amount used for all purposes previous to the advent of electric lighting and transmission of power. Every arc-lamp requires nearly a horse-power of electrical energy, and every incandescent lamp about a tenth as much; tens of thousands of electric motors add to the enormous consumption. It is doubtless safe to say that an aggregate of not less than a million horse-power of electrical energy is daily expended in the various electrical arts of to-day, of which amount certainly less than one tenth is required for the service of the telegraph, the telephone, and all other uses but those of light and power. The latter, ten-year-old industries, are therefore utilizing nine or ten times as much electricity as is required for all other purposes.

In the evolution of sciences and arts, such as form the topics of this season's course, there comes in a factor not found in the evolution of what is called the natural world—namely, the incalculable spirit of man. The *inventor* arrives. In the laboratory of the investigator, the workshop of the mechanic, the managing office of an industry, or in the quiet library of a student, a thought, an idea is born. If the time be ripe or the environment favorable, the idea may modify, or even revolutionize, a science; or may be embodied in a machine or device that will revivify a waning industry or found a new one. But, alas! the time is not always ripe nor the environment favorable; then, though the spirit do its work never so well, the thought, the idea, seems to perish, like useless variations in the evolution of nature. But, though useless at its birth, and perhaps during the life of its originator, it may in the fullness of time be found the one thing wanting in the thought or work of the world. A striking instance is found in the case of Thomas Davenport, a Vermont blacksmith, who died thirty-two years ago. We have now just become used to riding upon electric cars. In 1835 Davenport made and described electric motors embodying the essential features of the motors now in use. He exhibited several specimens within the next two years, running a miniature car upon a small circular track. But there was no adequate source of electricity to drive large motors; the dynamo did not exist. Davenport died poor and disappointed. To-day his thought, his idea, is serving us in all the manifold applications of electric power.

But for those who fail or fall in trying to make the world richer, more commodious, more beautiful, to make mankind better and happier, and for all of us, there remains the faith of the true evolutionist in the abiding quality, the permanence, of every true and good bit of work, whether in the realm of science, art, industry, or ethics.

The robust poet who left us a year ago thus sings through the voice of Abt Vogler, the inventor of a wondrous musical instrument, whose harmonies have entranced his spirit:

"There shall never be one lost good! What was shall live as before;
The evil is null, is naught, is silence implying sound;
What was good, shall be good, with, for evil, so much good more."

MR. T. C. MARTIN:

Mr. Martin said that the discussion of electricity in the series on evolution, at Christmas time and on the threshold of the New Year, was very happy and appropriate. The mission of electricity as a force and agent directly affecting human welfare was to promote peace on earth and good-will among men; its motto was: "Behold I make all things new." Electricity had been one of the principal means in bringing individuals and peoples together. Everything which broke down the walls of isolation and invited to freer social intercourse belonged to the higher influences, "not ourselves," but outside, making for righteousness and a perfected evolution of man and his world. So, too, electricity, in making all things new, was the latest of the great powers to be controlled by human wit and invention, succeeding others in due season, "lest one good custom should corrupt the world"; and teaching that the finite is the imperfect, of contentment in which we must beware. At the present moment the work of electricity lay chiefly in light and power, and it gave us purer, sweeter, subtler, gentler service than any of its predecessors had afforded. It could not but be that this refinement of service and influence would better and elevate all who enjoyed it, as taking us one remove further from the crude, raw, and barbaric. This messiahship of material things was borne in upon us in witnessing the advances of science, which, after all, meant nothing unless they purified and sanctified life. As one whose work lay in the electrical field, he found pleasure in thinking that such work, perhaps more than any other of its kind, laid hold on the future, with its promise of a nobler state of society than had yet been attained.

DR. ROBERT G. ECCLES:

Mr. Kennelly has in a clear and impressive manner carried us along the successive steps of the progress of electric science, and in showing its connection with the doctrine of evolution he has been ably seconded by the gentleman who opened the discussion. It is not possible for one scarcely an amateur in the subject to attempt any criticism of these experts, and it seems almost in the nature of presumption for me to even suppose myself able to add to the interest of the same. In one hour's talk, however, many things of great importance that might be advantageously dwelt upon to impress them the more firmly on the listener's attention are necessarily dismissed with the briefest notice. As an illustration we have the discovery of Oersted that a magnetic needle is deflected by a current of electricity, and if the current is strong the needle will set itself almost at right angles with the wire carrying it. It is safe to say that this evidence of the connection of magnetism with electricity is the trunk of the tree whose branches now fill the whole earth with telephones, telegraphs, burglar-alarms, electric lights, and all our successful applications of this force. From it can be traced the successive steps leading to the latest wonders of this kind and pointing toward many more yet to come. Some of the most recent attempts to chain this giant seem to border on the uncanny regions of fairy-land. To be able to send telegraphic messages from moving trains by induced currents is certainly a triumph to be proud of. Miraculous though it may seem, it is but a phenomenon of every-day experience with telephone-users who hear what is being said on wires contiguous to their own. Without apparent connection the message jumps from wire to wire through vacant space. But such telegraphing without wires has been discounted very much in the sending of messages to considerable distances across the sea without a cable. This was done not long ago from the Isle of Wight to the mainland of England. It is seriously proposed to adopt the same plan by ocean ships so that they can telegraph to each other on sight. A few years ago an enthusiastic individual suggested the possibility of sending oceanic electric currents from America to Europe by having wires and currents of sufficient power strung along the coasts of the Eastern and Western Hemispheres and grounded in the water at each termination.

In theoretical considerations this department of science has until lately made little or no progress. The two-fluid theory of Symmer and the one-fluid theory of Franklin, while held by various students and workers with less or more tenacity, were practically driven from the field by the doctrine of the conservation of energy. Educated electricians now generally believe that all they have to deal with is modes of motion in matter and in the universal ether. Clerk Maxwell's theory of light shows how it can be understood as related to and of a kind with electricity. The acceptance of this theory forces us to conclude that every chemical transformation sends out from itself two sets of strains on the ether answering to two forms of force, one of which we call heat or light, and the other electricity. One is longitudinal and the other transverse. It is not possible to give by mere verbal description to this audience other than a rough analogous adumbration of the theory. Imagine a set of elastic cogwheels reaching the length of the church and caused to revolve. The matter of the wheels goes up and down by their rotation. If at the same time they are crowded outward and give to the pressure, a to-and-fro movement of the substance of the wheels is added to the up-and-down movement of rotation. Some such two sets of movements are set up in matter and the ether answering to electricity and light. The truth of Maxwell's theory has almost met complete experimental proof within the last two or three years. Dr. Henry Hertz, in a communication to the Sixty-second Congress of German Naturalists and Physicians, which assembled at Heidelberg last summer, communicated the results of his experiments in this field of research. He showed that it was now possible to duplicate with electricity nearly every experiment depended upon to demonstrate the truth of the undulatory theory of light. Electric waves are shown under proper conditions to possess all the properties of light waves. They have been reflected, refracted, made to interfere, caused to cast shadows, and, in fact, to do everything that light can do. The dimensions of these waves have been measured and found to be much larger than those of light. A prism of asphalt refracts them as one of glass does those of light. A metallic grating polarizes them as a nickel prism does light. They separate, they combine, they re-enforce, they weaken each other. For a long time we studied the thermal qualities of bodies before we knew much of radiant heat, and for an equally long or longer time we have studied the electrical qualities of bodies, and have but just begun to appreciate the facts of radiant electricity. The science of electricity that began with the discovery that rubbing a piece of amber gave it the power to attract light bodies has gone on from this beginning until now it seems to embrace the universe. Strange that all powerful cosmic forces, because of such a beginning, should come to be classed as those of ambericity. Electron means amber. Every movement we make, every breath we breathe, every thought we think produces it.

Dr. William M. Hutchinson:

Frictional or static electricity, when applied to the surface of the body in the form of a spark, causes—1st, a sudden involuntary movement of the part irritated; 2d, a reddening of the cutaneous surface; 3d, a perception of a distinct sensation, either pleasant and invigorating or painful and depressing, as the case may be. That it causes a marked stimulating effect upon the function and nutrition of nerves and muscles is claimed by some and denied by others. It certainly will relieve the pain of some forms of neuralgia. As a means of producing marked mental impressions, and thus demonstrating the remarkable interaction between the mind and body by curing some forms of functional nervous disturbances, frictional sparks are often of service to the physician. It is probable, however, that this effect is purely mental, the result being produced by causing an expectant attention on the subject's part, as is done by the so-called "mind cures" or "hypnotic suggestion" methods.

Current or voltaic electricity, when passed through the body, produces three effects—viz., catalytic, cataphoric, and electro-tonic. The catalytic action may be slight if the current be weak, and, by increasing chemical reactions within the tissues of the body, it may serve to stimulate nutritive changes. If the current is sufficiently strong, intense effects are produced—the tissues are decomposed about each pole, blisters containing acid fluids forming at the positive pole, and alkaline fluids at the negative pole. This destructive effect is sometimes made use of in the breaking down of new growths, as tumors, and in the enlarging of contracted passages or canals.

By the cataphoric action of a continuous galvanic current is meant the property which such a current possesses of moving along with it fluids that lie in its path, and so, when applied to the body, of increasing osmoses. This action of this current may be also applied to carry with it medicinal substances into the tissues through the pathway of the skin.

The electro-tonic effects produced upon the tissues during the passage of a voltaic current are a diminished state of excitability at the positive pole, and an increased degree of irritability at the negative pole.

If this current be rapidly interrupted, or broken and reconnected, it appears to have the effect upon various organs of setting them to work. For instance, the muscles of the hand may be made to contract if this current be applied to the portion of the brain presiding over the hand, to the nerve trunk going to the hand, or to the muscles themselves. Again, if it be applied to special sense nerves, as the optic or auditory, the effect is to produce the sensation of a flash of light or certain noises. If this interrupted voltaic current be of high potency—500 to 1,000 volts—the effect is to produce such profound and sudden change of the molecular state of the tissues and vital processes that their activities instantly cease. The suddenness and painlessness of this death has caused the advocacy, by many electricians and physicians, of the execution of criminals by electricity.

Mr. Kennelly, in closing the discussion, held that it was probable that electricity would soon become the chief motor power in our cities, substituting both steam and horse-power. In this direction our Western cities were in advance of New York and Brooklyn. He also thought electricity the most painless and humane mode of executing criminals.

THE
EVOLUTION OF BOTANY

BY

FREDERICK J. WULLING, PH. G.

COLLATERAL READINGS SUGGESTED:

Article *Botany* in Encyclopædia Britannica; Gray's North American Flora, Structural and Systematic Botany, How Plants Grow, How Plants Behave, and *Statistics of the Flora of the Northern United States*, in Silliman's Journal, second series, vol. xxii; Henslow's The Origin of Floral Structures; Wallace's Island Life, and Tropical and Geographical Distribution of Plants and Animals; Sachs's Sketch of the Development of Botany from 1530 to 1860; Strasburger's Handbook of Practical Botany; Lester F. Ward's The Geographical Distribution of Fossil Plants; Grant Allen's The Evolutionist at Large; Lubbock's Flowers, Fruits, and Leaves.

THE EVOLUTION OF BOTANY.

By Frederick J. Wulling, Ph. G.

The history of botany portrays the gradual development of the scientific knowledge of the vegetable kingdom. Like that of many of the sciences, its origin is enveloped in the darkness of the early ages, but if considered in its widest sense it must have been contemporaneous with the origin of mankind. Before the discovery of the metals and the invention of the arts, and the employment of tools and weapons whereby man became dominant over the other animals, it must be assumed that he was largely if not wholly dependent upon the vegetable kingdom for his subsistence. Roots, fruits, and herbs must have at that time constituted his chief nourishment. As his powers of observation developed, he learned to know and distinguish such plants as were easily digestible and those difficultly so. He discovered that some, or parts of some, plants were cathartic or the contrary, that some were poisonous, while others were harmless. We must also be permitted to assume that the knowledge thus gained was transmitted from one generation to another. From later indications we also learn that the names of those who were fortunate enough to discover a new plant which furnished food or medicine were carried to posterity and succeeding generations. The veneration for these discoverers grew with each generation until they were, in some instances, revered as gods. Some of the gods of the ancients have been traced back to such an origin. In those early ages of mankind—indeed, as is yet the custom among some of the savage tribes of to-day—the collection and administration of food and remedies were always accompanied by curious ceremonies, for the people of that time were exceedingly superstitious and had peculiar ways of invoking the blessings of their gods, or of banishing a witch. For this reason the character of the priest was afterwards combined with that of doctor, and the sick would seek relief in the temples where the priest-doctors resided.

Pliny teaches that the Druids, that most extraordinary sect which once inhabited England, ascribed almost divine properties to the mistletoe, aconite, and samolus or water-pimpernel, and describes some of the ceremonies observed in their collection. The mistletoe had to be cut with a knife the blade of which was of gold; it needed to be collected when the moon was six days old. No one else than a priest was allowed to do the collecting, and for that purpose he was clad in white. The plant had to be so cut that it would fall into a white cloth which was always kept in readiness. Lastly, two oxen had to be sacrificed; and when the mistletoe was thus consecrated it was a remedy for barrenness and an antidote to poison.

The aconite (probably not identical with that we know to-day), after a previous sacrifice of honey, had to be collected in total darkness when neither sun nor moon shone, and the cutting had to be done with the left hand after a circle had been described around the plant. So collected, the plant would conquer fevers, neutralize snake-poison, and serve as an enchantment to gain the friendship of others.

The selago (probably one of our sedums) could not be cut with an iron knife without destroying its good properties, nor could it be touched with the bare hand. The collector had to array himself in white and perform the ceremonies which the superstition of the people prescribed, in bare feet, regardless of the possibilities of catching cold. If collected in this manner, and in this manner only, it would cure diseased eyes and serve as a charm against accidents.

Not alone the Druids, but it is fair to assume that all the primitive races knew a little concerning plants; there has been until now no nation discovered which was indifferent or negligent enough to have ignored health so much that it was not familiar with at least a few remedial agents Knowing something of the medicinal properties of plants implied as a consequence some knowledge of the physical properties as well; the ancients knew, for instance, that a plant collected at a certain time would be more active than if gathered at other times. They were familiar with the external appearance of these plants, and though they could not describe them as intelligently as we can, they yet must have had a way of communicating to each other the nature of a plant newly discovered to have remedial or nourishing value. In thus communicating with each other they must have invented and used terms of a descriptive nature, and descriptive botany would have been the first department of botany according to this logic; and it was so. The first works written on botany were only descriptive.

Thus the very earliest attention given to the study, if it may be so called, of plants, was bestowed upon those having or supposed to have medicinal value, and botany was therefore begun simultaneously with medicine. Although the progress in the beginning of medicine was very slow, the number of remedies, mostly though not wholly consisting of plants, gradually became larger. When medicine as a science began to assume form and to be taught in the schools of Greece, Hippocrates, the father of medicine, published the names of all medicinal plants known in his time, of which there were but 300. The various departments of botany were by no means instituted together or at one time; from antiquity until comparatively recent times the little attention given to botany was mainly devoted to a meager description, especially of medicinal plants. So Hippocrates's work gave only the description and supposed medicinal properties of the 300 plants known to him.

Aristotle, 350 B. C., seems to have been the first one who occupied himself with the study of plants, but, unfortunately, the results of his studies have been lost with other works of his. Those of his pupil Theophrastus have been preserved and are probably based upon his.

Theophrastus, besides indulging, in a purely philosophical sense, in a speculation upon the nature and origin of plants, describes about 500 species, the names of the most of which are not familiar to the botanist of to-day. Perhaps some botanist of the future will recognize in the plants described in these old books the ancestors of some of our present plants, and determine what changes evolution has wrought upon the former in twenty-two centuries. The works referred to above were published again, and in German, in the beginning of this century.

From Theophrastus's time there is no record of any work done in botany until the first century of the Christian era, when Dioscorides wrote his Materia Medica at Rome, in which he describes 600 medicinal plants. Though the number had swelled to 600, there was no advance in any other direction since Aristotle's time.

The beginning and spreading of the Christian religion checked the progress of the sciences exceedingly, and botany, in which considerable interest had been awakened through Dioscorides's works, with many of the other sciences, was neglected and allowed to recede into and remain in oblivion for a long time.

Again there is no record of botany until the twelfth century. The few who did interest themselves in it did so only to the extent of acquiring the little knowledge already possessed by men of Theophrastus's time, without entering upon any researches which would have enriched the fund of botanical knowledge. The dominant tendency at that time was to study the works of the old authors, among whom Dioscorides was recognized as the highest authority, and upon whose work many commentaries were written.

In the thirteenth century we find the German Albertus Magnus investigating and studying plant life, upon which he wrote seven books, which have since been published (1521) in twenty-one volumes. The voluminous character of this work hides its value as a botanical text-book, for which it is believed to have been intended.

When, at the end of the fifteenth century, the sciences began to revive and receive attention again, botany welcomed a goodly share. The Germans especially were instrumental in delivering botany from the fetters of the old school. The inadequacy of the teachings of Dioscorides induced several naturalists—among whom were prominent, Brunfels, Brunswick, Fuchs, Tragus, and Gessner—to examine and study the plants of Germany, with a view to publishing a work with illustrations and descriptions based upon their own researches. This they finally accomplished.

Gessner was the first to conceive the idea that the organs of fructification were the essential ones, and that a classification, the need of which began to be felt, should be based upon these.

These men were followed by Peter Matthiolus, A. Cæsalpinius, Alpino, Columna, Dodonäus, Clusius, Lobelius, Delachamp, Gerard, Camerarius, the brothers Bauhin, and others, through whose exertions the number of known plants at the beginning of the seventeenth century had reached 5,500. With this large number of plants little could be done if they were not classified, and some systematic arrangement became a necessity. The first attempt at a "natural arrangement" was made by Lobelius (1570), who classified plants into trees, grasses, ferns, lilies, etc., simply according to their external resemblances. A. Cæsalpinius, afterward named by Linnæus the "first orthodox systematizer," acted upon the suggestion of Gessner and employed the fruit and the essential parts of the seeds as a basis for his classification, which form of arrangement was retained by most of his followers. Cæsalpinius opened a new epoch in botany; he cared little for the description of individual plants, but rather sought to generalize from the individual. He aspired to a classification which recognized the internal nature of the plant, so to speak, and arrived, through Aristotelian philosophic deduction, to the conviction that a natural classification must be based upon the organs of fructification. His system contains as a consequence a series of most unnatural groups.

A little later the brothers Bauhin contributed a goodly share to the cause of botany. While John Bauhin, especially in his work Historia Plantarum Universalis, supported the views of Lobelius, and therefore aspired to a natural classification based upon general external similarity—that is, for instance, including in the class "trees" all plants that partook of the nature of a tree, including in another class all the grasses, in another all the ferns, irrespective of any other similarity than that of external appearance—his brother, Caspar Bauhin, not only increased the number of known plants by his investigations and discoveries, but also corrected the chaos existing in the very confusing synonymic of the time. The latter endeavored in his work Phytopinax to present a synopsis of all plants known up to that time, 1596; and in a later work, 1623 published the names of 6,000 plants with their many synonyms. The discovery of America more than a century before largely increased the number of known plants which were also included in the latter work.

Botanical enthusiasm ran high just at that time, and botanical knowledge spread rapidly, especially among the learned classes, who began to add botany to the branches taught in the higher schools. The universities had before that taught it. Botanical travels were undertaken by interested individuals, and scientific organizations sent out botanical expeditions to study the floras of surrounding countries. Clusius explored nearly the whole of Europe, and P. Albini most of the Orient, both with much success.

Clusius was one of those scientists who, after the Reformation, rescued the various departments of knowledge from the spirit of the old scholasticism, and taught that true science was the study of Nature herself, and not the study of the whimsical notions and theories of the old school. He was one of those reformers who instituted a practice of investi-

13

gating and testing the teachings of the old scholars, which practice brought to light and did away with many absurd intrusions upon science, and, on the other hand, served to widen scientific knowledge by the many new discoveries and inventions it brought about. In his travels, in France and Austria principally, Clusius was very successful in discovering new plants, which, upon his return, he classified with much labor, and described with more accuracy than had theretofore been employed in the description of plants. He published the results of his travels and succeeding labor in several books, of which the Rariorum Plantarum Historia contained most of the plants then known, with illustrations of those he discovered. It was the best exposition of botany in its time. Clusius also made an attempt at classification among plants of his own discovery, but which was not of much account. None of his contemporaries or predecessors can record the discovery of a larger number of plants.

Up to the first half of the seventeenth century only descriptive botany had received attention, and the classification was yet in a primitive condition. Of the structure of plants little or nothing was known until the invention of the microscope, which marked an important epoch in the development of the sciences. Indeed, botany benefited more by the introduction of the microscope than any other science. The invention of the microscope not only induced the study of the structure of plants, but was also an introduction to cryptogamous botany, the study of the flowerless plants, of which, until then, practically nothing was known. In the same degree in which the microscope was perfected did the knowledge of plant anatomy, the study of the structure of plants, increase.

As the founders of plant anatomy we must recognize N. Grew, Malpighi, and Leeuwenhoek, who simultaneously entered upon microscopical investigations, the results of which they published in 1670, 1671, and 1673, respectively, these works being the first of their kind. Malpighi first employed strong convex lenses, corresponding to our simple microscope of about 180 magnifying powers, to examine into the structure of human tissue. The experience he gained by thus studying the tissue of the lungs, brain, kidneys, intestines, and nerves, he applied vigorously to the establishment of plant anatomy; and his work Anatomica Plantarum may be said to have been the basis for the future and more exhaustive works by other authors. Nehemiah Grew also occupied himself very successfully with phytotomy—plant anatomy—of which he was one of the founders. He discovered the cell-structure of plant tissue, distinguished the parenchymatous tissue from the longitudinal fibers, the wood-bundles and ducts, and studied more carefully the relations which these cell-forms bore to each other in the various organs of the plants. His investigations brought to light much that we now know of spiral ducts. His book Anatomy of Plants, published in London in 1682, was an excellent work in that time. Leeuwenhoek, too, did much in developing microscopic botany. He was, at the time the microscope was invented, a modest book-keeper and cashier in an Amsterdam clothing-house, but he became so much interested in the new instrument that he set about manufacturing it for his own use, and making investigations therewith. Aside from the many discoveries he made, which widened the knowledge of human anatomy, the discovery of the spotted, spiral, and scalariform ducts in plants is ascribed to him. He was the first to point out the difference in structure between the monocotyledonous and dicotyledonous stem—i. e., the difference in stems of trees exemplified by the palm and oak. These discoveries were made with microscopes of his own make, of which he possessed about 200, in manufacturing which he displayed much skill and ability. If this enterprising Dutch investigator had had a good education, so that he would have worked systematically, he undoubtedly would have contributed even more to the advancement of botany than he did.

This period is followed by one in which classification received renewed attention, this time by Morison, Ray, Herrman, Boerhaave, G. A. Rivinius, and others. Ray, 1703, and Morison, 1715, accepted Cæsalpinius's arrangement, which they supported and developed more fully. The latter included in his method the formation of the floral envelope and its parts. Rivinius, earlier than that (1690), employed as standard for his system the regular or irregular form of the perianth or floral envelope.

An important progressive step in descriptive botany was made also, at this time, by Tournefort. He was professor of botany at the botanical garden at Paris, whence he was sent by the French Government to Greece and Asia Minor to study the floras of those countries. He spent two years, 1700–1702, in botanical explorations, and brought back with him representatives of 1,300 new species. He also devised a system for classification, based upon the floral envelopes and comprising twenty-three classes. Though his system gave little consideration to the *natural* relations of plants, a work which he wrote, Institutiones Rei Herbaria, received much recognition before Linnæus's time. Tournefort was the first before Linnæus to recognize the value of descriptive botany in determining the characteristics of the genera. The specific differences of the genera he treated as of secondary importance.

In 1789 an attempt was made by Magnol to arrange all known plants into real families. The attempt was a success to some extent. This system comprised seventy-six families, each family made up of species which resembled each other more than those of another family, especially in the flower and fruit. All the systems theretofore established had been found wanting, the constant discovery of new species soon proving them to be inadequate. So with Magnol's, though it was of some value when first established. New plants were constantly found which could not be included in any of the seventy-six families without disturbing the arrangement and rendering the system valueless even for the plants it included.

The fund of known species was about this time again greatly increased by botanical explorations into distant parts of the globe. The tropics especially opened up an immense field to botanical research, with an endless variety of vegetation, in which botanists soon discerned the entire inadequacy of all the systems of classification established up to that time. Rheede, Rumph, and Kampfer chose Asia as their field of labor and research, and Sloane and Plumier, Jamaica and America, respectively. Most of the plants Sloane discovered and collected he pressed and preserved, and finally described them in a work which treated of all the plants of Jamaica. These plants constituted a goodly share of his large collection of natural-history specimens which latter he sold to the English Government for a paltry sum, but for which he was better repaid by his success in founding the British Museum with it. Plumier summed up his work in three books, one of a descriptive nature on all the plants he collected in this country, another on the new plants he found here, and a third upon the American ferns.

An important epoch in the evolution of botany was the founding of botanical gardens in the larger cities, where not only the domestic but also foreign plants were cultivated and their habits and characteristics studied. Theretofore the study of foreign plants was limited to the favored few who could go to the native habitation of the plant for that purpose, but now the many scientists in the cities had equal opportunities for investigation and study. The number of men developing and advancing botany became largely increased by the introduction of botanical gardens, which were thus directly advantageous to the growth of the science. It is true that before this botanical-garden era under question there had been a few incipient gardens. One at Salermo was laid out by Matthew Sylvaticus in the fourteenth century, which was followed by one at Venice for the cultivation of medicinal plants. Both of these were very limited in their number of plants and contained few that were not medicinal. The real beginning of instituting botanical gardens was coincident with the revival of the sciences. The cities of Italy began to compete for excellence in planning and laying out gardens and in the number and variety of plants. *Here, as everywhere, competition was a factor in evolution.* Spain and France soon followed the example of Italy. In Ferrara, the Duke Alphonse Este was the first to found a garden, at which he worked with commendable energy and ambition, so that it was in its time recognized as the first one in Europe. The botanical garden at Paris was instituted in the early part of the sixteenth century. Its design and object were not, however, to advance botany, but to cultivate flowers, from which the royal dressmakers might take patterns wherewith to embroider the gowns of the court ladies and to embellish the coats of the court gentlemen. It was not until many years later that the garden was made a botanical one in a scientific sense, and named "Jardin des Plants," a name which it still bears. In Holland a garden was laid out as early as the fifteenth century, but Germany was not represented other than by several private ones.

By far the greatest eagerness in establishing botanical gardens was exhibited in the seventeenth century. An extensive garden was planned at Rome by Cardinal Farnese; the "Hortus Cattolicus" was founded by Prince della Cattolica at Messina; the Kew Gardens, by Queen Elizabeth; the Apothecaries' Garden at Chelsea, for the cultivation of medicinal plants, by the apothecaries of London; and the botanical garden at Amsterdam, which latter is to-day yet one of the richest in Europe. Many of the universities added botanical gardens—e. g., those of Leipsic, Breslau, Heidelberg, Giessen, Kiel, Jena. Of gardens founded by individuals, that of Bose, at Leipsic, attained European renown. In the struggle for supremacy in botanical gardens England attained and retained the lead in the eighteenth century. That at Chelsea, that of the brothers Sherard at Eltham, and the University Garden at Cambridge, were the foremost, not only in the extent but also in the choice and variety of plants. In the Netherlands, the gardens of Lord Clifford, at Hardecamp, under the management of K. Linnæus, gained quite a reputation; while the gardens at Turin, Pisa, and Florence in Italy, and Madrid in Spain, claimed much attention. Zurich, in Switzerland, began to boast of its garden when it came under the direction of J. J. Romer, and Dorpat, St. Petersburg, Wilna, and Moscow soon fell in line. Copenhagen, Lund, and Upsala instituted gardens, which soon were recognized throughout Europe. France received an additional one from the Empress Josephine, who founded one at Malmaison, which also attained considerable repute.

In the latter part of the eighteenth century Germany found nearly all of her universities with botanical gardens, and now none are without one. Berlin, Munich, Stuttgart, and Leipsic are especially proud of theirs at present, but the largest and most renowned of to-day is undoubtedly the Kew Garden, in England.

The Europeans are not the only ones, however, rejoicing in the possession of botanical gardens. The evolution of botany is marked by the establishment of extensive gardens in Asia at Calcutta, Madras, Ceylon, Batavia, Canton; in Africa at the Cape, Mauritius, on Teneriffe; in South America in Rio Janeiro; in Mexico at the city of Mexico; in Australia at Sydney, Melbourne, and Adelaide.

The first botanic garden in America was founded by John Bartram about the year 1730, and was most beautifully situated on the right bank of the Schuylkill a short distance below the city of Philadelphia. This garden, with all its interesting history and associations, was destined to flourish only a little more than a century. It scarcely survived the immediate family of its noble-hearted founder, and the past generation lived to see the accumulated treasures of a century laid waste. No motive availed, not even a feeling of State or city pride, to insure its preservation.

The second botanical garden established in America was that by Humphrey Marshall in West Bradford, Pennsylvania, now Marshallton. Marshall had before that indulged his taste for botanical collections in cultivating useful and ornamental plants at his father's residence near the Brandywine. His laudable example was not without its influence in the community where he resided, and among the number of incipient botanical gardens springing up around him, those of his friends William Jackson at Londongrove and Joshua and Samuel Pierce of East Marlborough, were conspicious.

In 1810 Dr. Hosack founded a botanical garden in New York upon the site now occupied by the Columbia College and surroundings, but it is only a bit of history now.

A garden was founded at Charleston, S. C., in 1804, but that too is of the past.

The one at Cambridge, laid out in 1805, was once under the skillful supervision of Asa Gray. It is yet an adjunct of which Cambridge is proud.

St. Louis has a botanical garden, the Shaw Garden, founded by Mr. Shaw privately, but lately made public. It is quite extensive and growing.

Philadelphia has her Horticultural Hall since the centennial exhibition, and Baltimore is soon to have a garden.

The city of New York, the metropolis of the American continent, the third now, soon to be the second, city of importance on the globe, the educational center of America, the home of learning and knowledge of this country, is without a botanical garden. May New York and Brooklyn soon enter upon an era of botanical gardens and museums.

In order to proceed in chronological order, let us go back again to the time when botanical gardens were beginning to become more numerous. The culture of foreign plants in these gardens contributed not a little to the progress of botany, but, in the same degree that botany was advancing, the lack of an adequate comprehensive form of classification became more and more felt. This want, and that for a general method for nomenclature (naming of plants), resulted in much confusion at times when the identity or names of plants were to be determined. This obstacle to the development of botany was especially annoying to Linnæus, who, in his endeavors to overcome this hindrance, originated a system (middle of the eighteenth century) which at the time fulfilled the needs admirably, and which bore his name and established his renown. The system, though an artificial one, and based upon the stamens and pistils only, was a sure and convenient one, and soon enjoyed widespread use among botanists and naturalists. Linnæus's greater merit, though, and because of which he was called "the reformer of natural history," was in establishing fixed rules regarding the scientific characteristics of the species and genera, and the correct terminology for these, which have yet to-day their value.

Among the opposers of the Linnæan system were such botanists as Ludwig, Gleditsch, Adanson, and Jussieu, none of whom, however, had before that a better classification to present. Linnæus himself looked upon his system as very imperfect, and he knew that to invent a natural system of some kind would be a problem for future botanists. The object of his artificial system was merely to furnish a simple and convenient method for finding out the habitat and name of a plant. He compared his system to a dictionary, as it distributed plants according to the number of stamens and pistils, just as in a dictionary words are arranged according to their first letters.

Many of Linnæus's scholars made it their duty to study the floras of foreign lands as well as that of their own, and Hasselquist, Forskal, Lõfling, Pallas, Brown, Jacquin, Commerson, Burman, Aublet, Scopoli, Pollich, Leers, Haller, and Gerard were especially successful in their studies, about which they wrote profusely.

Lightfoot investigated the flora of Scotland, Oder and Müller that of Denmark, Gunerus of Norway, Hudson of England, Martinez of Spain, Sequire of Italy, etc., and all contributed largely to the knowledge of the floras of the respective countries.

In Linnæus's time the lower orders of plants—the fungi, mushrooms, toadstools, mold, mildew, algæ, seaweeds, etc., and mosses—received detailed attention by Micheli, Scheuchzer, and Dillenius, who worked extensively in this direction. Dillenius examined most minutely the mosses, and elaborated much upon the little work done theretofore by English botanists, who were the only ones who had worked in that field at all.

Bauhin's Pinax register, mentioned before, contained only 50 species, so little attention had been given to the mosses. Ray's synopsis (1690) contained 80 species, and in 1696 the number had reached 170. Dillenius was the first, however, who considered and studied the generic characteristics of these plants, and who distinguished them from the fungi.

As an illustration of Dillenius's diligence and accuracy may be mentioned the fact that, in the neighborhood of Giessen alone, he discovered more than 200 species of mosses, of which 140 were theretofore unknown. Of fungi he found 160, of which 90 were not known before.

About this time is recorded the beginning of the experimental investigation into the physiology of plants, in which field St. Hales was the pioneer. He discovered the function of the sap in plants, and his experiments concerning the rising of the sap in trees are still celebrated.

In the following period the activity of botanists was mainly directed to the development and application of Linnæus's system. The increasing and widening knowledge of species was aided by the publication and continuation of Linnæus's Genera and Species Plantarum, to which Schreber, Willdenow, Vahl, Persoon, Romer, Schultes, Sprengel, Presl, D. Dietrich, and H. Richter contributed largely.

The study of the lower orders of plants was again resumed, in the beginning of this century, by Presl, whose works on the grasses and ferns are very interesting, and by Persoon and Sprengel, who were the first to describe the fungi. Persoon arranged and classified them into species and genera.

Late in the eighteenth century Kolreuter and Schmidel began to study the organs of fructification of the lower cryptogams (flowerless plants). Their works were factors in broadening the scope of cryptogamous botany.

The introduction of Linnæus's artificial system of classification led botanists to abandon their speculations on classification for a while, to devote themselves to the study of plants individually again, and, as we have seen, a period followed in which the investigation and observation of scientists were directed to the fuller development of the lower orders. The higher orders, though, were not neglected in the mean time, and new plants were continually discovered and new facts learned concerning those known. The vast accumulation of known species and the rapid development botany was enjoying soon convinced botanists that the Linnæan system, too, was becoming insufficient to answer its purpose, and that, sooner or later, a natural system would have to be instituted which alone could ultimately meet all the requirements.

Adanson, Oder, and Gārtner made several efforts to institute such a system, but all failed. Adanson in one of his works devoted much time and labor to a system which was conspicuous in its lack of adaptiveness. Gärtner, too, scored as his reward for his labors a signal failure in his attempt at classification, in which he employed the fruit and seed. The value of this system was not in the system itself, but in its contribution to the development of the morphology (form) of the fruit and seed. Gärtner distinguished with much clearness and accuracy between the spores of the cryptogams and the seeds of the phanerogams, and advanced a theory regarding the seed which was very comprehensive and with which we are all familiar.

The first successful attempt at a natural classification was made by Antoine Laurent de Jussieu (1789), but his system did not receive recognition at once; it was thirty years after that botanists began to appreciate its value. Among its advocates was Pyramus de Candolle (1813), who, though accepting all of Jussieu's arrangement, advanced many new ideas which he embodied with Jussieu's plan. De Candolle was a systematizer not surpassed by any of his predecessors or successors. He developed the theory and laws of our present natural system largely with much clearness and detail. He built not alone upon Jussieu's work, but based many of his ideas and views upon his own investigations of the morphology of plants, which, in doing much in aiding the natural arrangement, also became very fruitful to systematic botany. He first established the teaching of the nature of the abortive and rudimentary organs and applied the correct evolutionary meaning to them, recognizing also the transition of the organs into each other. He noticed, for instance, that in the lily there is very often such a transition between the calyx and corolla, or between the corolla and stamens, that it is difficult to tell to which set of organs a particular one belongs. In the best of his several works—Regni Vegetabilis Systema Naturale—De Candolle arranged all the phanerogamic plants according to his system, and described all genera and species then known. In plant physiology and geographical botany his works are conspicuous.

Besides Jussieu and De Candolle, there were others who endeavored to institute natural systems; among them were Oken, Lindley, Reichenbach, and Endlicher. The latter, in 1838, was especially successful in determining the natural families.

The proper system of classification was now arrived at, and, while its development and application were progressing, descriptive botany, too, was rapidly advancing. The floras of the various countries were under continual observation, not only to enlarge the fund of phancrogamic plants, but more especially with a view of learning more about the cryptogams or the lower orders. So Nees von Eiseneck, Tode, Bolton, and Corda very much increased our knowledge of the fungi. Eiseneck deserves much credit for his work in systematizing the fungi. He studied and elaborated upon the various stages of development of sweet-water algæ, systematized the sponges, and wrote the natural history of the liver mosses.

The beginning of the nineteenth century found the various established departments of botany receiving renewed attention, while a number of new ones were being founded. We find a series of botanists who made it their duty to study the internal structure of plants more fully. Among these may be mentioned Link, Rudolphi, Treviranus, Mollenhauer, Sprengel, Mirbel, and others. Link was one of the most ardent phytotomists of his time. He contributed largely to the knowledge of the way plants grow, and the various functions of the several organs. To his untiring study of the anatomy of plants we owe much of our present knowledge of the structure of plant tissue. He was a profuse writer on botanical subjects, and his Elements of Plant Anatomy and Plant Physiology, with a large supplement, were masterpieces of botanical work. Mirbel, too, was one of the foremost plant anatomists and physiologists, directing his attention mainly to the establishment of a theory regarding the organization of plants, which he published in several works.

Sprengel awakened much interest in phytotomy through his studies regarding the various cells and vessels and their structure. His uncle also devoted himself to botanical studies, and discovered the mode of fructification of flowers, or rather the ovaries, by the pollen, conveyed there by the wind, insects, and the many other natural contrivances.

L. C. Treviranus first occupied himself with phytotomy and plant physiology, but later lent his aid in determining and correcting the nomenclature of the species. He discovered the intercellular spaces and the structure of the epidermis, being the first to interpret the function of the stomata, or breathing pores, in the plant economy. In all of his works he emphasized and gave value to evolution as a factor in the transmutation of species. Much that we know of the organs of fructification we owe to him as well as to Sprengel. Treviranus's views on phytotomy seem to have been the basis for the theories which Mohl propounded later, and which led to his (Mohl's) discovering the primordial utricle. Mohl, too, worked a great deal with the microscope, and published a number of works on the anatomy of the ferns and on the anatomy of the cycas and palm stem. His scientific examinations advanced every department of botany, but phytotomy especially. The sclerenchymatic tissue was the object of the most minute and successful study by him. Mohl was a thorough evolutionist, who saw in all things evidence in behalf of natural development.

The work in microscopical investigation having been so successfully carried on, soon solicited the aid of such scientists as Meyen, Schleiden, Schwann, Unger, and many others, who continued the work, and to whom, with the previous workers, may be accredited the development which plant anatomy has reached to-day.

Plant *physiology*, now again taken up by Bonnet, Saussure, Duhamel du Monceau, Dutrochet, Senebière, Knight, and others, made big progressive strides, by the aid of the fund of anatomical knowledge, the result of the labor of the men just mentioned. Not only in the latter respect was physiology advanced, but also very materially by the development and application of chemistry. Boussingault and Liebig, the latter more especially, investigated the chemistry of plants, and determined the chemical processes going on within them. Liebig proved that plants needed certain chemicals in their food, and showed how they derived them from the soil. The knowledge he thus gained led to the use of artificial fertilizers, which restore the utility, for agricultural purposes, of soil deprived of its chemical constituents by many successive crops.

To Goethe's views and studies regarding the metamorphosis of the plant, and to the works of De Candolle, Robert Brown, Schimpers, A. Braun, and others, we owe the origin and development of the morphology of plants. A. Braun was very diligent in his endeavors to develop plant morphology, and it was he who discovered the regular arrangement of the leaves upon the stem—phyllotaxis. The cryptogamic morphology was the subject of his late studies; he studied especially the characeae. R. Brown busied himself in the same field; he determined the morphological relations in the organization of the seeds of monocotyledonous and dicotyledonous plants, determined the gymnospermous character of the *Coniferæ* and *Cycadaceæ*, and studied the nature of the fructification of the ovary through the pollen.

To this period (beginning of the nineteenth century) belongs also the origin of geographical botany, due to the work of A. v. Humboldt, while Schouw, Wahlenberg, Meyen, A. De Candolle, Grisebach, Hooker, Boissier, Asa Gray, etc., developed this department. These men studied the geographical distribution of plants and the effects of climatic changes, about which they wrote several books, the works of Grisebach being foremost.

The paleontology of the vegetable kingdom, the study of the fossil remains of ancient vegetable life, began to be pursued about this time by Brongniart, Unger, Göppert, Sapporta, A. Gray, and others. Brongniart, in one of his works—his best one—occupies himself with the history of vegetable fossils; in another he gives a systematic grouping of all the species known to him, with their probable history from prehistoric times. To this he added a chronological view of the periods of vegetation and different floras in their successive appearance upon the earth as far as that was possible. Sapporta, a pupil of the former, worked in the same field, giving his attention mainly to phytopaleontology. He wrote a number of works in which he accorded much value to the Darwinian theory, especially in his Evolution of the Vegetable Kingdom.

Göppert was one of the most ardent workers in this department of botany; he had made a very large collection of fossil plants which he compared in many works with the same species of to-day, bringing the Darwinian theory of transmutation to bear fruit. The formation of coal-beds was also a subject of his study. Göppert's Index Paleontologicum, a classification of all known fossil plants, with complete synonymic, published in 1850, is still the best work of its kind.

Structural and systematic botany, the latter more especially, enjoyed a goodly share of attention in the present century by a host of botanists, among whom Asa Gray and A. Wood rank foremost among the Americans. (See Sociology, p. 339.)

By the rapid advancement of the various departments of botany, they of necessity were made to occupy the rank formerly held by descriptive botany, although the latter was never underestimated during the progress of development of the other departments.

A special word about the American botanists and their work will be in order. One of the earliest, if not the first, description of North American plants was by a French botanist, Jac. Cornubus, who, it is believed, never was in America, but described the plants from specimens sent to him from Canada.

John Josselyn published in 1672 a work called New England Rarities. His book is interesting in its statement that "barley frequently degenerates into oats."

In 1680 the Rev. John Banister wroto the Catalogue of Plants of Virginia.

John Bartram, the founder of the first botanical garden in America, investigated the plants of America with indefatigable labor through a long course of years, and with amazing success. He probably detected and described more plants than any of his contemporaries.

Dr. Cadwallader Colden, an able and sagacious botanist, collected and described the plants in the region around his residence—Coldenham, near Newburg, N. Y.—and published his Plantæ Coldenhamiæ in 1744. Dr. Colden had a companion and assistant worthy of special commendation in his accomplished daughter Jane. She was the pioneer woman botanist of this country. In a letter from the distinguished botanist, Peter Collinson, to Linnæus, the former writes: "I but lately heard from Mr. Colden. He is well; but, what is marvelous, his daughter is perhaps the first lady that has so perfectly studied your system. She deserves to be celebrated." In another: "Last week my friend, Mr. Ellis, wrote you a letter recommending a curious botanic dissertation by Miss Jane Colden. As this accomplished lady is the only one of the fair sex that I have heard of who is scientifically skillful in the Linnæan system, you no doubt will distinguish her merits, and recommend her example to the ladies of every country."

Dr. John Mitchell, Dr. A. Garden, Dr. A. Kuhn, Humphrey Marshall, Dr. Hosack, Dr. Cutler, Thomas Walter, and Will Bartram, all wrote descriptions of local floras. B. S. Barton, Rev. Dr. Muhlenberg, De Beauvois, and others began to contribute valuable papers on botany to the Transactions of the American Philosophical Society toward the end of the eighteenth century. Thomas Nuttall also contributed to the Transactions.

In 1803 the first elementary work on botany was written by Prof. D. S. Barton. About this time President Jefferson projected an expedition, under Messrs. Clark and Lewis, across this continent to the Pacific. This was a means of introducing to the knowledge of botanists a number of plants which were previously unknown, though the principal collection made by these explorers was lost. That region was subsequently explored and vast additions made to our flora by Messrs. Nuttall, Nicolet, Frémont, and others.

Dr. Samuel L. Mitchell, Michaux (at Paris), Major John Le Conte, F. Pursh, Dr. Jacob Bigelow, C. S. Rafinesque, Dr. W. P. C. Barton, Dr. George Sumner, Rev. Lewis David von Schweinitz, and Stephen Elliott contributed papers on botany to the various scientific journals. S. Elliott published the Sketch of the Botany of South Carolina and Georgia, a work of value and indispensable in the investigation of Southern plants. Dr. William Baldwin aided in its preparation.

In 1819 Dr. John Torrey, with others, published a Catalogue of Plants growing within Thirty Miles of the City of New York, and in 1826 a Compendium of the Flora of the Middle and Northern States, and later several other works. We are much indebted to the labors of Menzies, Fraser, Lyon, Bradbury, Scouler, Richardson, Dr. F. Boott, Dr. J. A. Brereton, Prof. Short, Dr. Beck, J. Bachman, Rev. M. A. Curtis, Prof. John L. Riddell, Edward Hitchcock, Dr. John Torrey, H. B. Croom, Dr. W. E. A. Aikin, J. A. Lapham, W. S. Sullivant, Dr. George Engelman, Edward Tuckerman, S. T. Olney, and many more. These botanists all wrote papers on or catalogues of the floras of the various localities surrounding their homes, or of entire States.

About 1820 many of the schools began to teach botany, and soon a demand for suitable books arose. Among the most successful which appeared was the Manual compiled by Prof. Amos Eaton, of Troy. In 1842 Asa Gray published his Botanical Text-Book, and in 1845 Alphonso Wood published his Class-Book of Botany. Since then numerous botanists have engaged in botanical studies and made contributions to the science. Cook, Schrench, Coulder, Bastin, Rusby, and others are able botanists of to-day.

We see that America has and had several botanists who have done considerable original work in botany, but we all must acknowledge that we are decidedly behind European countries in this respect. Prof. W. G. Farlow, in a paper read before the American Society of Naturalists, candidly confesses that American botanists are not up to the European in original research. This, he thinks, is not due to lack of talent, qualification, or inclination among our botanists for research, but he attributes it rather to lack of opportunity. Those most eminently fitted are for the most part teachers, and in this country the demands upon the teacher are such that but little time and strength is left from the duties of teaching to carry on original researches. In Germany the greater part of the work of laboratory instruction is committed to assistants, while the professors are free to carry on important investigations which advance scientific knowledge and give luster to the institutions to which they belong. In America there is no due appreciation of the importance of endowing scientific research; hence the problems that ought to be solved by American botanists are left to be solved by Germans or other Europeans, working at a great disadvantage. Efforts should be made to create public sentiment favoring the endowment of original research.

Botanical investigations and researches are continuing in the various departments, the morphology, anatomy, and physiology of plants receiving the greatest attention. The theory of evolution; the laws governing the growth of the various organs and their deviation from the normal pattern; the molecular structure of the constituents of plant cells; the influence of environment upon plants; the intimate study of the fructification of the ovary; the application of chemistry to the determination and separation of the active medicinal constituents; the laws of heredity and variation; the circumscribed areas for certain plants and causes; the migration of plants, both terrestrial and celestial, and its causes; habitation in relation to composition, structure, and heredity; the relation of insects and plants to color and form; geological distribution compared to modern movements of plants, etc.—are subjects of present attention. A like activity is manifested in the study of the lower orders, of the fungi especially, and extensive work is being done in microscopical botany generally, including bacteriological botany.

The study of the diseases of plants and their treatment—plant pathology—especially of the cultivated and useful ones, and plant teratology (the study of malformations and monstrosities), are also receiving detailed attention, and laboratories for the physiological, anatomical, morphological, and pathological study of plants can now be found in all the great institutions of learning. In short, all departments of botany are being developed with the accelerating rapidity indicative of our present time.

We have thus briefly traced the historic evolution of botany from the earliest time—the time of its origin, which must have been contemporaneous with the beginning of man's cognizing powers—through the different phases of its growth up to the present time.

We have seen how it originated simultaneously with medicine, or rather how its origin and early growth were dependent upon the growth of medicine *at first*, and how afterward the growth of medicine was largely dependent upon the development of botany, especially after the discovery of the active medicinal constituents of plants.

We learned that descriptive botany was necessarily the first department, and that as the number of known plants began to increase, classification became a necessity, and that through many centuries various arrangements had been devised, each one succumbing to its successor, until finally our present one was arrived at.

We have reviewed the beneficent results for botany which the invention of the microscope brought about; how the knowledge of the internal structure, the anatomy of plants, was gained through its application and use, and how plant anatomy gradually served to develop plant physiology.

We learned of the many botanical explorations to the various countries, and how these opened up vast fields for the labor and research of botanists, and how, in order to facilitate and cultivate the study of botany, botanical gardens were instituted in the large cities where the nature and habits of foreign plants could be observed as well as in their native habitation. Then the cryptogams began to occupy the attention of botanists for a time, while morphology and systematic botany began to be developed, the other departments steadily advancing in the mean time. Then followed a series of important discoveries in the physiology of plants, and the application of chemistry was very helpful to the progress of the science. Geological and paleontological botany were next instituted, together with pathological botany, and *all* the departments are now in progress of still further development.

The history of botany is thus a veritable exposition of

the law of evolution. It shows the promiscuity and non-coherence of all *early* botanic work, and shows how indefinite the knowledge it conveyed was concerning the vegetable world as a whole; how before Jussieu the roots of the science consisted in a lot of arts and discrete discoveries, which, like roots, worked in the dark so far as scientific principle goes. With Jussieu the stem of the evolving tree made its appearance, and after him we find the stem grown into a trunk, with branches spreading, and all united as an organic whole in a tree of botanical knowledge.

The survival of the fittest is well illustrated in the survival of the natural over the other classifications. Its survival is intrinsically a most striking exemplification of evolution in that it arranges all plants according to the plan by which the vegetable creation evolved. The birth of botany as a science began with the development of the natural classification, and it is pleasing to notice the cohesion in thought which at once set in relating organically all plant life. The amassing of knowledge which followed forced the division of labor among botanists — a change from homogeneity to heterogeneity.

In conclusion, there is only time to allude, and in a general way, to the importance of botany to human life and well-being. If the hearer will let pass in review in his mind all that which contributes to his needs and comfort in his daily life, and select that directly dependent upon our present knowledge of botany, he can better comprehend the importance of this science to his comfort and well-being than words would enable him to do.

The production of most of our food is the direct result of our knowledge of agricultural botany, while much of our clothing is due to the discovery that the flax and other plants yield a fiber which may be woven into fabrics suitable for a thousand purposes directly increasing our comforts. The greater part of our materia medica—that vast number of medicinal bodies which alleviate bodily ailment and contribute to the maintenance and prolongation of bodily health—is due to our knowledge of the medicinal properties and of the active constituents of plants. Botany is, in short, the underlying basis of much of our wealth and comfort, and, aside from the aid it affords to horticulture and to the healing art, it claims a large share of the attention of every individual for the moral and intellectual culture which it is capable of imparting in an eminent degree. To the lover of nature no other department of the natural sciences affords more pleasure in its study than botany, and I can not think of a more fit closing than repeating the words of Alphonso Wood: "No science more effectually combines pleasure with improvement than botany. It conducts the student into the field and forest, amid the verdure of spring and the bloom of summer; to the charming retreats of Nature, in her wild luxuriance, or where she patiently smiles under the improving hand of cultivation. It furnishes him with vigorous exercise, both of body and mind, which is no less salutary than agreeable, and its subjects of investigation are all such as are adapted to please the eye, refine the taste, and improve the heart."

ABSTRACT OF THE DISCUSSION.

DR. ROBERT G. ECCLES:

In the absence of Prof. Ridenour, who had been appointed to open the discussion, Dr. Eccles was called upon by the president, and said, in substance: I desire to thank the lecturer for the condensed and admirable account of the evolution of botanical science which he has given us. I do not know that such a succinct and correct statement of the history of botany can be found elsewhere in the literature of that subject. In one sense botany antedates historical knowledge, and butterflies show an earlier knowledge of plants than man can boast. As a science, however, botany is of more recent growth. In the investigation of such subjects, one thing that strikes the student of nature is that everything in nature follows a single law of growth, progressing from homogeneity to heterogeneity, the same law that we see exemplified in its simplest form in the growth of a tree or shrub. Everything spreads, as it were, from a single trunk into branches, limbs, and twigs. We find the same principle illustrated in the form of the human body and in the structure of the brain—in the branching of the nerves from their central spinal axis—which is everywhere found in the plant world. The same phenomenon has even been observed in the lightning flash. When photographed, instead of presenting the appearance of a single line of light, it appears as if differentiated into tree-like branches. This principle of differentiation is also exemplified in the evolution of the science of botany. At first, as we have been told, our knowledge of plant-life was vague, homogeneous, and protoplasmic, consisting only in the recognition of certain familiar descriptive characteristics of well-known plants. As the science developed, its several departments were integrated and specialized. Now no single botanist can be a master of all branches of the science. He can acquire eminence only by perfecting himself in some one special department of research. The study of botany thus leads steadily up to evolution. Unless God designed to deceive the whole world, it is clear that the doctrine of evolution must be true.

In enumerating the botanical text-books published in this country, I think mention should be made of the valuable manual prepared by Miss Eliza A. Youmans, now a corresponding member of this association.

Mr. James A. Skilton:

Mr. Wulling has made it evident to us, in his thorough but condensed review, that the historic development of botany as a science has gone on coincidently with historic evolution in society and with all human progress during the last three hundred years. It is an important lesson for us also to learn that the evolution of botany has been co-ordinate as well as coincident with evolution and progress. Then the question follows: What will be the future history of botany, its evolution, and its co-ordinations? Prof. Mason, of the National Museum at Washington, has recently called attention to the fact that, as a result of our method of treatment, plant-life in the United States has declined in vitality and capacity for production, and that we have as a result a coincident and co-ordinate tendency toward barbaric conditions of individual and societary life. It is by no means a new thought that plant-life and its conditions have important relations to and with the moral status and general conditions of humanity. When Adam and Eve were driven from Eden the ground also was cursed, and it was said of it: "Thorns and thistles shall it bring forth to thee." Now, botanical science teaches us that "thorns" and "thistles" are the product of arrested development; and evolution, as well as "revelation," teaches us that human life and plant-life are so related in their totality that they prosper or fail to prosper together. And certainly no one who has seen and studied an "old field" cotton plantation can fail to realize that land can be "cursed" by some one—God or man.

A United States senator, discussing years ago a question concerning the introduction of free institutions into the West Indies, said, "Beware of the tropics." So long as we can not manage the plant-life of the temperate zone without drifting into barbaric conditions or tendencies, the legend is doubtless a wise one. But if the human race is to realize in fact the high development which evolution already foretells as possible, it will need to learn how to utilize all that the enormous and various plant capacity and production of the tropics, as well as of the other zones, is preparing and keeping in store for it.

From this point of view it must be evident that, great as has been development of the past, a compendium of which we have had presented to us to-night, the evolution of this science and of its cognate sciences can hardly be said to have yet begun.

Dr. Lewis G. Janes:

I am glad that the lecturer has called attention to the fact that it is impossible for investigators to become eminent in any department of original research while they are tied up to the routine of class-work in our schools and colleges. You will remember that Miss Youmans emphasized this fact last year in her paper upon Asa Gray. We need teachers in botany and in the other sciences who will do more than merely instruct their pupils in the contents of text-books—in what has already become common knowledge. We want teachers who shall be discoverers—masters in the field of original research—and who shall inspire others to this high order of work. This result can only be secured by emancipating our best men—and women, too—from mere routine work, by insuring them a competence, and bidding them devote their best energies to original investigation. I hope the time will come when our men of wealth will not only endow libraries and museums and college lectureships, but will give generously in support of original scientific research. Science is the fertile mother of progress—the foundation of our modern civilization. In no way can humanity be helped more effectively than by stimulating its beneficent conquests. It is one of our objects as an association, and by means of these lectures, to create a public opinion which shall demand the generous support of original scientific investigation. America, as the lecturer has said, is behind Europe in this respect, but no country owes more to science than America, none has more to expect in the future from the results of scientific progress. Let the wealth of America, therefore, be freely given in this behalf.

Col. William Hemstreet:

It would seem that the microscope applied to botanical studies should bring us very near to the secret of Nature as to the origin of life—its development out of inorganic matter. I should like to ask of any one competent to answer the question, whether any of the botanists eminent in microscopical investigations have observed the spontaneous generation of living organisms?

Dr. Janes:

The result of the most careful research thus far goes to prove that spontaneous generation, or abiogenesis, as a present fact, has not been demonstrated. Some eminent evolutionists, as Prof. Le Conte, go so far as to assert that the law of evolution, even assuming spontaneous generation as a fact of the past, necessarily makes it impossible under existing conditions; we have gone on beyond that stage in biological development. Bastian and others have claimed abiogenesis as an existing fact, but their experiments, in my judgment, were not sufficiently guarded to warrant the acceptance of their conclusions. I suppose all consistent evolutionists believe that somehow life began by an entirely natural process; but how and when that event occurred is now beyond our ken.

Mr. Wulling sustained Dr. Janes in his reply to Col. Hemstreet, and thanked the audience and critics for their kind reception of his paper.

ZOÖLOGY AS RELATED TO EVOLUTION

BY

JOHN C. KIMBALL

AUTHOR OF EVOLUTION OF ARMS AND ARMOR, ETC.

COLLATERAL READINGS SUGGESTED:

Spencer's Principles of Biology and Factors of Organic Evolution; Darwin's Origin of Species; Wallace's Contributions to the Theory of Natural Selection, Island Life, Tropical Nature, and Darwinism; Wilson's Facts and Fictions of Zoölogy; Huxley's Crayfish: an Introduction to the Study of Zoölogy, Evolution in Biology, and Man's Place in Nature; Karl Semper's Animal Life as affected by the Natural Conditions of Existence; Carpenter's Nature and Man, and Biographical Essays; Romanes's Animal Intelligence; Haeckel's Pedigree of Man and other essays; Lotze's Microcosmus; Cope's Origin of the Fittest; Whewell's History of the Inductive Sciences; McRae's Fathers of Biology; Cuvier's The Animal Kingdom; Murphy's Habit and Intelligence; Nicholson's The Rights of Animals; Powell's Our Heredity from God.

ZOÖLOGY AS RELATED TO EVOLUTION.

By John C. Kimball.

Man has always had a deep interest in animals. When he first woke to consciousness from the sleep of his own brute infancy in the early morning of the world's day, possibly its Tertiary hour, he found them already risen before him, a habit of precedence they still keep up, crawling as insects over his face, singing as birds in his ear, sporting as quadrupeds at his side. The oldest works of art found on earth, Pre-raphaelite by at least two hundred thousand years, as well as in other qualities, are etchings of their forms on plates of reindeer horn exhumed from anteglacial caves; and the liking for them and for pictures and stories about them, and the aptness for getting acquainted with them which all children exhibit to-day, are but the individual child repeating in himself, according to a well-known law of evolution, the intimacy and wonder for them which he learned originally in his childhood as a race. How close ever since have been his relations with them, how impressive to him their instincts and intelligence, so like yet unlike his own, how many and varied their contributions to the beauty and glory of his dwelling-place and to the comfort and joy of himself! Beneath all outward differences they have been his fellow-citizens in the great kingdom of Nature, his inevitable neighbors and associates, if not his recognized blood-relations, in the great family of life. Delegations of them have toiled with him at the plow, hunted with him in the chase, fed with him at the table, played with him at the fireside, traveled with him in the journey, fought with him on the battle-field. All the deeper experiences of his own existence—birth, growth, pain, pleasure, love's thrill, and death's agony—he has seen repeated in them. Language is filled with expressions for the qualities and activities they have in common—men, wolfish and foxy; bulls and bears in Wall Street; camels, "ships of the desert"; and ships in their turn "ocean greyhounds." Great nations have used them as the emblems of their power—made them play what a part in history as the Roman eagles, the British lion, and the Russian bear! Poetry has found in them some of its most suggestive themes, soaring with them how loftily in Bryant's Waterfowl, singing with them how sweetly in Shelley's Skylark, running with them how gracefully in Cowper's Hares, swinging with them how enchantingly in Lowell's June bird "atilt like a blossom among the leaves," and galloping with them how gloriously in Sheridan's steed bearing its rider and victory to Cedar Creek and a flying army thirty miles away! Who would lose out of fiction Ulysses's faithful dog, or the lesson-teaching asses, apes, and foxes of Æsop's Fables, or Don Quixote's Rozinante, or the Cid's Bavieca, or Scott's The Antlered Monarch of the Waste, or Dickens's Boxer and Jip, or Poe's croaking Raven, or, later, Mrs. Sewell's Black Beauty, or even Mary's Little Lamb? With what a wealth of vigor and grace they have lent themselves to painting in the canvas of Landseer and of Rosa Bonheur, and to sculpture in such marbles as The Plunging Horses and The Farnese Bull! Astronomy has taken them as its helper into the far-off skies, bidding the North forever know its place with a Great and Little Bear, covering the earth in its cool autumn nights with an Eagle's starry wings and establishing in the solemn heavens the never-stopping merry-go-round of its Zodiacal Ram, Bull, Crab, Lion, Scorpion, Goat, and Fishes. And even in the midst of Religion's grand service and majestic thoughts they have occupied how large a place both as the victims offered the gods and as the very gods they were offered to—even in our Christian faith have borne on their backs what mighty doctrines as the Serpent, the Worm, the Dove, the Lion of Judah, and the Lamb of God!

It is out of this great wonder realm of animal life, associated with man in so many ways and of which he himself is so vital a part, that Zoölogy has arisen, seeking to arrange its objects, to discover their structure, relations, and laws, and to get at their cause and reason. There is no other branch of science which alike in its materials and in itself is so full of interest, no other which embodies so completely the great world-wide principles of evolution and on the field of which the battles against it have been so fierce and the victories for it so brilliant, no other which lets the student in so close to the very workshop and elbow of Nature and so near to the great mystery of life, no other which opens so suggestively into the whole philosophy of man's own being, both physical and mental, individual and social, as this; and a lecture devoted not so much to its details, needing years of study, as to its growth and larger teachings and to its bearing on these other themes, may have its modest place, even when the lecturer's qualification for it is only a love about equally divided between its outside live objects and its inside live truths.

I. Looked at historically, the growth of the science itself has been along the direct lines not only of evolution, but of evolution in its Darwinian phase of mounting up from species to species through variation, modifying environment, a struggle for existence, and natural selection. In its beginnings and first forms, the same as with life itself, it was vague, nebulous, protoplasmic, consisting for ages of only such acquaintance with the habits and structure of animals as the hunter and the herdsman following them in the chase and the field, and the priest and the householder cutting them up for the altar and the table, would be likely to acquire, and of such accounts of them as wonder and amazement would be likely to suggest. Even after collections of their varieties began to be made it was as objects of curiosity and amusement rather than of study; and in regard to their very names, if it is not a puzzle as to how they were obtained from their more waspy, bearish, and uncommunicative owners, as it was to John Phenix how astronomers ever got at those of the stars, it is one, certainly, as to which animals those used in its earlier books were really meant for, so loose is their description.

Aristotle (384–322 B. C.), that mountain mind which caught on its brow so many of the beams of wisdom's rising sun a thousand years before they touched the vales below, was the first observer to look on animals with the really scientific eye, describing minutely their wonderful varieties, and, by his divisions of them into oviparous, viviparous, and the like, recognizing the need, if not the method, of their classification. It was a work in which Alexander the Great was his friend and patron, putting at his service, it is said, millions of money and thousands of men, specimens also of all the new animals and plants found by him in the countries he ravaged; and it is an interesting fact that while the empires over men that the great Macedonian established have long since passed away, and the glory that he won as a warrior become only a blot on the page of history, the little he did among the brutes was the founding of a kingdom that has gone on to gather all lands into its sweep and is the sole thing remembered now to his credit.

But Aristotle, like advanced thinkers in all departments of life, even in religion itself, if a great help to progress, was also a great hindrance; if a mountain to catch long beforehand the beams of the rising sun, a mountain likewise to throw long afterward a deep darkness over the plain. For two thousand years men lingered in the shadow of his great name, studied what he had said about animals rather than animals themselves, and trembled lest in going beyond Aristotle they should go beyond truth. It was not till the seventeenth and eighteenth centuries, and with them the advent of Ray and Willoughby in England, Buffon in France, and pre-eminently Linnæus in Sweden, that the science resumed its growth, one of the many instances in known history of a leaping from mind to mind over whole centuries with hardly a connecting link between, which ought to remove all difficulty about missing links in the ages before history when in accordance with the same law the leap was from species to species and from form to form.

The great service of Linnæus (1707–1768) to zoölogy, the same as to botany, was his well-known twofold one of classification and of nomenclature. He was a new Adam in the Eden of science before whom each of its creatures passed again to be named, a scientific Napoleon in the kingdom of nature, who took its myriad inhabitants as a mob and organized them into the divisions, brigades, regiments, and companies of a vast army, each with its own distinctive uniform. And though his organization, while serving well on some fields, has proved inadequate for science's advancing needs, his system of double names—one for genus and the other for species—has been of immense permanent value, and illustrates strikingly the new power that words with fixed meanings have to make charges with, bayonet-like, in the battles of thought.

The work of Linnæus was taken up and carried on yet further by Cuvier (1769–1832), the third great name in zoölogy. A new and vastly improved system of classification, based on the structure of its objects as a whole, rather than on a single feature of them, was added by him to its growth. The idea of its kingdom as a regular series, *scala naturæ*, ascending from zoöphyte to man, which had hitherto prevailed, he supplanted with the conception of it as a tree-like structure, having four distinct branches—Mollusk, Radiate, Articulate, and Vertebrate—an immense gain. He was the first zoölogist to enter the great nature-built museum of the rocks and recognize the exceeding value of its fossil treasures as the antecedents of living forms; and his skill as a comparative anatomist is indicated by the fact that while his predecessors had mistaken the bones of creatures as wide apart as the elephant and the salamander for those of men, he out of a single tooth could reconstruct the whole body of an animal otherwise unknown.

It was under him that zoölogy reached the maturity of its second great form, that of organized knowledge, Natural History; and who can compare it with what it was to begin with, a mere unassorted collection of strange stories about animals, and not see that it was as much a transmutation of species as any that the primitive amœba ever underwent in mounting up from its original protoplasm to be an organized mammal?

Side by side with this process of classification, however, another one still more striking had already begun—that of asking what was the origin and cause of classes, and of trying to get at the laws and forces by which they had naturally come. As far back as the time of Linnæus—not to go back to that of Hippocrates and Lucretius—Buffon (1707-1788) had given the question birth. He is usually ridiculed as a dreamer rather than a scientist, a man who in studying animals vivisected them unopened with his imagination as a scalpel, and arranged them unpunctured with his philosophy as a pin; and indeed as a dealer with facts he is not for a moment to be compared with Linnæus and Cuvier. But he got hold in his dreaming of some things in nature that they with their eyes wide open for facts were utterly blind to; he was a babe in zoölogy as compared with them, but, like the primitive anthropoid, the babe of a new species. He reached forward in fancy to almost the exact thing that Darwin later found in fact, expressing it, however, as he had to, in the subjunctive mood of church fear rather than with the indicative of scientific manhood. "If," he says, "we did not know the contrary to be the case by sure warrant, we might easily have concluded, so fallible is our reason, that animals always varied slightly, and that such variations, indefinitely accumulated, suffice to account for almost any amount of ultimate difference"—words that for delicate ingenuity in hinting a truth so as not to hurt a prejudice, serving God and yet not offending Mammon, even a minister in the pulpit could hardly rival.

The new species of zoölogy thus feebly begun developed in the time of Cuvier into a great school of brilliant thinkers who in their aims and methods were widely differentiated from the old stock. On the side of the past were the patient observers and careful experimentalists who held to the traditional doctrine of species as the immediate work of the Creator, and believed in letting new theories about causes alone and in confining themselves to the collection and arrangement of facts. On the other side were the bold speculators and nature-philosophers who believed in studying the causes which underlie the facts, and in all species as originating through natural laws out of a primitive stock, a side which embraced such advocates as Erasmus Darwin (1731–1802), who believed in a slow inward variability as leading to their differences; Lamarck (1744–1829), who ascribed them to the efforts accumulating through inheritance of the animals themselves; St.-Hilaire (1772–1844), who emphasized the action of the environment; Oken (1779–1851), who taught the doctrine of protoplasm and the cell; and Goethe (1749–1832), who explained the skull with all its wonders as only an enlargement of the upper spinal vertebra. The antagonism between the two schools widened gradually from word and work into feeling and friction; and at last, in 1830, it broke out on the floor of the French Academy in an open dispute, headed by Cuvier on the one side and St.-Hilaire on the other, which for violence and ferocity the beasts themselves could hardly have excelled, the famous dispute which Goethe at his home in Weimar looked upon as of so much more importance than the French Revolution breaking out at the same time, that he could hardly imagine how his friend, when he spoke to him of "this great event," could think he referred to the mere political outbreak.

Cuvier won the victory for the time in hand, nothing being able to withstand the torrent of facts that his brain, made on the mitrailleuse principle, was able to pour forth; and for thirty years he was the hero, the world over, of conservatism and the church. All the same, however, the new phase of the science kept on with its growth. Von Baer (1792–1876) opened and read the testimony of embryology; John Miller dissected and described, with an accuracy unknown before, the animal body; Richard Owen

(1804–18—) pointed out the distinction of analogous and homologous members in comparative anatomy; Schwam (1810–1882) discovered with his microscope the starting-point in the cell of all animal life; and Herbert Spencer formulated the great principles of biology in his new synthetic philosophy. Then evolution, having done its work with observation and speculation separated, took its next great step in order—that of integrating them in a man who, with a minuteness and accuracy of observation which place him at the head of all fact-gatherers, united a skill of interpretation and a boldness of generalization which place him at the forefront of all truth-finders—Charles Darwin, the fourth great name in zoölogy; and the result was The Origin of Species and the transmuting of what with others had been a brilliant guess into a statement of the very laws and principles by which as a fact it had been brought about. It was itself another phase of its own doctrine—raised zoölogy to be a new species of science as distinct from those which had gone before it as ever man was from monkey. In its first form it was natural knowledge, in its second natural history, in its third natural science; in its first fact, in its second order, in its third truth; in its first an unorganized amœba, in its second a vertebrated animal, and in its third an intelligent man. It exists in all three of those forms to-day, just as other derived species do; has its museum and picture-book species, its cabinet and school-book species, and its ethical-society and philosophical-lecture species; and people are interested sometimes in one, sometimes in another, and now and then in all three.

With the proclamation of its new truth there came in natural order its struggle for existence, the world's modern thirty years' war. Against it have been brought to bear all the thunderbolts of theology, all the flippancies and squibs of the newspaper, all the stupidities and timidities of society at large, and all the arguments the conservative side of science could find in its arsenal. Agassiz's great work on Classification, the crowning effort of zoölogy's old dispensation, was published by a striking coincidence the same year that gave to the animal world its new Evangel; and even he had to say "Darwinism is a burlesque of facts," and "science would renounce the claim which it has hitherto possessed to the confidence of earnest minds if such sketches were to be accepted as indications of true progress" — words that evince how distinctly a man may see facts and yet how utterly blind he may be to truths, how accurately know the trees of the forest and yet how ignorant be of the forest itself.

On the other side have stood from the start such names as those of Wallace, Spencer, Tyndall, Huxley, Haeckel, themselves masters in the realms of thought. Little by little Cuvier's great victory on the floor of the French Academy, gloried in for thirty years as the triumph of fact over theory, observation over speculation, has been turned to defeat. The facts themselves, whole regiments of them, enlisted so carefully under the banners of observation, some the very ones that Agassiz himself gathered, have mutinied against their own leaders and have put in their sturdiest blows in behalf of theory. Darwin's doctrine, whether or not it is regarded as the whole truth about descent, is held, almost without exception, to be a large piece of it, the grandest generalization yet reached in zoölogical progress. And Darwin himself stands forth to-day a testimony forever to the value of the speculative reason, as well as of the plodding, practical, fact-gathering senses, as an agency in winning victories even on the fields of material science.

But while recognizing thus the inward growing force of zoölogy's great names and the struggle for existence it went through, there is another element of evolution working with them in producing its changes, which is not to be forgotten —that of its environment and of the world's general unfolding knowledge. Meat-eating, and with it the need of cutting creatures up, making in every butcher's shop a dissecting-room; medicine, and with it the study of man's structure; vaticination, and with it the inspection of animal bodies, each of these, must have contributed largely at the start to its knowledge of facts. The discovery and exploration of America in the fifteenth, sixteenth, and seventeenth centuries, bringing to its hands a multitude of new animals, brought about almost as a necessity the classificatory stage into which it then developed. And geology, revealing a score of other new worlds with their missing links under the old one's feet; the microscope, revealing still another score in the old one's every drop of water; astronomy, explaining with its nebular hypothesis the origin of a myriad worlds from one primal mist; chemistry, explaining with its atomic theory the origin of a myriad substances from possiblyone primal element; Lyell, explaining with his uniformatory doctrine the production of all the varieties of rock from one central mass; Harvey, explaining with his circulation of the blood the moving of a thousand little drops from one common fountain of life; and Herbert Spencer, explaining with his grand synthetic philosophy the evolution of the universe as a whole from one starting-point of matter and force,·all sweeping along in the same path of a single natural cause for a series of widely different results—all surrounded zoölgoy with an atmosphere which inevitably helped to sweep its thinkers on to Darwin's like new truth.

Even the changing climate of the religious world was not without its modifying effect. The zoölogical mind, the same as the thinking mind everywhere, felt the inspiring warmth of the new summer, the delicious trouble in the moral ground, that with the Reformation began coming to the world of men. Ideas that Buffon could only hint in the cellar, Darwin could proclaim unhindered on the housetop The skepticism of religion became the faith of science. And just in proportion as the Church got rid of its doctrine that man had gone down from his primitive perfection to being "a worm of the dust," it became possible for the lecture-room to show that his being a worm was the very condition from which he had come up.

Nor were humbler agencies lacking as contributors to the grand result. Darwin notoriously was started on the track of his doctrine of how species originate by what he found in the farmyard and the garden. The experience of breeders down through long ages had accumulated a vast fund of practical knowledge on the subject, overlooked by other scientists, that he was not ashamed to sit at their feet and learn. Hodge was found not to have raised his pigs through so many generations only for pork. The story of the crafty Jacob in the sheepfolds of old Laban was discovered to have a truth in it beyond anything the most inveterate believer in biblical infallibility had ever dreamed of. Doves, drawing of old the chariot of Venus, drew for him the fairer one of Wisdom. Mares bred to win prizes at the Derby were taught under his touch to win them on the race-course of science. And while other men had sought truth by converse with the gods, and thought of it as too holy a thing to be enshrined in aught but learned tongues, its nineteenth-century disciple found it, like the Magi of old, cradled in a stable and uttering itself in that most despised of all things, "horse talk," illustrating anew Emerson's words:

" 'Tis not in the high stars alone,
  Nor in the cups of budding flowers,
Nor in the redbreast's mellow tone,
  Nor in the bow that smiles thro' showers,
But in the mud and scum of things
  That alway, alway something sings!"

II. Passing now from what zoölogy has been historically as an embodiment of evolution to what it is scientifically as a field for it, how widely already has it opened its gate for its entrance! It is not indeed the whole of its sphere. The starry heavens, the rock-ribbed earth, the chemical elements, the vast realm of botany, and who shall say how largely the kingdom of mind, are other rooms in its great house. But it is one of its most important departments—one that, with the great mystery of life already its occupant, it seemed beforehand almost impossible for it to enter. All its great fundamental principles—homogeneousness at the start, differentiation, rhythmic movement, the multiplication of effects, integration, and then dissolution and the use of its materials over again in a new series—all these, with some others, as natural selection, peculiar to its own realm, it illustrates with marvelous beauty alike in the individual and the race, evinces it as holding good in the realms of flesh and life as well as in those of matter and force, shows that what made the star made the soul, that what organized the earth organized its inhabitants, and that the highway of creation trod out of primal fire-mist over whirling atom, tenuous nebula and blazing sun, over cooling planet, heaving continent and quaking rock, was not ended or interrupted when it came to man and mind. It is not strange that to the world at large Darwinism means the same thing as evolution. Without the Origin of Species to lead the way it is doubtful whether The First Principles of a New Philosophy would have ever got beyond the scholar's study. It was its victory on the field of zoölogy that forced it into the ears and faith of the general public. With the citadel of life carried by its logic and the myriad armies of the animal world made its captives, it was felt that the whole vast fort of the universe might as well be surrendered to it at once as wait for an assault it now became certain nothing could resist. And so, if Spencer is to be regarded as the Messiah of evolution, Darwin must be set down as at least its Apostle Paul.

What a field, too, it affords for its further progress! Darwin's discovery, with all it did for it, was but a stage along its way, not by any means its goal. It gives us the doctrine of animal descent, starts the student on the right track for all coming investigation; but the actual lines of their descent, the ages and order in which their different classes, families, genera, and species have branched off from the common stock and from each other; in short, the construction of that vast genealogical tree, world-wide and ages high, on which each member of the animal family shall have its place marked—that, except it be in Haeckel's imperfect outlines and with a few ancestors of the horse, is as yet hardly touched. Departments for its study that were thought of old to be outside of zoölogy are brought by The Origin of Species directly within its sphere. Ontogeny, the science of the individual, is made by its principles as much a part of it as is phylogeny, the science of the race. Embryology, once regarded as hardly a fly-leaf in its mighty volume, is found under it to be a most precious table of contents, repeating with the child in a few months what it took ages to accomplish with its parents, and giving in its summary whole chapters again, ages long, which in the book itself earthquakes have blotted out and oceans covered up, opening, therefore, what a new world for evolutionary eyes! Morphology, the science of structure, the study of the origin of the organs inside of the body—as much species as the animals which are outside of it—what made them vary from their original homogeneous protoplasm into all the complexities of their present condition, three hundred thousand fibers, for instance, in a single optic nerve, and why it is that each animal and each species has the exact size and shape and number of limbs and of senses that it does—all as much a matter of law as the shape of crystals or the orbit of planets—all this is legitimately within its zoölogical sphere. Then, with man as an animal, sociology, the study of the laws and forces which evolve society, is surely as much a part of it as is the study of those which gather the bee in hives and the ant in hills; and especially comparative sociology, an investigation of the common elements which run through all collections of animals from those of the insect up, how much has it got here to learn—what a help, also, find from it in solving some of the social problems that we are vainly now seeking wisdom for among ourselves, giving a new point to old Solomon's words, "Go to the ant, thou sluggard, consider her ways and be wise." And, crowning all, psychology, the marvels of mind and soul, the wonder that fills and overflows this wonder of body—consciousness, love, thought, aspiration—how they unfolded out of protoplasm with the body, what they root in and what they lead to, all these have got to be studied henceforth in connection with animals—are for some future Darwin to make discoveries in as much beyond The Origin of Species as The Origin of Species is beyond the animal pictures that the old Troglodytes drew on their half-eaten bones in the caves of Dordogne and La Madelaine.

III. Proceeding from the historic and scientific aspects of the subject, we find it unfolding into still another species of truth, one which in some respects is the most interesting and important of all. Evolution is not only a history and a science. It is also a philosophy. It embraces not only facts and causes, but with them reasons—asks not only what and how, but, likewise, why. And after giving us in its department of zoölogy the natural history of animals and the methods and causes of their origin as species and individuals one from another, it is met at once with the further question of why their existence and descent in this way, what the object of the myriads of them that lived and struggled and died before men came on earth, as well as of the myriads that are doing it now—a page of Nature written how deep in blood—what the philosophy of their different forms, many of them so repulsive and monstrous, and of man's being born out of their loins, as Darwin represents, instead of his coming up directly out of the dust and with a human shape to start with, as theology so long has taught.

There is doubtless a sense in which animals are their own end, a side of philosophy which must recognize that, like beauty and the multiplication table and man himself, the ugliest beast and the humblest worm are their "own excuse for being."

"Know Nature's children all divide her care;
The fur that warms a monarch warmed a bear.
While man exclaims, 'See all things for my use.'
'See man for mine,' replies the pampered goose."

And yet it is not the less true that a secondary purpose, a vein, if not of the old, Paley, watch-maker teleology, yet of practical good sense and of a reason for things, does run everywhere through Nature. And it is this that evolution finds shining out as a vein of gold from the dark strata of paleontology and from the forms even of the most monster-like brutes.

Not to dwell on their work in making the earth's continents and soils, and in elaborating its crude inorganic elements into nourishing foods, the why of their existence, of their forms in the past, and of the whole process of their growth from moner up to man, is to be found in Darwin's doctrines of variation and heredity—in their acquisition of organs and qualities by variation step by step in the only environment that was fitted for their production, and then in the transmission of them by inheritance from species to species up into higher surroundings and finer shapes, and at last into their existing completeness. Animals have been not merely the lineal ancestors, but beyond this the necessary makers of humanity, the only possible builders not only of man's dwelling place and man's food, but of man himself. Nature's method of phylogenic growth, made inevitable apparently by her own inherent laws, has been herself to push forward an organ a little way and then to set its recipients to using it with their own will-power over and over, till at last, like the beating of our hearts, it unconsciously did itself, and then to employ her vitality, released from this work, in pushing out still another organ on which the process was repeated; and so on, the gain of one generation being transferred by inheritance to the next, a thing impossible, you see, under the old idea of species as independent creations. The uniting of its four great elements, in some respects the most refractory of Nature, into the original protoplasmic mortar out of which all animals are built up, had probably to be done millions of times by its low amœbic forms before they got the habit of staying united; and every step of the wonderful organization and functioning to which it has now arrived in humanity has been taken by having myriads of animals along the way go through with its various operations of digestion, respiration, nerve-action, sense-perception, blood-circulation and the like, again and again till what at first was direct effort—done by giving their minds to it—became at last involuntary action, done without a thought. Man is indeed a bundle of habits, and a bundle formed not only by himself, but by all the multitudes of creatures that are in the lines of his descent back to the first amœba that ever ate its bit of brother slime. A few years ago, as a German naturalist was watching the hatching of an egg, he noticed that after the shell had broken apart, and while the chick was yet in one side of it, a fly lighted on the other. Instantly the little creature, not wholly hatched as yet, darted its bill out for the fly and caught it and ate it up; and in doing so, the naturalist reckoned that it must have made, bodily and mentally, at least three thousand co-ordinated motions, each one of them absolutely perfect. Where did it get its skill? "Instinct," said old ignorance. "Inherited habit," says new evolution. Millions of mature chickens in the generations before it had spent their lives in catching flies, and the skill they had acquired came down to their descendant in its blood. So with man in his facility for catching flies, whether they be in the shape of milk on his mother's breast, or of base-ball on the playground, or, further along, of crinkled lightning on the breast of earth, it comes how largely from the skill of muscle trained into him by the brutes. We live not only outwardly on strata of rock filled with their bones, but inwardly on strata of flesh filled with their deeds. The whole marvelous story of paleontology is recapitulated in every babe that creeps, the four-footed ways of its fossils in the very creeping itself. Honestly indeed, as the saying is, do boys come by the monkey tricks and the habits of sliding down banisters and climbing up trees, reckless of clothes, they are so notorious for, acquired in far-off tropic forests when literally it was "Rock-a-by, baby, in the tree-top," and when the only nursery tales they had to amuse themselves with were what they carried appended to their own bodies, and the only pantaloons to tear, those which their mother Nature had made. Primeval heats, which blotted all traces of the Eozoon out of Laurentian limestone, left the marks of it cindered on the inner, more imperishable bed-rock of the geologist himself who goes out in its search. And live men are not only "dead men warmed over," as Holmes has expressed it, but with them dead animals warmed over, whose subtler selves, never dying, still wriggle and crawl and climb in our every bone and nerve.

The value of the unconscious automatic functioning thus established in the human body it is hardly possible to overestimate. Suppose that man had to superintend and execute each act of his physical living by the direct conscious exercise of his own will; suppose the sailor, reefing the topgallant sails of his ship in a tornado, with the masts swinging through the air like whips and the lightnings jabbing through it like bayonets, had at the same time to keep the pumps going of his own heart; or that the orator, while filling his audience with inspiring thoughts, had with every respiration to give part of his mind to the filling of his own lungs with breath; or that the poet, right in the midst of his subtle fancies and revelings in the ideal world, had ever and anon to turn his eye in a fine frenzy rolling down on to his liver to keep it from idling, or in along his digestive apparatus to make sure its thousand little nutrients were not sending his nourishment off to the wrong places—what power or time would they have left for success in their immediate human work? More to us than any outward legacies from human parents are these inherited habits within that we are all born to from our animal progenitors. It is because they used their volitions and vitality so well in the establishment of such physical ones that we are able to go on and use ours for the establishment of those that are intellectual and moral. Out of their awful conflicts in the long past, seemingly the expressions only of ferocity and cruelty, have come to us for use in the mighty moral conflicts of civilization

"The wrestling thews that throw the world."

"Thirty centuries look down upon you," said Napoleon to his soldiers as they went forth to the battle of the Pyramids. Thirty eons look down upon—nay, join you and fight with you—evolution says to every man who goes forth to the battle of life. And with such an inheritance from the brutes is it a thing very discreditable to us that we have had them as our ancestors—a philosophy wholly without significance which shows thus the reason for Nature's method of human descent?*

* The line of thought here presented does not depend for its truth wholly on how the question is decided which is now under discussion among zoölogists, as to whether qualities acquired by use are transmitted by inheritance, or only those acquired by variation. As showing man's indebtedness to animals, it is in a measure true either way; but of course as a philosophy of life running up even into human activity it is more complete and emphatic under the view that both kinds are transmitted, a view which has on its side the great names of Spencer and Darwin. Most of the arguments against the transmittableness of use variation are based on the assumption that the characteristics of animal nature were the same in the past as now, always a dangerous assumption. When a species is new, all its acquisitions, whether by variation or use, are vastly more unstable than when it is old. There is a continual tendency in the generations which immediately follow a recent species not only to revert back to the old stock, but to vary away from it yet further, as many a breeder who has tried to perpetuate a valuable variety either of animals or plants has sorrowfully found. It takes Nature's streams a long while to wear down new channels into its bed rock, but just in proportion as they are worn it becomes more and more difficult to change them either by variation or use, a fact which explains not only why acquired qualities are so little transmitted now, but why in the early history of life variations were

It is a philosophy, moreover, which holds good not only with reference to those species of animals which are in the direct line of man's origin, but in some measure of all the side ones, also, that have branched off from it and ended only in themselves. Mr. Dawson urges it as an argument against Darwinian evolution that the trilobite, after existing all through the Silurian and Devonian ages, finally died out without giving rise to any new forms of life. It is a kind of reasoning which hardly looks further than their own stony eyes. The trilobites did their work and answered the why of their existence by the nutriment they afforded the surviving main stock of animal life. It is a part of the magnificent economy of nature, one of the reconciling features in its horrible system of having animals eat each other up, that its very failures are used thereby to make its successes—its creatures that perish in their struggle for existence are made to live and triumph in those which survive. The distinction between eater and eaten, as we go down the scale of being, grows continually less and less. Reproduction by nutrition is only the opposite side of reproduction by fission. When a big amœba eats a small one, the result is a new creature almost as much as when higher up the two parents unite their lives in that of a child. Indeed, there are some cases where the new food is a direct agent in producing a new species. Inheritance in nature is from branches as well as roots, from uncles and aunts as well as from fathers and mothers. The lower limbs of a forest tree are not the less necessary for its growth, nor the less represented in its final fruit, because its top boughs grow on it elsewhere, leaving the bottom ones to be overshadowed and die. And whole species of animals have done the same thing for man's stock in the past that individual animals and plants are doing now—elaborated its food and food qualities out of coarse, inorganic elements up into what was most akin to its own flesh and blood.

Of course the process has been a very slow one—myriads of animals to establish a single habit, ages of time to deposit

so many and rapid. The truth of the matter seems to be that the two methods of change work together. Nature makes the variation at birth, and then use comes in to establish its functioning as a habit. If the stock is young and vigorous, the variation advantageous, and its use continued long enough, then the whole thing, both the original variation and its acquired strength, are transmitted by inheritance, otherwise the reversion is back in the offspring to the channel in which the life stream first flowed. It is precisely what is seen in the individual—acquisitions of knowledge and character much more easily made in childhood than in age, but retained and made a part of their acquirer only by their constant use; and it is all expressed in the familiar saying that "it is hard to teach an old dog new tricks," the dog being in zoölogy the species and the race.

a single organ. But time with those animal antediluvians was of no especial value, a million years but as a watch in the night, and a small eternity but as yesterday when it was passed. It was the one thing and the only thing that in those days they had to do; and it was what right in the midst of their frolicking and fighting and eating each other up they could go on doing just as well. And here again is where Nature's economy comes in and the reason comes out why the originators of man were brutes instead of higher beings and why he was not set to build himself. It was as brutes with brute shapes and brute tastes that they could best make what is animal in man. It was protoplasm alone that was plastic enough to begin with, protoplasm alone that could be the flask in which life could imprison the four great genii of matter. Rough claws shaped parts of man grandly where fine fingers would have miserably failed. And what would have been the sense of having a creature with fifty ounces of brain in his skull at work generation after generation on the stomach, lungs, heart, and eye just to establish in them the habit of involuntary action, when a ganoid fish with a pennyweight of skull-stuff, or a megalosaur reptile with all the cycles of Cathay at his command, could do it vastly better? I have a young friend, a machinist, who keeps a few barn-yard fowls for his amusement, and who, like most amateurs in that line, became fascinated one year with the idea of raising young spring chickens ahead of Nature by means of an incubator. So one Sunday morning, disregarding the remonstrances of mother, wife, and sister, he went to consult a friend in the city who already had one on his hands. His friend showed him his instrument, its spirit-lamps and steam-pipes and hundred eggs in their compartments, and then told him how careful he had to be in its management, sitting up all night to watch the thermometer and feed the lamps and to keep everything right, and then took him solemnly out into the back yard where were two other sets of a hundred eggs all spoiled, one because he had left the apparatus fifteen minutes in the care of a small boy who had let them roast, and the other because he himself had gone to sleep a moment or two the twentieth night and let them chill. "Now, Joe," said he, with a melancholy air, "if you will take the benefit of my experience, so long as your time as a machinist is worth more than that of an old setting hen as an incubator, I should advise you to stick to your lathe and let the old setting hen hatch the chickens." And that is what Nature did in hatching the chicken qualities of her myriad creatures in the early spring of life—used not her thinking man, but her brooding hens to be their incubator. And slow and muddle-headed as they were, how grand is the resulting body which has come out of their nest! How supple and varied its powers, how marvelous its organization! What a strain it has stood of battle-fields and long abuses and accidents by field and flood, what a foundation proved on which to build the enormous structure of mind, what a new significance given to the pious hymn of good old Dr. Watts that alike saint and scientist can for once unite in singing—

> "Fearful and wondrous is the skill that molds
> Our body's vital plan,
> And from the first dim hidden germ unfolds
> The perfect limbs of man!"

And with all the work there is still before it as the agent of mind, all the business cares and social problems and weights of philosophy and science, all the marvels of our coming civilization, that are yet to be piled up on its brain, who shall say it is a particle too strong, who feel that those old brutes with their myriad years took for its building one hour too much, who not fear, with it breaking down so often even now, that the future may show that those Tertiary anthropoids who put on it its final touches before the superstructure of reason was begun, hurried up their part of the work a little too fast?

Nor is it body alone that man owes to the brutes. In them, too, were laid all the great foundation stones of mind, heart, and soul! And how far back in their blood do some of the qualities reach which seem now to be most distinctively the badges of human superiority! Little did that old amphibian think, when he saw under far Devonian skies the fish-fins with which he had come out of the water separate into the ten phalanges of his fore limbs, that he was laying the foundations of an arithmetic that was to count at last the stars of heaven with its digits and measure the distances of Sirius and the nebulæ with its multiple; little those "dragons of the prime that tare each other in their slime" imagine that out of their conflicts they were storing up in their blood a courage, energy, and pluck that were to fight the great battles of liberty when bayonets were to be the claws and steam rams the tusks, and win victories for truth when ideas should be the horns and arguments the jaws; little that early batrachian, who called his mate to him with a croak, foresee that his vocal faculty was to go on developing itself through human voices till it broke forth in the eloquence of a Demosthenes, drove reform to its mark in the sarcasm of a Phillips, and went up to heaven in a song the angels might hush their own to hear of a Nilsson and an Abbott. Love, with its mother tenderness and its sex-passion climbing in humanity to what splendors of poetry and romance, has its root down how far amid the tenants of the rocks. Society and its duties, and that "social contract" about which philosophers have had so much to say, were made for man by the Rousseaus and St. Simons of an ancestry that went on all fours—had already been in existence millions of years at the period when the great Frenchman thought of them as being formed, and can no more be overturned now than our human nature itself. A large part of our moral uprightness antedates our walking physically upright. A few years ago a family on the Hudson, going away for their summer vacation, left in their cellar a piece of meat which they showed their pet dog as the food he was to live on in their absence. The dog, however, mistook their gestures and supposed it was food he was meant to guard. Three weeks afterward, the family returning, found the faithful creature's starved bones beside the untouched meat. Who does not wish that at least an equal share of the fidelity which had thus come down to the little dog out of his brute ancestry had descended to some of the bank presidents and insurance-company trustees that are set to watch people's financial meat? Even as regards religion, not from the lips of angels, but very possibly from the insight of animals, did its first knowledge come. The terror they manifest in the presence of objects which to them are uncanny, as when a horse shies at a bit of whirling paper or at anything in motion whose propelling power he does not see, in spite of the other explanations given of it, is impressively like the dread which lies at the base of all savage worship and which civilized man, his children especially, who repeat in so many ways their far-off ancestral experience, feels in the dark and at the hearing of strange sounds. It suggests, how inevitably, their common origin in a four-footed worshiper who was their common progenitor—is "a fear of the Lord" starting in the awful shadow of primeval woods that was the beginning of a wisdom which is to sing and soar at last in what splendors of Christian day!* And with such inheritances, bodily and mental, received from animals, is it not about time that the words brutal, beastly, and the like, as designating what is worst in man, should have a rest? The really brutal and beastly qualities we have derived from them are often a hundredfold more and better than the human ones that the persons thus described have added to them since. Our animal infancy as a race is just as honorable to us and just as worthy of being referred to with tender regard as our animal infancy as individuals, the two being exactly of a piece. And instead of making it our aim, "working out the beast, to let the ape and tiger die," ought we not rather to keep them in us tamed and civilized as the beasts of burden to carry us on their backs, as no outward ones can, in the long, long way our human nature is yet to travel?

IV. It is a question which opens up into the last and crowning phase that zoölogy as interpreted by Darwin has entered upon, and that is a morality that shall include animals as well as men among its objects and a religion that shall save civilized brutes from the hell so many of them are now in as well as savage heathen from the one they are threatened with by and by. What hitherto has been only a kindly sentiment warring against the wretched cruelty that in so many forms they have been subject to is based by The Origin of Species and The Descent of Man on a solid foundation of science. Sharing with them the membership of one larger animal body, we inevitably share with them also the great Divine law, alike natural and scriptural, that "if one member suffer, all the members suffer with it, and if one member be honored, then all the members rejoice with it." A lady, on getting a kitten for her little boy to play

* It is a sensation that the deep woods, which, according to Darwin, were the probable abode of man's immediate progenitors, seem to have pre-eminently the power to produce. Who, when wandering alone under their stately arches, has not felt in some degree its return—a consciousness of something not found in the open fields, creeping over even his civilized and perhaps skeptical nerves? It suggests the reason why "the groves were God's first temples," and why Gothic architecture has always been recognized as so specially consonant with the more solemn forms of worship. And is it not also an explanation of the fear and credulity with regard to witches, hobgoblins, the Evil One, and an uncanny supernatural presence that are so conspicuous an element in the second generation of our New England ancestry—the overpowering influence of the primeval forest, sweeping the soul back to that brute sense of a more than earthly presence pervading it, in which religion began? Subtle and wonderful the agencies and paths which led the anthropoids of our race up to be men, their long sojourn in their arboreal wilderness not only giving them their upright bodily attitude and developed hands, but awakening at the same time, as nothing else could, their germ of soul, going so fitly with the hands and with the bodily uprightness.

with, told him as a means of keeping him from doing it harm that only half of it—the hind half—was his, and that she was going to keep the other half—its head—as hers. The next day, sitting in the parlor, she overheard a terrible cry of animal pain coming from the play-room, and exclaimed: "O Tommy, Tommy! what are you doing to my end of the kitten?" "I ain't doing nothing to your end," was the answer. "I only pinched my end, and it was your end that squawked." And that is what Darwin has taught us with regard to the whole animal kingdom, man included, that it is only a larger kitten, and that cruelty can not pinch the meanest worm at its tail without having its farthest human end squawk, can not do any part of it needless harm without having it react through nerves subtler than those of flesh and harm the harmer also—the frightened calf poison its eater, and the whip that scars the horse's flesh at one end ply an unseen lash at the other, scarring with its every stroke the driver's soul. Revealing our origin from a common stock, it is not only the good Samaritan, but his good ass also that is made by it our neighbor; not only the savage man, but the savage beast that is our brother; not only at the tomb of Adam in Palestine, but at the tomb of the Eozoön, Nature-built, in the primeval rock, that we can stand, weeping, if we will, and say, "A distant relative to be sure, and yet a relative." And all the reasons that ethics can show based on self-interest, gratitude, blood connection, and the mystery of a common life-tie for the exercise of justice, kindness, and the golden rule toward the lowest man, it shows hold equally good for their exercise toward the humblest brute. Philanthropy is widened by it into zoöphily; humanitarianism into panzoicism; altruism between man and man into altruism between man and all that lives. It completes the great circle that theology has traveled from its finding of Deity at first in animals out in its search for Him into the Infinite, and then back through man to its finding of Him in their life again—makes it the word of science as well as poetry that

> "He prayeth well who loveth well
> Both man and bird and beast."

And though its practical influence in doing away with cruelty is yet only partially felt, it has the potency in it of truth, and it is as sure at last to bring about a reform in their treatment as Christianity is in that of human beings.

Darwin was the apostle to the gentiles of the forest, field, and flood; the Light of Asia to the darkened world of the brute; and as he "passed on" to his great discovery it is not difficult imagining their myriads as doing for him what Arnold represents them as doing for Siddârtha of old:

> "Large wondering eyes
> Of woodland creatures—panther, boar, and deer—
> At peace that eve gazed on his face benign
> From cave and thicket. Bright butterflies
> Fluttered their vans, azure and green and gold,
> To be his fan-bearers. The doves flocked round,
> And e'en the creeping things were 'ware and glad.
> Voices of earth and air joined in one song
> Which unto ears that hear said, 'Lord and Friend,
> This is the night the ages waited for.'"

And now, under the reign of those new influences in their behalf, what does evolution point to as likely to be the whole final outcome to animals from their long struggle for existence, what their own place at last on the great life-tree they have done so much to nourish—a look into their future which surely may not unfitly close our look into their long past? Philosophers are not wanting who have held that, sharers of man's mortality here, they will be sharers of whatever immortality awaits him in the realms beyond. Mourners of household pets have easily agreed with the poor Indian

> "Who thinks, admitted to that equal sky,
> His faithful dog will bear him company.'

And there are some sportsmen, I verily believe, animated with a somewhat different shade of interest, to whom heaven would lose half its attraction if they thought its river of life was to have no speckled trout in its waters waiting to be caught, its tree of life no robins and squirrels among its branches placed there to be shot at, its New Jerusalem no blooded trotters on its golden pave to be bet upon, and its fields of amaranth and asphodel no flying fox and hunting hounds to gallop over in the merry chase.

But without speculating on their condition beyond the realms of time, we can reasonably look forward, under the light of evolution, to their developing side by side with man in the long future which is before him on earth, and to their sharing with him—at least their more saintly representatives—that ideal state, the golden age of heathendom and the millennium of Christianity, which beyond question our existing world is to ripen into before it passes on to its final stage. Mosquitoes may not tune their voices in its dewy airs, nor rattlesnakes join their harps in its choral song, but it is hard to think of a perfect earth, even with its silver questions all settled and its social problems all solved, that is not to be musical with the song of birds, graceful with the forms of quadrupeds, and alive with myriads of the happy things which have labored so long to build it up—as hard as it is to think of a flower, however fair, that is not the fairer when encircled with its chaplet of leaves. Its poisonous reptiles, its pestiferous insects, and its more ravenous and untamable beasts, unrepenting sinners of the swamp and fen, will doubtless die out, for universal salvation, however true it may be of man, and even of the old theological serpent, can hardly be stretched out wide enough, even by its most determined advocate, to cover the snake in the grass and the worm in the flesh—killed off not so much by human hands as by the earth's changing clime. But with these gone it will be all the easier for its better ones to survive, preserved alike by Nature's softened laws and man's co-operating care. Its woods will still be merry with the frisky squirrel and its airs sweet with the song of birds; its brooks still alive with the silver gleam of scales and its meadows with their painted butterflies and golden-trousered bees; its tropics still have their winged rainbows and feathered gems; and its mountain thrones and courts of snow their eagle kings and nature-ermined lords. The same principle of ripened stock, better living, and more mental activity that operates among men to lay the Malthusian specter of over-population some philosophers are now troubled with, will obtain among animals to keep their numbers from ever crowding the earth. Death will round off their old age with its sleep the same as it will that of human beings even in their perfect state—a death as painless as that which the cells of our bodies in passing from living tissue to waste matter already every day undergo. With the earth's grains and fruits perfected and the chemical means discovered of producing artificial nitrogenous foods, all need of their slaughter and all taste for their flesh will have passed away. Othello's occupation in the shambles and at the meat market, as well as his like one on the tented field, will be gone. We shall look back then on the days of humanity's roast mutton with as much horror as we now do on those of its roast missionary. Sportsmen will find a pleasure in watching the habits of animals out in the millennial woods such as their predecessors never thrilled with in accomplishing their destruction. John Smith will no longer write proudly to his British newspaper, as he does now, that he has "shot a nightingale in Devonshire, the first one that has ever strayed there, as it was singing on a thorn-bush." "Deer assassins," "bird murderers," "fish pirates," and "buffalo thugs" will be the names given by the newspapers of the nineteen hundredth century to the killers of animals, and we shall then say of vivisectionists and of ladies with birds in their bonnets, as some people now do of the Indians, that "the only good ones are the dead ones." Cruelty in the treatment of them will everywhere give place to kindness; dread in their demeanor to confidence. Monkeys will no longer examine the cakes given them by little boys to make sure that they contain no red pepper, or cats go a roundabout way to their lying-in places to keep their kittens from being drowned. The phrase to "lead a dog's life" will denote in that age a very desirable kind of existence; and such proverbs as "slaving like a horse," "uneasy as a toad under a harrow," and "getting the wrong pig by the ear," will need for our children's children in the thousandth generation a dictionary of the dead languages for their explanation. Good society will open its doors to take in other and worthier representatives of their race than the poodles and lap-dogs its "four hundred" are so intimate with now. Traits and qualities which exist in them at present only as a germ will develop under the touch of kindly companionship into forms of unsuspected beauty. They will unite in drawing all together as one mighty team, without lash or goad, the great car of progress. And at last, with the material world all perfected, as some day it must be, and our human world all freed from its sins and shames and wrongs, as some day it shall be—

> "Every tiger madness muzzled, every serpent passion killed,
> Every grim ravine a garden, every blazing desert tilled,"

love shall have in the animal world all forms of life as its own;

> "The spirit of the Lord
> Lie potent upon man and beast and bird";

and in no small degree literally as well as figuratively, old Isaiah's prophetic vision shall be fulfilled: "The lion shall eat straw like the ox; the wolf shall dwell with the lamb, and the leopard shall lie down with the kid, and the fatling and the young lion together, and a little child shall lead them, and they shall not hurt nor destroy in all my holy mountain, saith the Lord."

ABSTRACT OF THE DISCUSSION.

Mr. James A. Skilton:

In this instructive and delightful essay Mr. Kimball has again shown, as he did in that delivered before the Association last year, not only familiarity with the scientific side of his subject, but a unique talent for the popular presentation of it; and again he leaves little if anything to be added, and nothing to be criticised. He has doubtless led every one of us to think of our animal pets, associates, and friends of the present or of the past. It may not be improper, therefore, for me to offer, for you and for myself, some testimony in regard to character as exhibited by animals.

I have this evening had recalled to me the experiences of youth beyond the teens, a time when servants had not yet usurped the privileges and opportunities of the service of sons to fathers, and when I had the constant, sometimes laborious, but always enjoyable, companionship and charge of horses. Not all my teachers were as good teachers as they. By their docility, fidelity, and obedience, and by their exhibitions of endurance, power, and speed, they not only taught me, by the Froebelish method of example, in the minor virtues, but they sometimes fired my young imagination with a high sense of the heroic. One among them was Prince by name and prince by nature. It often became our joint duty to bring succor to the sick, and more than once to bring life to the dying. He was a tall and powerful dapple-gray of great speed and with a grand action touched with something like refinement. A blow of a whip seemed to arouse in him a sort of divine rage terrible to the beholder and combined with a sense of unmerited dishonor and injustice impossible to be endured, while a touch of caress was met first with a look and next with a gentle nip, as much as to say: Please let me do my duty without any petting and for the pleasure of that alone.

In some subtle way he seemed to know how to gauge emergency, and on our errands of mercy and succor, rushing through the streets, there were times when, with that dancing white mane, proudly carried tail, and grand air, he seemed to my boyish thought to have almost the port and stride of an archangel.

Even after he went blind as the result of hard work, he always pressed straight forward in the harness, without faltering or turning to either side, but with a sort of sublime trust in his driver, using his whole energy to perform the task put upon him. I am not ashamed to say, then, and you will not be surprised to hear me say, that when in later life the burden has been great, the road long, and the lash of brutality has seemed about to strike, I have sometimes thought of that noble horse, his great endurance, his unconquerable pride, his spirit and his fidelity, as supplying examples not unworthy to be cherished and followed. Indeed, I presume the question must have arisen in the minds of most of us: Would not the state of the world be greatly better than it is if men had lived and done as nearly up to their capacity and duty as some animals constantly do?

My own early experiences, then, join with evolution in teaching me that character is a common possession of men and animals; and also, possibly in rudimentary form, of vegetal life as well. I should say that all three belong not to the "Kingdom," but to the Republic of Nature, if evolution and its necessary implications are true. In that republic equal justice to all is the ruling principle, as in all other republics. The essayist has suggested that in the "good time coming" animals will not be slaughtered for food as they now are. It is by no means the least function of applied evolution to effect the accomplishment of this result, and also to transfix and overthrow the Malthusian dragon that in so many other directions blocks the way not only of human life, but of all life and societary progress.

I thoroughly believe, with the essayist, that when the time shall have come in which justice shall in universal practice be done to animal and plant life, the vegetal world will furnish, and best furnish, the necessary foods for men of the highest possible development, and that not till then shall we have "Peace on earth, good will to men," and to every living thing, in the most complete sense of the word "living." In fact, it is one of the lessons of the gospel of evolution that if man had been as true to the law and the opportunity of his being as animals and plants have been to theirs, we should now be approaching that better and possible Eden which is already disclosed as we look steadily and carefully along the evolutionary vista. Indeed, it is my own firm belief that it was along a similar vista the incomparable man was looking when he said, ages ago, "The kingdom of Heaven is at hand."

It seems to me, however, that the animal belongs to a class the future of which may be said to be in the main behind it. Wild animals certainly disappear before advancing civilization, and they reappear again before retreating civilization. They have even disappeared before it already to some extent, and apparently must do so in the evolutionary civilization we ought to have; and so do domestic animals in proportion as, through invention, machines and other products of invention come to take their places and perform their functions. As we have already learned in another connection,* as soon as the rational faculty in man reached such a stage as to enable him to invent and use implements and tools, he began to become independent of his own muscular development, which practically ceased at that point and permitted a new state of things to grow out of the new co-ordinations developed thereby. Animals have furnished man with a part of his muscular outfit in the earlier stages of his evolution, but it would seem that the copartnership of man with animals must diminish more and more, in its relative co-ordinations at least, as man develops and makes use of the new co-ordinations.

Has not the animal, then, done a large part of his work, and is he not in great part and except in the lower forms to go out, leaving the future largely to man and to vegetal life?

While, then, zoölogy as a science may continue to make progress for a season, are not animals as such largely destined to extinction, having had their day and done their work, if the human race is to continue on its evolutionary march, and is not zoölogy therefore to become more and more palæontological—a science of fossil and extinct forms of life?

Dr. Richard B. Westbrook:

I have the honor to be an officer of the Wagner School of Science in Philadelphia, and with much pleasure attended a course of lectures in that institution on the development of man and the relations between the lower animals and human beings. I think the ancients exceeded us in their love for the brute creation, and even the pagans of to-day are in that respect in advance of our boasted Christian civilization. The Buddhists build hospitals for their domestic animals, and the Hindoos so reverence the life of brute creation that they will not permit them to be killed for food. The ancient Egyptians embalmed some of their domestic animals and revered them as symbols of the Divine power. I am glad to have had an opportunity of attending a meeting of this association, of the work of which I have known something through its publications, and have listened with great pleasure to the lecture of the evening; and though I came to listen, with no expectation of being called upon to speak, I am glad to say a word in favor of the higher development of our American people in that department of ethics which treats of the love and care due to the brute creation.

* See essay on Mechanic Arts, Sociology, pp. 196, 197.

DR. LEWIS G. JANES:

That I have greatly enjoyed the able and suggestive paper of Mr. Kimball goes without saying. I find little in it for dissent or criticism. Possibly I may not carry my millennial expectations quite so far as the lecturer has indicated, but I think we are making some progress in recognition of our relationship and duties to our brute neighbors. Indeed, I go so far as to dissent from the last speaker and to believe that we are in advance in this respect not only of the ancients, but of the pagan world of the present day. I doubt very much whether the ancients or the modern Buddhists were and are as kind to their animals as we have been led to suppose. In the matter of ethical sanctions we constantly find two diverse attitudes illustrated—that of authority arbitrarily imposed, the "Thou shalt" and "Thou shalt not" of an arbitrary moral code, enforced usually by religious aid, and that of the higher law of spontaneous right action which bids us serve the right for love of such service and which ultimates in the extinction of the sense of constraint and obligation. The ancient Egyptians and the Buddhists were commanded by their religion to honor certain animals and refrain from killing them, yet Prof. Haeckel, in his Voyage to Ceylon, speaks indignantly of the cruelties inflicted by the Buddhists of that country on their domestic animals which only stopped short of the infliction of death. They seemed to see no wrong in torturing and maltreating dumb creatures provided they did not actually kill them. Their obedience was to the "letter that killeth"; ours, yet far from complete, is, so far as it is effective, intelligent, and ingrained, a recognition of the spirit which giveth life. The lesson of the duty of kindness to our dumb relations, however, is yet needed, and can not be too strongly and frequently enforced.

DR. P. H. VANDER WEYDE:

I had anticipated listening to a lecture of a somewhat different character this evening—to a more strictly scientific discussion of the evolution of animal life. As life develops from its lowest forms, it differentiates into several distinct families or divisions based upon peculiarities of structure. The lowest of these are the radiates, of which the star-fish is a familiar example, their organs and limbs being built up around a central axis as a plant grows. Next we have the articulata, illustrated by many insects and worms, constructed as it were in distinct, articulated sections; and these are followed by the mollusca, or oyster class. I once listened to a lecture by Prof. Agassiz which was devoted to proving that a clam was more intelligent than an oyster. So good an observer could see distinctions not obvious to the common mind. Nature apparently tries to show in how many ways she may exhibit her powers of variation. Above the mollusca, in the order of evolution, we have the vertebrata—first the fishes, then the reptiles and creeping things, followed by the quadrupeds, at last rising erect in man. In the development of the higher organisms the strife of Nature to produce a higher intelligence becomes evident, the brain becoming more and more predominant, until in man, where intelligence reaches its highest point, it is placed on the very apex of the spinal column. According to Agassiz, this indicates the final effort of Nature in the evolution of life; we can go no higher. (Dr. Vander Weyde exhibited and explained a number of diagrams, enlarged from Haeckel's Evolution of Man, showing the remarkable similarity of the chicken, dog, reptile, and man in the earlier stages of fœtal development.) Man, said the speaker, advances through all the stages of the lower animals, and then goes a step beyond them all. In no other animal does the brain occupy relatively so large a place as in man.

Mr. Kimball replied briefly, thanking the audience for its attention and the critics for their aid in the development of the topic under discussion.

FORM AND COLOR IN NATURE

BY

WILLIAM POTTS

AUTHOR OF EVOLUTION OF VEGETAL LIFE, THE SOCIALISTIC METHOD, ETC.

17

COLLATERAL READINGS SUGGESTED:

Darwin's Origin of Species, and Sexual Selection; Wallace's Darwinism; Grant Allen's On the Colors of Flowers, and The Color Sense: Its Origin and Development; Lubbock's Flowers, Fruits, and Leaves; Peckham's Sexual Selection in Spiders; Eimer's Organic Evolution as a Result of the Inheritance of Acquired Characters; Hinton's Life in Nature.

FORM AND COLOR IN NATURE.

BY WILLIAM POTTS.

THE subject seems a very simple one, but when I place it before me and try to orient myself, the simplicity measurably disappears. I am to deal with something which is both subjective and objective, with something which is both cause and effect, with that which is mental and that which is physical. And at the very outset of my exposition I am met with the inquiry, "What is Nature?"

Should I ask you this question, you would probably reply that I am absurd—that I know perfectly well what Nature is; that it includes, for example, all the birds of the air. Very good; is a fantail pigeon, then, a part of Nature? "Certainly," you would probably reply. Then I should say, But a fantail pigeon is simply the result of man's ingenuity in the application of the laws of selection and growth. What is the Sistine Madonna but the result of man's ingenuity in a like application of the laws of chemical and mechanical combination? Is there anything with which you deal which is not a part of Nature? Is there any power which you apply to that with which you deal which does not come from Nature? "Even that art which you say adds to Nature is an art that Nature makes." It seems to me not quite so easy a matter arbitrarily to set aside a certain field and say, "This is Nature," and another and say, "This is not Nature."

I want to emphasize this a little in the interest of *my* monistic philosophy—to enter a protest in advance, as it were. I confess in very real earnest that I should not know where to draw the line; that I should only find myself limited by lack of time and space. I suppose that, in the choice of the subject which has been given me, there was simply embodied an intention to set aside, for future treatment, the arts of painting, sculpture, architecture, etc. I am to speak of such simple matters, for instance, as a flower. Ah! how easy!

> "Flower in the crannied wall,
>   I pluck you out of the crannies—
> Hold you here, root and all, in my hand,
> Little flower—but if I could understand

What you are, root and all, and all in all,
I should know what God and man is."

But to my work.

First, as to the concrete meaning of our other terms. By *form* we mean usually that which occupies space with two dimensions—length and breadth; or with three dimensions—length, breadth, and thickness. Your mathematical professor will talk to you learnedly about the fourth dimension of space, but we, who find it difficult enough at times to fill out our three dimensions, will not envy him his fourth.

I shall use the term to mean that which has length, breadth, and thickness—which has perceptible limitations in all directions.

Anticipating somewhat for the sake of completeness, I will add that we can perceive form in two ways: through vision and through tactual perception or touch.

By *color* we mean a modification of that which we call light, the character of which I should experience difficulty in defining, and of the definition of which I am happily relieved at the moment, as I hope, by your knowledge.

So far as I am aware, we perceive this modification of light solely through vision. Going one step farther back, we apprehend light, and color as a resultant of light, as produced by waves or pulses of exceeding minuteness and great rapidity, in a hypothetical medium called the ether, which is supposed to pervade all space, and therefore to penetrate at least between the particles of so-called solid bodies, if it does not pass through these particles. For I must call your attention to the fact that the deeper we go in the investigation of matters of this character, the more we are thrown back upon hypothesis, and the wider will be found the differences between the theories of different investigators. For example, you will note at the outset two diverse theories of the constitution of what we call matter; one, that it consists of extremely minute particles or atoms, separated from each other, and in constant agitation; the other, that these atoms are themselves simply vortices, or centers of a peculiar motion.

(And perhaps I had better state thus early that this essay must of necessity be an almost inextricable tangle of fact and hypothesis. In many directions we are merely guessing the unknown from the known, and you will doubtless find that I have mingled my own guesses with those of others. I have simply, to the best of my ability, tried to indicate what now seems to me to be true concerning the matters before me.)

These light waves in the ether correspond with the slower sound waves in the air, which we perceive by means of the ear. And as these sound waves differ in length and rapidity, thus producing the effect which we recognize as high and low tones, light waves also differ in length and rapidity, and thus produce the effects which we recognize as the several colors. This can be illustrated by the division of the light ray through the interposition of a prism, thus producing the spectrum.

With this crude explanation of our terms as a foundation, let us try to progress systematically.

We divide matter, possibly somewhat arbitrarily, into two classes, which we call, respectively, the organic and the inorganic. We place at the bottom the inorganic, and raise upon it our ladder of life.

This inorganic matter we subdivide into various classes in various ways: according to its mechanical situation, so to speak, as solid, liquid or gaseous; according to its chemical constitution, as metallic or otherwise—copper, sulphur, oxygen; or, again, according to its composition or supposed origin in a crude sense, as mineral, etc. To inorganic matter in all its forms we attach the relation of color. We perceive such matter by light, either transmitted or reflected. In either case the light has had impressed upon it a certain character which causes in us the sensation of color. If we see a beam of clear light through a translucent substance, such as glass, or a membrane, it either appears clear to us, or we have an impression of color, caused by the fact that certain waves are allowed to pass freely, while others are intercepted. If we look upon an object upon which clear light strikes, it either appears colorless, or we have an impression of color, because certain waves are absorbed, or pass into the object, and others are reflected, or thrown back upon the eye. And according as the surface upon which the light falls is rough, or smooth, or polished, according as it may be crossed by fine lines, or may be delicately laminated, will the color vary. And all conceivable changes may be rung upon the colors which appear.

And so as to form. What form is not to be found in the inorganic world? Omitting the gases and the liquids, the boundaries of which may be roughly considered as formed by the solid bodies against which they flow, in the solid matter alone with which we are familiar the forms are practically infinite. These may be divided primarily into crystalline and non-crystalline. The great body of matter, as we know it, comes within the non-crystalline class, and much of it might be called amorphous.

Thus we have the inorganic world, characterized by form and color in infinite variety, and governed by laws a part of which we know and of much of which we are ignorant. Still trying to view our subject systematically, and looking back into the dim past as far as we can safely speculate, we may imagine a nebulous body of diffused matter, inspired by, led by, animated or endowed with, certain tendencies. I care not what expression you use; I simply care about the thought: of substance, or that which for the sake of convenience we may call substance, characterized by certain tendencies—the various attractive forces, the chemical forces, the vital forces, call them one, call them many—they are all one to me; for at the earliest point at which my mind can have relation to the universe I must assume it to be already possessed of the promise and the potency of all that is to come of it. I do not say that I can understand this; I do not say that it makes speculation easy. As I have stated here before, I can not go back in my thought to a time where I do not touch upon that which to my mind is impossible and inconceivable; nor do I believe that any one else is better off than I.

I am informed that there are those who do understand all these things, and who could have given points had they been called upon for their advice at the proper time. The pity of it is that this appears not to have been thought of, and we are left to mourn our fate as denizens of an imperfect and faulty universe. In the evolution of language certain popular phrases, one after another, appear and disappear, having while they are current a certain expressiveness, tickling, as they do, our jaded fancies. If I might borrow one of these of recent origin, I should say that "I have no use" for the pretended evolutionist, who, standing upon this globe and conscious of the whirling, living universe of which he is a part, feels no sense of an awful power, infinite and incomprehensible, which eye hath not seen nor ear heard, and the nature and attributes of which it hath not entered into the heart of man to conceive. At the only beginning of which I can think, the universe was throbbing with this power. I imagine the nebulous body of which I have spoken revolving, condensing, dividing, as you have heretofore heard described by other lecturers. The first form which emerges is the sphere or globe, one of the "Heavenly bodies," say the Sun, or our Earth.

We may suppose the various chemical constituents acting and reacting upon one another, combining, disintegrating, recombining; affected now by heat, now by electricity, now by gravitation, now by chemical attraction; at one time by these several forces in co-operation, at another in conflict.

Approaching nearer to the present, we find that this earth of ours has taken a definite shape, with an extended solid crust, resting upon an interior in regard to the condition of which we can only speculate, and holding in the depressions upon its surface vast expanses of liquid.

The result of the conflict of the various forces operating through it has been to leave most of it in what may be called an amorphous condition. But while this is so, on the other hand we find on every side the phenomenon of crystallization; we find that as it worked heretofore, it still works in a multitude of ways, but that ever the same substance obeys the same imperious command. And how wondrous, how beautiful is the result! Who has not looked curiously into the treasures of the snow? Many, I fear—but I hope that none who are here are ignorant of them. Examine the fleecy stranger upon your sleeve, and if he has fallen gently he will reveal a marvelous beauty. Look upon your window-pane and see forests of luxuriant palms and ferns, the very tropics in ice. Glance even at the flagstones at your feet, and find the same delicate tracery. Does this insensate matter take this form for any other reason than because—so help it God—it can do no otherwise? And so with the diamond and the chrysolite, and the emerald and the malachite, and hundreds and hundreds of other crystals which you dig from the earth, or which form themselves in the chemist's laboratory, form themselves not as he wills, but as they will. Form and color both are here! Such form and such color!

We stand at the parting of the ways: on the one side "mere dead matter," as people are wont to say; on the other "life." For some inexplicable reason, it is easier for many to understand, or to think that they understand, that which takes place in the inorganic world, than that which takes place in the organic world, but why, I can not comprehend. It is all a mystery. We see an order of events, and in some cases we see that a certain result not only follows, but is produced by, a certain cause. But why? I defy mankind to answer. Anything which happens, anything which ever will happen or could happen, is as simple and as easy as the action of the chemical laws and of the laws of attraction in their most familiar operation. When, therefore, we take the step across the Rubicon which we have reached, we certainly touch that which is remarkable, but that which is no more remarkable than what we have already known. We are upon the very border-land of what we consider the kingdom of life. We consider it so simply because here we begin to find traces of the operation of a tendency which hitherto we have not observed. And in what do we find it? In an albuminous substance which appears in water or other liquid, which we can not recognize as animal or vegetable, and which has no apparent organs or distinction of parts. Huxley, indeed, says that there appears to be no organic substance which we can examine microscopically which does not seem at least to have some distinction between the surface and the interior; but this is all.

Haeckel assumes that the ordinary chemical and attractive forces with whose operations we have in a certain sense become familiar upon the other side of the line are all sufficient to account for the origination of the organic compound, and that simple pressure and condensation complete the process of the formation of the earliest living individuals. It may be so. It is an interesting speculation, but I do not see that it much matters. This could not happen of itself without a *tendency*, whether through the known laws or through the unknown law, any more than a man can lift himself up by the straps of his boots. All that we surely see is an order of development.

The first individuals which we can examine are unicellular, are without distinction of parts so far as we can judge, and are without distinction of function, excepting that the surface incloses the interior. Being composed of the same constituents as inorganic matter, they are subject to the same or similar laws as to exhibition of color.

These cells are driven hither and thither by currents through the liquid in which they float, changing their shape by protrusion of parts, absorbing nourishment and increasing in size, and multiplying in numbers simply by division. Sometimes, however, although divisions are formed, the cells remain attached, and the individual becomes a congeries. Affected by forces upon every side, a differentiation gradually takes place; certain portions of the surface become firmer, others softer; food is taken in at certain particular points, or at one point alone—a division of function has arisen. A distinction has also arisen between the animal and the vegetable, and with this distinction comes a difference in constitution, effecting a distinction in color. The vegetable forms contain an ingredient called chlorophyl which reflects the green rays; the animal tissue reflects the brown and gray. I speak, of course, in general terms.

Before these changes have taken place and while they are proceeding, we notice that sensation has arisen—that is, a response to external impressions. And here let me pause to call attention to the nature of physical impressions, or sensations, as we know them. We speak of our five senses: of sight, of hearing, of touch, of taste, and of smell, not meaning that these terms indicate all the impressions which we perceive, but merely using a traditional expression describing certain obvious classes. All these are the result of different qualities and quantities of motion. Now, it is extremely difficult, perhaps impossible, for us to pass back through the various forms of life and tell with any certainty just when any particular sense had its beginning, or what was the nature of that beginning. We can only perceive these things when they have acquired a certain definiteness and stability. Nevertheless, we can with some degree of clearness trace their development, and can, I think, safely assume that the first of them which was acquired was touch, or that mere susceptibility to impression in general which, in default of a better term, we may entitle touch. I think it is evident also that whatever sensitiveness existed at the outset was equally present in all parts of the individual.

But as the unicellular individual gave rise to the aggregation of such, and as in this aggregation the individuals gradually surrendered their independence and assumed specific functions, in the way of surface protection, of the management of the commissariat—the receipt and disposition of food; as the avoidance of obstacles and the search for sustenance gradually gave definiteness and direction to motion, the sensations of different parts became gradually differentiated. It would be natural—that is, in accordance with experience—to expect that there would be a special concentration of sensibility in that portion which was ordinarily directed forward, where food was received, and where good and evil influences would probably oftenest make themselves felt.

We know nothing of the origin of the sense of taste, but happily it seems least to require an exposition. The sense of sight is connected intimately with our subject, and is indeed of the first importance. Let us see, if we can, what was probably the method of its production.

Doubtless most of you have noticed potato vines which have sprouted in your cellars, or have seen other vines or plants growing in rooms which were dimly lighted from one small window or other aperture. If so, you have probably also noticed their lack of color, and have seen that they were struggling toward the opening. Even these vegetable growths are responsive to the light, and the same fact you have seen evidence of, if you have not noticed it, a thousand times, exhibited in many ways. Do you not place your vase of fringed gentians in the full light of the generous sun, and do they not promptly open their chalices to drink in the welcome flood?

Now, this sensitiveness to the influence of light, in the beginning shared alike by vegetable and animal, becomes greater with the more active organism and greatest in that portion of its surface which is most generally sensitive to all impressions. By the time that there is a certain differentiation of function in the parts there seems to be the initiation of a nervous system with centers of activity and channels of communication. The reaction of the surroundings upon the individual rapidly tend to the perfection of the system. (Of course, in describing all these processes, I am following the development of forms, not giving the history of the changes in a single individual.) Now, hitherto, such color as appears is of the nature of that of which the biologists speak as "adventitious"—that is, resulting from the nature and distribution of the ingredients, without any special relation to function, or to specific causes which materially affect the welfare of the individual.

But investigation seems to show that there appeared a greater degree of sensitiveness to the influence of light in certain otherwise unimportant pigmentary deposits. This greater sensitiveness having once been initiated, its development by natural selection seemed to follow as a matter of course. The motion of the light-waves impinging upon the surface and thus affecting and exciting the nerves, resulted by wholesome stimulation in increasing their sensitiveness. So gradually arose a condition which enabled the individual to perceive an object before it, perhaps, as one biologist says, about as we perceive our hand when it is passed between our closed eyes and the light. Such an amount of vision, although seemingly of slight importance, was, we may infer, sufficient foundation for the structural changes which have followed, resulting in the formation of the eye and connecting visual organs, as we know them in the higher animals.

Please note that it is not the eye—it is the brain which sees. The eye, with its connections, its lens and coats and nerves, its rods and cones (which I am sure you would not thank me to attempt to analyze and describe), is a highly developed mechanism, although, says Helmholtz, very imperfect, whose function is to convey the motions of the ether to the brain, which must interpret them.

I apprehend that anybody who has not wholly forgotten his skating days can remember times when he has seen a great light "which never was on sea or land," and which was not at all dependent upon the ordinary action of his visual organs. This light was clearly traceable to motion, but to motion anything but ethereal in its character. I will say nothing of many spectacles which we have all of us seen with our eyes closed, both while awake and in "the visions of the night when deep sleep falleth upon men," since these involve other questions.

How far the senses of smell and hearing may have been developed before organic life passed from the water into the air I am not aware that any one has attempted to investigate, or even to state in the form of speculation. They are foreign to the field allotted to me, and I will only note incidentally one or two points. Sound is a mental impression resulting from wave motion in the air, as light and color are mental impressions resulting from wave motions in the ether. An odor is a mental impression which appears to result from motion produced by fine material particles which impinge upon the proper organ, as taste is a mental impression which appears to result from motion produced by a material substance applied to the palate.

But sound may be perceived without the intervention of the ear, through which it is ordinarily conveyed, as taste and smell may be perceived without the direct excitation of those primary membranes which are their usual agencies.

There is every reason to believe that these senses also were gradually developed through the reaction of the individual to the environment, as has been described in the case of the sense of sight.

You will hardly expect me to go through all the arguments for the credibility of the development theory. This straw has already been threshed over among us many times, and the belief in the theory is now so universal among scientific men that it seems as useless to enter into argument upon it as to attempt to wrestle with Brother Jasper. That there are many differences in the manner in which this theory is accepted among scientific men is most true. Cope is opposed to Wallace, and Eimer to Weissman; the strict Darwinian out-Darwins Darwin, and some of the neo-Lamarckians hark back of them all. And as to pretty nearly all alike, we sometimes feel that in their arguments it is "heads, I win; tails, you lose," so ready are they to account for apparent exceptions to their rules. It is somewhat as in the management of the restless child—after trying in vain to keep it in its place they say: "Then get up and run about, for I *will* be minded."

Sometimes it seems to us that their difficulty consists in being too near to the subjects of their investigation; they are like our venerated friend Yankee Doodle, of whom it is said, as you will remember, that "he could not see the town for so many houses."

For myself, as a sympathetic pupil and not an original investigator, I may say that, after a pretty wide survey of the field and of the evidence adduced, my leaning is toward the later Darwin and, measurably, the neo-Lamarckians.

As you are doubtless aware, the main contention is around the question whether natural selection has been practically the sole agent in the modification of species, or whether some considerable credit is also to be given to use and disuse and to inheritance. There is also a struggle over the question whether there is an inherent tendency to vary in a certain direction.

Lamarck's principal cause for the development of species was functional activity and habit, acquired in adaptation to environment and fixed by inheritance. Darwin realized and pictured the intensity of the struggle for existence which inevitably results from the immense productivity of animal and vegetable life, showed in great detail the amount of variation which is constantly occurring, and therefrom conclusively proved the inevitableness of natural selection and the survival of the fittest as an important controlling factor in the development of species. He never, however, contended that this was the sole factor, and, with the freedom from bias which always characterized him, during his later years he was disposed to grant more importance to use and to sexual selection than he had formerly been ready to allow. Wallace, his co-discoverer of the principle of natural selection, has not been disposed to accompany him in his later conclusions, and in his "Darwinism," printed last year, he reiterates and argues at great length for his thesis that natural selection has been the principal, and practically the sole, cause of development. I think, however, that it is impossible to read his work without being impressed with the strength of his bias, and to me the alteration of his attitude when he comes to treat of mental phenomena and of man is almost ludicrous. I can not think of it as otherwise than strikingly inconsistent.

Those of you who heard Prof. Cope's lecture in this place a few months ago will remember into what detail he entered in confutation of Mr. Wallace. Mr. Cope is perhaps disposed to go further even than Darwin in the direction of Lamarck. Herr Eimer also is a neo-Lamarckian, laying great stress upon the effect of use and habit and upon the inheritance of acquired characters. He has done a most useful work in the accumulation of evidence upon the latter point, and among this evidence there is not a little of seeming incontrovertibility touching the inheritance even of physical mutilations, such as the loss of a finger or a scar upon some particular part of the person, as well as of a tendency to certain diseases.

Eimer contends that there is a principle of growth or development in organic nature which corresponds with the inorganic tendency to a certain form of crystallization, and that natural selection acts upon the variations thus produced and sifts out those which are to endure. I can not discover anything so heinous in this theory; on the contrary, it seems to me most consonant with that which we see in other fields, of an all-controlling law or living presence, a persisting force which produces results through an intricate system of checks and balances.

Herr Weissman, on the contrary, whom Wallace quotes

with approval, believes in natural selection and pammixis, or the combination by marriage of varying types alone, as the causes of the origin of species, and wholly repudiates the inheritability of acquired characters. He develops a peculiar theory of the continuity of the germ-plasm—that a portion of the original germ itself and not a new germ passes from individual to individual in the line of descent, and that modification comes alone through the crossing of varieties in the germ. That this is an absolutely unproved, if not an absolutely unprovable, hypothesis is perhaps its weakest feature. Possibly the best sentences in Mr. James Hinton's curious, interesting, and very disappointing book, Life in Nature, are these: "Let it be assumed, for argument's sake, that all the phenomena of life could be traced back to chemical and mechanical powers, what would follow? Simply that all the wonder and admiration with which we now regard the living body would be extended with increased intensity and elevation to those powers which we call chemistry or mechanics, but which we would then perceive we had entirely underestimated." Whatever differences there may be in regard to more or less, I suppose that most of our men of science of good standing are agreed that the struggle for existence, variation in individuals from whatever cause, natural selection, and the survival of the fittest, are stages of the most important process in the development of species. Variation in minor particulars is shown to be of the widest occurrence. Those variations which prove useful in any way tend so far to give the individuals in which they occur an advantage over others, and so enable them to leave posterity; and a repetition of the same variations, accompanied by similar advantages, tends toward permanency and toward an increase of the acquired peculiarities.

If I should now attempt to do badly what was so magnificently done last winter by Mr. Kimball in relation to an important branch of the development of form, I certainly should not thereby establish a reputation for wisdom. If there be any present who failed to hear Mr. Kimball's fascinating essay upon The Evolution of Arms and Armor—the finest piece of work which has ever been done in this field—I should advise him or her to lose no time in reading it. Its burden is the burden of war: how the struggle for existence led to attack and defense, and these to alterations in structure for the one purpose or the other, each keeping pace with each, as the rifled cannon and the dynamite gun with the ironclad. This was done by him in so masterly a manner that I will pass on to other phases of the matter.

The wealth of materials which has been gathered in illustration of the various branches of our subject is such that one is at a loss to select from it. Perhaps I can not do better than to take up the development of flowers and fruits and their relation to insects and birds. In this field Mr. Darwin, Mr. Grant Allen, and Sir John Lubbock have all been industrious workers.

Broadly speaking, the order of the changes in the method of reproduction in organisms has been as follows: First, through mere multiplication by fission or division; then through the conjunction and blending of apparently similar individuals; then through the combined action of certain specialized organs in the individual; and, finally, through the co-operation of distinct and different individualities. There have been and are some cases which must be considered more complex than the foregoing statement implies, but for the present this is sufficient for our purpose. All these methods are still in use and their operation may in a measure be followed. Now, as organization has become more complex, investigation seems to show that vigor has resulted from cross-fertilization even where both elements were to be found in the same individual. This conclusion and the circumstances connected with it can best be traced in the vegetable world, where the various processes are to a degree open to inspection.

Making a long stride over the less elaborate forms, where the causes of change have been more obscure, and taking up the phanerogams or true flowering plants, we are at once met with a question as to the origin of the primitive flower. It is commonly held by botanists that all the parts of a flower of the more familiar kind—the sepals, the petals, the stamens, and pistils—are simply modified leaves. The original flower was undoubtedly a very simple affair compared with that which we now see, and we may liken it to a bud, which consists of an unfolded cluster of leaves. Still more bud-like is something which is found on the common violet. This blossoms profusely, but ordinary flowers in certain species produce but few seeds. There is upon the same plant, however, another class of flowers called cleistogamic, which do not open, but nevertheless produce seeds, and these are occasionally found below the surface of the soil. Some other plants produce seeds under ground without opening flowers. A most curious case of quite a different character is the common ground-nut or peanut, dear to the gallery gods, which forms a yellow flower in the axil of the leaf, and the stigma, then lengthening into a tendril-like form, buries itself in the ground and develops the fruit at its extremity. A bud which never becomes a flower is the bulblet which forms itself in the axil of the leaf of the tiger-lily and then becomes detached, ready to produce a new plant.

The ordinary color of vegetables is green, with more or less tendency toward yellow, though many plants sometimes show red or some other color at certain points. In the ordinary processes of vegetation carbon is absorbed and oxygen is given out. When for any cause this process is reversed, it is held by some authorities to be proved that there is a tendency to the production of other colors. Such is the condition in the process of flowering and fruiting.

The original flower was probably minute, and consisted of the representatives of the male and female elements alone. Instances of this kind are now to be found. The first variation of color was probably to yellow. Supposing that vigor was the result of cross-fertilization, those plants which varied so as to make cross-fertilization probable were most likely to gain a strong foothold. The earliest method of cross-fertilization seems to have been by means of the wind, and so we find a large class of plants, many of them with greenish or yellowish blossoms, individually inconspicuous, but frequently collected in numbers in aments or catkins, the anthers hanging loosely and scattering a shower of pollen on the air. The risk of loss by this process is so great that a prodigious waste must be suffered in order to insure success in effecting the object. The crowded grasses are of this class, but there are also many large trees which bear their blossoms high in the air where the wind may have free access to them, and these frequently tint the ground around them with their pollen. This, however, is a very expensive way of providing for fertilization. An animate helper with a brain, or its equivalent, is more economical than the inanimate wind, and so it happens that the insect world was brought into relation of interdependence with the vegetable world, to the wonderful transformation of both. In all probability the beginning of this process was of the simplest character. Some one plant, or some hundred or some thousand plants, exuded a drop of sweet sap about the imperfect blossom, and wandering ants, or bees, or butterflies happened upon it, and found it good. Having emptied one, the most natural thing in the world was to try another. The pollen accidentally caught upon the head or the wings was carried along, and cross-fertilization was effected. Time will not permit us to follow all the steps, necessarily hypothetical, though substantially evident. It is sufficient to point out that the plants which were thus aided would be likely to perpetuate their race and to develop their peculiarities; that the insects which were benefited were likely to acquire the habit of visiting the flowers which had proved valuable to them; that those flowers, in turn, which most quickly and certainly attracted the attention of their useful guests would be those which would most profit by their visits. Thus there does not seem to remain a shadow of a doubt that by reciprocal action on the part of the insects and the flowers the showy petals and their varied colors were produced. At first the petals were inconspicuous or absent. When they appeared they were separate. As the development proceeded they began to coalesce, and this tendency became greater and greater, until in some instances the individual petals totally disappeared, or left mere traces, as in the tubular flowers. At the same time regularity of form gave place to irregularity in many instances, and this coincided with insect changes. As the tube of the flower lengthened, the proboscis of the insect lengthened likewise, and certain flowers became the feeding places of special insects, upon which they wholly depended for fertilization. In some instances the most elaborate arrangements have been evolved to prevent self-fertilization and to insure fertilization by the special insects upon which the flower relies. The number of flowers of which this is true is enormous, and these among the most common, as well as among the most rare. A special study was made by Darwin of the orchids, the arrangements in which family are of the most curious and elaborate description.

You will readily see that it is impossible for me to enter upon detailed descriptions of these cases, of which the books are full, and which any of you can observe for himself. And no description can be needed to show you the nature of the process. Take, for instance, the matter of color in the blossom. We know that at this moment most flowers tend to vary more or less in color or tint. Such tendency doubtless always existed. Suppose that at some time a variation in color occurred simultaneously with an increased secretion of honey, as we call it, an occurrence which we may assume would inevitably take place. This variation would tend to be perpetuated and to increase, because it would be as a signal held out for assistance, to secure extension and propagation. So in regard to increase in size on the part of the flowers, or other changes to meet the necessities of the situation, and make sure the perpetuation of the race. At the same time adaptation to the surroundings must have continued in other directions, and forms and habits must have been varied accordingly.

Now, these modifications of color would have been of no possible advantage in the direction which I have indicated unless the insects could recognize them. It therefore follows that as the colors were developed, by reaction the color sense was developed and increased in the insects. Some naturalists have seemed to doubt whether any real color sense or enjoyment of color exists on the part of insects. After the investigations which have been made during late years, however, there is no longer any possible room for doubt as to the existence of the sense, at least. Among other experiments, those made in regard to the color sense in wasps, by Mr. and Mrs. Peckham, of Milwaukee, were extremely painstaking and elaborate, and should certainly set this question at rest forever. As to the matter of enjoyment of color, that is, of course, a far more difficult question to answer. Grant Allen's theory is, that the exercise of the color sense, developed in the manner which I have indicated, became a natural function, and that all natural functions in their normal exercise are pleasurable. He assumes, therefore, that it is not extravagant to believe that, even in organisms of no higher stage than this, an actual taste for or enjoyment of color may have arisen, and that this may have had a not unimportant effect upon the color of the insects themselves through sexual selection, a subject in regard to which I shall have more to say in a few moments.

So much, or so little, for the flowers and the insects; the fruits and the birds seem to have had a somewhat similar relation. But the fruits have sought to secure their distribution in many other ways besides. Technically, the fruit is the seed vessel with the seeds. Primarily, it was probably very minute and simple, and the seeds when ripe fell directly to the ground and quickly germinated. But as space became crowded, no field was left for the new-comers; not even standing room was to be had, and any variation which made dispersion probable tended to perpetuate itself. Thus many seeds gradually developed plumes or membranous wings, and so, borne on the wind, were carried to "fresh woods and pastures new." Others developed curious spines or hooks or viscid exudations, by which they caught in the hair or wool of animals, and were carried away. Others again accumulated edible substance, by which birds or mammals might be lured, and many of these, to draw attention to them among the surrounding leaves, put on contrasting colors of yellow, or red, or purple, or blue—an enormous variety. And all sorts of devices were used to make the fruits attractive. Sometimes, as in the apple, it was the calyx which gathered nourishment, increased and softened and enveloped the seeds which were inclosed within a scaly sack; sometimes, as in the fig, a large number of blossoms and seed-vessels were inclosed within a common receptacle, which likewise developed. Sometimes, as in the raspberry, a multitude of seeds, each surrounded by its own fleshy pulp, were clustered upon the receptacle. Again, as in the strawberry, the receptacle itself became fleshy and bore the seeds in depressions upon the surface—the fig, as it were, turned inside out. And to protect the seeds from destruction by the animals which swallowed them, they were often very minute, and were usually covered with a hard, scaly shell. Then again, as in the peach, the seed has become large, but the shell is of great density and difficult to break. Then, as in many of the nuts, the kernel is first protected by a hard shell, and this in turn is covered with a bitter rind. In the case of the cocoanut, the tree bears its fruit far away from all enemies excepting the monkeys, at the summit of a tall, slender stem, and then protects it with a hard shell, and covers this again with a thick fibrous matting, which prevents it from splitting when it falls to the ground. You can readily see how minute variations in all these directions, by providing increased protection to the seeds, and therefore insuring germination, would tend to increase, and become more and more distinct and peculiar.

The birds have had most to do with the smaller fruits, the berries, etc., and mammals with the larger ones.

Fruits of many kinds have tended to accumulate sugar and other nutritious substances, sometimes in the seed itself, often in its protective covering, and this of course has been usually the attraction. A large share of our own diet, and of that of other animals, is of such a nature. It has only been made possible for man to continue to find nourishment of this character through the care which he has himself taken to insure the supply, by special cultivation of such crops as wheat, etc. In the case of the nuts, which have been in the special charge of the squirrels and their like, it is supposed that the trees have found their profit through the squirrel's habit of burying nuts for future reference, and then frequently forgetting their hiding place.

It was believed by Darwin, who supported his opinion by a vast amount of evidence, that a great part of the variety of color found in the animal kingdom, and no insignificant portion of the variety in form, were due to sexual selection —that is, to the accumulation of minute variations in these particulars, through the exercise of a certain degree of choice in mating, on the part of the sexes. This hypothesis has been supported by Grant Allen, Mr. Poulton, Prof. Peckham, and others, and very vigorously opposed by Alfred Russel Wallace, although, as it seems to me, in a somewhat halting fashion, and with concessions which seriously damage his argument.

Mr. Darwin's investigations seem to show the exercise of a certain choice on the part of the female as to her mate, even as low down in the scale of development as the fishes, and in more stylish circles a noteworthy amount of fastidiousness is exhibited, often, it is claimed, accompanied by a careful consideration of personal appearance. Mr. Wallace doubts if the female in the lower ranks of animal life has any æsthetic preferences, but, if she has not, it would seem that there is a sad waste of time in the preliminaries of courtship upon the part of the males. The details which have been recorded by different observers are in many cases extremely curious, and seem very significant. It is true that in some contests Mars has been the victor rather than Apollo or Adonis, and from jousts upon the field of war between ambitious suitors have doubtless been derived, in part at least, the horns of the deer, the ox, and other animals, the mane of the lion, and other features. But a vast part of the decoration of birds and beasts—consisting mainly in the arrangement or coloration of the feathers and hair, or in curious and apparently useless excrescences, and in most instances much more striking in the male than in the female—seems to be fairly accounted for as an accumulation of minute differences which have found favor in the eyes of the softer sex. Even in the human race it is said that personal appearance is not wholly unconsidered at the mating season.

It is Darwin's theory that when peculiarities arise late in life they are more apt to be transmitted only to the sex in which they first occur. It is well known that many peculiarities which pass from sire to son appear at a similar age in each. When the male and female differ greatly, it is usually the male which departs most widely from the type of the family to which he belongs; he is the most brilliantly colored, and this peculiarity frequently is not greatly marked until about the period of maturity. I wish it were possible for me to give a fair statement of the evidence which has been accumulated upon this point, but I must confine myself to a very few cases. It is plain that in innumerable species the male exhibits himself very elaborately to the female before he finds favor in her eyes, and postures like a veritable coxcomb. Of the more curious cases among birds, the most frequently noted is that of the bower-birds of Australia. These, of which there are three species, build an elaborate bower upon the ground, or sometimes raised upon a platform of sticks. Their nests are formed in the trees. The bowers are places of assembly for the sole purpose of courtship. Both sexes assist in the erection, but the male is the principal workman. In the fawn-breasted species the bower is nearly four feet in length and eighteen inches in height. "Each species decorates its bower in a different manner. The satin bower-bird collects bright-colored feathers, bleached bones, and shells; 'these objects are continually rearranged, and carried around by the birds while at play.' The spotted bower-bird lines its bower with tall grasses, kept in place by round stones, which are brought from great distances, together with shells. The regent bird makes use of bleached shells, blue, red, and black berries, fresh leaves, and pink shoots, the whole showing a decided taste for the beautiful!"

Among other birds, "the males sometimes pay their court by dancing, or by fantastic antics performed either on the ground or in the air." The capercailzie and blackcock, which are both polygamists, have regular appointed places, where during many weeks they congregate in numbers to fight together and to display their charms before the females. "The elder Brehm gives a curious account of the Balz, as the love dances and love songs of the blackcock are called in Germany. The bird utters almost continuously the strangest noises; he holds his tail up and spreads it out like a fan, he lifts up his head and neck with all the feathers erect, and stretches his wings from the body. Then he takes a few jumps in different directions, sometimes in a circle, and presses the under part of his beak so hard against the ground that the chin feathers are rubbed off. During these movements he beats his wings and turns round and round. The more ardent he grows the more lively he becomes, until at last the bird appears like a frantic creature."

The modes of courtship among spiders as described by Prof. Peckham are very varied and very curious. The males engage in fantastic dances and posturings, exhibiting their peculiarities of coloring or form in the most elaborate ways, and sometimes many hours or even days are consumed in these performances. The females seem attentive observers of these antics, and it is hardly possible to understand them excepting as efforts to excite a personal interest through some impression upon the sense of sight, which would appear to involve an appreciation in some sort of color and form. These efforts are usually successful, but not always. In many species the female is much larger and more powerful than the male, and sometimes while he is absorbed in his efforts to please she will adroitly pounce upon him, and then gently dismember and devour him. I am well aware that "evil communications corrupt good manners," and I mention this habit with hesitation. I beg to assure the young ladies before me that I do not indorse it, and should greatly regret that any word of mine incautiously spoken should lead to its general adoption.

It is perhaps not too much to say that there is strong probability in the theory that great modifications, both in color and in form, may have resulted from sexual selection following or accompanying a decided development in the color sense. But of perhaps equal importance (Wallace says of controlling importance) are mimicry and protective resemblance.

Of course these are only phases of ordinary natural selection. They are found widely prevalent throughout animated nature, and present some of the most marvelous instances of elaborate adaptation which are to be found.

It may perhaps be fairly assumed that butterflies and

many other insects originally acquired brilliant colors, more or less resembling those of the flowers which they chiefly visited, as a protection from the birds by which they were sought. And as one part of the evidence in this case it is noteworthy that certain butterflies which have acquired a nauseous taste, and are therefore not sought after, are very marked in their coloring, and make no effort to conceal themselves. And as an instance of protective mimicry it is to be added that the females of certain other species have sought or found protection by closely imitating the marking of these, which differs greatly from the type to which they belong. This is a form of mimicry of which there are many instances. Then there is the imitation of vegetable colors and forms in many inhabitants of trees and smaller plants, in caterpillars and in larger creatures as well—imitations so close that even the eye of a practiced naturalist is sometimes deceived. And the colors frequently change according to the season. But, most marvelous of all, numerous careful experiments made upon larvæ by Mr. Poulton and others have shown that their color can actually be altered from day to day by changing the colors surrounding them. These changes occur in the individual creature experimented upon, and therefore differ from the cases of color acquired through development, with which mainly I have been dealing. Their method of production is one of the many items in the study of natural history which require a vast deal more investigation than they have yet had.

The case of the chameleon is a peculiar one. This lizard has long been a synonym for variability in color, and it is only within a few years that it has been discovered that it has two or more sets of pigment cells, so placed that they can be projected in turn and at different angles to the light, and that it is by the use of these that it can totally change its appearance at will.

In mammalia the colors are generally more subdued than they are in the case of birds and insects, and there is some doubt whether their sense of color is quite so strong. The color is frequently protective, as shown, for instance, in the brown or tawny tints of those animals which live upon sandy deserts, the tendency to stripes found among those living among reeds, etc. These general characteristics are modified in individual cases, as they are among nearly all species in all families, by what are called recognition markings, which are supposed to have been acquired or retained for the purpose of keeping up family intercourse between near relatives or friends.

I have said but little of the development of organic form excepting incidentally. To do even scant justice to this side of the subject one should have at least an evening. But Mr. Kimball's lecture to which I have referred you treats one part of this question, and, beyond what I have already said, I can only call your attention generally to a few points.

Upon the earth there are four fields in which organic functions may be exercised—in the liquids, in the solids, on the surface of the earth, and in the air. Organic life seems to have originated in the liquids, where, in the beginning, substances having the same specific gravity were borne about freely by mechanical causes, and thus brought into contact with the ingredients which they required for nourishment. What has been already said, coupled with the exercise of a little imagination, will lead you to see the natural sequences of modification in this earliest medium, under the influence of natural selection. The manner of production of organs for locomotion and for grasping prey as well as for perceiving it, together with the simultaneous specialization of function in the internal organization, do not call for any unusual exercise of the powers of comprehension so far as we can comprehend them at all. Nor does it seem difficult to trace the steps by which some forms were induced to attach themselves to the rocks and so live a stationary life, and by which others living close to the shore, and from time to time left bare by the tide or the drying up of shallow waters, should have become accustomed to a terrestrial life. That some should remain amphibious, and that some, both animal and vegetable, wandering inland, should become wholly acclimated there, being modified to conform to altered circumstances, we can realize. Bearing in mind the extreme minuteness of the individual changes, and the enormous period of time during which they have occurred, there seems little required of our imagination excepting that which is in tolerably close accord with our ordinary experience. Even when we contrast the worms and other inhabitants of the soil, or of living or dead organic matter with mammalia, both terrestrial and aërial—such as the bats, flying squirrels, and lemurs, or the reptiles and their glorified descendants the birds, or the insects—we are no longer greatly troubled by their differences.

As for the vegetable kingdom, little more needs to be said than has already been stated. The geological record and the world before us show a systematic development of certain forms from the simple to the complex, the origin, growth, culmination, and decline of races, in accordance with the conditions to which they were at the period exposed. A certain degree of sensation in the vegetable kingdom is beyond question, but sense-perception therein we can hardly believe to exist. Sensibility to touch and sensibility to light can not be doubted; but there is no evidence indicating anything in the nature of sight, and we can not therefore predicate any reflex action in the acquirement of color from this source.

I do not intend to poach upon the territory of the lecturer upon painting, but it is clearly within my province to touch at least upon the material which the painter has to handle, and to allude to its reaction upon the human being. I have not a shadow of a doubt that the same omnipresent, unfaltering, and irresistible power — that power which is to any force that we can define, as a universe to an atom—which is responsible for the development which we see throughout the whole of nature outside of the human race, is responsible for the development of that race itself. I can not conceive of two conflicting primary powers in the universe; two Kings of Brentford sitting on one throne.

It seems to me that while it is quite possible that any one of the senses may be developed to a higher degree in some of the lower animals—as, for instance, the sense of smell in dogs, the sense, whatever it may be, which enables carrier pigeons to reach their homes in a few hours after they have been carried several hundred miles in a closed basket —there can be no doubt that all the senses combined have so far found their highest development in man. Yet in man we find this development must be characterized by degrees, and in some it has been checked at an early stage. Sometimes this is simply temporary and accidental, sometimes it appears to be functional. It is well known what a wide range of capacity exists in relation to the appreciation of sound. So in a measure in relation to form, much more in relation to color. We all know those who can not discriminate between certain colors which to us have the widest distinction. In some instances the power of perception in these could doubtless be educated. In others there seems a numbness of nerve which must forever stand in the way of a response to certain characteristic vibrations. But in the race as a whole, through inheritance of that which had been acquired by earlier types, through use and constant reaction to the multitude of impressions from surrounding objects, there has been developed an acute perception and enjoyment of color and form, and there has been formulated within us a sense of beauty, including grace and fitness, which has acquired the power of that which we call an instinct.

The lines of the mountains and the valleys, the forms of trees and plants and every object which opposes our view, the motion of the sea or of waving grain, the gradations of the distance, the colors upon the softly rounded cheek, upon flowers and fruits and birds, and in the evanescent glory of the sunset, appeal through the sense to the heart of man, and find their heaven in his spiritual nature. Stimulated by their influences as by all that come to him from the wondrous universe in which he is placed, palpitating in every part with that fresh new life which is the life of ages, should he not aspire to something more than is now visible to him? Should he not compel a future for his race upon this earth worthy of the past which has nurtured him?

"Can rules or tutors educate
The Semi-God whom we await?
He must be musical,
Tremulous, impressional,
Alive to gentle influence
Of landscape and of sky,
And tender to the spirit-touch
Of man's or maiden's eye:
But, to his native center fast,
Shall into future fuse the past,
And the world's flowing fates in his own mould recast."

ABSTRACT OF THE DISCUSSION.

DR. ROBERT G. ECCLES:

The lecturer of the evening has given us an admirable statement, in the main, of some of the ways in which form and color in Nature have been evolved. He has also touched briefly upon the psychological principles involved in this process, in so far as it is related to the animal world. The result of my own studies in this field has been that I have broken with the idea broached by the lecturer, that the sensation of feeling was the primary sensation developed in conscious organisms. To my mind it would appear that taste would naturally precede feeling, since the earliest activities of sentient creatures are devoted mainly to the search for and appropriation of nourishment. Even in the most primitive micro-organisms we observe a capacity for distinguishing between that which is suitable for their food and that which is not. The lecturer has well shown that the various parts of Nature are so dovetailed together that the insect could not be what it is without the flower, and *vice versa*. In illustration of this fact we have the statement that when Mr. Alfred Russel Wallace was on board a ship off the coast of Madagascar, a theretofore unknown insect was brought to him, which he carefully examined, and then proceeded to sketch a flower which at that time had not been seen by any white man, but which he declared must be somewhere on the island, as this insect was peculiarly adapted for fertilizing such a flower. The correctness of Mr. Wallace's views was afterward proved by the discovery of a plant such as he described. I believe that an exact relation, which may be termed mechanical, exists throughout the universe, so that if we were sufficiently intelligent, and could view all the forces operating in the world from the nebula up, we could predict the existence of form and color in Nature exactly as we now perceive them.

DR. LEWIS G. JANES:

I think we must all agree that Mr. Potts has given us a suggestive and admirable paper upon the topic of the evening. I was particularly pleased with his clear statement of the grounds for a belief in a Power transcending our modes of sense-perception. In regard to our "five senses," as they are ordinarily enumerated, I think, while they represent certain of the more obvious distinctions in our modes of contact with the external world, it is a mistake to assume a too rigid limitation and differentiation of their activities. Modern physiology shows that the sense of touch, for example, is not a uniform thing iu all parts of the body—that certain superficial areas respond more promptly to sensations of heat, others to cold, others to titillations, etc. The divisions between the senses are, perhaps, not so rigid as we are disposed to think. It is possible that the sense of muscular contractility—that sense by means of which we are enabled to judge of weight and resistance—should be differentiated from the ordinary tactile sense. As to what constituted the primitive mode of sense-activity I should, perhaps, not agree wholly with either the lecturer or Dr. Eccles. I can not think that the developed sense of touch, as we understand it, existed in primitive organisms, or a distinct sense of taste, either. The mode of perception of such organisms may, perhaps, be best regarded as a vague, undifferentiated sense of feeling, which combined the germinal forms of both taste and touch—indeed, of all the special senses. Binet regards sight as the earliest of the special senses to be evolved. If this is the fact, it is somewhat remarkable that it is still in some respects the most undeveloped and defective. As to the order of their development, there seems to me to be a wide range for speculation and hypothesis. It may be more correct to regard their evolution as in a large degree simultaneous.

Mr. Potts, in reply, said that in the matter of the senses he had used the term "sense of touch" as being the term of the simplest character, intended to convey the idea of a general sensibility to impressions which seemed to him nearer to our sense of touch than to anything else. He did not intend to imply that the lowest organisms possessed a developed tactile sense, such as the higher mammals now exhibit, however. His paper had taken a form quite different from that which he originally had in mind, and he was glad if it had proved interesting and provocative of thought.

OPTICS AS RELATED TO EVOLUTION

BY

L. A. W. ALLEMAN, M. A., M. D.

COLLATERAL READINGS SUGGESTED:

Tyndall's Lectures on Light, and Light and Electricity; Stokes's Burnett Lectures on Light; Articles *Light* and *Optics* in Encyclopædia Britannica and American Cyclopædia; Whewell's History of the Inductive Sciences; Lommel's The Nature of Light; Thomas's Revised Theory of Light; Brewster's Optics; Bailey's Paradoxes of Vision; Leibnitz's Letters on Light.

THE EVOLUTION OF OPTICS.

By L. A. W. Alleman, M. A., M. D.

The first great landmark that the student of the history of optics encounters is the name of Sir Isaac Newton. Up to his time this science had made a slow and halting progress. The meager knowledge of the ancients—which consisted in the observed facts of the rectilinear propagation of light, reflection, and refraction—had been greatly supplemented by the labors of Alhazan, an Arabian philosopher, who lived about 1200 A. D. He wrote a valuable text-book on optics, and by an anatomical demonstration proved the absurdity of the popular theory of vision—viz., that a visual ray was shot out from the eye to grasp the picture of external objects.*

After Alhazan follows a long period of inactivity. Then came Roger Bacon, Vitellio, and Kepler, each contributing his share to the fund of knowledge, out of which Newton was to elaborate a science of optics.

In 1625 Willebrod Snell enunciated the law governing refraction, which Tyndall terms the "corner-stone of optics," and which connected together all the measurements relative to refraction executed up to his time. This law was "that at any angle of incidence the ratio of the sines of the angles of incidence and of refraction is constant for the same two media, but varies with different media."

A new life was now infused into the work, and a master mind appears capable of using to best advantage the material collected ready to his hand. The figure of Newton rises like a massive peak, supported and sustained, as says Tyndall, by the high table-land of knowledge which had already been attained.

We can not here attempt even a brief review of the labors of Newton, inviting as is the subject. It is a chapter filled with interest, alike to the student of optics and of human progress. It teaches the wonderful possibilities of

* It is an interesting fact that no one before the time of Aristotle seems to have had the practical sagacity to ask why, if this theory be true, we could not see in the dark.

one human mind; its wide-reaching influence, the heritage of intellectual wealth which one man may bequeath to all who come after him. The failures, too, are as instructive as the greatest triumphs. What more eloquent protest against the domination of authority in scientific inquiry could be found than is contained in this chapter of the history of optics? The weight of Newton's authority served to uphold almost to our own day the corpuscular theory of light. It blocked paths of investigation which led to very treasure-houses of discovery. His masterful intellect impressed with equal force error and truth.

Newton's great contribution to the science of optics was his demonstration of the composite nature of light. He showed white light to be a mixture of different kinds of light of varying refrangibility; he made his demonstration conclusive by analyzing and then recombining the constituents. To explain the phenomena of light, Newton constructed the emission theory. Conceiving light to consist of small particles shot out from luminous bodies, he explained the phenomena of reflection by elastic collision, and refraction by an attractive force similar to that of gravitation.

This theory Newton developed with great ingenuity, and by it many of the phenomena of light were seemingly explained; where it fell short, Newton supported it with a weight of argument which for a time successfully bore down all opposition. But new discoveries were constantly adding difficulties to the acceptance of this theory. In 1676 Römer had proved, from observations of the eclipses of Jupiter's satellites, that light traveled with the velocity of some one hundred and ninety thousand miles a second. Now, it was very difficult to conceive that matter, however minute, traveling with this enormous velocity, could be received without injury upon the delicate tissues of the retina. A rival theory of light, destined in time to supplant the emission theory, had already been proposed. In 1664 Hooke had suggested, as a happy guess, the proposition that light might consist of undulations in a homogeneous medium, and a little later Huygens had developed this theory in a very masterly manner, and showed that it offered a much more rational explanation of light than did the emission theory; he investigated the phenomena of double refraction, first observed by Bartholinus in 1669, and showed that this could be explained by the wave-theory. In fact, Huygens seems to have possessed a very accurate conception of the nature of light, and in his hands the wave-theory fell but little short of that positive demonstration which it was destined to receive years after from Young and Fresnel.

Newton urged against the wave-theory that, were it true, light should bend round opposing obstacles, as do the waves of sound, and this objection Young for the first time satisfactorily answered.

From a careful study of the phenomena of sound, he was led to a comprehension of the phenomenon of the interference of light-waves. He showed that such a bending of the waves as Newton had suggested *did* take place, but that the light was destroyed by the mutual interference of the waves. He showed that light added to light under certain circumstances could produce darkness, just as sound added to sound may produce silence.

There is, perhaps, no man of equal merit so little known and appreciated as Dr. Thomas Young, whose name is so intimately associated with the development of the undulatory theory of light. In Music, Art, Literature, and Science he was illustrious. The unraveling of the puzzle of the Egyptian hieroglyphics was an achievement upon which any man might have rested his claim to distinction, yet this was but one of Young's interests.

The wave-theory of light has proved a key for the unlocking of Nature's language. It has done for the science of optics what Young's reading of the Rosetti stone did for the meaningless hieroglyphics; it has made all the phenomena of light intelligible; it has reduced a jumble of curious facts to an eloquent demonstration of scientific truth. Yet Young was scarcely known to his contemporaries. It was sufficient to say, "Who is this man that pretends to be greater than Newton?" and the upstart and his work became objects of popular contempt. But the theory could not be thus snuffed out, although Young might be temporarily deprived of his due share of credit.

About this time Fresnel, a young French engineer, was pursuing investigations which led to similar results. He likewise demonstrated the truth of the wave-theory, and to him is usually assigned the honor of its discovery, but, be it said to his credit, he fully acknowledged Young's claim to priority.

The labors of Young and of Fresnel served to establish the wave-theory of light, than which few more important hypotheses have ever been enunciated. It embraces at once conceptions of such astounding magnitude and minuteness that the mind is utterly incapable of representing to itself many of the quantities with which this theory has to deal. Yet the difficulties which the theory presents to our understanding are no valid arguments against its acceptance, and by that crucial test of all physical theories—its ability to explain all the known phenomena, and even to predict results which must follow in given cases—the wave-theory of light has established its claim to our acceptance With the final triumph of this hypothesis we bring the science of optics to a comparatively recent date, but we have omitted many considerations which belong properly to such a record. There have grown out from the science of optics, by a natural process of differentiation, new sciences, made possible by its achievements, which rival the parent in interest and importance. The employment of lenses in the correction of visual defects, and the combination of lenses and mirrors for assisting the eye to pry into the secrets of the sublimely great and the equally marvelous minute, have played a mighty *rôle* in the development of man's intellect. Try to conceive, if you can, the history of scientific thought without the revelations of the microscope and telescope.

Again, spectrum analysis furnishes one of the most beautiful examples of the interdependence of kindred sciences. Astronomy had elaborated a theory containing many propositions beyond all hope of demonstration, when its sister science steps in and enables us to subject the most distant luminaries to a chemical analysis much as we would a specimen brought to us in the laboratory We can read in the heavens the history of our own system, we can find worlds in various stages of evolution, and the theory of the astronomer receives the confirmation of the physicist.

It must not be inferred that in the history of optics proper the record is closed, for it is only with the wave-theory that the real history of optics may be said to begin.

The wave-theory introduces order and harmony into the phenomena of light. It shows that what was once considered light is but that very little part which the eye is capable of appreciating, of a continuous series of waves extending from the invisible so-called chemical rays to those which our senses interpret as heat. Having thus far triumphed, it now proposes to occupy new territory, to bring light and electricity under one common governance, and in this land of promise, in the field of electro-magnetic phenomena, no doubt lie some of the most important future discoveries, some of the greatest achievements of the science of optics.

In our consideration of physiological optics we shall not formulate any theories or attempt any explanation of the marvelous transformation of ethereal vibrations into light-sensations. Such an explanation belongs rather within the field of physiological psychology. We will first take up and briefly describe that organ in which the first step of this wonderful metamorphosis is accomplished and by means of which the ether wave-energy is converted into nerve activity.

In these days of amateur photography the comparison of the eye to a photographic camera will enable almost every one to form a clear conception of its structure. A camera consists essentially of a box lined within with some dark material, having on one side an opening into which are fitted a series of lenses so arranged as to throw an image of the desired object upon a sensitized plate, which is to receive the picture, situated at the opposite side from the lenses. A diaphragm or shutter to regulate the amount of light admitted to the camera and some arrangement for adjusting its focus for both near and distant objects is also present. Now, this is practically the same mechanism that we find in the eye. Corresponding to the box, we have in the eye a strong fibrous coat, the sclerotic, commonly called the white of the eye, in the front of which is situated a transparent portion known as the cornea. Back of this cornea hangs a curtain, the iris, with a small circular opening in the center, the pupil, which diminishes or increases automatically in response to more or less light-stimulation. This arrangement is approximated in some of the most improved photographic cameras by what is known as an iris diaphragm; but this has not yet been sufficiently perfected to work automatically. Back of the iris is a lens of such power that in a normal eye rays of light are focused upon the background of the eye, where is situated that structure which corresponds to the sensitized plate. This is known as the retina, which we may consider for the present to consist of the delicate terminal filaments of the optic nerve that, curiously enough, spreads itself out on the front of the retina and turns its sensitive tips away from the light back into the retina. A layer of pigment gives the eye its black lining, and the greater part of the interior is occupied by a semi-fluid mass, the vitreous humor. Now we have all the apparatus necessary for giving us distinct pictures of distant objects.

Let us now look at the important mechanism by which the eye is enabled to adjust its focus to both distant and

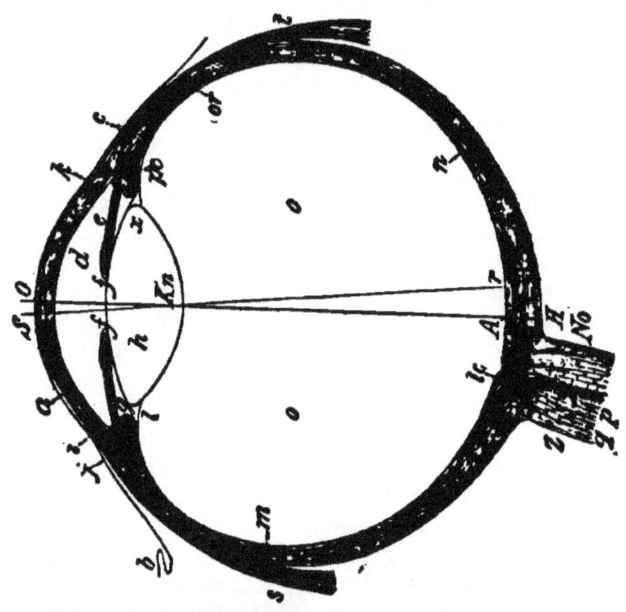

Fig. 1.—Horizontal section of the right eye (Landois). *a*, cornea; *b*, conjunctiva; *c*, sclerotic; *d*, anterior chamber containing the aqueous humor; *e*, iris; *ff'*, pupil; *g*, posterior chamber; *l*, Petit's canal; *j*, ciliary muscle; *k*, corne-oscleral limit; *i*, canal of Schlemm; *m*, choroid; *n*, retina; o, vitreous humor; *No*, optic nerve; *q*, nerve-sheaths; *p*, nerve-fibers; *lc*, lamina cribrosa. The line *O A* indicates the optic axis; *Sr*, the axis of vision; *r*, the position of the fovea centralis.

near objects. For our purpose we may consider the dioptric apparatus of the eye as constituting one single lens, although in reality the cornea, lens, and humors of the eye each contribute their share to the result. We assume rays of light coming from a distance—that is, from more than twenty feet—to be parallel, and in a normal eye to be sufficiently refracted to form a clear image of the desired object upon the retina.

Now, it is manifestly impossible that without some adjustment this same apparatus should give us clear images of nearer objects, because the rays of light from a nearer object are more divergent and require a stronger refracting agent to focus them. To accomplish this purpose the eye possesses the power of accommodation corresponding to the focusing apparatus of our camera. This is effected by means of the crystalline lens, which hangs suspended, as we have seen, behind the iris, and upon which the suspensory ligament exercises a constant traction when the eye is in a state of rest. At the attachment of this suspensory ligament is situated a muscle which surrounds the lens. When we wish to adjust the eye for near objects this muscle contracts, and, as a necessary result, the traction exercised upon the suspensory ligament of the lens is relieved, and by its own resiliency the lens assumes a more convex shape, just as a rubber ball upon which you have been pulling if released springs back to its original form (see Fig. 2). The convexity of the lens is thus increased, and consequently its refracting power, so that the diverging rays of light are now focused upon the retina, the accommodation effort being exactly proportioned to the nearness of the object upon which the eye is directed.

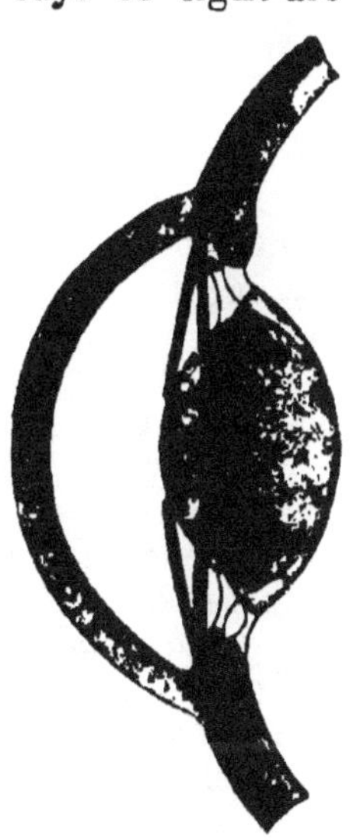

Fig. 2.

This in its simplest form is the mechanism of accommodation.

The eye which we have thus far considered is the normal or ideally perfect eye. But, as met with in actual experience, eyes vary widely from this standard. The most common defect is that known as hypermetropia, or far sight, the latter term being somewhat misleading, because such eyes do not always possess perfect vision at long range, nor is their vision for near objects necessarily imperfect. A far-sighted eye is simply a flattened eye (Fig. 3), and the retina is situated in front of that point to which the rays of light are converged when in a state of rest. This defect is most usually compensated by a constant accommodation effort of the focusing muscle and the individual is not conscious of any visual defect.

Myopia, or near sight (Fig. 3), is that condition in which the length of the eye is too great and the rays of light are focused in front of the retina. With such an eye it is impossible to obtain a clear picture of distant objects, and the eye, according to the degree of myopia, is normally adapted for objects more or less near.

Still another defect more annoying than either of the foregoing is caused by the fact that the curvature of the anterior surface of the eye is not symmetrical — that is, should we make a section of the eye in the horizontal and again in the vertical meridian, we would find that one segment was longer than the other, because the cornea is more sharply curved in one direction than in the other. As a necessary result, the light entering the eye in these different meridians can not unite in one focus—that is, it could no longer be a point, but a line of light—and from this fact the defect is called astigmatism, the name signifying *without a point.* The annoying visual disturbance which this defect causes is very frequently overcome by an unequal contraction of the focusing muscle, making the lens cylindrical to compensate for the corneal defect; but when not so corrected it gives rise to very curious visual impressions. For example, it is sometimes impossible for such a person to see the hands of a clock save when they are turned in one direction, being able only to tell the time, say, at twelve and six o'clock. Astigmatism may occur in connection with either far or near sight, or both defects may be combined in the same eye, one meridian being short-sighted, the other long-sighted.

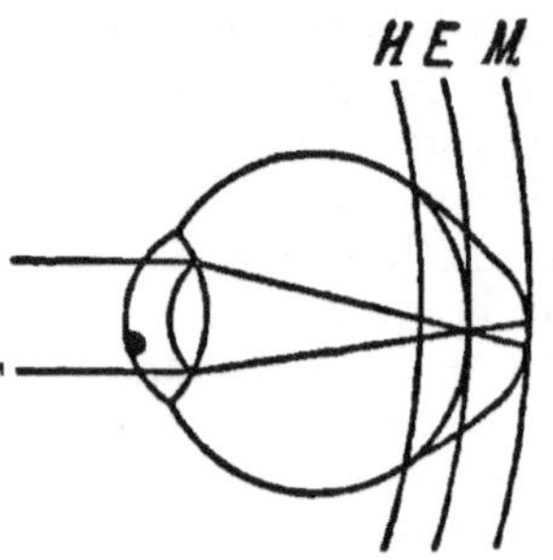

FIG. 3.—*H.* = hypermetropia, or far-sight; *E.* = emmetropia, or normal; *M.* = myopia, or near-sight.

But such defects of form are by no means the only ones which the eye presents when considered as an optical instrument. Although the visual field of the human eye is very large, that portion of the sensitized plate capable of appreciating clearly defined images is very small, because one portion of the retina has become more highly specialized than the remainder; this spot is called the *macula lutea*, and it is only in the comparatively restricted portion of the field which this macula commands that the most perfect visual acuity is reached. It is consequently necessary, when carefully examining any object, that the eye should be directed in turn to each point which we wish to observe. This restless motion of the eye gives what we know as expression, and it is this movement, this constant attention to the different parts of the picture, which we miss in blind or very defective eyes. Again, as the terminal filaments of the optic nerve are alone sensitive to light, it follows that at the point where the nerve enters the eye and spreads out upon the retina there is a portion of the background of the eye which is entirely blind, and you have no doubt all demonstrated the existence of this blind spot for yourselves by that simple and familiar experiment made with a dot and a cross upon a piece of white paper.

Since light of varying wave-lengths is unequally bent in passing through a refracting substance, it follows that light having passed through a lens will not be united in a single focus, but, we may say approximately, in different foci, corresponding to the different colors; this gives us what is known as chromatic aberration. It was once supposed that the eye was free from this defect. This, however, is not the case, as may be easily demonstrated; but it is an interesting fact that the supposed freedom of the eye from this defect led to its imitation in the manufacture of lenses. Lenses of different materials were thus combined, and with the most happy effect, as is witnessed by our present highly perfected achromatic objectives.

From any point of view save that of evolutionists these defects are inexplicable. What useful purpose can be served by the facts that but one little spot on the retina possesses accurate vision, that one portion of the field is entirely blind, that the retinal vessels cast shadows upon the retina, which, if we were conscious of them, would give us the impressions of viewing the world through the branches of a forest? Why should not the optical apparatus be corrected for color and for form? It signifies but little that these defects are compensated in one way or another; there is no excuse for their existence unless we look at the eye as a nerve of common sensation which has been developed and modified through various steps of evolution, and which, from mere light-perception, has come by gradual stages to its present visual perfection. When we understand this, our criticisms are turned to admiration, and we look upon the eye as one of the most wonderful, one of the most instructive, of all Nature's works. Darwin has well said that "it seemed quite inconceivable that such an organ could be developed; but," he continues, "reason tells me that if numerous gradations from an imperfect and simple eye to one perfect and complex—each grade being useful to its possessor—can be shown to exist, as is certainly the case; if, further, the eye ever slightly varies and the variations are inherited, as is likewise certainly the case, and if such variations should ever be useful to any animal under changing conditions of life, then the difficulty of believing that a perfect and complex eye could be formed by natural selection, though insuperable by our imagination, can not be considered real." It is impossible, as Mr. Darwin has said, in studying the gradation through which any organ has passed, to look exclusively to its lineal progenitors; we must look to the collateral descendants which may have preserved the organ in its rudimentary form, and pick up, whenever we can, any instance which will throw light on its manner of evolution.

In our consideration of this subject one fundamental fact should be kept clearly in mind: the development of the visual organs is always dependent upon and correlated with the power of locomotion possessed by the animal. The greater its extent and rapidity in any given case, the greater, consequently, is the advantage of accurate vision; obstacles are more easily seen, enemies discovered and avoided; while in the pursuit of its prey, an animal which possessed at the same time superior powers of locomotion and more accurate vision than its fellows would of necessity triumph over them and be victorious in the struggle for existence. If functional activity leads to modification, what more powerful stimulus can we imagine than that which has been operative during countless ages for the development of the eye, always seconded by the most vigorous application of the law of natural selection?

We find that the first suggestions of a visual organ make their appearance very low in the scale of animal life. It has been suggested by Mr. Spencer that in animals whose cutaneous surface is everywhere sensitive to light the development of specialized nerves for light-perception has been determined in those parts of the animal which were exposed to the greatest contrasts of light and shade. Should some opaque particles of pigment deposited in certain parts of the skin, suggests Sir John Lubbock, arrest and absorb light, its effect would be intensified; and should there be a depression in the skin at this point, these cells would be better protected. Epithelial cells frequently secrete more or less matter, which, forming a ball, would act as a condensing-lens, and the cells immediately subjacent might develop into special nerve-tissues; and to show that this is not imaginative he cites eyes representing these various types, and shows that the eye of a snail, in its development, passes through these very stages.

The most rudimentary form of eye with which we are acquainted is such as that found in the *Medusa*, which we can scarcely term an eye at all, but simply a nerve, which responds very slowly, as shown by Mr. Romanes, to light-stimulation by a contraction of the body. Such an optical apparatus would seem to be of very little utility to its possessor; yet the simple eye-speck of the oyster, which is superior to this only in giving a quick response to light-stimulus, we can readily understand to be of great value, for the oyster is seen to close its shell, when the shadow of an approaching object falls upon it, long before the disturbance of the water, through the sense of feeling alone, could give it warning of the danger.

Over such a simple eye-speck an advantage would be gained by the thickening of the covering epidermal scales, which would tend to concentrate the light upon the exposed nerve, thus obtaining a greater intensity of stimulation. These stages we have seen actually occurring in the lower animal forms, and embryology tells us that, in our own eyes, the crystalline lens is formed by such a folding in of the epithelial layer.

From a simple light-receiving organ it is but a short step to one in which the lens serves not merely to concentrate the rays of light upon terminations of the optic nerve, but likewise to form some rude image of external objects. Such a visual organ would no doubt tend to greatly modify the habits of any animal in which it was developed. The increased facilities for finding and selecting food would powerfully modify its habits. It could with greater safety increase the latitude of its excursions, and this change in environment would tend to still further modification. All these causes would no doubt exert a powerful influence upon the development of the visual organ.

In endeavoring to trace the development of the eye through its various stages of evolution one very important fact is met —viz., the eye, in its progress toward perfection, has not always traveled in the same lines. Under varying stimuli different reactions have taken place, and we find two well-marked types of the visual organ—one, the invertebrate eye, which has probably arisen, as we have already said, as a modification of dermal structures and a nerve of common sensation, and in which the nerve is distributed at the back of the retina and the terminal filaments extend forward toward the light; the other, the vertebrate eye, which in its development is a portion of the brain, and in which the nerve is distributed upon the anterior surface of the retina and the tips are turned down into the substance of the retina and away from the light. Many explanations of this curious phenomenon have been attempted, but none are altogether satisfactory. It has been suggested that the primitive vertebrate must have been a transparent animal, and that the eye or eyes were situated inside the brain, as in the ascidian tadpole, which would explain the fact that the light-receiving portion of the eye is, in its development, an offshoot of the brain. This whole subject is extremely interesting, but it has not been as fully and definitely elaborated and explained as we could wish.

Among the invertebrates the greatest variety of optical apparatus is met with. In most lower forms the eye-speck is found with or without a condensing lens, and vision probably amounts to little more than ability to differentiate between different degrees of illumination. The usual type of eye is the one found on the invertebrate plan, as we have already mentioned; but to this the eyes of *Pecten* and a few other classes form exceptions, for in them the optic-nerve terminals are turned away from the light as in the vertebrate eye. The nerve does not, however, pierce the retina from behind, as in the latter type, but bends over from the side. In certain Southern snails we find an eye still more closely resembling the eyes of the vertebrata, for not only is the distribution of the retinal elements the same, but the nerve also enters from behind, as in the vertebrate eye. But this is seen to be only an arriving at the same goal by different routes and not an evidence of relation, for the eye in its development is a dermal structure, a true invertebrate eye.

We may take the eyes of insects as typical examples of the invertebrate eye, for in this class the eyes have obtained great perfection. The eyes of insects are of two kinds—the simple eye or ocellus, and the compound eye. Ocelli differ somewhat in structure, but consist essentially of a corneal lens, either spherical or cylindrical, a mass of transparent cells, a retina, optic nerve, and pigment. This eye sees as does the human eye—that is, by a reversed image—but is very near-sighted and possesses at best but imperfect vision. The compound eye (Fig. 4) consists of a number of tubes—sometimes as many as twenty-five thousand—arranged side by side, with such a disposition of the lenses, pigment, etc., that only those rays of light falling on the axis of the tube may reach the retina. (This is represented diagrammatically in Fig. 4 *a*.) There has been much discussion as to the method in which vision is accomplished in these

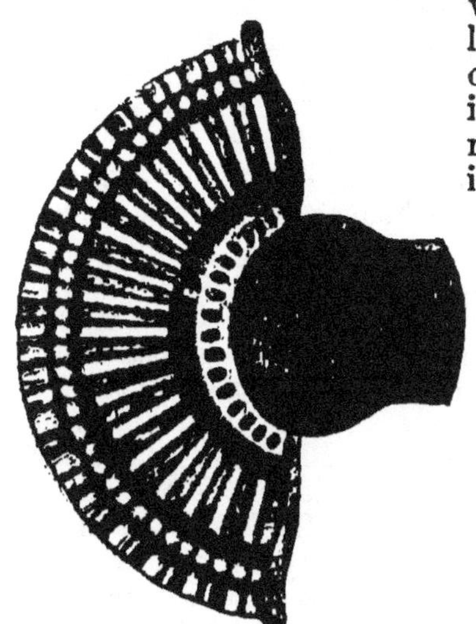

a

Fig. 4.

eyes, but it seems most probable that, as suggested by Müller, the vision of the compound eye is a mosaic, each segment of which corresponds to the field directly in line with the axis of each tube. That each division of the compound eye produces its own image seems highly improbable from the fact that in many compound eyes the image would not fall on the retina, and no arrangement for accommodation seems to be present, while the nature of the crystalline cones and the retina itself is such, in many cases, as to preclude the possibility of a clear image. It seems probable that Müller's theory is correct, that the compound eyes produce single upright images, and that the ocelli, when present with the compound eye, as is sometimes the case, are useful for vision at very near range.

A brief description of the eyes of spiders may not be uninteresting in this connection, as a typical instance of the manner in which the location of the eyes has been determined by the structure and habits of their possessors. "Spiders which hide in tubes or lurk in obscure retreats, from which they only emerge to seize a passing prey, have their eyes aggregated in a close group in the middle of the forehead, as in the bird spider. The spiders which inhabit short tubes, terminated by a large web exposed to the open air, have eyes separated and more spread upon the front of the cephalo-thorax. Those spiders which rest in the center of a fine web, which they frequently traverse, have the eyes supported on slight prominences which permit a greater divergence of their axes; this structure is well marked in those species which lie in ambuscade in flowers. Lastly, the spiders called *errantes*, or wanderers, have their eyes still more scattered, the lateral ones being placed at the margin of the cephalo-thorax." *

The eyes of vertebrates differ from those we have just been considering both in their type and method of development. All vertebrate eyes are not identical in structure, but for the most part we find the same essential features as in the human eye, which we have already considered, while each class presents some slight modifications which are usually intelligible from the habits of life of the animal.

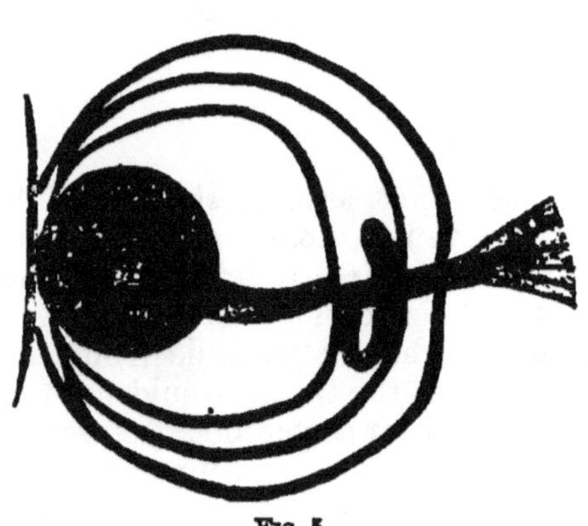

Fig. 5.

The eyes of fishes (Fig. 5), for example, are flattened in their anterior segment, thus diminishing liability to injury during the rapid movements of the fish. The eyes are set in bony sockets, and the sclerotic is still further fortified by osseous or cartilaginous plates. In the water, vision at great distances is impracticable, and we find that the eyes of fishes and most aquatic animals are so formed as to adapt them for vision at comparatively short range. The flat cornea is compensated by a globular lens, making the animal naturally near-sighted. The pupil is usually round, but in some flat fishes which grovel at the bottom of the water there is a peculiar fringed process from the margin of the iris which can be drawn up or let down at will, thus regulating the amount of light received. The lachrymal gland is of course absent, being unnecessary in aquatic animals; but in some fishes—as, for ex-

* Owen.

ample, sharks—a nictitating membrane or third eyelid is developed. This is a thin membrane situated at the inner angle of the eye, and which can be drawn across the globe in a direction at right angles to the external lids. We find in some species of reptiles a muscle by which the eye is retracted at will, being prominent when in the air, and withdrawn from danger when in the water.

The eye of the lizard is peculiar in that it possesses a macula, and the two eyes have an independent movement. Many reptiles present nictitating membranes, and those living upon land a lachrymal apparatus.

The eyes of birds (Fig. 6) are conspicuous for their large size and prominence, as we would naturally expect from the habits of the animal. In some aquatic species we find a flat cornea, but, as a rule, the anterior segment of the eye is prominent and the cornea convex.

Fig. 6.

The coats of the eye are supplemented by a layer of osseous plates, which are situated in the sclera; there also exists a peculiar muscular arrangement which makes traction upon these scleral plates, compressing the globe and rendering prominent the cornea, thus quickly adapting the eye for near vision. It is alleged that in birds the act of accommodation is largely dependent upon this bulging forward of the anterior segment of the eye to produce near vision, and it is possible that the pecten, which is a vascular loop extending into the interior of the eye, is of service in keeping up the intra-ocular tension during such extreme changes in form.

In mammals we never find any development of bone in the sclerotic, and the eyes are usually well protected by a bony orbit. In animals of nocturnal habits the cornea is proportionately larger and more convex; the lens is likewise more globular, thus adapting the eye for vision at nearer range. In aquatic mammals the eyes more nearly resemble those of fishes in form, the cornea being flat and the lens globular. In timid animals, and in those who defend themselves by kicking, we find the eyes lateral and prominent, which enables the animal to watch for the approach of a possible enemy from behind. The retractor muscle of the eyeball is present in all mammals up to the *Quadrumana.* In the catarrhine *Quadrumana* and in man we have that specialization in the function of the retina which gives us what we know as the macula; this pit is not developed in the embryo, and is inconspicuous in childhood.

In some of the mammalia, especially in the carnivora, there is on the inner surface of the choroid a patch of brilliant pigment of metallic luster called the tapitum. This assists the vision of the animal in a feeble light by reflecting forward the rays of light as from a mirror.

We find in the eye many interesting examples of retrogression and atrophy from disuse. Very frequently, when an animal is freely moving in its larval state, the eyes which it then possesses are lost later on with its power of locomotion, as, for example, in the ascidian. The rudimentary character of the eyes of animals living in dark caverns is well known. In those forms living at a great depth beneath the surface of the water, where little light can penetrate, one of two adaptations usually occurs: the eyes either atrophy, the animal finding it safer to depend on the sense of touch alone, or else they become very large, to catch all the rays of light possible. Sometimes these deep-sea animals possess their own luminous organs, which are useful not only in the search for food, but likewise as weapons of defense, and which, like dark lanterns, they flash upon their frightened enemies. Again, other species hang out their lanterns to tempt their unwary prey within easy reach. In certain lizards there are found concealed beneath a scale in the center of the head the atrophied remains of what was a perfect median eye in the now extinct ancestral forms. This eye is connected with that curious and unexplained organ the pineal gland, which has at least served a useful purpose as a target for theory makers. It was in this organ, you will remember, that Descartes located the seat of the soul, and we now find it connected with a once functional window of that elusive phantom. This pineal eye has been studied in several reptilian forms by Mr. Spencer, who concluded that it is identical with the median eye of the ichthyosaurus and allied extinct *reptilia*, in which it attained large size.

As we ascend in the animal scale we find the pineal gland becomes more and more rudimentary, although present in the higher animal forms up to man, in whom it is a small, apparently functionless remnant. It is interesting to note that the pineal eye when found is formed after the invertebrate type, thus differing from the two lateral eyes in the same animal.

Certain flat fishes, notably the *Pleuronectidæ*, furnish an interesting example of adaptation to changing condition of environment. The young of these fishes are symmetrical, swim in an upright position, and have an eye on either side of the head; but, from the habit of groveling upon the bottom in search of food, by which the lower eye is exposed to constant danger of injury, the skull undergoes such a modification that in the adult fish, which swims on its side, the eyes have swung around, so that both eyes appear on the upper surface of the head. And we sometimes see in man, when the upright position of the head is interfered with by the scars of burns or other contractions, a somewhat similar modification of the bones of the cranium. We have referred several times to a nictitating membrane, a third eyelid which is found in many lower animals, where it exists in a state of perfection. In man and the *Quadrumana* this is present only as a rudimentary organ, a small functionless fold at the inner corner of the eye, an ever-present reminder of our relation to the lower animals.

While discussing the subject of the developmental stages through which the eye has already passed, the question naturally arises, "Has our own eye reached its final and most perfect form, or is it still in the process of evolution?" As we have seen when considering the human eye, the ideally perfect organ when in a state of rest is adapted for vision at infinite distances. It is the eye best suited for the savage in the chase or in war, to the sailor, to any man who leads an outdoor, country life; but in the process of civilization the eye is put under conditions to which it is by no means so well adapted. In the crowded city the eye is constantly directed through all the waking moments to objects at short range. Its longest distance is across the narrow street, while its most usual range is from the desk or book to the limits of a room. The result is that the focusing power is called constantly into play. The muscles which converge the eye exercise a constant tension upon the globe, while the enervating habits of city life do not tend to fit the organ to withstand this increased strain. The result is that the eyeball gives way beneath this pressure; it becomes elongated, and in its position of rest is now adapted for the perception of near objects. It is an undoubted fact that near-sightedness is on the increase among the more civilized races. It develops usually in childhood, and statistics show that in school-children the degree of near-sightedness is directly in proportion to the number of hours of study.

It might at first appear very desirable that the eye should thus adapt itself to the work it has to do; and so, no doubt, it would be were these near-sighted eyes healthy and perfect organs. But, unfortunately, this is not the case. The development of near-sightedness is attended with grave dangers. It means a giving away of the firm fibrous capsule of the eye and always endangers the delicate nervous elements beneath. The near-sighted eye is a diseased eye and is always liable to still further deterioration. The process is distinctly hereditary, the children of near-sighted parents being frequently born near-sighted, and when born with normal eyes earlier develop more aggravated cases of near-sightedness than the children of healthy parents. Thus Nature's latest attempt to improve our visual organs is of but doubtful utility.

The problems of physiological optics thus far encountered are much less involved than those which arise in connection with the color-sense. Anything approaching a connected and logical statement of this subject would require a much more elaborate treatment than is here possible, and I shall be obliged to omit many facts which I fear are almost essential to a rational presentation of the subject.

From the time of Thomas Young to a comparatively recent period the ability of the retina to differentiate color has been practically unquestioned. Young saw the logical necessity for retinal elements capable of receiving each phase of vibration of a continuous spectrum, but believed it impossible that so many different retinal elements could exist. He therefore assumed arbitrarily the existence of three sets of fibers corresponding to what he called the three primary colors—red, green, and violet. Another theory somewhat similar was suggested by Herring, which, in place of retinal elements, assumed the presence of three chemical substances which were supposed to have certain positive and negative reactions to light. Neither of these theories has any discoverable foundation in the anatomical structure of the retina, nor are they supported by any known facts as to the nature of light. The presence of three kinds of retinal elements or of three chemical substances can not be demonstrated. Neither can any division of light-vibrations corresponding to three primary colors, nor, in fact, to any color, be found in the spectrum.

When the spectral band falls on the retina, the material with which the retina has to deal is simply a series of ether-vibrations of varying periods, and in this series we find those waves which we see as one color differ as widely from each other as they do from the vibrations in the next adjacent color band. The difficulty seems to be that, having started with the assumption that the power to differentiate color resided in the retina, a retinal structure has been assumed to correspond to the theory; but why this work has been assigned to three sets of nerve fibers or chemical substances is not clear. I see no escape for those who hold this theory but the assumption of a retinal substance attuned to each vibration in the visible spectrum, for, as we have before said, no breaks occur corresponding to the color bands with which we are acquainted in experience.

There has been much good work done of late in illuminating this dark field of color-perception, and the theory that seems most acceptable to our evolutionary ideas is that which transfers the seat of color-differentiation from the retina to the brain. All the retina has to do is to receive the rays of light which fall upon it, and which create, according to their wave-length, a characteristic molecular disturbance, thus making the function of the eye a refined temperature-sense, and the translation of such impressions into what we know as color a purely psychical phenomenon.

That we do see definite bands of color, and that our ordinary division of the spectrum must have a basis of fact somewhere, seems self-evident. The explanation of this phenomenon has been very ably given by my friend Dr. Gould, and I would recommend his instructive monograph on the human color-sense to all who are interested in this subject. He starts with the fundamental idea that our color-sense must be the organism's response in reaction under stimulus. It has arisen as a response to light-stimulus; not to the stimulus of pure white light, but to the light that we see every day in nature.

"Sunlight, we are told, is composed of the following parts:

54	Red.
140	Orange-red.
80	Orange.
114	Orange-yellow.
54	Yellow.
206	Greenish-yellow.
121	Yellowish-green.
134	Green and Blue-green.
32	Cyan-blue.
40	Cyan.
20	Ultramarine and blue-violet.
5	Violet.
1,000	

Condensing the intermediates with the principals, we have:

Red colors	194
Golden colors	454
Green colors	255
Blue colors	97
	1,000"

The explanation of such a grouping of light-waves is taken to be due to the fact that, among the color stimuli which the eye has received, the golden stimuli have largely predominated. The ordinary diffused daylight is slightly yellowish, and obscuration, as from a turbid atmosphere, increases this hue. The rising and the setting sun floods the earth with golden light; again, the yellow light of fire has, since the first dawn of civilization, played a most important place in man's history. By fire-worship, by burnt-offerings in almost any form of religious belief, the golden firelight has impressed itself on man's attention.

The next most important class is that of the greens—which are abundantly present in nature, being the predominant color in vegetation.

The next class is that of the reds, where we meet with a very interesting and important fact. Were any of us asked, "Which is the strongest color?" I think we would reply, "Red," unless we had looked into the matter a little critically, and we would be surprised to find that red is not a color of high luminous power, nor can the feeling of the striking and important nature of red be due to the fact that the quantity of the red stimulus in nature has been powerful enough to give it this exalted place in our estimation.

The explanation of this fact Dr. Gould finds to be

in the part that blood has played in the world's history. Throughout the long struggle for existence among the higher animals bloodshed has ever been the constant accompaniment of strife, has stained the weapons of the victor, marked the defeat of the conquered.

Throughout the history of all religions and all social customs we find that blood has always played a most important part. We read of "the blood-drinking, blood-baiting, blood-ransoming, blood unions, blood compacts and friendships, blood sacrifices and blood suppers, blood burials, blood cures and sprinklings, bloody hands and uplifted arms, blood transfusions, human sacrifices and cannibalism, bloody burnt-offerings and blood-stained ark of the covenant, bloody passions and bloody atonements"; and thus throughout the long and passionate strife of mankind has the red burned itself deep into the human soul and has come to occupy this prominent position in our estimate of color while only possessing that luminous intensity to which its comparative infrequency in nature would entitle it. "The portion of spectral blue is small in extent and weak in power. It has a character of distance and impersonality, exactly corresponding to the sources whence this color has reached the eye. The sky is above, but man's eyes are seldom raised to it. At the horizon it often fades into violet, in which the spectrum likewise passes out of sight."

Dr. Gould concludes: "Waves of more or less extended differences of length are perceived as a single color, just as the bulk of the waves from each of these classes of objects have been most uniformly and persistently reflected into the eye during the growth of the race. Nature has acted upon the organism in these continuous ways, and the cerebral product is the spectral colors in the proportions and with the characteristics we find appearing in consciousness. The largest and most persistent stimulus has been that of the gold rays—the varied shades of the diffused light of day or the ever-present mystery of fire. These have been poured in profusion into all eyes, comprising nearly one half of their total stimulus, while the green rays make up a fourth, the red less than a fourth, and the blue a still more limited amount."

We likewise find the objective luminous intensities to bear the same relations to each other.

We can not enter further into this interesting discussion, but I think we may safely assume that this theory offers the most satisfactory explanation of the origin of our color-sense.

It is asserted that color-vision is a later and more refined sense than the vision of form, and it is well known that it is presided over by a separate cerebral center. It is also subject to very frequent modifications; for example, among the sect of Quakers, which has existed only for a comparatively short time, and who so religiously avoid all use of color in dress, color-blindness is said to be proportionately greater than among other communities. It is much more frequent among men than among women, whose habits render color-vision more important to them; it is frequently transmitted in the male line of a family through females possessing perfect color-vision.

The color-sense is certainly capable of great education, although it seems to be developed in the lowest races of mankind. Goethe tells us that the mosaic workers in Italy are in the habitual use of fifteen thousand varieties of hues, each variety comprising fifty tints, a perfection of color-sensation which is truly marvelous.

We can scarcely argue from the color-vision of man to that of the lower animals. The color-sense is most highly developed, no doubt, in many lower animals, but that their perception of color is identical with ours is by no means proved. In some cases we know definitely that the limits of the visible spectrum are not the same. Lubbock has shown this to be the case with ants by a series of very interesting experiments. This fact alone should make us extremely cautious in assuming such identity.

The eye, as we have seen, has developed in various classes of animals in a somewhat different way, and it seems probable that color-vision, which is a later development—a refinement, as it were—of light-perception, has been modified by the structure of the eye and the habits of its possessor. It seems much safer, therefore, to explain the human color-sense in the manner we have just outlined than to trace it, as is sometimes done, from animals far removed from man in the line of descent.

ABSTRACT OF THE DISCUSSION.

Dr. George M. Gould:

The excellent lecture of my friend Dr. Alleman is so complete that we who follow can find but little to add. I can not let the present opportunity pass, however, without protesting a little against my friend's passive assent to mechanical and materialistic explanations.

To the belief in evolution I heartily subscribe. But I am also a believer in logic and the laws of thought; a firm believer in never going into captivity to a popular craze, or *Zeitgeist*, or disbelieving what I see and know, even though all the Darwins and Spencers and Lubbocks of the world should tell me it is not so. My friend quotes, with apparent consent, the explanation of the origin of the eye as due to certain opaque particles of pigment deposited in certain parts of the skin—purely accidentally, is the *sous-entendu* inference—which would arrest and absorb light, and that if this rudimental accidental eye should perchance be attended by an adjacent depression of the skin, these cells would be better protected—the protection being again a little matter of pure mechanical chance. Now, so far as the origin of the organ of vision or of any organ is concerned, people are fast beginning to suspect the utterly asinine quality of such explanations. If you take up the works of a large class of science-plebificators you will find instances, like the above, of how a little learning may make one mad. I found, in a popular little book of one such, the other day, the amazing, imperturbable, impertinent saying that chemistry had shown that there is no essential difference between the organic and inorganic, and that the sensitiveness of protoplasm explains all biological phenomena. Of course, if one have poise, self-possession, eyes of his own, a logical mind, he soon comes to see the fallacy of the modern popular unscientific science of the day, as illustrated in this outrageous nonsense. The sad thing is, that many people take such explanations and the animus of such explanations on trust, and drift into materialism—the absurdest of all creeds, as Huxley says. Young people should be taught that the covert and assumed mechanicalism of these pseudo-explanations is not only unjustified by good science or by good scientists, but is a crude eighteenth-century infidelity masking in a nineteenth-century science-cloak. I have not the faintest objection to materialism, mechanicalism, or atheism, if the facts of life warrant them—or if they are true. The fact is, they are *not* true. Sensitive protoplasm explains all, if sensitiveness be explained and if we are told how protoplasm came into existence. Chemistry has no more conception of the chemical processes of organic metabolism than have birds on telegraph wires a hint of the messages going through their feet. The bit of "opaque pigment" and the "depression" were no more fortuitous results in the evolution of the eye than the electric button of your Edison light is a chance accident of house-building. Function always precedes organization. Life always precedes function, and purpose rules every step of evolution. Where purposiveness, there mentality. Selection requires a selector, and natural selection, as a blind force or mechanical explanation, never modified an organ or begot an adaptation. Living matter and dead matter are the most dissimilar things in this world, and to explain life as a function of matter is the height of absurdity. Evolution can not evolve what was not previously involved, or what was not within the evolving thing; the effect exists potentially in the cause. I look upon the origin of the eye as of that of every organ—as a designed tool of intelligent, ingenious life. The pigment spot was located in the best place by a mentally equipped protoplasm * or purposive power, and its outfitting is a beautiful example of intelligence.

As regards the varieties and modifications of eyes found in animals, Dr. Alleman has brought out clearly the laws expressing or causing them. The first and most important consists in the influence of locomotive powers or habits. The greater and swifter and more complicated the movements of an animal, the more perfect the organ of vision if light be present. This fact was forcibly brought home to me very lately. I got from the United States Fish Commissioner some little brook-trout eggs. They were about a sixth of an inch in diameter, almost transparent. Putting one under a one-inch objective, you could see the wonderful little being all formed, and could even see the blood-corpuscles and currents sweeping through the tiny blood-vessels like sand through an hour-glass. Most astounding, however, were the tremendous great eyes! So important is vision to the "speckled beauties" in catching flies and escaping enemies and obstacles, so quickly must they move among the pebbles of their home, that Life had thus early had to make the eye her chief work of formation and arrangement. I hatched the little fellows out, and, despite their big yolk-sacs, when the light comes they run like mad for a protecting pebble. So it is all through the animal kingdom. Visual power and perfection had to keep pace with or precede the necessities of quick

* A word nobody knows the meaning of, and a thing nobody knows the chemical construction of, and which no two persons would apply to the same substance. It is a name not understood, given a thing not understood by persons not understanding.

motion and precise action. I suppose there is no organ in the universe responding with such lightning-like precision to such infinitely small and infinitely quick stimulation as the eye of a humming-bird. One is simply appalled and thrilled by such an astonishing miracle. So important is accurate vision to birds of prey that they have two fovea, an explanation of which fact is not at present quite clear. The remarkable adaptive power of life is shown by the change life has had to undertake in the evolution of her eyes. Dr. Alleman has admirably made clear the difference between the construction of the two types of eye, the invertebrate and the vertebrate. The fact seems to show that the perfection of eye required by the vertebrate could not be gained on the invertebrate type or plan, and a complete about-face was undertaken and carried through. It is extremely suggestive that the retina and lens of the invertebrate eye are developed from the epidermal structures, while in the vertebrates the retina is developed from the brain. In other words, in invertebrates the light goes into the brain to affect it, but in the vertebrates the brain comes out to see! The fact, like many another, shows also that Life, though intelligent and ingenious beyond any human conception, is yet not omniscient. Neither is she omnipotent; she is always working under difficulties and with inexhaustible cunning, doing the best she can with the materials at command. We are at present incapable of catching the least glimpse of a reason why the optic nerves and organs constituting the retina should in vertebrates turn backward and the light be thus forced to pierce the numerous layers of the retina until it reaches the final pigmentary layer into which the rods and cones dip. It looks like a very poor plan indeed, but it is because our little minds are so poor that we think so. It seems to work pretty well—perhaps better than any plan we could have devised. You have all heard of the noble Castilian who wished he had been present when God created the world—he could have given him such excellent advice! The modern pseudo-scientist is filled with that spirit, and, on the assumption that God is omnipotent and omniscient, the point becomes less vulgarly impertinent; but if the demiurge is neither omnipotent nor omniscient, but works, as he evidently does, under difficulties, then the impertinence becomes the most colossal impudence. In illustration of the influence of locomotion upon vision the following instances are noteworthy:

Sacculina, a degenerate parasitical crustacean, in its early life moves freely about with complex organs of locomotion. It fastens upon the crab's tail and loses its organs of locomotion, losing also its eyes and other organs of special sense.

The *Pinnotheridæ*, a family of crabs, have vision while moving about, but when they settle down in the lungs of the Chinese sea-slugs the brow grows over the eyes.

There are three families of vertebrates that live as parasites in ants' nests. They are blind, or nearly so, two having lost their limbs. Indeed, it is the rule that the young of most blind parasites have eyes. The number of such blind degenerate species tells a sad story of the fall of animals as profound as any "fall of man."

All these facts are corollaries of the great law that use develops function and disuse is followed by atrophy. Another controlling law operating under and with this law consists in the influence of diminished and denied light. The most interesting examples of this law are the eyes of deep-sea fish. A writer in the Cornhill Magazine has thus stated the facts:

"Fish that live at very great depths have either no eyes at all or enormously big ones. Indeed, there are two ways you may get on in these gloomy abysses—by delicate touch organs, or by sight that collects the few rays of light due to phosphorescence or other accidental sources. Now, as we go down in the water we find at each depth that the effects produced upon the eyes of fish are steadily progressive in one direction or the other. Species that live at a depth of eighty fathoms have the eye already a good deal bigger than their nearest representatives that live at or near the surface. Down to the depth of 200 fathoms, where daylight disappears, the eyes get constantly bigger and bigger. Beyond that depth small-eyed forms set in, with long feelers developed to supplement the eyes. Sight, in fact, is here beginning to atrophy. In the greatest abysses the fish are mostly blind, feeling their way about entirely by their sensitive bodies alone over the naked surface of rock at the bottom. Some of them have still external relics of functionless eyes; in others, the oldest and most confirmed abysmal species, the eye has altogether disappeared externally, though its last representative may still be recognized, imbedded deep in the tissues of the head."

You all know about the blind fish of the Mammoth and other caves. Before birth the optic nerve is connected with the eye of the mole, but during adult life it is usually atrophied, and the mole is of course blind. The *Spolax d'Olivier*, or mole-rat, also lives underground, and is blind, though having some rudiments of eyes left under the skin. An aquatic reptile Proteus, living in obscure caverns, has only traces of the organ of vision. The number of blind or partially blind species is said to number hundreds. So fearfully does the law of hunger sacrifice everything else to its implacable rule. A remarkable illustration is also that of the African tunnel ants, or termites. No one can ever forget Drummond's beautiful essay on them. There are three intolerable mysteries about them that puzzle me beyond measure: First, how do they construct covered ways by the million whose engineering difficulties and tremendous labor exceed those of the Mount Cenis tunnel by man, with never a mining or building worker showing itself to view? How do they build from an incomplete tunnel-end without exposure to light? Second, how do they, absolutely eyeless, know darkness from day? Third, and most wonderful, why does the huge queen, whose whole life is spent in one spot, in the dark, and in laying eggs, have eyes, and her progeny have none?

Lastly may be briefly noticed some of the ingenious ways by which Life has outwitted darkness and made it possible for her children to see in spite of denied or diminished light. These devices consist principally of three classes:

1. Widening of the iris, diaphragm, or window-curtain of the eye, so to gather a larger quantity of weak light. Every child knows the remarkable power of the cat to widen the pupil in darkness and narrow it to a mere thread-like slit in the light.

2. Increasing the size of the whole eye with the same object in view and synchronous with the enlargement of the pupil also.

3. The creation of the *tapetum lucidum* in nocturnal vertebrates, such as the tiger family, dogs, etc. This, as Dr. Alleman has pointed out, is an organic concave mirror usually about one third the size of the retina, situated at the back part of the eye, and gathers to a focus in front of the animal the little light that may enter the eye in the dark. It is a structure too little studied and understood. One can not comprehend how the same light can be used to stimulate the retina and also be reflected out of the eye. This physical difficulty has always made me wonder if the light it throws in front is not phosphorescent or self-created.

4. The development of the function of phosphorescence. No human chemist or physicist has ever been able to understand how these numerous animals can create light without at the same time creating a burning heat. The Edison who does this for our street and house illumination has awaiting him a fortune greater than that of Jay Gould and Vanderbilt combined. We are some way behind the glow-worm yet, despite the naturalists.

5. Finally, the hypertrophy or refinement of the tactile and other senses may in part compensate for the loss of sight. The antennæ and feelers of many insects are doubtless thus used. The acuteness of the sense of touch of blind people is well known. Blind men have been authorities in the science of conchology, in numismatics, in botany, etc., and something akin to the distinctions of color are credited to some blind people. The timbre of the sound of a struck object aids

the blind man tapping the pavement with his cane to keep him in safe or known ways. It is said that Laura Bridgman could tell idiots or insane people by the feeling of their hands. I believe it has been demonstrated that eyeless bats escape obstacles in their flight by the fact of the increased atmospheric pressure near these objects, which is perceived by the hypersensitive interdigital membrane.

My friend has alluded to that curious structure, the pineal eye, and was doubtless laughing slyly at me when he spoke of this organ being a good target for theory-shooters. I have had my say about it, and, while far from dogmatic, I still suggest that it may have something to do with the perception of the magnetic currents of the earth and with that exquisite, wonderful, beautiful mystery, the homing instinct.

But I am very proud of another theory I have been guilty of fathering, and also proud that it has received the approbation of your lecturer. This theory of mine in regard to the origin and significance of our human color-sense unfortunately appeared years ago in a periodical that in publishing it did in fact bury it, and I firmly believe that it is worthy of the serious consideration of students of science, evolution, and æsthetics. I hope to see it some time resurrected, not so much as a salve of slightly wounded vanity, but because it seems to me to be a great and valuable truth. It is strictly in the line of the teaching of evolution doctrine, harmonizes with archæology and history, and is adequate. I have great respect for that acute and genial observer, Grant Allen, but his theory of the origin of our color-sense seems to me trivial, inadequate, and unworthy of his genius. It is an explanation that explains nothing. I think the mystery of our color-sense is due to the effect of the great orders of natural and historical color-stimuli that have poured into the human eye and brain in the past ages, and with these streams of stimuli have also been deposited in the human mind the influences that now make the symbolism of color.

Allow me to read a few sentences from my pamphlet: *

"If we ask what great color-classes of visible objects have most occupied man's eye and mind in all past history, we are certain the answer will be something like the following:

"The first in overwhelming importance is light and fire; the second, the world of vegetation; the third would be blood, as the concrete representative of war and struggle and superstitious symbol; the fourth, the sky above with its reflection in the waters of the earth. It would be difficult to name another class, for whatever other colors Nature may have presented to the eye of historic man, they must have

* The Human Color-Sense considered as the Organic Response to Natural Stimuli. By George M. Gould, A. B. (Reprint from the American Journal of Ophthalmology, September, 1886. Reprinted entire by Dr. S. Dudley Reynolds, in Progress.)

been mixtures of these, or unimportant exceptions that have left only a small and inconsiderable organic response in the psychic mechanism.

"Nature has acted upon the organism in these continuous ways, and the cerebral product is the spectral colors, in the proportions and with the characteristics we find appearing in consciousness. The largest and most persistent stimulus has been that of the gold rays—the varied shades of the diffused light of day, or the ever-present mystery of fire. Those have been poured in profusion into all eyes, comprising nearly one half of their total stimulus, while the green rays make up a fourth, the red less than a fourth, and the blue a still more limited amount.

"Gladstone, as a Homer student, and on simple philological evidence, tried to show that 'they who fought at Troy' were as blind to certain colors as Homer himself (supposably) was to all. Dr. Magnus, in Germany, drew the same conclusion from a wider sweeping of word-lore. The whole affair was a dismal collapse, and Allen pricks the bubble with justifiable satisfaction. It was hardly to be expected that if ants, bees, and birds had such highly developed chromatic powers, even savage men should be so far behind them. Present-day barbarians have essentially the same power in this respect as ourselves, though extreme delicacy of perception is, to be sure, not so highly developed, and their nomenclature would of course be very faulty or deficient, as Gladstone and Magnus might have supposed. The savage's delight in color, as shown in tattooing and decorating his body, presupposes the ability to feel the differences in color quite as accurately as the birds whose bright plumage he adorns himself with, and who have no words for colors either. The development of color perception lies far back of all this, and is as old as hunger, in satisfying which, and by the attacks and escapes of enemies, it quite certainly took its rise. The sobering remark of Wallace is also *à propos*, that it is the absence of color that would require accounting for; he says that the most conspicuous pigeons, whether by their color or by their crests, are all found where they have fewest enemies."

Allow me a few words upon the future of the organ of vision, or upon what might be called *The Eye and Civilization.* Dr. Alleman has used words implying that myopia is Nature's attempt and failure to adapt the eye to the demands of civilization. I do not agree with this view. The oculists' patients are always asking why so many more people have now to wear spectacles than was formerly the case. This, in substance, is the answer I have given perhaps a thousand times: Life created the eye for the work the eye had to do—that is, seeing more or less distant objects. All animals, all savage and uncivilized peoples, all civilized babies, are far-sighted. The majority of civilized people are also hyperopic. Suddenly comes civilization, within fifty or one hundred years, with its printing, reading, writing, commercialism, cities, schools, and indoor life, demanding constant use of the eye upon objects within a foot or two, and keeping the ciliary muscle in a state of abnormal continuous tension. The habits and structures of millions of years' formation are in a few years forced to do a work of a very different and straining sort. Give Nature time and she will turn a pseudopod into a seal's flipper, a horse's foot, a bat's wing, or a man's hand. But in the instance of the eye no time has been allowed. Civilization was never foreseen by evolution. Civilization, like a footpad, has darted upon the eye and delivered it a vicious blow, demanding, "Your vision or your life." Myopia is one of the direct results of the blow, not the failed effort of Nature to heal the wound of the blow. It is always a disease, never a healthy adaptation. Nature has been given no time to make modification. Will she be able to do so? What is to be the result of this wolf-and-lamb controversy? As I am not a Brooklyn oculist, I may be pardoned the vulgarity of "talking shop" a minute, and of not assuming the modesty of my friend who lives among you. Indeed, I believe thoroughly in risking the crude suspicion of advertising and of being credited with hobby-riding, by proclaiming as from the housetops a truth of profound and tragic importance. There are thousands of people in this city to-night who have suffered a life of misery from headache, sick headache, nervous troubles, and lessened vitality simply because they are trying to look at a microscopical specimen with a telescope. They have been leeched, blistered, and cupped; have taken bromides, nux vomica, caffeine, iron, antipyrine, cod-liver-oil, and tonics for years; they have wrapped their heads in whisky-soaked towels, gone to bed a day or two every week, taken trips to the sea-shore or mountains, become chronic invalids, or have been attacked by some serious disease that is always looking out for a weakened organism in which to settle. It was all of no avail. They wanted a microscope, and Nature had made a telescope for them. A good oculist would make a fortune in a year if he could, or would, have every case of headache in the community to treat on condition that he should get fifty dollars for every cure, and give one hundred dollars for every failure to cure. From fifty to eighty per cent of all school-children and city folks are to-day undermining their health, depleting their assimilative and nervous systems, laying the sure foundations and preparations, either for themselves or their children, of ill-health, disease, and early death, simply and solely from lack of a proper pair of spectacles. Does that seem like crazy quackery and hobby-riding? It is the truest truth I know. Give Evolution a little affair of a hundred thousand years and she may lengthen the eyeball a little in a healthy way, or, more properly and more probably, will develop the Müller ring-fibers of the ciliary muscle to stand this great task. But at present, so sudden has come the frightful strain of civilization that there ensues a multitude of evils whose existence is not a quarter suspected by the world, and only half suspected by the medical profession. The great concealing, deceiving fact about eye-strain is that the eye itself does not complain or suffer so much as other organs. This fact makes every patient say: "My eyes are all right; do not pain me at all," and yet that same patient's life and happiness may be destroyed by eye-strain. What is the reason of this anomalous fact? These are three chief of many reasons: 1. Eye-strain is due to no disease whatever, but to overuse and misuse of an organ created for a different kind of use. 2. The enormous and preponderant importance of the function of vision to the life and welfare of the organism makes Nature throw the brunt of the burden upon other organs. If eyesight were ruined, then all is ruined; other organs, chiefly the nervous system, can afford to suffer better than the eyes. 3. Healthy-looking eyes are the very essence of beauty; the eyes are truly "the windows of the soul." Sexual selection has been willing to sacrifice everything to maintaining pure, clear eyes, and has therefore switched the morbid results of eye-strain to other parts rather than mar the beauty of those superb structures. Hence the creation of the great brood of reflex ocular neuroses. I am as convinced as I am of my own existence that a great deal of the headache, anorexia, dyspepsia, the reduced vitality, the hysteria, the neurasthenia, the anæmia, the now morbidly exalted and now morbidly depressed nervous energy, characteristic especially of the modern woman, are due to the persistent influence of eye-strain. Of course, whisky and corsets and laziness are also powerful causes. But the worst about eye-strain is that it does not kill directly, but creates the neurotic type, perverts and *morbidizes* the assimilative and nervous systems, reduces healthy vitality, and manures the field for a prolific crop of pathological weeds.

Dr. Robert G. Eccles:

While I agree with Dr. Gould that function precedes organism in the processes of organic evolution, I am also a believer in the absolutely mechanical structure of the universe. The introduction of the psychological element does not abolish the necessity for the search for efficient causes all along the line of biological development. I can not see in what way the eye could have been evolved except as shown by the speaker of the evening. There are purpose and intelligence manifested, doubtless, in all biological processes, but not necessarily the purpose and intelligence of a mechanical creator, outside the organism. I do not see how we can draw the line between consciousness in the life of an organized creature and consciousness in the atom. I believe that each atom is endowed with a consciousness of its own—that their structural combinations are thus intelligently guided in a manner similar to that in which individuals unite to form societies and states. Every consciousness, however, works in an orderly manner, according to laws strictly mechanical in their nature. The problem is immensely complex; but if we could grasp all its conditions we could trace the operation of cause and effect throughout the entire process, even up to the development of the highest qualities of sense-perception and psychical activity.

MR. ELLSWORTH WARNER:

I must express my dissent from one of the conclusions of the lecturer—that involved in his advice to resort to the use of spectacles to correct the tendency to near-sightedness arising from the artificial conditions of our civilized life. I believe the true method is to compel the eye to do its work, and thus the organ will in time adapt itself to the necessities of its new situation. If the eye gets strained or wearied by the necessity of viewing near objects in the daily routine of life, let the person go out into the fields and among the hills, and rest it by the contemplation of natural scenery. If we resort too early to the use of spectacles, we encourage and increase the very weakness and defect which we desire to guard against.

DR. ALLEMAN, in closing, said that, in presenting the theory that the eye was evolved from certain opaque pigments deposited in certain parts of the skin, he had offered the only explanation of the evolution of the eye with which he was acquainted. He failed to see that Dr. Gould had presented a more plausible theory. We must guard against those theories which do not explain anything scientifically—which are merely confessions of our ignorance. Replying to Mr. Warner, he said, if we could betake ourselves to the woods and lead an out-of-door life we could, doubtless, get along without spectacles, but in the present state of civilization that solution of the difficulty is hardly possible.

THE
EVOLUTION OF ART

BY

JOHN A. TAYLOR

AUTHOR OF THE EVOLUTION OF THE STATE, ETC.

COLLATERAL READINGS SUGGESTED:

Taine's Philosophy of Art, and Fiske's review of the same in The Unseen World; Lübke's History of Art; Reber's History of Ancient Art, and History of Mediæval Art; Freeman's Effects of the Norman Conquest on Art, in History of the Norman Conquest; Article art, in Encyclopædia Britannica; John Stuart Mill's Logic and Essay on Art.

THE EVOLUTION OF ART.

By John A. Taylor.

The continuing wonder of mankind is man. What he has achieved in the past is at once the inspiration and the harbinger of what he shall achieve in the future.

The history of human effort is briefer than we are wont to realize. Speaking within the chronicles of recorded history, more has been produced by man during the past five centuries of the hundreds of thousands of years during which he has walked upright upon the earth than during all the previous period. Indeed, it might be possible to demonstrate that the century now entering upon its last decade has witnessed the creation of more potent instruments of human advancement than all its predecessors combined. And, in the broadest sense in which it is permitted to speak of art, it may be safely asserted that at no age of the world has human effort been more abundantly crowned with success than in the present.

Art is the consummate product of the human being. It presents itself as the result of all the knowledge of the past, of all the opportunities of the present, and its possibilities for the future constitute one of the chiefest motives for human effort.

Nature is the great laboratory in which stands man, the chemist. Her laws are all about him, her substances are his to mold and combine, her glorious skies bend over him to thrill his soul with images of beauty, her abundant harvests sustain his waning strength, her violent catastrophes set limitations to his ambition. What he shall do with these supplies at hand has measured, and will forever measure, his own creative skill. And yet all the grandeur and beauty of Nature are, in a sense, subservient to the adaptive skill of man. Mr. Chadwick, in an off-hand speech, not long since, said: "Not what he can get out of it, but what he puts into it, is what makes a good artist." And is it not this creative power which has had most to do with the evolution of the race?

Was there not much truth in the enthusiastic outburst of

Tickler in that remarkable symposium on nature and art which is one of the most pleasing of all the Noctes Ambrosianæ: "Who planted those trees by that river-side? Art! Who pruned them? Art! Who gave room to their great arms to span that roaring chasm? Art! Who reared yon edifice on the cliff? Art! Is that a hermit's cell? Art scooped it out of the living stone. Is that an oratory? Art smoothed the floor for the knee of the penitent. Are the bones of the holy slumbering in that cemetery? Art changed the hollow rock into a tomb, and when the dead saint was laid into the sepulchre, Art joined its music with the torrent's roar, and the mingled anthem rose to the stars which Art had numbered."

When we contemplate the numberless æons during which our progenitors lived and walked among the most majestic scenes of Nature, and remember that none of the great divisions of the fine arts have flourished much beyond a score of centuries, we must admit that it is in the growth and development of human art that the great elements of progress have found their most efficient exposition.

The relation of art to Nature is, in great part, that of an interpreter. "Art performs the same office for the mind," says Jarvis, "that speech does for the ear. It is a variety of language, sometimes requiring sound, as in music, for its alphabet; form, as in sculpture; and form and color combined, as in painting." From the picture-writing of the earlier Egyptians to the slave-ship of Turner, the one object of the artist is to communicate his new thought to the observer. Century after century, mankind lacking this interpretation have groped blindly along, entangling themselves more and more in the complex web of human passion and desire, until at great epochs the great interpreter has arisen who has sung the song, builded the temple, painted the picture, carved the statue, or written the poem which has riven the cloud of ignorance and engraved his name among the great artists of his century. In the broadest sense, all such are artists. Whoever creates, whether in the field of fancy, art, science, religion, statecraft, or war; whoever shows a new method, discloses a new beauty, contributes a new impulse to his fellow, is an artist.

The poorly-equipped peasant walks, perhaps, for thirty years beneath a midnight sky and never looks higher than the low thatched roof of his cabin. Whoever points him to the glittering pageantry above and reveals to him the matchless beauty of the stars is an artist. The lesson may come to him from the trite couplet of an old Greek poet; it may shine out from the glowing canvas of a Titian; it may be born in the fervor of eloquent speech—if only he be lifted up to see the new beauty, to be possessed of the new thought, the true artist has done his work. Nature has found for him its interpreter; thenceforward he is more reverent toward her; all her ways take forms of lasting beauty in his sight; he has been shown the way.

Using the term art, then, in its broadest signification, the evolution of art would be commensurate with that of man, since what man has done constitutes the all of human history. So competent an authority as Sydney Colvin has said that art comprises "every regulated operation or dexterity by which organized beings pursue ends which they know beforehand, together with the rules and the result of every such operation or dexterity."

The art of war, the art of government, the art of worship, the inventive arts, the art of navigation, the fine arts of music, poetry, painting, sculpture, and architecture, all are within the definition. Most intimately connected with all these latter arts are those of government and invention, as affecting the environment, which, encircling man at different stages of his history, have constituted important modifications of his creative skill. It will be assumed, however, that our inquiry this evening is to be confined to palpable art creation as represented in one of the five great departments of human skill, the exercise of which finds embodiment in a symphony, a painting, a statue, a building, or a poem. All these will be found to be absolutely determined in their results by the controlling ideals of the artists, and these in turn to be largely modified by contemporaneous wants.

At the outset let us observe that all the arts are dependent upon two classes of persons for their existence and survival—namely, artists and art-lovers. The one can not exist without the other. The last man in the world will neither write, sing, paint, carve, nor build. Demosthenes, training his voice at the shore of the sea, heard above the tumultuous fury of the breakers the swelling applause of Athenian audiences. That was his objective point, and all great artists dedicate their work to the art-lovers of the race at large—whether in alien states or in generations unborn. And this distinction must be kept in mind in order rightly to weigh or judge the varying conditions of mankind.

Consider for a moment the state of government, the habits of life, the narrow horizon of that cultivated people who carried the realm of taste in the early age of Greece to such a height that in all the long centuries which have succeeded them no more perfect conception has been known, no more skillful hand has executed than that which buried its identity in the charming outlines of the Venus of Milo, so that in an age which boasts of the elevation of its masses and the erudition of its scholars, which has cloven the bed of ocean for the passage of its thought, its most hopeful students of art are sitting at the feet of artists dead for two thousand years, and are faithfully copying the clear lines and proportions of the human form laid down for them on the banks of the Mediterranean centuries before the Christian era.

There also had thriven painting, poetry, and architecture, and the race that crowded the halls of the Parthenon at its dedication had heard for fifteen generations the mellow Grecian syllables of Homer repeated in all its households.

Now, this people was largely an enslaved race; their inventive genius was still slumbering; the husbandmen of that day plowed, sowed, and reaped with the rudest devices; the most limited forms of communication existed; communion with the outer world, and especially with other nationalities, hardly existed at all. No true conceptions of statecraft were known to their rulers. They had no dealings with humanity in the aggregate. A few independent cities, allied by the most slender threads of mutual interest, constituted their entire state. Their habits of life were of the simplest kind. Their moral culture was at so low an ebb that they banished the wisest man among them from their chiefest city because they were tired of hearing him called the just. And yet the universal consensus of cultivated people is that in beauty of outline, in matchless expression, in absolute perfection of delineation, their art stands unapproachable as yet in the history of the world.

What, then, was the producing cause of their creative effort? Let it be noticed first that the achievements of this age were valued by a limited class of people. It is possible that not a hundred thousand Grecians ever saw all the great works of art which came from the cunning hands of Scopas, Lysippus, or Polycleitus during the lives of the artists, and of these, few, perhaps none, had any conception of the posthumous glory which was to immortalize the names of men then walking in their midst, and the principal feature of the situation, as it impresses one who searches for the impulse to this art, will be seen to be that it met the current demand of the ruling sources of power.

The upper life of Greece was given over to sensuous delight and to one phase of that ambition—that of form. It was reserved for the Roman artist to glut the senses of a later people with the glowing hues of the canvas. Rubens, Titian, and Raphael were to make the coming centuries radiant with their brilliant devices of color, but the luxury of the Greek delighted itself with graceful flowing outlines. The balmy atmosphere, the languid temperature, the softly breathing winds from the Ægean waters, were an ever-present inspiration to well-rounded shapes, and the artist of that time studied industriously the human form and wrought with such matchless cunning that the demand of his generation congealed into the simple, graceful beauty of the disentombed statues of the Greek temples.

And yet for fifteen centuries before the walls of the Parthenon rose in that golden age of Pericles, when Phidias—sculptor, artist, and architect—was rearing his monuments of wonder and beauty, there had stood on the banks of the sluggish Nile the most colossal product of human hands, and two hundred years after the walls of the Parthenon were to be shattered by gunpowder the prying eyes of the present century were to explore for the first time the hidden recesses of the Egyptian pyramids. But, if we seek for the beginnings of art, we shall wander back into the age of myths and romances.

It is impossible for any historian, archæologist, or evolutionist to assert as an established proposition that what we call civilization has not attained heights in the past far beyond the possibilities of the present to conceive; and even the signal products of art which are preserved to us may be but the lesser productions of some preceding age, the glories and beauties of which are locked deep in the foundations of the earth. No greater error can be made than to consider our own as the apex age of the world; for, however humiliating may be the fact, candor must compel us to admit at the outset that in architects, sculptors, painters, poets, and musicians the centuries already closed stand pre-eminently above the present epoch.

What greater names have we to-day than Wren in architecture, Mozart in music, Shakespeare in poetry, and Rembrandt in painting? This is not to say that the artistic sense is not to-day far more widely spread than in any previous age. Rather it is to say that when we speak of the evolution of art we are recognizing that the knowledge of art has grown, that its borders have increased, that its area of influence has widened. It is not to say that by any known processes of nature or of human conduct the great artist has been brought forth as a clearly discerned effect from an all-sufficient cause; for nothing in science, religion, or evolution has ever been able to uproot the old Roman aphorism as to the birth of poets.

The true theory undoubtedly is that the exceptional man of any age has set the ideal not only for his contemporaries, but many times for the centuries to come. It is the art-lovers who are increasing even though the colossal artists are becoming less frequent. And this limitation must be kept in mind in considering for a moment the relation of art to civilization.

Civilization must be measured in the last analysis by the extent of its influence upon the largest number of human beings. The civilization which is of value to mankind at large is not that which carries a select few nearest heaven, but that which lifts the ignorant mass farthest from earth. The true relation of civilization to art, then, has been to increase its admirers, to extend its audience, to make possible new but not greater masters by bringing to its promoters larger accessions of people. The advantages of the last two centuries have manifestly been not to overtop the great artists of the past, but to greatly multiply their disciples and admirers and thereby elevate and dignify the æsthetic quality in humanity.

Take an illustration from our own country. In 1790 Franklin presented the first petition to Congress to abolish slavery. In 1792 Whitney invented the cotton-gin. Then began a contest between a principle of human rights and a product of human art. The art thrived, the right was overcome. The nation, bent on keeping alive, approved the one and ignored the other, but the seed of right, long dormant, blossomed into war and fruited in victory. The money-getting power of the cotton-gin had given way to the moral power of righting a great wrong.

While such a contest was raging in a new land with lives to preserve and fortunes to gain and maintain, is it any wonder that the fields of the highest arts were sterile, the fountains of beauty ran dry, and the deep-thinking man of the present can find no phenomenal greatness in its artists? Even now we are sustaining, by the wisdom of our national legislature, the Chinese wall against foreign paintings and sculpture which our fathers timidly reared. Let us not be deceived. We must look for our great artists—in heaven.

The prevailing tendency in our country to-day is one of practical betterment in goods and estates. It is the fame of the soldier, the wealth of the millionaire, and the power of the politician that captivates the eye of our growing youth. The press and the pulpit are disputing supremacy, not in the realms of classic art, but in the arena of commanding results, and the results to be commanded are safety in government, safety hereafter, economy in the management of public affairs, and such a development and extension of the facilities of money-getting as will most largely benefit the common people. The daily aim and object of the average citizen of the world in this present year 1891 is to get above his fellows in power, and power with a vast majority means money. The overburdened tax-payer cares not who is mayor of his city so long as his tax-rate is lowered. Four centuries before Christ the citizens of Cnidus were offered by Nicomedes the discharge of their entire debt in exchange for a statue which Praxiteles had created, but they kept the statue. What works of art in any of our great cities would weigh for a moment in value, taken together, against its debt, in the opinion of its suffrage-brokers?

To this end the thrifty arts are those which obtain a market—the useful arts, as the authorities classify them. The man who can invent the liveliest egg-beater rides in his carriage, while the artist, from the soft eyes of whose creation the soul of centuries shines, walks afoot, content if he be allowed his modest share of the king's highway. A patent car-coupler, a talking-machine, increasing a hundred-fold the contact of man with man, putting vast continents in touch with one another across intervening oceans, carries with it the capital prizes of wealth and honor, and the mean soul who has nothing to offer but the perpetuation of some phase of natural beauty on his canvas sits hungering in his dingy garret, wondering why his benefactor, the tariff-tinker, does not protect him better.

I have said that art is the interpreter of Nature. The primal medium of this interpretation is imitation. Burke says: "No work of art can be great but as it deceives; to be otherwise is the prerogative of Nature only."

He that has looked farthest into the material heart of the world shall most correctly interpret her secrets. A writer of prominence has said that "Purcell, Handel, and Bach wrote every combination of musical notes that down to our latest times has ever been employed with good effect," and yet the last of them has been dead more than a hundred years; and Jarvis has said that "all that is noblest in art took its origin in the thirteenth century."

It is the first necessity of our improvement in art, to clear the way for our great artist, if he is ever to be, that we shall frankly disassociate our artistic genius from the deceiving glamour of the national ensign. What callow youth in America does not feel the insignificance of Ruskin when he writes in Fors Clavigera that "though I have kind invitations enough to visit America, I could not, even for a couple of months, live in a country so miserable as to possess no castles"? And with what pride he turns to the divinity of Shakespeare, who consoles him with the gracious aphorism that "the art of our necessities is strange that can make vile things precious"! And yet Ruskin might well be referred to an older country than his own—Japan—where the temple of Todaiji, older than any cathedral in Europe, retains, almost unimpaired, the perfection of its structure and the brilliancy of its decoration.

But is there not something beneath the gibe of Ruskin that rankles of reality? Is there not a background of experience and of history, of storied memories and regnant battle scenes, as necessary to the loins out of which a great artist is to spring as to the finished product of a Claude Lorrain? If we believe with Charles Sumner that "that quality or characteristic called experience is the highest element of art," can we not well understand that the humanity of ages past must look out from the painter's pigment if it is to catch the eye of the true lover of art?

The germs of high art, then, have been lying latent in the soil of all the centuries, and have been hindered, encouraged, overwhelmed, and developed by the fundamental elements of manhood in association. We have high authority for asserting that "the appreciation of art and the art impulse are inherent in the nature of man, and are not the products of civilization." If, as Taine observes, "a work of art is determined by a condition of things combining all surrounding social and intellectual influences," then the quality of the artist himself should be largely affected by these changing conditions.

Perhaps some light may come to us in following this theme by considering a little more carefully the sources of art.

We have already found that the arsenal of the artist is furnished by Nature. She is the tutelary saint entitled to his grateful worship. But the inspiration that informs the pencil or the chisel of the artist, whence comes it? Why does Correggio outshine Guido, or each of these another? So long as artists have painted, sung, or builded, Nature has lain before them in the same transcendent beauty. The limpid moonlit stream which the poet and the artist of every age have striven to re-create was running clear and shining in the ages long before the Sphinx, and tells its enchanting story anew to every succeeding generation. Whatever new standards in other things have been erected, the copy-book of Nature remains substantially the same. Is it not then safe to conclude that there is something beside the imitator and the imitated which largely modifies the resulting work of art?

Mr. Taine says: "If we pass in review the principal epochs of the history of art, we find the arts appearing and disappearing with certain accompanying social and intellectual conditions." It must be clear that while men were in the savage or even pastoral stage of living, no want of art was felt. It was only when a fixity of abode had been determined upon that any of the fine arts began to develop. The demand for shelter was the first necessity, out of which came in time Westminster Abbey. Two upright posts, perhaps the stumps of trees, supporting as a rude lintel a log thrown across, was the first step taken toward the Coliseum of Rome, covering its eighty thousand people.

Given, then, the artist born, his ear attuned to Nature, his imagination kindling at her suggestive mysteries, his heart throbbing responsively to all the sweet influences of her great magazine of forces, still the product of his art is to be largely modified and its ultimate evolution to be prescribed by his environment, and it is the evolution of this environment with which we are chiefly interested. Four great controlling influences will be seen to be effective in shaping it—religion, government, locality, and the prevailing judgment of the time.

Let us consider these separately.

Taking, in the first instance, religion, it will be found that it has furnished at times the only opportunity for art to live. Letters, architecture, poetry, sculpture, and music, like the hunted criminal of the early centuries, all found sanctuary at her shrine. True, she has imposed in many instances the most morbid conditions on the sons of genius. Michael Angelo, ordered by Leo X to quarry with his own hands the Pope's monument, comes down to posterity himself immortalized, the Pope forgotten. So out of joint was he with the times in which he lived that it is no wonder that he wrote upon the pedestal of his sleeping statue—

"Sleep is sweet, and yet *more* sweet it is to be of stone while shame and misery last."

And Raphael, compelled by the same pope to interpolate the burly pontifical figure into his matchless fresco in the Vatican, is heir to all the greatness of his deed. And while we may not believe that Dalmasio, an early painter of Bologna, gained art efficacy by fasting every day while painting the Holy Virgin, yet the Church as a conservator of art must be given credit for offering the opportunities which she undoubtedly has to the earnest art creator.

To the Church, indeed, we are almost exclusively indebted for the evolution of the Gothic type of architecture, from the simple pediment of the Grecian temples to the great cathedrals of Europe. And while religion protected the artist by its strong and effective patronage, it also furnished the opportunity for widening the scope of his genius. The mysterious ruins at Stonehenge are supposed to have been the meeting places of a rude people for religious rites. Nor was it only in the art of building that religion has been preservative, not to say productive, of the works of genius. The wonderful frescos that glorify the roofs of her Florentine chapels; the statues that dignify her great cathedrals; the majestic poetry of Job; the sweet songs of David, and the glowing fervor of many a Hebrew scripture, have all been preserved to us by various religious sects. The curiously carved wooden temples of India; the imposing monolithic structures of Egypt; the quiet, simple beauty of the Grecian porches that dignified the approaches to the summit of the Acropolis, alike attest the intimate dependence of art upon the patronage of the worshipful impulse in man.

And may it not be asserted with equal truth that to-day the commanding influence of the mother Church is largely dependent in turn upon the art creations of which she so freely avails herself? He who, susceptible to deep religious awe, enters some great cathedral of to-day, is divided in homage between his supernatural sense of the divine presence and his appreciative delight of that which the cunning skill of human art has devised for its embellishment. Poetry marries itself to music in the deep-swelling harmony and rhythmic flow of sentences which answer from the organ loft above to the dim recesses of the chancel in the apse. The deeply groined roof, planned by the skillful architect, is glowing far above with the transcendent brilliancy of the sunlight which brings in strong relief the enchanting figures of departed saints with which the painter has crowded the stained windows of the clearstory. From all these brilliant accessories of art, does not the belief of the actual presence of the Christ in the wine and water of the host derive much of its supernatural conviction, and would not the same ceremonies, transferred to the barren simplicity of a Quaker church, lose much of their influence upon man's emotional nature?

However this may be, the fact remains that in no age, at least of the Christian era, has the Church divorced from her services the aid of art. And if time sufficed, it might be approximately demonstrated that this art environment has in all ages been largely shaped and colored by the dominant religion of its time.

The huge monolithic temples and excavatory tombs of ancient Persia were the tangible expression of their simple pagan beliefs, and the wonderful temple at Karnak, on whose rugged pylon, sixteen centuries before the Christ was born, Thothmes the Third had carved the history of his military expeditions, and within whose spacious outlines two cathedrals as large as St. Peter's of Rome could be builded —represented faithfully the prevailing temper of that theology which dedicated its walls to Chons, the Deity who possessed the highly convenient attribute of expelling evil. There was no room in an age when the millions were burden-bearers, and the few wearers of purple, for art to lift itself toward heaven, and to these people was unknown the pediment or arch in architecture, meter or rhythm in poetry, or harmony in music.

All the noteworthy products of Gothic architecture date their origin less than five centuries ago, and found their opportunity and inspiration in the great established churches of their periods. Indeed, we have the best of authority for asserting that secular art was comparatively unknown until the seventeenth century.

This brings us to notice the second element of art environment—namely, government. An absolute form of government deputed the power to fix authoritatively the fashion of the time to the monarch. It likewise furnished him exclusively the revenues of the realm to execute such conceptions of art as his fancy chose to promote. Thus it was that art was degraded by the selfish vanity of Romish popes, and the artist was only permitted to survive upon a slavish complaisance with the caprices of power.

The vacillating Dryden, tuning the lyre of his mellifluous poetry to the changing dynasties of Puritan Cromwell and Episcopal Charles, is an instance among poets of this controlling power; and wherever the people have been free to choose, with the added capacity of knowing how to choose, there the artistic sense has reached its highest development.

There can be little doubt that the objects to which the creative and executive powers of man are devoted have increased in diversity and importance with the growth of civilization, and, upon familiar rules of evolution, this should have resulted in an increase in the complexity of the art product. And a modern writer of standing has declared that "the further research is pursued, alike into the habits of living races of savages and into the characteristics of the oldest traces of primitive art, the more clearly becomes manifest a process of development from the first rude working in stone to the highest art of the skilled metallurgist."

Clearly, also, art is dignified or disgraced by the objects which it seeks to accomplish, and what these shall be are almost altogether determined by the average good taste or judgment of the special time. Modified in large part by these considerations, the knowledge of the classic arts borrowed from older Egypt increased and throve in Greece and Rome. Sometimes it followed in the wake of victories, as when the Romans invaded the British Islands, and again it survived the defeat of cultured people, as when Rome, conquering the Athenian cities, discovered her imperishable arts—arts which long after survived the devastation of Rome herself by the barbarous Northmen.

Engulfed in the general ruin of the middle ages, it came to new glory in the latter centuries, always and everywhere determining the real status of art.

Of locality as an environment, it may be further observed that it has largely modified art by prescribing its objects and limiting its possibilities. The northern half of Germany being devoid of stone, all its buildings of magnitude are composed of brick, which constitutes a limit of material. Obviously in warm countries the less substantial structures of wood would meet all immediate necessities, while in temperate zones, like our own, the fullest scope for material of all kinds would be furnished.

A fourth element of art environment has been mentioned as the prevailing judgment of the time. This must be seen at once to be largely determined by the auxiliary conditions of science, the minor arts, and especially the arts preservative and distributive of art productions. Poetry found an expansive outlet in the art of printing; architecture, painting, and sculpture in the various inventions by which the stability of nations has been increased or the products of art distributed. Science, "upon which," says Spencer, "the highest art of every kind is based, and without which there can be neither perfect production nor full appreciation," has brought, by its development of the skillful arts, the productions of the great artists to the knowledge and apprehension of all classes.

The subsidiary arts of engraving and photography, especially the perfective arts of chromo-lithography and the artotype process, have literally carried to the firesides of the poor the costly exclusiveness of the Vatican, and there lie on the tables of more than half of the skilled mechanics of the world to-day more really beautiful art representations than were in the castles of the English barons of the sixteenth century.

While, then, we may deplore the dearth of highly creative artistic genius, we must acknowledge the increasing evolution toward a more perfect apprehension of true art ideals of the prevailing judgment of the time. The great foundation stones of all true art—simplicity, truth, expression—long buried by the *débris* of decaying taste and a corrupt standard of excellence, are finding once more an appreciative recognition. Even the necessities of commerce itself have brought about changes in standards of art which have found a response in the taste of the people. Whoever stands in the City Hall Park of New York, and, appalled at the grotesque ugliness of the Post Office, fails to understand why the builder could not have opened his eyes to the simple and chaste proportions of the City Hall across the Plaza, can find a sure relief by crossing the Wall Street Ferry and feasting his eyes upon that modern wonder which swings its fair proportions above the vehicles of traffic that ply their complex passage beneath—the Brooklyn bridge. Here necessity, many times the cruel tyrant of art, has imposed conditions upon the builder, the result of which has challenged the artistic homage of the world. It most effectually satisfies the two great essentials of art—simplicity and unity of design.

Now, this average judgment of the times, called by some good taste, is subject both to complete submergence, as in the centuries before the Renaissance, and to epidemic diseases due to changing environment and to sporadic art-fashions.

Modern Italian art, especially in sculpture, exhibits one of these, and in our day the rank contagion of an unnecessary realism in art offers a conspicuous illustration. We have among us quite a scholastic contingency, who have fallen in love with that kind of interpretation of Nature which reproduces with photographic minuteness all her minutiæ of incident and fact under the plea that it is a necessity of truth.

Tolstoi, Zola, and Whitman, in literature, are the apostles of what seems to their disciples to be a new era in art, the province of which is to tell some secret of Nature hitherto decorously concealed. They attach themselves to the realistic school of art and carry the wholesome doctrine of anti-sham production to an extreme which would be ridiculous if it were not disgusting. Nothing is to be left to the imagination of the reader. The most offensive details of immorality, the by and forbidden paths of infamy and vice, are dragged festering to the light of day, under as conscientious a disregard of the decencies of society as if the artists had been sworn in a court of justice to tell the truth, the whole truth, and nothing but the truth. Under the fostering protection of many men of genius, our book-stalls are infected with the vilest suggestions of indecency, and publishers vie with each other in running as near the condemnation of the law as their fear of its punishment will permit them to do.

Now, let us not ignore the facts of nature; vice, crime, misery, obscenity, unfortunately exist. Through the threescore years of human life they will often enough protrude themselves as uninvited guests upon all of us, but the heresy of this school of art is found in its degradation of the art object. The notion that, for any purpose, or to accomplish any end or aim of true art-pleasure, the artist should find it necessary, or in the least degree helpful, to draggle his muse in the mire, is one utterly unsustained either by the healthy intuitions of mankind or by empirical reasoning.

The constantly increasing effort of every true disciple of art, whether Olympian creator or humble admirer is to soar above the limitations of to-day; it is to direct the impulses of humanity toward better things and not to call their attention to meaner, not to say unclean, objects; it is to reveal to man the benignant significance of Nature rather than to invite his attention to her morbid excrescences; and every great artist who has touched the heart of his own or succeeding ages with a commanding influence has used in the accomplishment of his worthy purpose the chaste weapons of honor, truth, simplicity, and sincerity. He has fixed his gaze upon the shining purity of the Pleiades rather than upon the unhallowed depths of human weakness and crime.

Is there really so much danger that the coming generations shall be too refined or virtuous or high-minded, that we must temper their noble aspirations with literature so rankly questionable that it is most safely placed on the high shelves of our libraries? The alleged necessity of realism, which, masquerading under the clean name of truth, gluts itself with the disgusting putridities of vicious hearts and vicious minds, is the product of as diseased a condition of the true art impulse as it is a subtle impeachment of our common humanity; and it finds its most ardent and effective support, not in the high-minded men who are blinded by its seeming fidelity to the truths of Nature, but in the scurvy camp-followers of art, who gorge themselves upon the offal which is sometimes created by the mistakes of its masters.

This school of realists is by no means new to the fields of art. The churches of Naples and Spain in the sixteenth century colored and draped their statues. Jarvis describes a mosaic on the ceiling of the Baptistery of the Duomo of

Florence, representing the realities of a local hell-fire as follows: "A huge figure of Christ clad in robes of deep blue and red, and displaying his pierced hands and feet, is the prominent object; above him is a representation of the Almighty as an old man in a red frock with a carefully trimmed beard holding the book of life; on each side are attendant cherubs and seraphs. Beneath the Saviour is the scene of the resurrection; angels are helping the good to rise from out of their tombs on his right hand, while on his left great green devils with bat-like wings are eagerly pulling sinners from their graves. Satan, as a huge monster of like color, is seen sitting in the center of hell munching human beings; on either side of him are serpents and hideous imps pursuing the damned, who escape their fury only by plunging into lakes of fire. Above the infernal regions the apostles and saints sit in stiff rows with books in their hands, while archangels lead the saved in crowds to join them." And this was a fair illustration, adds the author, of Florentine art and theology in the thirteenth century.

Let it not for a moment be supposed that any word here spoken is to be taken as ignoring in any degree the true school of realists in literature and art. Homer, Shakespeare, Dickens, and all the noble names in literature were in a true sense realists, if by realism be meant a faithful representation of the incidents and circumstances of the world about them; but it is the crowning glory of Dickens that in no single paragraph of his voluminous writings has he found it either desirable or necessary to pander to the meretricious taste; and the name of Howells, among American realists, is equally suggestive of clarity and a sound mind. Mark it well, friends: when a teacher of the public heart and mind begins to discuss with himself the decency of the scene or illustration which he is to employ, he is in the same situation with a holder of public office who finds himself splitting hairs as to the right or wrong of some proposed official action. In the one case as in the other, the only safe course to be pursued is to put under his feet with a lofty scorn the questionable proceeding, disenthrall his mind and heart from the ignoble temptation, and walk resolutely forth into the clear, still air where conscience breathes, and where the holy promptings of his truer and better nature find a responsive audience.

And now, without in any sense, either complete or incomplete, having demonstrated how art has grown to be what it is, or through what varying conditions of intelligence, government, religion, or other environments the products of art which bless and dignify our own age have been developed, we are brought to the close of our fifty minutes' consideration of our subject.

Briefly considered, it would appear that the artist, by which is meant the art-creator, is not the product of any known cause; that he visits unbidden and unaccounted for the haunts of men; but, on the other hand, the art-lovers are largely the product of favoring or unfavoring influences of widely different education, leisure to observe, capacity to value, and desire to possess the products of artistic genius. To the furnishing of this environment have contributed all processes of nature, all inventive genius, all improvements in mechanism, all tendencies which shorten the hours of necessary labor, reveal to man new opportunities, or bring within his reach new art-creations. Out of the first necessities of man arose the first products of his hands, and out of this gratification of his necessities has developed this increasing desire, which has been called the "play-want" of mankind, for the ornamental as distinguished from the useful. It had its rude beginnings in the uncouth decoration of the tattooed savage, it rose to sublime heights in the Athenian courts, it went down in the despairing darkness of the middle ages, it revived in the glories of the French renaissance, it was planted upon firm foundations in the Elizabethan age, it crossed the ocean to the New World, and is to crown at last its new environment with ever-widening beauty and grandeur.

Seeking thus for the seeds of culture, refinement, and beauty out of which have blown the precious products of the artist's soul, we have found them beneath alien skies, among foreign peoples, and in older times. It may well be worth our while to ask of the future what it has in store for the latest home of art.

Reasoning from such premises as the fundamental doctrines of evolution can furnish, what should the answer be? If from any soil there are to spring more fruitful products of the human mind than all the past can furnish, here is the clime, here will be the environment. Art, in the sense in which we have considered it, is the crowning product of a great people. He who reads aright the labors of our fathers must discern that we have but cleared the forest and laid the foundation stones of our American Pantheon. We have determined a few political postulates which were necessary to our existence as a state. We have climbed from the position of a poor relation in the confederacy of the world, to become the arbitrator of the wealthiest nation of Europe. The children of Rubens's genius, repeated by art-processes unknown but a score of years ago, look down from the walls of the humblest peasantry all over the land, the thoughts of all the great poets inspire the rudest people of the frontiers. In whatever waste cavern of the continent the child of genius hides, a ray of light is sure to touch him from the ubiquitous newspaper, for in the advancing army of intelligence at the very front is the column of the press. We have just begun to possess a leisure class, without which, as furnishing art-lovers, no art can flourish. True, our leisure classes are quite often, and sometimes justly, mistaken for loafers, but they are here and have come to stay. They are finding out the charms of Nature and are rapidly possessing themselves of her domain. They have fallen in love with Art and are transferring her treasures from private cloisters to public museums. They have begun to house in seats of learning our masters of letters, and to erect the busts and statues of the sculptors within our public parks. They are placing in the way of all the people the highest interpretations by art of Nature. Upon the use which they shall make of this opportunity is to depend the destiny of art, and out of this destiny is to emerge the coming artist. Greater than Shakespeare's may be the song which is to entrance the peoples of the thousand years to come. Greater, higher, stronger than all the past has known must always be the possibilities of the future. Let no man, surveying the present, dare to boast of its starveling products as the best that is in the capacity of men. Rather let us with candor confess that in the unwritten volumes of the coming years shall be found the fruitful nepenthe for the present. Contented, happy, hopeful, may that man or woman well be who shall have listened reverently to the lessons of the past, in whom the sublime vision of beauty shall have found loving recognition, and who can with kindling heart and sincere feeling repeat as his own the language of another but little paraphrased:

"So venerable, so majestic is this living temple of art, this immemorial and yet freshly growing fabric of beauty, that the least of us is happy who hereafter may point to so much as one stone thereof and say, 'The work of my hands is there.'"

ABSTRACT OF THE DISCUSSION.

MR. Z. SIDNEY SAMPSON:

While I have been deeply interested in the able paper of Mr. Taylor, I must dissent from his pessimistic view of the present condition of the artist in America. The high prices obtained for objects of art at recent sales is an evidence, it seems to me, that the condition of the artist is improving.

One of the basic principles of evolution is the law of differentiation, as expressed in Herbert Spencer's well-known formula. This is true not only in biology and sociology, but also in the development of art, as illustrated by the lecture of the evening. As art becomes complex and highly organized, it differentiates into opposing schools, resulting from differences in local environments.

As regards realism or naturalism, against which the lecturer has animadverted, as I understand its devotees, they hold that art is concerned with truth rather than with morality. In literature, at least, they profess to be educators of their readers. In order to educate them in a knowledge of life, we must analyze life, and if we truthfully portray the facts derived from our analysis, we must record and portray the details even of vice and crime. Such writers do not claim the name of artist so much as that of educator and truth-teller.

MR. DANIEL GREENLEAF THOMPSON:

I have listened with great pleasure to the scholarly and beautiful lecture of Mr. Taylor, and will merely amplify one or two thoughts which he has presented. In the familiar line of Keats,

"A thing of beauty is a joy forever,"

are set forth two of the fundamental characteristics of art: first, in the word "joy," which expresses the principle that there must be in all true art the quality of agreeableness, and, secondly, in the word "forever," which indicates the universality of art. A work of human skill, to be art, must be beautiful; the disagreeable as it exists in Nature or in fact must be eliminated. Realistic art, so called, thus fails to be real art. Yet we are bound to realize the fact that tastes differ at different times, and that which one generation applauds may be condemned by another. Many of the pictures to be seen in foreign galleries are to us expressive only of the horrible, presenting as they do phases of military and religious life that we have ceased to admire yet when they were painted they were an inspiration to the beholders living in environments totally different from ours. In our day realism takes a form less disagreeable to us, though perhaps not less objectionable on that account. After all, we must not quarrel with the artist, but with the people or civilization whose habits he depicts. In the future, Art will ally itself to Science, interpreting and explaining the latter—combining the highest art with the highest scientific truth. The most finished work of art will always be a noble human character.

Mr. Ellsworth Warner:

I think the lecturer has not dwelt sufficiently upon the relation of art to morality. In the discussion of the evolution of art before an ethical association that point ought not to be slighted. Does the development of the artistic feeling conduce to the higher evolution of man as a moral being? Viewing art historically, were those ages most distinguished for its development remarkable also for purity of morals? In Greece, for example, the over-development of the art-feeling was certainly coincident with the fostering of a love of pleasure rather than a sense of duty. The Puritan period, in which, whatever may have been its faults, the idea of duty was paramount, was not an art period. The field of art, as it appears to me, is narrowing by the application of mechanical devices in the production of the beautiful. If recent reports of success in photographing colors are correct, a great step will be taken toward the disuse of the pencil and the brush.

Dr. Lewis G. Janes:

I have greatly enjoyed the lecture of Mr. Taylor, and heartily agree with him in his main positions. I was particularly glad to hear his characterization of our modern realism in literature. I can not refrain, however, from protesting against the association of the name of Walt Whitman with those of Tolstoi, Ibsen—and Zola, I presume, should be classed with them, though I have never read a page of Zola myself. I have read Walt Whitman, and his realism—virile and optimistic, full of the healthy, natural flavor of the woods and fields—it seems to me, should not be confounded with the morbid pessimism of the realistic novelists, which smacks rather of the over-heated, ill-ventilated study. I confess that I can not always see poetry in Whitman's productions, but his realism seems to me expressive of an ideal totally different from that of Tolstoi and Ibsen. If he exalts the sense-life in man, it is because he sees in it that which is healthful, natural, and good. Whitman is the prophet of Democracy; his protest is against that morbid asceticism, born of a false theology, which assumes man's total depravity and sees naught but evil in his bodily passions. You nowhere find in his writings apologies for or glorifications of the sensual, as such, in an evil or degrading sense, or minute delineations of vice and crime, or pessimistic views of life or its conditions. The praise of pure-minded Emerson, and of such able art-critics as John Addington Symonds, shows that I am not alone in my judgment.

MR. WILLIAM POTTS:

I wish to add a word of thanks to the lecturer for his vigorous denunciation of the barn-yard school of literature. I can not say with the president that I have not read a page of Zola; I have read many pages; but I do not regard him nearly as disgusting as Tolstoi. I disagree with Mr. Warner in his implication that we may be injured morally by too much love of the beautiful. The moral is itself the beautiful in character, and naturally allies itself with all other forms of beauty. As regards photography, in a certain sense it is art, as are also the so-called mechanic arts. In the highest sense, however, art is Nature as seen through the medium of the artist. The personal note is the main thing in art of the highest character. I do not think, with Mr. Taylor, that art necessarily reached its highest development in the past. Following the natural law of evolution, art has become specialized, and while we may not have great all-around artists, we have great specialists in art. In dramatic music, for instance, I think most competent critics will agree that in Richard Wagner this art has reached its highest exemplification in our own day. And in landscape painting no previous era has equaled our own.

DR. ROBERT G. ECCLES:

I am surprised that no word has been said in defense of Tolstoi from the strictures that have been made upon him. I think he is the only really consistent Christian writer of our time. I do not believe he is guilty of intentional grossness. While I do not myself accept Tolstoi's conclusions, I believe him to be honest and consistent. I believe he is following, sincerely and logically, the teachings of Jesus Christ and of St. Paul.

MR. J. HOWARD COWPERTHWAIT:

I wish to enter my protest against eulogizing the Puritan, and extolling his spirit and influence as of superior morality to that of our own time. I think the Puritans wrought great mischief by their teaching that all pleasure is wicked. Their appearance of superior sanctity was superficial. Like all asceticism, it covered grosser immoralities of conduct than those which characterize eras of larger freedom. The Puritan should be taken down from his pedestal, and Art placed thereon instead.

Mr. Taylor, in closing, replied briefly to his critics, defending the positions taken in his lecture. He thought Mr. Warner confounded the natural effect of art with that of the prostitution of art. As to Tolstoi and Whitman, he regarded them as geniuses—particularly the former. The latter was undoubtedly original, but was he a poet? The great poet might analyze, but Whitman's analysis ran into inconsequential details that were no more poetry or art than was an auctioneer's catalogue. Mr. Taylor closed with an amusing parody on the poetry of Whitman.

THE EVOLUTION OF ARCHITECTURE

BY

JOHN W. CHADWICK

AUTHOR OF THE BIBLE OF TO-DAY, CHARLES R. DARWIN, EVOLUTION AS RELATED TO RELIGIOUS THOUGHT, ETC.

COLLATERAL READINGS SUGGESTED:

Lübke's History of Art; Reber's History of Ancient Art and History of Mediæval Art; Freeman's The Effects of the Norman Conquest on Art, in History of the Norman Conquest, Chap. XXVI, and Historical Sketch of Architecture in Great Britain, in Bädeker's Great Britain; Fergusson's History of Modern Architecture and Palaces of Nineveh and Persepolis; Article *Architecture*, in Encyclopædia Britannica; Viollet Le Duc's Discourses on Architecture and Story of a House; Herbert Spencer's Sources of Architectural Types, in Illustrations of Universal Progress; Wilkinson's Architecture of Ancient Egypt; Parker's Introduction to the Study of Gothic Architecture; Street's Gothic Architecture in Spain; Moore's Gothic Architecture; Murray's Handbooks of the English Cathedrals; Montgomery Schuyler's Modern Architecture in America.

THE EVOLUTION OF ARCHITECTURE.

By John W. Chadwick.

To any rational understanding of the evolution of architecture no one can help us less than the philosopher whose name is associated with the doctrine of evolution more honorably than any other. Mr. Spencer has written briefly of the Sources of Architectural Types. The following are the results which he contributes to our edification: "Buildings in the Greek and Roman style seem, in virtue of their symmetry, to take their type from animal life. In the partly-irregular Gothic, ideas derived from the vegetable world appear to predominate. And wholly irregular buildings, such as castles, may be considered as having inorganic forms for their base." Mr. Spencer has little sense of humor, but Sidney Smith never wrote anything funnier than this. We are not told what particular animal is resembled by the Parthenon. "Analogies do not go on all fours," said Whately, and certainly the Parthenon does not. It is more centipede than quadruped. But its sides are alike, and its back and front are different. Certainly it resembles a quadruped to this extent, and this is all that Mr. Spencer's analogy amounts to, all that he claims. The inference that the Greek went to the animal world for his architectural scheme is a conjecture as absurd as that of the Christian father Irenæus, to the effect that there must be four gospels because the wind blows from four quarters. For proof that castles of irregular construction are copied from "inorganic forms" Mr. Spencer offers the fact or fancy that the more irregular they are the better we are pleased; and that is so with inorganic forms. But is it so? From the whole range of crystalline perfection comes an emphatic No. But Mr. Spencer was evidently thinking more of great masses of inorganic matter, of mountain scenery. Is it true of that, the more irregular the better? Or do we never tire of our Monadnock's symmetry, or of such splendid cones as Hood and Fusiyami lift into the upper air? A certain "protective resemblance" in castles built on cliff or crag goes but a little way in proof of Mr. Spencer's generalization. The account he gives of the origins of the most symmetrical and the most irregular forms is at least original, and his claim to it does not invite dispute. But, as for the resemblance of Gothic architecture to vegetable forms, he is one of many in remarking the analogy between a groined nave and an avenue of trees with interlacing branches, and in contending that the former is a copy of the latter. But "an avenue of trees" is quite as artificial as a cathedral nave, and, while it is possible that the latter suggested the former, it is certain that the former did not suggest the latter. We know perfectly well how the groined nave arose, and we know that its actual origin furnishes illustrations of the doctrine of evolution second in force and beauty to no others in its imperial range. One approaches the west front of Winchester Cathedral from a magnificent avenue of trees that interlace their branches overhead. Entering the cathedral, you find the nave, I can not say built, but decorated, in the perpendicular style. England has nothing else to show so like an avenue of trees. But how feeble is the impression in comparison with the avenue without! Man's art, though at its best, is ever feeble when compared with the majestic handiwork of God.

It is an interesting comment on Mr. Spencer's account of architectural origins that Mr. Sidney Colvin, who is "wise unto salvation" in such matters, classifies architecture with music as a non-imitative art. He is well aware that in the pastoral symphony and elsewhere there are imitations of natural sounds, and that in architecture, especially in decoration, there is much imitation, more or less conventional, of vegetable and animal forms. But these facts do not affect the main conclusion that as music in general "appeals to our faculties for taking pleasure in non-imitative combinations of transitory sound, so architecture appeals to our faculties for taking pleasure in non-imitative combinations of stationary mass"—"combinations of line, light and shade, color, proportion, interval, alternation of plain and decorated parts, regularity and variety in regularity, apparent stability, vastness, appropriateness, and so on." Further than to set architecture with music as a non-imitative art over against the three other fine arts—sculpture, painting, and poetry, which are non-imitative in this matter of classification—I do not care to go. The different classifications have been almost as many as the attempts to classify. That men so radically different in their methods as Comte and Hegel arrived at very similar conclusions gives to their classification a special interest. This, proceeding from the lowest to the highest, was architecture, sculpture, painting, music, poetry. But here the personal equation accounts for much. No great architect or sculptor would allow of such subordination to his favorite art. So with the passive, non-creative artists of the world—those who enjoy what the creative artists make. For them the highest art is that which they enjoy the most. Thus, if I were going to classify the arts, I should say, beginning at the top, poetry, architecture, sculpture, painting, music, but I should know that my classification was purely subjective after its highest term. That poetry is absolutely the highest of the arts I have not a particle of doubt, and not much that music is the lowest. And for this reason the confusion of poetry and music by such poets as Poe and Swinburne and Sidney Lanier seems to me a very lamentable result.

That architecture is the only art of those ranked as Fine Arts of the Primary Order that has any implication of utility, is a circumstance which has frequently prevailed with those who have assigned to it a lower place. And one of these contends that architecture is pure art only in such constructions as are useless or very nearly so, and these are religious edifices and monuments. According to this dictum, the Roman Catholic church in which the priest does the worship is a much better field for the pure art of architecture than a Protestant church where "the word preached" is an essential part of the worship. Cardinal Newman said: "A church wanted for human use can not compete with a sacred building not wanted by men and women; for in the latter case it is built for the honor and glory of God, which is a much higher end of action than the convenience or service of men." Such a church would furnish a basis for the ideal purity of architectural art without any hindrance of utility. It is a wiser thought that architecture finds nowhere a more sacred law than in the fitness of its constructions for the ends which they are meant to serve. That is the best architecture in which we do not have to write under the separate buildings, "This is a church," "This is a bank," and so on, because a dominant style has imposed itself upon the city. The uniformity of Paris is considered classical, but we have reason to believe that Rome and Athens loved variety, especially of elevation. Nothing could be more different from the one level of the Louvre or Versailles than that glorious jumble which the so-called palace of the Cæsars must have been in Rome, a group of palaces, no two upon one level; and the Acropolis of Athens presented a similar effect. Use in architecture is not necessarily the enemy of beauty. For all its technical defects even so useful a building as our capitol at Washington is very nobly beautiful. Very beautiful also were the town halls of Flanders, in Brussels, Ghent, Liege, Louvain, and Oudenarde. Chicago has no church, even the most useless, that is so beautiful as the great storehouse for dry goods which Mr. Richardson built for Marshall Field. Nor are the arches of our Brooklyn Bridge less admirable as architecture because they serve the daily use of thronging multitudes.

Much better than to define architecture as the art of those constructions which have no use is it to say that it is the art of building with an eye to beauty without sacrifice of use where there is any use to serve—"a shaping art of which the function is to arouse emotion by combinations of ordered and decorated mass." And what is meant by the evolution of architecture is that in its historic changes there is nothing accidental; that each present form of it is rooted in some past and has its bearing on the future; that here also there is a struggle for existence and the preservation of the fittest to survive, which may or may not be the most beautiful; that there is a development of degeneration as well as of progress, as in animal and vegetable evolution; that here, as there, we have fixity of type and the tendency to variation, and that the selected variations make new species in the course of time. Indeed, there is hardly any principle of the general philosophy of evolution which does not find some illustration in the history of architectural form and decoration.

I do not propose at every stage of my discourse to point the moral, but to give you a broad outline of the course of architectural development, and let you make the application for yourselves, with here and there a more explicit word.

Building is not architecture till it makes for beauty, not for use alone. Could there have been preserved to us any of the caves, or huts, or tents, of the primeval races, we should doubtless know that this "making for beauty" was at an early stage. From the fact that the cave-dwellers of Europe ornamented their tools and weapons it is a safe inference that they strove to beautify the caves in which they lived.

The shaping force of the environment determined the kind of habitation; with wood abundant there was the wooden hut; with wood scarce and stone abundant, the hut of stone; where wood and stone alike were scarce, the skins of beasts stretched upon poles furnished the primitive tent. Survival is a proof of evolution second to no other. Thoreau's trout in the milk is not better circumstantial evidence of it. Now that we have in the temples of Egypt, if not of Greece, the stone hut or cave magnified and improved, in the structures of India and Persia the wooden hut enlarged and glorified, there can be no doubt; but it is the architecture of the pagoda and the mosque that most obviously tells the story of its origin; one sees the tent in them with half an eye. The Lycian tomb in the British Museum is an object-lesson of remarkable significance. Built of stone, its whole construction is a reminiscence of the carpenter. That the temples of Greece are reminiscential in the same way I may not dare to say, because two such eminent authorities as Viollet le Duc and Dr. Franz von Reber are of opposite opinions, each absolutely sure that he is right. I must confess that Reber, contending that the stone-work of the Greeks was but a modified carpentry, appears to me to make out his case much better than Le Duc.

The earliest architecture, properly so called, with which we are acquainted is that of Egypt, and this is far removed from any of the rude beginnings of mankind. The oldest buildings stand upon the youngest earth, the alluvial deposits of the Nile. Chaldea may have preceded Egypt with a splendid architecture, but she built of sun-dried bricks where Egypt built of stone, and offered premiums on oblivion by that method, the only one at her command. By what steps of strength and beauty Egypt climbed to that plateau of architectural splendor on which we find her sitting proudly at the dawn of history five thousand years ago it is not given us to know. If we could believe that any architecture was a revelation of the Infinite Beauty and had no progressive development from less to greater things, we should believe it of the architecture of Egypt, not only because we find none of the steps that led to it, but because from the period of our first acquaintance with it it reveals so little change. With such immobility preceding the oldest monuments as we have succeeding them, no time seems long enough to have developed the architecture of those monuments. There must have been a time when every present did not slavishly reproduce the methods of the past, and there must have come some terrible experience to chill invention to the bone, and it could have been no brief experience. Look at it any way we will, the monuments of ancient Egypt have their foundations in a past that baffles the imagination. From the time they rise on our astonished gaze until the beginning of our era—that is to say, through the entire course of their history—they afford such an illustration of the principle of fixity of type, so central to the doctrine of development, as only China can begin to match in other fields of human nature's self-expression. If we had to judge from their monuments we might confound Egyptian dynasties one and two thousand years apart. The most tremendous revolutions came and went, and still the architectural type remained unchanged. Pygmalion falling in love with the statue he had carved would fain have given it life. Egypt reversed his mood: falling in love with her creations, she fain would have them stiffen into death, and so they did. The sameness of her skies, her seasons' habits of invariable drought and flood, no doubt expressed themselves in the uniformities of her intellectual history. The temple, the obelisk, and the pyramid are the three splendid forms in which she expressed the ruling passions of her life for worship, for remembrance, and for the mystery of death. The work of human hands presents no simpler illustration of the course of evolution than the development of the pyramid from the little mound of earth which the displacement of the body makes above a new-made grave. The next step was to heap the earth a little higher; then, seeking greater permanence, men raised the cairn—the heap of stones. But from these rude beginnings what a march to the pyramids of Dashour and Gizeh! The final geometrical form with those long, slanting sides was probably determined by its resistance to the desert's stupid rage. Tenterden Steeple was the cause of the Goodwin Sands. Inversely the sands of Egypt were the cause of the pyramids' unbroken lines and surfaces. Any irregularity invited the blowing sand to come and bury the monument and defeat the monarch's pride. No senseless piles are these which ignorant slaves could heap course upon course with stupid iteration; nay, but marvels of a constructive genius that must have loved its work as only the true artist can. For intelligent adaptation of the artist's means to the ends he clearly had in view, there is no work superior to this.

Egyptian monarchs did not monopolize the pyramidal

tomb; they only insisted that their pyramids should come to the point; an easier thing to accomplish with a pyramid than sometimes with the living man, as many a woman knows. But rock-hewn tombs were the more common form of burial for heads that did not wear a crown. The square pillars that support the roofs of these burial chambers mark the beginnings of Egyptian temple architecture. As those piers were treated in one way or another they evolved into the proto-Doric or the more characteristic lotus-stem column of three thousand years. Along one line the corners were chamfered away again and again till the pier became round, and then "its sleek rotundity" was channeled with a greater or less number of perpendicular grooves. In the square piers, the eight and sixteen sided polygons, and the round columns with their various flutings, we have a chapter of evolution in which there is no missing link. We have another equally interesting and complete in the evolution of the painted pier. The graver's tool followed everywhere in the footsteps of color, and nowhere more obviously than here: a favorite painted ornament was the long stems of the lotus with their flowering tops bound into a sheaf. This ornament was reproduced in stone. The bunch of blossoms was the capital; the binding fillet grew into its hypotrachelion—i. e., the convex ring between the capital and shaft. Another and most happy step made the shaft one gigantic stem and the capital one gigantic blossom, and the Egyptian column had then reached its most characteristic form, which rises in our minds as quickly and distinctly as the pyramid whenever the subject of Egyptian architecture is named; or as the obelisks which stood in pairs before the pylons of the temples, those great truncated pyramids which made the temple's front, approached through rows of sphinxes asking upon either hand the everlasting questions which the priests within answered as best they could. We see with our minds and not merely with our eyes, and seeing so (especially since the Egyptian obelisk came to stay with us, and we know how difficult it was to handle the great monolith), can we admire too much the energy and skill that quarried this and all its splendid fellows from the rocky borders of the Nile?

Any detailed account of an Egyptian temple would exhaust the time I have at my command and still be incomplete. Passing within its monstrous portal, one entered first the peristyle or outer court, and then the hypostyle or inner, *par excellence* the hall of columns. This at Carnac was truly a forest of columns—one hundred and thirty-eight in all—the larger seventy feet in height with capitals of twenty feet diameter. It may well be doubted whether the world has ever known another architectural effect so grand and so imposing as this must have been, seen in its glorious prime. No wonder it became a type so fixed that it withstood even the onset of the Roman power which carried everywhere else throughout its wide dominions the hybrid forms of its own art. Egyptian art under the Ptolemies was Egyptian still; the temple of Edfou its most characteristic work, which, till the reading of its inscriptions, the archæologists fancied of an earlier date than the temples of the Theban dynasty two thousand years before. It was Cleopatra's nose, they say, that changed the world; but these Egyptian builders changed Cleopatra's nose; made her Egyptian utterly, and dressed her in the clinging garments of old Rhamses's queen, who had been dead about three thousand years.

In the last analysis we should, no doubt, be able to detect a great many actions and reactions of European and Asiatic architecture upon each other, but the main stream of architectural evolution, which is all that I can hope to trace in one short hour, was, with one exception, not seriously affected by Asiatic influences, great builders though the Hindoos and Iranians and Assyrians and Sassanians unquestionably were. Westward the star of architectural empire took its way. In our Metropolitan Museum we see the struggle for existence between the sculpture of Egypt and Assyria, with the gradual emergence of the Hellenic type. This struggle must have had a wide extent, and architecture as well as sculpture must have been affected by it in both Ionian and Doric Greece. In Ionia, upon the western coast of Asia Minor, we should expect to find the Oriental influence more evident than in Attica, and it is so. If the tombs of Lycia on the southern coast of Asia Minor, with their Ionic columns imperfectly developed, do not mark a station of the western march of architectural forms from Mesopotamia, they are "a distinct parallel development of the most primitive Ionic forms," and their Oriental origin in either case admits of little doubt. But Greece touched nothing that she did not beautify; and the difference of the completely developed Ionic column and its order from the primitive forms of Lycia and Ionia is a difference which makes for symmetry and beauty in every least particular of change. But the Ionic column with its order was never the most characteristic of the Hellenic genius; it never could compete with the Doric in European Greece. But the Doric, even more obviously than the Ionic, was a borrowed form, and Egypt was its original home. There it was the proto-Doric column which was, as I have said, developed by the chamfering off of angle after angle of the square pier till it was practically round, and then grooving it to obviate its "sleek rotundity." The monuments of Beni-Hassan prove that Egypt reached this proto-Doric form a thousand years before the architects of Greece. Shakespeare was not so royal a borrower as the Greeks, nor so justified his borrowing from the clumsy playwrights who furnished him with his various plots by his imperial transformation. As with the Ionic column, the capital took on an ever purer grace and the entablature added a member of the first importance, the wide frieze, a necessity of the roof and ceiling, where the Egyptians had them both in one, and flat, encouraged by their rainless skies. Then, too, the Greeks were practical idealists. They knew that things are not what they appear and contrariwise, and so they gave the shaft an entasis—i. e., bulged it out a little so that it might not look as if it were hollowed in; and in the same spirit they inclined the columns a little inward (a very little, $\frac{1}{180}$ of the height), so that they might *look* exactly vertical. It can hardly be regarded as an Egyptian reminiscence that the Doric column was so sturdy in its strength. The most perfect architects "by their loved masonry approved" this sturdiness, the columns of the Parthenon, in which the Doric style reached its perfection, being about five diameters in height, a happy mean between the earliest and later forms.* It was no foolish fancy that the Doric was to the Ionic column as masculine strength compared with feminine delicacy and grace, and the comparison held good of the entire order, which in the Ionic was proportionately delicate in every part as in the Doric it was proportionately stout and strong. Both the base and capital of the Ionic column prove its Asiatic source. But as the Egyptian proto-Doric suffered a Greek change into something rich and strange, so did the primitive Ionic. The round base-molding got the under concave plinth, its horizontal groovings bringing it into harmony with the perpendicular groovings

* Four at Corinth; six at Sunium.

of the shaft. These were different from the Doric flutings and different from the Persian, which, like the Doric, met in sharp arrises. The perfected Ionic left a band of the original cylinder between the flutings. The capital has suggested ram's horns and the curling locks of lovely woman, but it is the inventor of such silliness who here stoops to folly. The volutes were originally the spiral ornaments of Persian chairs. The Ionic order was harmonious throughout, the entablature sympathizing with the column in its delicate beauty. This statement would be truer turned about, for, as in the Doric, it was the weight and character of the entablature that determined the character of the column, a first principle in logical building. In Attica the Ionic order never competed successfully with the Doric, and the Corinthian had a much more limited vogue. This was not in reality so much an order by itself as a variation of the Ionic in the capital. It was of late origin, reaching its normal type about 250 B. C. The earliest examples are more like the lotus-capital of Egypt than like the typical Corinthian, and this suggests a far more probable history than the very pretty, very silly one for which we are indebted to Vitruvius—viz., that it represents a basket of toys on a sprouting acanthus, which a nurse had set upon the grave of a young girl. It was simply "a fanciful and ever-varied decoration of foliage around a concave calyx." It was Antiochus Epiphanes, the Glorious or the Mad, the same that roused the Maccabees to victorious insurrection in Judea, who built the Corinthian Temple of Olympian Zeus in Athens about 170 B. C. This was on the very eve of the Roman conquest, and strangely enough the architect was a Roman. The capitals were of the most florid style, and when the columns were carried off to Rome by Sulla they furnished the Romans with a type after their own hearts—superb, magnificent, and easily abused.

If time allowed, it could be shown how Greek architecture was throughout obedient to the principles of evolution in the struggle for existence between rival forms, the preservation of the fittest being steadily assured. The course of development was extremely short; a century or less to match each slow millennium of Egyptian art. Homer knows nothing of columnar architecture, and in four centuries the Parthenon crowns at once the Acropolis and the completest cycle of development. The modern archæologist was not considered in the least by the builders of the age of Pericles.

In the rage for architectural beauty everything short of the ideal was swept away as proudly as the Saxon churches of England by her Norman conquerors. Happily the Roman conquerors of Greece did not *destroy*, they *stole* her temples and her statues. Of the latter, 70,000 have already been exhumed in Rome. The worst they did was to debase the architecture of Greece on her own soil. They did not know the best, and so they left the Parthenon, "the glory that was Greece," to shame "the grandeur that was Rome" for twenty centuries of wondering time.

The origins of Roman architecture are much more clearly defined than those of Greece, and its borrowings were much more conspicuous. These were from the Etruscans, their next neighbors on the north, and from the Greeks, who, long before their conquest by the Romans, had covered southern Italy, called Magna Græcia, with great examples of their architectural taste and skill; that of Pæstum witnessing to us how glorious they could be. The general popular impression credits Greece with much too large a part of Roman architecture. The Grecian part was superficial, decorative. and this part has obscured the other, the fundamental, the structural, in which Rome achieved a very great distinction. But here again she was no more original than in her use of Grecian elements. We penetrate the secret of her greatness, if I may say so without offense, by way of the Cloaca Maxima, the gigantic sewer built for her by Etruscan engineers under Tarquinius, well named Superbus, if for no other reason than because he built this sewer, without which the seven-hilled city would have sunk into the ooze of the surrounding plains. It would have been a fortunate thing for Rome if she could have developed her architecture wholly from this root. Then it might have had its own appropriate decoration, which, if less beautiful than that it borrowed from the Greeks, would have been more rational and organic. It made use of the Greek forms in the main only to debase them and to hide the structures which were characteristic of its genius and could not have been too obviously revealed. It made use of its Etruscan origins so freely, so boldly, so splendidly that the credit of its ultimate performance can no more be given to the Etruscans than the credit of Greek architecture can be given to the Egyptians or Iranians. Great architects in the æsthetic sense the Romans never were, and here the comparison with Greece was greatly to their disadvantage. But they were great builders. They built with tremendous vigor, boldness, grandeur, ingenuity, and here the comparison with Greece, so limited in her structural range, is greatly to their advantage. In those stupendous heaps of brick and rubble which alone remain to us of the palace of the Cæsars and the baths of Caracalla, the appreciative mind finds all that was foreign to the Roman genius stripped away, and what remains is superb in its magnificent suggestion of the highest things.

In Roman architecture we have five different columns and their respective orders, the latter much confused, and even the former borrowing freely from each other back and forth. Those unknown to Greek architecture were the Tuscan with its round unfluted shaft, and the Composite, which topped the acanthus capital of the Corinthian column with the volutes of the Ionic, a combination suiting well the Roman passion for excessive ornament. This was the passion of imperial days. That, in the simpler days of the Republic, the Doric order, of which southern Italy and Sicily had so many brave examples, did not attract the Roman builders is perhaps accounted for by the fact that in the unfluted Tuscan they had an even simpler form. Certain it is that when they came to borrow largely from the Greeks in the third century B. C., it was not the Doric but the Ionic that they borrowed. This they not only borrowed, but debased, placing the volutes on all four sides, thus making them as merely ornamental as they had been in their original Asiatic forms. But the Corinthian soon displaced the Ionic in the general taste, and when the two had been united in unlawful marriage, the offspring—the Composite—was as magnificent as the proudest Roman could desire.

But none of these forms was used in that logical and organic spirit which was so characteristic of the Greeks. Meantime it was not in their sacred buildings that the genius of the Romans naturally displayed itself. Their religion was a function of the state, an economy, a convenience, and the idea of use was central to their architectural genius. Use, power, pride, luxury—these were the ruling passions of imperial Rome. The strength she felt in every limb of her political organization she loved to manifest in the structure of her aqueducts, her basilicas, her triumphal arches, and her baths. And the initiative of this splendid manifestation came from the arch and barrel vault of her Tuscan neighbors, who were her earliest architects. It was not until the second century B. C. that the cross-vault with its important corollaries, the apse and dome, gave an immense extension to those possibilities of internal grandeur which were to the Roman all that the possibilities of external beauty were to the Greek. And it was with bricks and mortar that these possibilities were realized. The Romans were essentially a brick-building people, and the loss of their great art of making an adhesive, binding mortar was one which to later builders was incomparably great. Marble in Rome was very scarce indeed, and used for little else than ornament outside and in.

Sewers and aqueducts were the first colossal works in which the Roman passion for the useful found expression. The first great aqueduct, however, was more than two centuries later than the first great sewer, the Cloaca Maxima. The next four hundred years (from 300 B. C. to 100 A. D.) saw thirteen of these gigantic works threading the Campagna, some of them bringing their crystal flood from mountains forty miles away, and they still bring it (some of them) after the lapse of some two thousand years. The great city did not need a third of all the water they brought for its necessities. It needed all the rest for its eight hundred and fifty private baths, opened to any one who could pay the modest price, and the great imperial baths that welcomed all alike without a fee. The present Pantheon is the best preserved of all the imperial baths, though what is left is merely the great central hall, one of the noblest interiors in the world. The grandeur of this was much exceeded by the baths of Caracalla and Diocletian, the latter capable of entertaining three thousand bathers at once. From the love of pleasure and the admiration for physical courage and the political necessities of the times—"*Panem et circences*"—came the whole system of buildings of which the theatre of Maxentius, the Circus Maximus, and the Flavian Amphitheatre or Colosseum are great examples; triumphs of constructive energy and skill, incrusted with architectural columnar ornaments, having no structural function to perform. Such monumental columns as those of Trajan and Marcus Aurelius are as peculiar to herself as anything that Rome can show. The triumphal arch is almost equally her own. It is her own as being a massive building with a decorative screen; her own as an expression of her conquering zeal and pride. The pyramids of Egypt do not tell the story of their origin in the burial mound more clearly than the arch the story of its origin in the festal wooden arch, a painted compliment, or wreathed with flowers and green. We have had a very recent object lesson in this kind of evolution. I refer, of course, to the centennial arch of 1889 set up in Washington Square, New York. The people liked it and said: "Come, let us put it into stone." The arch of Constantine is very beautiful to look upon, if one is not a purist in his architectural ideas. Nevertheless, as one passes under it he passes out of Roman architecture into a period of architectural darkness centuries long. The arch of the first Christian Emperor, it is built out of the stolen substance and decorated with the stolen ornaments of the arch of Hadrian. What better symbol could we have of that "unexampled poverty of artistic invention" which marked the development of Christian Rome for an ill thousand years?

And still the line of evolution did not break. But the Roman building to which it attached itself was neither aqueduct, nor amphitheatre, nor bath, nor arch-triumphal. It was the basilica, the name of which passed over with the thing, and it is of the Basilica of St. Peter's that we hear in our time. But the evolution followed the line of Christian worship, which, beginning in the private dining-room, passed into the private basilica, or ceremonial hall. This and not the public forensic basilica fixed the type of the early Christian churches of the West. We have still remaining splendid examples of those churches in San Pietro in Vincolo, in Santa Maria Maggiore, and in St. Paul's outside the walls. The last, although well-nigh destroyed by fire in 1823, has been restored in perfect sympathy with the original design. In the other two, when you go to see Michel Angelo's "Moses" or the mosaics of Cimabue, you have on either hand majestic columns that have served their present use some fifteen hundred years, and before that they had some centuries of history as the bath or temple columns of the pagan city.

The sixth century was one of the great building centuries of architectural history; hardly less so than the century of Pericles in Greece and Hadrian in Rome, and the thirteenth century, which saw Amiens and Salisbury and Burgos rising simultaneously into the wondering and astonished air. It was the century of Justinian, the Eastern Empire's most imperial man, during whose reign and by whose inspiration twenty-five churches of magnificent size and splendid decoration were built in Constantinople, all in the Byzantine style. This style was very far from being a debased Roman style, as many enthusiasts for the Gothic and the Greco-Roman have too willingly believed. It was more Roman than the Roman. It recognized the superficiality of the Greco-Roman decoration, a veil that hid the structural properties of a constructive art that had no call to be ashamed. It stripped away all this, or kept only so much as served a purpose. Ravenna and Milan (the Christian church of San Lorenzo) and Constantinople are rival claimants for the honor of this new departure. But what is certain is that Constantinople developed it the most freely and that there the decorative qualities of the style were taken on. I say "were taken on," for that they were original with Byzantium no one has so far essayed to prove. They have a distinct Oriental quality. The capital especially has no classical traits. Judea has been treated so contemptuously by the architectural critic, as if she had no architectural life in herself, that her horn may well be exalted by the suggestion of Viollet le Duc that Byzantine ornament detached itself from the friezes, capitals, and spandrels of Jerusalem, where their derivative history is lost in the dim labyrinth of Oriental art.

Meantime Germany and France were carrying on the development of the old basilica by methods which received only the most superficial aid from the Byzantine school—the development which is called Norman, as it was, in England, but in Germany and France is known as Romanic, or more commonly as Romanesque. If these designations are not altogether vain, the line of evolution was not broken here any more than it had been between Egypt and Asia and Greece, or between Greece and Etruria and Rome, or between Rome and the Byzantine architects, who were truer to her genius than she was herself. But Romanesque is itself a species which has several distinct varieties, as different as the Cathedral of Pisa is from Speyer and both from Durham, while southern France has its own special traits. In southern France there were more Greco-Roman architectural remains than Italy could boast. And from the influence of these the Provençal architects could not escape. They clung to classical details. If they did not incorporate the columns and the entablatures of old Roman buildings in their churches, they copied them with free or careless hand. But at the same time they engaged the column that had been merely ornamental and gave it real work to do—something to actually support—and the beginnings of all possible sincerity were in this half-unconscious step. Necessity is the mother of invention, and as the paucity of Roman ruins in Ravenna put her architects upon their mettle till they said "So much the better!" so in Germany the same paucity, the same lack of Roman material to steal or copy, brought about a much more original style than southern France or Italy attained. But this German Romanesque, which reached its climax in the noble symmetry of Speyer, the cathedral of that city, was, after all, a primitive Romanesque carried to its farthest point of characteristic excellence. It is a Romanesque that has a closer cousinship with the towers of Lombardy and of Saxon England than with the sturdy strength of Caen and Durham. And here again we have a capital illustration of evolutionary principles. The type became so definitely fixed that there was no chance for the varieties. The consequence was that Germany never developed a type of Romanesque so liberal and expansive as that of France and England in the eleventh and twelfth centuries: So joined was she to her idols, that the Gothic could not persuade her to abandon them. The German Gothic of Cologne and Strassburg and Freiburg is merely a French importation, not a native growth.

For beauty of Romanesque detail we go to southern France, but for the free development of a Romanesque, as self-centered as the Gothic in its magnificent virility, we must go to Normandy and to the England of the Norman Kings. In Caen and Durham we have the best examples of this noble and impressive style. Why call it Romanesque? For one thing it reproduces the forms of the Roman basilica, where the Byzantine rooted back into such Roman circular tombs or mortuary chapels as those of S. Constanza and Minerva Medica. For another thing it is essentially Roman in its construction. It is more frankly Roman than the Roman. It confesses its structural character where the Roman architecture of the Empire disguised it with a veneer of lying ornament. In the nave of Durham and the transept of Winchester there is nothing to remind us of Rome's borrowed ornament. There is everything to remind us of the Rome that built the aqueducts of the Campagna and the arches of the Colosseum. Reversion is a principle of evolution of which Darwin had a good deal to say. In Norman Romanesque we have a reversion to the Roman type of simple strength, unspoiled by foreign drapery.

If I had time I should like at this point to make a brief excursion into the field of Moorish architecture. It has no structural logic that we should desire it. It needs all the beauty of its flat or colored decoration to distract us from the ugliness of its pendentives and other forms which seem to ape the crystalline drippings of some wondrous cave. But the decoration is marvelously beautiful and has an evolutionary tale to tell of great simplicity; for it is evident that in this decoration we have a survival of textile fabrics hung upon the walls of mosques and palaces. In the wide family connection of those who are only happy when affronting some received opinion, there are those who think that all the credit of Gothic architecture belongs to the Mohammedans. These are those who think Bacon wrote Shakspere, and Thomas Paine the Letters of Junius and the Declaration of Independence, and that Jesus of Nazareth is a poor copy of Gautama Buddha. Unquestionably the Mohammedans used the pointed arch. They had borrowed it, as nearly all their architectural forms, from Oriental art. Mohammedan architecture is ten times as much indebted to the Christian art of Byzantium as is Christian architecture to it. But nothing could be more absurd than the idea that Gothic architecture came from the borrowings of the pointed arch or from any special fondness for this particular form. Such an idea is of a piece with the old biology which classified animal life by its external forms until Buffon decided that the crocodile was "altogether too terrible an insect" to be classed as one. Gothic architecture was another daughter of necessity. We might never have had it if timber roofs hadn't had such a vile way of burning up. Again we might never have had it if the builders of the eleventh and twelfth centuries could have made as good mortar as the Romans did who built the Pantheon. To replace timber roofing with stone vaulting was the problem of the mediæval architect. To do that, he strengthened the side-walls of his cathedral. But this device was both costly and insufficient. His next move was to abandon the continuous barrel vault and take to groining, opposite the thrusts of which he placed external buttresses. This was the Norman Romanesque. Then he perceived that the walls between his buttresses had no functional character. They were almost as useless, save to keep out the weather, as the ornamental incrustations of imperial Rome. Thin walls would do this as well as thick, and glass as well as stone. Glass would, moreover, let in the light, and this glass could be stained "with forms of saints and holy men who died, here martyred and hereafter glorified." Such was the evolution of Gothic architecture. If the primitive Romanesque had its complete development in Germany, culminating in the Cathedral of Speyer, and the later Romanesque had its complete development in England, where Durham is its great example, Gothic not only had its complete development in France, but it had it only there, the Gothic of Spain and Germany being almost wholly French and only different to be less, while the Gothic of Italy and England is never structurally Gothic in the fullest sense, but a matter of Gothic ornaments and details inhering in a building of Romanesque construction. Gothic architecture in France was first distinctly and systematically applied to a great edifice in the building of the Notre Dame of Paris. There the system of opposing thrusts was everywhere substituted for the inertia of great masses. In Amiens the new system reached its most complete expression in the thirteenth century. The building of Salisbury was almost exactly contemporaneous with that of Amiens and Burgos—from 1220 to 1260. But both Salisbury and Burgos are essentially walled buildings; that is, their strength depends largely on their walls, not on the opposing thrusts of their functional frame-work. This does not prevent their being buildings of marvelous beauty.

The Gothic had an internal evolution, more or less significant as it was here or there. In France it passed from the early decoration to a more elaborate, from the flame-like character of the window-tracery called flamboyant. In England also the different stages are named after the tracery, which, beginning with the lancet, single or in groups, passed into the decorated, in which flowing lines predominate; thence to the perpendicular, in which the flowing lines are cut by perpendicular mullions and there is a general accentuation of perpendicular and horizontal lines. The evolutionary principle of correlated growth finds many happy illustrations in this process, as where the flattening of the roof over the aisles extinguished the triforium, the arcade between the lower and upper stories of the cathedral nave or choir.

The architecture which followed Gothic was the Renaissance. It was a dubious return to what was worst in the Greco-Roman architecture of the second century, and hence its name. Therefore as a *re-birth* it was far less truly Roman than the Romanesque. Superficial in its very nature, it began very superficially. You are assisting at its birth in England when you are standing by the tomb of Henry VII in his famous Chapel at Westminster, a sample of the Tudor Gothic gone to seed. No wonder that men wished a change. Inigo Jones plastered a classic portico on the front of old Saint Paul's which the Great Fire of 1666 mercifully destroyed, though it threw out the baby with the bath—destroyed the building altogether. In France the marrying of Gothic structure with classic ornament produced some beautiful results, especially in domestic architecture—the sixteenth century chateaus. Of the completed Renaissance development, St. Peter's is the most stupendous, St. Paul's the most symmetrical example. In our own time England has had a Gothic revival, of which the best result has been the restoration of her cathedrals. It is, or was, one aspect of the mediæval revival of which the Oxford movement was a part. William George Ward was one of Newman's followers who came in ahead of him in the race to Rome. "To think of such a man as Ward living in a room without mullions!" said Pugin, the Gothic architect. But when Newman went to Rome he abjured Gothic for the Renaissance, "the architecture of pomp and pride." The Houses of Parliament are certainly an imposing example of the perpendicular style, though their horizontal lines are most conspicuous and aggressive. William Morris does not like them and contemplates with complacency a future when they will be economized for the storage of manure. But his dislike of the laws made in them, and in fact of all laws, may have much to do with this.

Of our American reversions and revivals I should like to speak, but my hour is out and there is one coming after me who will be preferred before me. I console myself with thinking I know as much about his architecture as he does about my theology.

I trust I have made good the title of my address. I trust that I have shown that architecture has had an evolution and not merely a history; that with much of imitation there is much more of genetic relation; that every present brings something from its past and leaves something for its future; that the evolutionary principles of fixity of type and variation, struggle for existence, preservation of the fittest, reversion, correlation of growth, influence of the environment, are not strange to any part of the long course over which we have passed so hastily. If the time had been sufficient for me to speak elaborately of transitional forms, and if I could have accompanied my text with illustrative plans and sketches, the evolutionary character of the record would have been much more pronounced.

ABSTRACT OF THE DISCUSSION.

Mr. Albert L. Brockway:

I must beg to differ with Mr. Chadwick in the idea that architecture has been the field of an evolution similar to that in the organic world and in the scientific sense. In the organic world evolution has resulted from the action of inherent forces. Architecture has been created by an external power. It is the work of men's hands and minds. Any evolution in architecture—using this term in the sense of growth or development—has been the result of man's mental activity. The growth, therefore, is not inherent. The combination of arch and column was not an inherent product in the Greek temple. We now can see the possibility of the combination. The so-called Romanesque vault did not imply the Gothic vault. Evolution or unfolding we can find in any architectural style from its inception to its decline, but as we advance from style to style we do not necessarily go on from perfect to more perfect with occasional backward steps, as we do in the organic world. It may be admitted that there is evolution backward as well as forward, but the grand general trend is onward. Who can presume to say that the most perfect Gothic cathedral is more perfect than the Greek Parthenon? Yet from the evolution point of view it should be so. Each is a growth, in its style depending upon considerations of climate, customs of people, and material at hand.

Architecture is essentially a product of the people. It grew as they grew. Painting and sculpture were allied arts, and decorative rather than substantial and useful. From the first necessity to protect and cover himself, to making a fit place for showing his love and reverence for a Divine being, the building has grown. When the Communes were established in France, but more particularly in Flanders and the Low Countries, we see the beautiful town hall spring up to meet the want. The church of the middle ages may resemble the Roman basilica, but constructively it differs widely therefrom. The very rise in power of the bishops by associating with the kingly power against the abbots, who were generally powerful barons, is a very potent factor in the springing up all over France in particular and Europe in general of the vast cathedral churches. Here again it was the growth in the people that induced the growth in the art.

The plan is the essential feature of an architectural production.

The elevation expresses, in a general artistic and constructive way, the disposition within. The plan is the characteristic note, the motive of the creation, and that arises from the surrounding conditions and circumstances of the daily life. Our American house-plans and office-building plans are essentially American and are indigenous. To cover them with a face consisting of some Romanesque or Gothic detail and call them, accordingly, Romanesque or Gothic, is therefore a misapplication of terms. I wish to affirm that there is an American architecture, at least in infancy, and it is a well-developed infant, too.

MR. CHADWICK, in reply, said: There is an evolution of degeneration as well as of advance, and the doctrine explicitly recognizes both of these processes. A Gothic cathedral, for instance, is not a finer piece of architecture than the Parthenon, though it is of later origin, yet both are products of evolution. Over and above the evolution or decay of special or local types there has been a broad evolutionary line of architectural development from Egypt to Greece, Rome, Byzantium, and the later Western European forms. The great churches all root back into the basilica, though widely separated in locality and time. Architecture, in its various forms, undoubtedly expresses the dominant life of the people. Where that dominant life was religious we find it expressed in churches and cathedrals. The dominant life in America is the business life; hence we find that architecture in this country takes its most characteristic form in our business buildings and private houses. Architecture, in its earlier stages, however, never was a popular art. The great monuments of Egypt were built under the lash. In Rome the noted buildings were erected by the rulers, not by the populace. The Gothic cathedrals, on the contrary, were built by the Communes.

THE EVOLUTION OF SCULPTURE

BY

THOMAS DAVIDSON.

COLLATERAL READINGS SUGGESTED:

Articles *Archæology* and *Sculpture* in American Cyclopædia and Encyclopædia Britannica; Lübke's History of Art and History of Sculpture; Harriet Hosmer's *Process of Sculpture*, in Atlantic Monthly, vol. xiv, 1864; Miss Harrison's *Sculpture in the United States*, in Atlantic Monthly, vol. xxii, 1868; Grattan's Book on Sculpture; Jacob's Wealth of the Greeks in Plastic Art; Flaxman's Lectures on Sculpture; Perkins's Tuscan Sculpture; Robinson's Italian Sculpture of the Middle Ages; Westmacott's Schools of Sculpture, Ancient and Modern; Ruskin's Aratra Pentelici; Agincourt's Histoire de l'Art.

THE EVOLUTION OF SCULPTURE.

By Thomas Davidson.

When we speak of the evolution of anything due to conscious human exertion, we mean at bottom the evolution of a certain human faculty. The product of this faculty is merely the means and proof of its development, and this development is the real end of the product. In all things done by man, man is the end, and his deeds and products are but means. Man does not exist to develop the world; the world exists to develop man; for the world is made for man, and not man for the world.

The law observed by Aristotle to hold good for political institutions is universal—viz.: this, that all human faculties and products are at first developed by physical needs, and, when so developed, are transferred so as to subserve the evolution of spiritual faculties. The faculty that held together and governed the Roman Empire, the faculty that sustains this great Republic, started in its career in the humble form of sexual and domestic instinct holding together and ruling the family. The faculty that shaped the marbles of the Parthenon and the Praxitelean Hermes began by molding soft clay into rude drinking-cups and chipping flint for arrow-heads to kill game for food. The faculty that composed the symphonies of Beethoven and the operas of Wagner began by singing lullabies to restless babies. And so on through all the arts.

So long as human actions and products are the result and satisfaction of purely physical needs, they do not essentially differ from the actions and products of the lower animals; but, as soon as they rise above this, the former enter the sphere of ethics, the latter the sphere of art, both of which belong to man only as an eternal being, having no meaning for any other.

Art begins when physical things—clay, wood, stone, color, sound—are used to give expression to thoughts or conceptions, so that they may be reflected back upon the artist, or upon men similarly endowed, through their senses, and thus permanently grasped and realized. Art is human creation in the strictest sense. The product of art is always a mirror held up, not to nature (for that is already a mirror, the mirror of God), but to the soul of man, so that it may behold and know itself—become self-conscious.

I wish to insist particularly upon this point, because it is fundamental in any conception of art, and must be clearly grasped before the phrase "evolution of art" can have any intelligible meaning. Art is an expression of man's inner nature imprinted upon matter, so as to appeal to his senses, which deal only with matter, and through which he obtains experience. Whatever fails to do this is not art. Whatever is a mere copy of outward nature, such as the sun can imprint upon a photographic plate, and whatever shows only the action of physical forces, whether in nature or in man, has no claim to be called art. All this is simply nature, and art, as Goethe says, is called art just because it is not nature. The more fully, deeply, accurately a human product bodies forth man's inner nature, his freedom, his love, his wisdom, the more truly is it a work of art; and no amount of technical skill in the way of imitation can vindicate for art a work in which these attributes find no expression. For this reason the rude reliefs which we find upon the clay tablets of Babylon and Nineveh are far more truly works of art than many of the works of sculpture and painting which adorn our museums, and excite our admiration by their technical skill, but are void of content. Skill is not art, but only art's handmaid. The workman who has only skill, but nothing worthy to express thereby, is no more an artist than a fine penman is a good correspondent or journalist.

The human soul realizes itself in matter in various ways and by various means, and this realization has in each case an evolution and a history, which begin at the point where a process previously used to satisfy a physical need is employed to express a spiritual act. The transition is by no means an abrupt one, and there are many primitive objects of human shaping of which it would be hard to say whether they belong to the region of art or not. Of this nature are the rude faces and figures upon funeral urns. Is the purpose of these to alleviate physical suffering or grief, or is it to express a spiritual hope? Who can tell? May it not be partly both? Is not the hope originally born of the grief? Is this not the very function of grief, to mother hope? Of the same doubtful nature is much of the architecture and pottery of all ages. It is difficult to say when a building or a race rises above physical usefulness into expression. All depends upon the aim which the artist has set himself.

So much for art in general. My theme at present is sculpture and its evolution. For the sake of freedom of treatment, I shall make sculpture include all the arts termed plastic, as distinguished from the graphic, literary, and musical arts. Indeed, the evolution of sculpture could hardly be treated without this extension. By sculpture, then, I mean the molding or cutting of solid matter with a view to making its form express some inward idea or emotion of the soul. It is evident from this definition that the evolution of sculpture will include three elements: (1) Evolution in the choice of materials; (2) evolution in manipulatory processes; (3) evolution in ideas to be expressed. Roughly speaking, these three elements develop simultaneously, although sometimes one outruns another. As men's ideas deepen, so their power to fashion matter increases, and hence they will go on choosing matter more and more difficult to fashion.

The first material of sculpture was, in all probability, soft clay; the first process, molding with the fingers; the first embodied ideas, the rude conceptions of beings in the unseen world—men, animals, monsters. In saying this, I do not mean to imply that men did not copy things in the seen world before they tried to body forth things in the unseen; but I mean that the former process was not art, and therefore not sculpture. Art begins with the first attempt to portray the unseen as it lies in the human soul. At first the unseen world is conceived very much after the fashion of the seen, and this could not be otherwise, for obvious reasons; only the conditions of life in it are conceived as more attractive and easy. It contains sun and moon, men and animals, which, accordingly, are the earliest objects represented. The number of clay men and animals that have come down to us from the prehistoric ages is very great. They are to be found in almost every museum of palæontology. Along with these rude, clay-molded products, and perhaps originating later, are figures scratched on sandstone and on bone, many of which have been found in caves and near the dwellings of primitive men. In these we find a forward step in technique—the use of a sharp instrument—but we find no advance in thought or imagination.

The first material *cut* into shape for art ends was almost certainly wood. This, however, is of so perishable a nature that few, if any, very ancient or primitive specimens have come down to us. Molding, scratching, wood-cutting, were the three primitive, we might say preparatory, forms of sculpture. It is not uninteresting to observe that they are all three still used as preparatory to sculpture. The pencil sketch drawn by the artist represents the scratching, while the model composed of wood (or iron) and soft clay recalls the other two processes.

There can hardly be any doubt that in the art progress of all civilized nations there has been a molding and scratching period, succeeded by a wood-cutting period. By the end of the latter men have begun to conceive the unseen world as in many ways different from the seen—its denizens as different, especially in the direction of power, swiftness, etc. Hence we find growing up what we may call the monstrous —men with numerous arms, legs, and even bodies; men with bodies of horses, lions, oxen, and even serpents. The monstrous in strength is the first element that differentiates the unseen world from the seen. It is at this date that all such things appear as hundred-handed giants, centaurs, minotaurs, priapi, seraphim, cherubim (which is the same word as griffin), and dragons of all sorts. They are all expressions of power, mere brute force, the first form in which the unseen is recognized. The *fear* of the Lord is the beginning of art as well as of wisdom. At this stage art has nothing whatever to do with beauty, for mere brute force is never beautiful. Although we have few or no wooden sculptures from ancient times, we know, from the contemporary myths as well as from the rude sculptures of semi-barbarous peoples still existing, what those early sculptures were like. Moreover, the monstrous is carried over into the next period, to be there gradually contrasted with, and elevated by, the principle of that period. The principle of the period of human history which succeeds that of fear and force may be called that of cunning, which means of reason without love. The beginning of this period coincides, roughly speaking, with that of the employment by art of hard materials—stone, bronze, etc. And it is easy enough to see why this should be the case. Until the reign of force and fear is at an end, there is not settled life enough to enable men to manipulate hard materials, or to inspire them with any wish to construct things that shall endure. It is in building walled towns and fortresses that men learn to hew and cut stone, and so prepare the means for the more enduring forms of sculpture.

The earliest stone sculptures of Greece are contemporary with the earliest stone walls. And so it is everywhere: first use, then art.

I have said that the age of force and fear is succeeded by the age of cunning. Our American use of that word, to mean 'pretty,' shows how we feel the connection between cunning and art. And cunning workmanship is a common biblical phrase. We may further call attention to the word "craft." Cunning applied to life means the subordination of the members of society to a head—the ordering and governing of the many by one. In a word, it is order established from one point, in a sense from without. In art it means that order and harmony which we call beauty. Beauty is order, and order is the outcome of cunning.

The process by which men passed from force to cunning is a slow one, and involves a struggle between the two principles. So in art, the struggle between the expression of force and the expression of order—between the monstrous and the beautiful—is a slow one. It generally appears as a struggle of gods or men with monsters—of the gods against dragons or giants, or Titans; of men against hydras or dragons, or centaurs or minotaurs. Of course, the victory is always with the higher principle. If we examine the early stone sculptures of Babylonia, or Egypt, or Greece, or Scandinavia, we shall find the same subjects in all—cunning and order struggling with, and overcoming, brute force. And the same thing is reflected in all early literature, even in the Bible itself. Egypt, and Babylonia with its successive kingdoms, are the lands wherein this struggle is carried on for all human history. In neither does beauty ever completely conquer force. The sphinxes of Egypt and the winged, human-headed horses of Assyria are compromises between brute force and beauty. But, even where the human form displaces the monster, made up of man and beast, it does not attain to true beauty; only to a kind of mathematical proportion, which is the earliest form of order. The figures and groups of the two river civilizations are all mathematical. They have proportion but no life. They are purely conventional. We do not know, I believe, the name of a single artist belonging to these two countries, and this for the reason that there is no life or originality in their art. It is an interesting fact that in those countries sculpture never gets disengaged from architecture, but always follows its law, which is that of simple proportion. Egypt and Babylonia show no free-standing figures in art. All are connected with some building, or attached to some stone to represent a building. This means that man has not yet learned to stand free from his surroundings: he is part of his house and follows its laws. He is a mere attachment to a strong-walled edifice of institutions. It is by no mere accident that in the tenth commandment a man's house is mentioned before his wife.

The struggle between cunning and force, so long maintained in Egypt and Babylonia, is taken up by Greece and by her decided in favor of the former. Greece is the land of the sculpturesque. Her sculpture stands to-day unrivaled, nay, unapproached. And all her art, even her music and poetry, was sculpturesque.

At first her sculpture differs in no essential particular from that of Egypt and Assyria. It is formal, mathematical, lifeless, and attached to buildings or stones. The sitting figures from Miletus, and some even from Greece proper, are in no way different from those of Egypt. Greece too has her sphinxes, centaurs, and other monsters. But, as Greece realizes her true character, all this gradually disappears. Even the monsters gradually assume a certain beauty. Let any one compare the centaurs of the temple of Assos with those of the temple of Zeus at Olympia, and with those on the metopes of the Parthenon. Gradually, too, the figures get detached from buildings and stone blocks; gradually mathematical proportion gives way to a sense of life, first in the limbs and then in the face. It is most interesting to watch this process as it shows itself in the Cyprian statues now in the New York Metropolitan Museum. In the earliest of these the heads are mere stone bullets, with features, hair, and coiffure rudely indicated; the bodies are simple blocks, with the arms parallel, perpendicular, and clinging to the body, and the legs and feet unseparated; the clothing is indicated by ridges or grooves, and shows no muscular frame beneath. Gradually the faces begin to assume the half-idiotic smile, the earliest attempt at expression; the pendent arms are partially separated from the sides by the cutting out of oval holes between the elbows and the body, leaving a ridiculously attenuated waist. One foot begins to advance a little; one hand begins to rise and hold something, then both hands. Then the folds of the drapery begin to be marked, until at last the figures begin to show signs of life. But in Cyprus sculpture never gets beyond

Oriental stiffness; never belies its medium. Indeed, even in Greece itself it has not done so in the earliest art-products known to us—e. g., the Spartan grave-reliefs, the Agemo of Asea, the Apollo of Tenea, and even the so-called Marathonian soldier.

But a time finally comes when Greece breaks through the bonds of Orientalism, when she rises above the stiff, mathematical order to the order of life and its beauty; when the human spirit for the first time becomes conscious of its freedom. When the cunning of Themistocles enables a handful of freedom-loving Greeks to baffle and rout all the brute force and stiff despotism of Persia, the cunning of Phidias overcomes all the brute forces that he finds in stone and bronze, and makes them vehicles for living and breathing thoughts of freedom. The one is the counterpart of the other.

When we speak of the sculpture of Greece, we at once think of the Parthenon marbles, the Hermes of Praxiteles, the Venus of Melos, etc. But these mark the ripeness and decay of Greek sculpture, not its evolution, which is all prior to the Parthenon marbles. Indeed, we can trace the whole history of sculpture in Greece itself—growth, ripeness, decay.

In the tombs of Mycenæ, Tiryns, Nauplia, and other places, we find small clay images, rude as can be, the earliest attempts to body forth the unseen. They are doubtless images of gods and ancestors, such as were to be found in every family. We hear of them among the Hebrews as *teraphim*, among the Etruscans and Romans as *lares* and *penates*. The Greeks had, no doubt, similar things from very early times; but it is curious enough that in Homer we find no mention of idols of any kind, except the Palladium, which seems to have been of wood. And doubtless by Homer's time the clay images had to some extent been superseded by wooden ones. How rude some of these were we may understand when we hear that the statue of Hera, at Samos, was a mere board, and those of the Dioscuri, at Sparta, little better than rude crosses. Yet such things were held very sacred, and were worshiped even after art had advanced to a far higher stage. The improvement of these rude statues is connected with the half-mythical name of Dædalus. He is the reputed originator of those *xoana*, or wooden statues, which were the chief objects of worship in very many Greek temples. None of these remain to us, but we may judge of their character by certain reliefs found at Sparta, which were plainly copied from wooden originals. That the *xoana* were rude, stiff, and expressionless we know. Perhaps they were enlivened by being painted. At all events, they served to enable the consciousness of the invisible to fix itself to form, and that is the purpose of all art. A great change took place in Greek art somewhere about the year 600 B. C. It appears to have been about that time that two new materials and several new processes came into use. The materials were bronze and stone; the processes were beating and casting for the former, hewing and sawing for the latter. Of course all these processes had been known elsewhere long before that; indeed, they had been known, most of them, in Greece itself, but not by the Greeks. For them they were lost arts recovered. It is at present impossible to say whether the bronze or the stone statues are of more ancient date. It is certain, however, that bronze-beating preceded bronze-casting. The oldest bronze statues were formed of sheets nailed or riveted together, and some of the earliest stone statues bear evidences of having been copied from originals of beaten bronze. A great technical advance was made when the arts of casting in bronze and of sawing marble into blocks were discovered. From that time on sculpture, and statuary in the narrower sense, steadily progressed. Advancing skill goes hand in hand with advancing life and advancing thought. The spirit of freedom that now stirs in Greece shows itself at once in all the arts. The very gods renew their form and become beautiful as well as strong. It was a saying of Plato's that the state is but the individual man writ large. We may reverse this and say that in these times the individual statue, with its balance and proportion of life, is simply the ordered state of freedom writ small. Just in proportion as Greece advances in true freedom, her sculpture gains life and beauty; yea, and when freedom dies, sculpture dies; all the arts die. True art is always the expression of freedom, because it is the expression of man's spiritual nature, and that is freedom.

Enough still remains to us of Greek art to show by what steps it passed from the rude stone block to the finished art of Phidias. These steps are better presented to the eye than to the ear.

There is, however, one important series of steps that can not be presented for want of material. It is characteristic of all rational advance that, when the new is found, the old is not thrown contemptuously away, but glorified in the light of the new. So the Greeks, when they learned to make statues of bronze and marble, did not cast aside their old wooden *xoana*, to which so much religious feeling clung. On the contrary, they worked up the *xoana* into something of surpassing beauty. The truth is, the two most famous statues of all the ancient world, the colossal Athena and Zeus of Phidias, were merely improved *xoana*—improved with ivory and gold. And it is a matter of the deepest interest that in these two statues Greece embodied her two ideals, power and wisdom. Power is the father of wisdom. The whole of Greece is in these two statues—her strength as well as her weakness. She has power and wisdom, but she has no love. Ere that come, the world will have to be turned upside down, and Greece will have to perish. The age of Phidias marks the culmination of Greek sculpture, which in him expresses all that Greece is and loves—power and wisdom. The next age, that of Scopas and Praxiteles, exquisite as its works are, already shows signs of decay, or, at any rate, of over-ripeness. What is even more interesting is, love now comes in as a subject of representation. This is not only the age of the great Aphrodites and Dionysuses; it is also the age of the Niobe Group, with its wonderful conflict between power and love, and of the Hermes of Praxiteles, with its pathetic human tenderness. With love the pathetic enters into art. But Greek sculpture never could embody love for want of a type. No such type was given to it. The Greek can never separate the divine love from the animal, and animal love can never be a subject for art. Scopas and Praxiteles do all that Greeks could do to embody love. Their efforts are worthy of all respect and admiration; but they never reach the true ideal. And it was just for want of that ideal that Greece fell into decay. The truth was that, when love did come, it set to work to break down all natural limitations, and that too from its very nature.

The sculpture of Greece after Phidias and Praxiteles is just what one might expect from a nation that had finished its task, worked out into clear visibility its own inner nature. Originality is henceforth impossible for it, and so it goes on repeating old ideas in new and striking forms, making up by technique what it lacks in content. Just as previous to Phidias the content had been too much for the form, so after Praxiteles the form is too much for the content. This is always the sure sign of decay in art.

In Phidias and Praxiteles art reaches its zenith. The monstrous is completely banished from it, except as something overcome. Beauty—calm, dignified, self-poised—reaches its highest expression, and reaches it by a simple idealizing of the natural. In the works of this time there is no effort to arouse a numbed æsthetic sensibility by a false effectiveness, or by appealing to tastes lower than the æsthetic. But after Praxiteles all these tendencies show themselves more and more. Now is the time when Colossi and other monstrous works begin to appear, catching a vulgar attention by their mere size. Now appear the statues familiar to us in all Italian museums, with limbs unnaturally long and heads unnaturally small. Now appear those Herculeses that are mere masses of bones and muscles, and those Venuses that are mere flesh. The downward process begins under the Macedonian Empire, but, checked in part by the full taste of the Greeks, becomes accelerated under the Romans, who appear to have had no taste for anything but the colossal and the meretricious. Ere the Christian era arrives, art is dead, its form being thenceforth only galvanized to fabricate portraits of emperors and their minions, or of fashionable ladies on exhibition.

Such is a very brief and imperfect sketch of the history of Greek sculpture, which may, for several reasons, be taken to represent the history of sculpture generally. Let us enumerate its steps once more. They may be divided into two groups: (1) Steps of growth. (2) Steps of decay. The former may be counted along the line of technical process, or on that of ideas expressed. We have perhaps said enough about the former. Looking at the latter, we find (1) an effort to express an idea in mere static form, first by copying nature, and afterward by introducing monstrosities. The latter is intended to express force. It is only by a very slow and laborious process that art learns to express its ideas without resorting to the monstrous. When this is completed, art (2) tries to express human action—that is, rational action, action ordered for a purpose. It is here that beauty makes its appearance, for beauty is but the expression of ratio or reason. Having accomplished this as it did in the marbles of the Parthenon, it attemps a bolder task, trying to express emotion—at first emotion as a condition, and afterward as a cause of action. So long as this is kept within limits, it is attended with admirable results; but no sooner does the emotion become boisterous than it goes beyond the limits of sculpture. The Hermes of Praxiteles and the Niobe Group are still works of art; so is the Apollo of the Belvedere and the group it belongs to; but we begin to feel a revulsion when we come to the Laocoön, and turn altogether away from the Farnese Bull. In these and other works of the same ages we see the steps of decay—(1) the effective, (2) the harrowing, (3) the gigantic, (4) the meretricious, (5) the meaningless, or merely pretty or curious, (6) the fashionable, (7) the revolting, as so much of the Pompeian sculpture is.

Ancient civilization perished for lack of love. Ancient sculpture perished because it had accomplished its task and could go no further. As ancient civilization died out, Christianity, the religion of love, gradually took its place, and prepared the way for a new and higher civilization. It might, accordingly, have been expected that as the new civilization arose, sculpture would arise with it. But this was by no means the case. The Christianity of the first fifteen hundred years shows no sculpture worthy of the name, and, indeed, in this art Christian civilization has nothing to set alongside Greek sculpture. And the reason of this is by no means difficult to understand. Christianity contains an element—indeed, its essential and characteristic element—which refuses to be represented in sculpture at all. The just and rational naturally appear in sculpture as the beautiful, and this we have in its utmost perfection in Greek art; but love or the holy can not be made to appear in sculpture. The author of the Hebrew decalogue felt all the difference between the just and the holy, the beautiful and the adorable, when he forbade his people to make graven images; and the same is true of Zoroaster. The Greek and Protestant churches felt the same thing when they banished idols from their places of worship. And even the Roman Church, which retains them, shows that it feels their inadequacy by painting them and hiding the body with clothes.

Architecture, dancing, and sculpture are the arts of the just, beautiful, and graceful, and in these the Greeks stand to-day unsurpassed and unsurpassable. The arts of love and holiness are painting, poetry, and music, and in these we moderns as far excel the ancients as they excel us in the other arts. Raphael, Dante, Beethoven have no rivals among the ancients, just as Iktinus, Theodorus, and Praxiteles have no rivals among the moderns. Modern art—which, when it knows itself, is the art of the holy—rises higher in proportion as it uses less material.

We can never dispense with architecture; but it may well be doubted whether we can ever carry it as an art beyond the perfection reached by the Greeks. Dancing we can well afford to dispense with, both as art and as amusement; it is the childish art. And even in sculpture we never can excel. We may use it for portraits, for pretty conceits, and for decorative purposes; but it can never be the expression of what is deepest in our life, never an art for us.

In the Belvedere of the Vatican, along with such works as the Laocoön, the Apollo, and the so-called Antinous, are two statues by one of the greatest of modern sculptors, Canova—two boxers. He was a cruel foe to Canova who put them there. When one suddenly comes upon them they cause a revulsion so great that one feels as if the place had been desecrated. This tells the whole story. And I do not believe that the case can ever be otherwise. We may equal the Greeks in technique, we may make beautiful things by slavishly imitating them, as Thorwaldsen and Jerichau did; but beyond that we can never go. The age of sculpture is past, just as the age of pyramids is. Reason as well as strength must give place to love. Sculpture remains with reason and justice upon the earth; love carries us to heaven, and requires an art that can go thither with us.

Can any one imagine a piece of sculpture creating the same profound interest as the tiny Angelus? No; and why? Because the Angelus expresses the holy, that response of the soul to God—an element which no sculptor, be he ever so deft, can embody in his art—an element which interests us more than any other, which, above all others, it is important that we should unfold in ourselves.

ABSTRACT OF THE DISCUSSION.

Mr. Lysander Dickerman:

I think the audience must have been greatly impressed, as I have been, with the force, beauty, and philosophic thought manifested in the lecture of Prof. Davidson. I can speak only in commendation of his carefully considered and matured conclusions. Since he has drawn his illustrations and traced the line of evolution mainly from the art of Greece, it may be of interest to note its characteristics in an older country—in Egypt. Had I selected my own views, however, I should have made a somewhat different choice. I must use the material at hand as best I may. [A series of about twenty-five views of Egyptian sculpture was placed upon the screen, and explained by Mr. Dickerman. They comprised three views of the Sphinx, several portrait statues, and figures of the gods and goddesses.] In regard to the portrait statues Mr. Dickerman said: The object of the Egyptians in making these statues, which are usually found at or near their burial places, was to prepare an abode for the *Ka*, which was the fourth principle composing the personality of the human being, the other three being the body, soul, and mind. The *Ka* was something like our conception of a ghost; it may have been what Paul meant by the "spiritual body." When the person died it must have an abiding place prepared for it until it should again be united with the soul and body at the resurrection; it must not be left to wander about at a distance from the body. Hence it was the aim of the Egyptian sculptor to make a correct likeness of the deceased: and it is noteworthy that in the oldest of these statues the expression is dignified and life-like. I think we do not find anywhere in Egyptian sculpture the conventional silly and inane expression to which Prof. Davidson has called your attention in these early sculptures of Greece and Assyria. This wooden statue is 6,000 years old—three thousand years older than the earlier products of Greek art; yet you observe that the arms are separated from the sides, without destroying the symmetry of the body; one foot is advanced, and the whole attitude is natural and life-like.

There is a difference between the Greek sphinx and the Egyptian sphinx. The former may have symbolized brute force, as Prof. Davidson has assumed. The latter was simply the symbolical representation of the god Horus—*Har-em-akhu*—the rising sun. It is not true, I believe, of any period of Egyptian history, that that people worshiped animal forms or idols in the ordinary sense. Animals and images were to them symbols of certain divine powers or characteristics, and no more idols than are the lamb and dove in Christian symbolism. This form of idealism, or religious symbolism, was largely the inspiration of Egyptian art.

DR. LEWIS G. JANES:

It is an interesting fact that some of the very oldest products of the sculptor's art, if we may trust the archæologist, have been discovered in this country. Many of you have perhaps seen the little image, now in possession of Prof. G. F. Wright, of Oberlin College, which was dug up in one of the Western Territories during the boring of an artesian well, from a point 400 feet below the surface of the earth. Prof. Wright and other archæologists regard this as the very oldest extant product of the sculptor's art. Rudely sculptured heads of anthropoid apes, regarded as very ancient, have recently been found in the valley of the Columbia River, Oregon—a region in which no such animals have lived in recent times. You are familiar, also, with the rude carvings of animals on bones, found in the caves of Europe.

The noteworthy superiority of the early art of Egypt over that of Greece, of a much later period, and the unquestioned fact that Egyptian art crystallized into conventional forms under the influence of the prevailing religion and civilization, while Greek art, under conditions more favorable to free development, rapidly evolved to the highest perfection, is destructive of a false conception of evolution which sometimes prevails, implying a world-wide seriality of development, and constantly progressive attainment. The evolution of an art merely implies its natural genesis, development, maturity, and decay, as influenced by its local and temporal environment, the prime factor in which, of course, is mental and spiritual. The relative perfection of extant early Egyptian sculptures may be accounted for, perhaps, as suggested indirectly by Prof. Davidson, by the fact that more primitive products were of wood and have been destroyed. I think he is mistaken in supposing that the name of no Egyptian artist has been preserved. If I remember rightly, we have the name and pedigree of at least one architect of note, given at length in the inscriptions.

If I were to criticise the admirable essay of Prof. Davidson at any point, it would be in questioning his right to draw a rigid line of demarkation between an imitative copying of nature and a conscious striving to realize spiritual ideals in art. In the earlier stages of art these two impulses seem to me to be everywhere interblended. Probably the imitative impulse at first predominates; nevertheless, we have in its outcome, I think, the substantial beginnings of art. The gods themselves are pictured most frequently in human form, and clothed with human attributes. The early artist creates both his gods and their artistic symbols in his own image. He can do no otherwise. Even the composite symbolism of later times is made up of distinct natural elements, each copied from some real object. But if all art is in part imitative, so all—even the rudest—is in part, in very large part, symbolic and idealistic. The child who draws his first picture of a man—a rude three-cornered head, with two dots for eyes, single lines for mouth and nose, two horizontal strokes for arms, and two perpendicular ones for legs—exhibits the germs of a genuine artistic impulse. He has symbolized what are to him the living, active, expressive features of his subject—the thinking, speaking head, the moving limbs. These are to him the whole man. The body, the trunk, is quiescent; it is the seat of functions mainly automatic, and concealed from view—so he leaves this out of his picture.

THE
EVOLUTION OF PAINTING

BY

FORREST P. RUNDELL

COLLATERAL READINGS SUGGESTED:

Lübke's History of Art; Drs. Woltmann and Woermann's History of Painting; Twining's Philosophy of Painting; Blanc's History of the Painters of all Nations; Buchanan's Memoirs of Painting; Heaton's Concise History of Painting; Jervis's Painting and Celebrated Painters, Ancient and Modern; Radcliffe's Schools and Masters of Painting; Hamerton's Thoughts about Art, and A Painter's Camp; Eastlake's History of Oil Painting, and Ruskin's Review of the same in the London Quarterly Review. Articles *Fine Art*, *Painting*, *Schools of Painting*, and *Archæology*, in Encyclopædia Britannica; Article *Painting* in American Cyclopædia; Barry's Lectures on Painting; Fuseli's Lectures on Painting; Kügler's Handbooks of Painting; C. E. Clement's History of Painting, and Handbook of Legendary and Mythological Art.

THE EVOLUTION OF PAINTING.

By Forrest P. Rundell.

Painting has been defined as "the art of representing on a flat surface, by means of lines and color, objects as they appear in nature—that is to say, in such a manner that the picture produced shall within certain limits affect the eye in the same way as do the objects themselves." During its early history, painting was everywhere wholly decorative in character. In some countries it has not yet advanced beyond the decorative stage. This is especially the case in China, and to a certain extent also in Japan. In most countries painting was at first closely allied with sculpture and architecture. In Egypt, Assyria, and Greece both painting and sculpture were subsidiary to architecture, being chiefly used to ornament tombs, palaces, and temples. The bas-reliefs and earlier statues were painted. The practice of coloring statues continued in Greece until after sculpture became differentiated from architecture.

The subjects of the early paintings were of a simple character. They consisted chiefly of figures with few or no accessories. When trees were first introduced they were treated in the most conventional manner. Each tree was of the same size and had the same number of leaves as all the other trees in the picture, and all were represented as in the same plane.

With a knowledge of perspective came the introduction of backgrounds; and when skill had been acquired in treating the backgrounds, they were gradually separated from the figures, and in course of time were themselves used as subjects for pictures.

At a later period artists devoted their attention to special features of landscapes. Some painted only marine pictures, others mountains, others flowers or fruits. Spencer's definition of progress was never better illustrated than in the history of painting. There has been a constant differentiation of forms, a constant change from the homogeneous to the heterogeneous.

If time permitted, we should find it profitable to trace the history of painting back to remote ages, and to discuss its progress among semi-barbarous peoples.

An exploration of caves in western Europe has brought to light many interesting remains of early art. These remains belong to the Pleistocene period, and prove beyond question that the so-called cave-men had great natural aptitude for art. In speaking of the cave-men, John Fiske says: "Many details of their life are preserved to us through their extraordinary taste for engraving and carving. Sketches of reindeer, mammoths, horses, cave-bears, pike, and seals, and hunting scenes, have been found by the hundred, incised upon antlers or bones, or sometimes upon stone; and the artistic skill which they show is really astonishing. Their drawings are remarkable not only for their accuracy, but often equally so for the taste and vigor with which the subject is treated."

Sir John Lubbock, in describing these remarkable drawings, states that "in some cases there is even an attempt at shading."

Coming down to historic times, the earliest art is to be found in Egypt. Pliny tells us that the Egyptians boasted of having been masters of painting more than six thousand years before it was acquired by the Greeks. We would doubtless agree with Pliny that this was a "vain boast," because while many of their paintings date back several thousand years, they were never masters of the art.

The remains of Egyptian paintings are found mostly on walls of tombs and temples, on cases and cloths of mummies, and on papyrus rolls. Their pictures are not works of art in the ordinary sense; they are merely symbolic writings which record the social, religious, and political life of the people. The pictures consist merely of outline diagrams arbitrarily colored

The Egyptians knew nothing of perspective, or the science of composition, and very little about the use of colors. They were conventional in their treatment of the human face. Woltmann, in his History of Painting, says: "One face wears almost always the same fixed expression as another. A king, whether we see him engaged in prayer, or sacrifice, or confronting the enemy in the onset of battle, or marching in triumph after his victory, or sitting upon the seat of judgment in the character of an avenging deity, invariably bears upon his countenance the character of inexpressive and conventional rigidity, beneath which our modern eyes seem to detect something of a sensual and self-complacent smile."

The Egyptians made little or no progress in either sculpture or painting during a period comprising thousands of years. Artists were regulated in their work by rigid rules prescribed by the priesthood, and all innovations were expressly prohibited. Plato says in his Laws: "The art we have proposed for the education of youth was known long ago to the Egyptians. This people having fixed by statute what forms and what music should be licensed, they had them represented in their temples. Nor was it lawful for painters or other inventive artists to make the least deviation from the authorized standard. Upon careful examination, indeed, it will be found that the pictures and the statues made by this people ten thousand years ago are neither an advance upon nor inferior to those they now execute."

The Greeks borrowed their art from Egypt; but in borrowing the art, they left behind the religion. The Egyptian seed was planted in a fertile soil, and in a congenial climate like that of Greece it soon produced a flower of great beauty. Unfortunately, no remains of masterpieces among Greek paintings have been preserved. In judging of the merits of these works we are obliged to rely largely on the descriptions of contemporary historians. The remains found at Pompeii and in the Catacombs belong to a period of decline, and, although some of these are copies of earlier Greek paintings of note, they are mostly the works of inferior artists.

As might have been expected, the Greeks were several centuries in acquiring their knowledge of painting. They were pioneers, and their advance was slow. The gradual growth of their knowledge has been summed up in an admirable manner by Barry. In one of his lectures he says: "Here we find them beginning with an outline. They write down the names of their objects for fear of mistake. A Corinthian and his followers first attempt to fill up this outline with one color. An Athenian makes his men different one from another. A Cleonian acquires the ability to draw his figures in different postures, distinguishing the joints and parts of the body, and making folds in the drapery. Others come to have an idea of light and shadow; they no longer use simple colors, but mix and compound them one with another. Apollodorus is distinguished for a judicious choice of nature; Zeuxis, for good coloring.

Parrhasius is first remarkable for symmetry and expression. Pamphilus joins the study of mathematics to art. Pausias excels at foreshortening his figures. Euphranor introduces majesty, and Apelles grace." It will thus be seen that their final success was the work of progressive and accumulated experience.

There has been much controversy regarding the relative merits of Greek paintings when compared with the works of modern masters. Greek writers bestow the same high praise upon the work of their painters that they do upon that of their sculptors. Nevertheless, it is generally agreed by modern writers that Greek painting did not reach the degree of excellence attained by sculpture.

An interesting story has come down to us regarding a trial of skill between Zeuxis and Parrhasius. Zeuxis painted some grapes which were so natural in appearance that birds came to eat them. Parrhasius then painted a curtain and was so accurate in his execution that even Zeuxis was deceived. When Zeuxis was invited to the room to view the picture, he asked that the curtain be drawn aside so that the picture could be seen. The contest was decided in favor of Parrhasius, because he had deceived Zeuxis, while Zeuxis had only deceived the birds.

The complicated problems of scientific perspective were unknown to the Greeks, and there were perhaps some weaknesses of coloring. Woltmann tells us that "in the pictures having definite backgrounds and a complete pictorial purpose, the evident blunders in perspective, the false foreshortenings, rudely managed distances, and inefficient conduct of light and shade, are very disturbing." As the Greeks were not very ambitious in the matter of landscapes, many of these defects were not often apparent. And Woltmann gives the opinion that if we could "look upon some great series of masterpieces by a Greek artist we should not be struck by any technical shortcomings in his work, but should place it by the side of the most finished performances of all times or races."

After the third century B. C., Greek art began to decline. The general debasement of morals and the political revolutions and changes of dynasties which convulsed Greece accelerated the decline; and finally, at the time of the Roman Conquest in 146 B. C., the spoliation of the art galleries, public buildings, and temples tended to crush the art of painting everywhere.

After the conquest of Greece, statues and paintings were carried to Rome by tens of thousands. As a result of plundering the entire East, Rome became the center of art. The Roman art was all stolen, however. Even the painters themselves were Greeks. Not a single name of a Roman painter of eminence has come down to us.

When the Emperor Constantine made Byzantium the capital of the empire, Rome itself was plundered to supply the new capital. Soon after this the barbarian invasions commenced. In the year 410 Rome was sacked by the Goths under Alaric. In 455 Rome was again plundered, this time by the Vandals, and the destruction of art in the West was then complete.

From this time until the thirteenth century the principal seat of art was at Constantinople. The painters were mostly monks or persons connected with monasteries, and painting was practiced almost wholly for religious purposes. What is known as the Byzantine style was developed, which became almost as fixed and conventional as the style employed in ancient Egypt. "The characteristics of the Byzantine school are length and meagerness of limbs, stiffness of figure, features almost devoid of expression, long, narrow eyes, a disagreeable blackish-green coloring of the flesh, various conventional attitudes and accessories having no foundation in nature, and a profusion of gilding."

The capture of Constantinople by the Crusaders in 1204 opened channels of intercourse with western Europe. Many Byzantine artists settled in Italy and Germany, and schools of painting were established in the flourishing cities in these countries.

At first the Byzantine style was servilely followed. But finally the study of ancient Greek art was taken up, and this, in connection with the direct study of nature, led a few men of genius to reject the prevailing style. New methods were gradually adopted until the foundations of modern painting were laid.

Cimabue, who lived in the latter part of the thirteenth century, was one of the first Italian painters to break away from the Byzantine style, and many writers speak of him as the father of modern painting. Others accord this honor to Giotto, a pupil of Cimabue. Giotto was a thorough student of nature, and he greatly improved upon the work of his master. From this time the development of painting was rapid, and the great schools of Italy were soon established.

In the fifteenth and sixteenth centuries we meet with Leonardo da Vinci, Michel Angelo, Raphael, Titian, and other great masters.

In summing up the work of the Italian painters of this period, N. d'Anvers says: "We find a simultaneous fulfillment of all the great principles of painting; form, design, and expression had been perfected in the Roman and Florentine schools by Michel Angelo, Leonardo da Vinci, and Raphael; and coloring and chiaroscuro in the schools of Venice; Parma by Correggio and Titian and Paolo Veronese; spiritual beauty had found its noblest exponent in Raphael, and corporeal in Titian; the art of portraiture had attained its highest development; landscape painting, properly so called, though not much practiced, had been greatly improved, and genre painting had been introduced. The religious subjects almost exclusively favored in the thirteenth century had given place to some extent to those of antique mythology and history, and a general love of art pervaded all classes."

Raphael died in 1520, and soon after this a rapid decline in painting took place in all parts of Italy except Venice. A large portion of the country was devastated by war. In 1527 Rome was sacked by Charles V. The city never regained its former splendor. The art schools were dispersed and ruined, and the artists found no other center of encouragement and support. Florence was captured in 1530. The desolation of war was supplemented by the horrors of the plague, and the ruin of art in Italy was for a time nearly complete. The Italian civic states were supplanted by petty despotic governments of foreign extraction, which ruled in the interest of the trading class, and the public patronage of art wholly ceased.

The decline of art in Italy was nearly contemporary with its spread over northern and western Europe. Gothic architecture, which had been adopted in northern Europe, was unfavorable to the development of painting. The large colored glass windows in the churches left little room for pictures on the walls. Furthermore, the influence of classic Greek art was felt sooner in Italy than in Germany. For these reasons painting had a slower growth in northern Europe than in Italy.

Flanders emerged from the barbarism of the middle ages sooner than most other countries. The great commercial and manufacturing cities established there attained a high degree of civilization in comparatively early times, and the art of painting developed earlier than in Germany. The paintings of the earlier Flemish artists were nearly all destroyed by Christian iconoclasts, and little is known of the painters living previous to the fifteenth century.

The brothers Van Eyck, who were born in the latter part of the fourteenth century, discovered a new method of applying colors with oils, and carried the art of painting to a high degree of perfection. After the death of these artists painting rapidly declined. But two centuries later we find two of the great names of history—Rubens of Belgium and Rembrandt of Holland.

In Germany, painting reached its highest development in the beginning of the sixteenth century. Albert Durer and Hans Holbein are its great masters. After the death of Durer, in 1520, Germany was convulsed by the religious wars and social revolutions of the Reformation period, which had a destructive influence upon art.

The art of painting made little headway in Spain until the sixteenth century, and owes its origin largely to Italian and Flemish influences. It was not until the seventeenth century that the great names of Murillo and Velasquez appeared. As a portrait painter Velasquez has had few equals and perhaps no superiors.

Although French writers claim an early origin for the practice of painting in France, it appears that the early French painters chiefly excelled in glass painting and in the illuminating of manuscripts. There seems to have been no distinctive French school until a comparatively recent period. Francis I did much to encourage art in France. He invited Da Vinci and other Italian artists into his service. A great part of Michel Angelo's designs and cartoons and two cases of his models were taken to France, and also a large number of antique statues and busts. Florence was stripped of paintings and statues. Raphael painted his Transfiguration and other works for France. The superficial character of the French people, taken in connection with unfavorable social conditions, has done much to retard the growth of art. But France can boast of many painters of great merit, and at present the French school is perhaps the leading school of the world.

Painting in England is of recent growth; in fact, it belongs almost wholly to the last century and a half. The growth of art was very much retarded by the many religious and political revolutions to which England was subjected. While Francis I was encouraging art, Henry VIII was engaged in a hot controversy with Luther, and a little later he had a hotter controversy with the Pope. While the French were bringing works of art from Italy, the English were burning paintings and covering the pictures in their churches with a coat of whitewash, and putting up Scripture texts in their places. The Madonnas were replaced by the second commandment. Barry maintains that if the ancient Greeks had been of the same leaven as the original English Quakers or Puritans, they would never have excelled in art.

The first English painter to attract attention was William Hogarth. His work was all done in the eighteenth century. Since the time of Hogarth, England has produced many painters of note. Sir Joshua Reynolds and Thomas Gainsborough excelled in portraits, Landseer as a painter of animals, and Turner in landscape. Ruskin mentions Reynolds and Turner as the only supreme colorists among true painters outside of the Venetian school, and gives it as his opinion that Turner was the greatest painter of all time.

While the people of the United States have given their attention largely to trade and manufacture and the development of the country, they have by no means neglected art. We have already many painters of real merit, and the future is full of promise.

There has been much discussion regarding the influence of climate and other physical causes upon the development of art. Buckle states that earthquakes have had a stimulating effect on the imagination, and that this particularly accounts for the genius displayed by the Italian and Spanish painters. Taine attributes the superiority of the Flemish and Venetian painters in coloring to the hazy atmosphere which prevailed in Flanders and Venice. He asserts that Rubens and Titian merely copied nature as they saw it. It may be added that Taine, in his lectures on the Philosophy of Art, has carried the materialistic theory of progress to its extreme limit. He maintains that the art of a period is the product of all the physical, intellectual, and social forces of the time. That the Last Supper of Da Vinci was as much the product of all the forces of his time as was a stratum of Potsdam sandstone of the age in which it was formed.

Religion has everywhere exercised great influence over art. In Egypt painting was under the immediate control of a religion which paralyzed the artistic genius of the people by making all innovations a crime, and by making the profession of the artist hereditary and compulsory. Dissection was prohibited, and therefore a knowledge of anatomy was rendered impossible.

In India religion ever soared to the unnatural and the prodigious, and consequently art was completely turned away from nature. The faculty for accurately copying nature was lost, and the imagination of the artist reveled in the grotesque and the terrible.

The Koran contains the following: "O ye faithful, of a truth, wine, gaming, images, and the casting of lots are things to be held in abhorrence." Another declaration of more emphatic character was also attributed to the Prophet: "Woe unto him who paints the likeness of a living thing: on the Day of Judgment those whom he has depicted will rise up out of their graves and ask him for their souls. Then, verily, unable to make the work of his hands live, he will be consumed in everlasting flames." The baneful effects of these prohibitions are seen wherever the religion of Mohammed has prevailed. The art of painting has never flourished in any Mohammedan country.

The influence of the Hebrew religion was in the same direction. The commandment, "Thou shalt not make unto thee any graven image or any likeness of any thing that is in heaven above, or that is in the earth beneath, or that is in the water under the earth," had a repressing influence upon both painting and sculpture. Origen says that artists were forbidden to enter the Jewish state.

The religion of Greece, on the other hand, was especially favorable to the development of both painting and sculpture. Being nearly a pure nature worship, it led directly to a careful study of nature. Beauty was the highest object of worship. The deities were represented in human form and were models of physical excellence.

All manual labor being performed by slaves, the free Greek was able to spend his time in the gymnasium and bath, and in training for athletic games. Greater attention was given to the development of the body than to the cultivation of the mind. The athletic games occupied a large place in the life of the people, and physical strength and beauty were held in the highest admiration. The clothing worn on ordinary occasions was of such a loose character as to expose a large portion of the body, and in the games the participants appeared perfectly nude. In the gymnasium, which was one of the sacred institutions of the country, both men and women appeared nearly if not quite naked. As a result, the ideas of modesty were transformed. Nakedness was associated with dignity rather than with shame. The gods, it was said, were naked, and they were so represented in art. To represent a king naked was deemed the highest form of flattery, because it was to represent his apotheosis.

Under these circumstances the human body reached a perfection of form which has never been attained in any other country or age, and artists were constantly furnished with the most perfect and beautiful of models. The human form was glorified and idealized, and every effort was made to secure perfection in its representation in sculpture and painting. The statues and paintings thus produced have served as models during all subsequent time, and have exercised a lasting influence upon the art of the world.

There is one unfortunate circumstance to be noticed in this connection. The Greek idea of modesty is not in harmony with that of the Christian world. The students of Greek art have had a constant struggle with our modern civilization. The Christian world has always been opposed to nude figures, especially in painting. Italian morals in the fifteenth and sixteenth centuries were so lax, and the influence of the painters was so great, that the feeling of the Church was to a certain extent overcome. But even Michel Angelo's influence was not great enough to prevent his figures from being draped by order of the Pope. It is probable that if our ideas of modesty had prevailed among the Greeks they could never have boasted of a Phidias or an Apelles, and perhaps Italy would never have had a Michel Angelo or a Titian. But be that as it may, it must be admitted that the three hundred good mothers in Philadelphia who protested the other day against the pictures of naked figures which were on exhibition in that city are more in harmony with our civilization than the committee which denied their petition; and undoubtedly they represent the judgment of a large majority of the people of our country.

The discouraging influence of the second commandment upon art was not confined to early Jewish times, but was extended with the spread of Christianity and was felt as late as the seventeenth century.

Although the early Christian painters were pagans by

education, the effect of the new religious ideas was at once apparent. Christianity opposed the pagan mythology and idolatry, and the early Christian artists were not allowed to represent the Deity in human form. This led to the use of symbols. Christ was represented by a lamb; the Holy Ghost, by a dove; purity, by a lily; immortality, by a peacock; sin and paganism, by a serpent or dragon; zeal or fervor of soul, by fire; God was sometimes represented by a hand pointing to a cloud. In 692 a council of the Church authorized the direct representation of Christ instead of a symbol.

Many of the early church fathers considered the second commandment a prohibition of all painting and sculpture, and an effort was made to enforce it. Good Father Tertullian did not hesitate to denounce artists as persons of "iniquitous occupations." He expresses himself in the following vigorous language: "There was a time past when the idol did not exist; the sacred places were unoccupied and the temples void. But when the devil brought in makers of statues and images and all kinds of likenesses on the world, all the raw material of human misery and the name of idols followed it. And ever since then any art which produces an idol in any way is the source of idolatry. It makes no difference whether the workman makes it in clay, or a sculptor carves it, or if he weaves it in Phrygian cloth, because it is no consequence as to the substance an idol is formed of, whether it be plaster, or colors, or stone, or brass, or silver, or canvas." Furthermore, Tertullian did not hesitate to prove his faith by his works. He would not allow any artist to be baptized until he had foresworn his art, and if any artist was found in the Church he was excommunicated.

The opposition to painting and sculpture was based principally upon the fact that it was supposed to promote idolatry. The war against "images" extended over a large part of the Christian world at one time or another. The use of sacred pictures in churches aroused the greatest opposition. St. Augustine says there were many worshipers of tombs and pictures in his day; that the Church condemned them and strove to correct them. Sirenus, Bishop of Marseilles, ordered all the images in his diocese to be destroyed. Among the decrees promulgated by the Council of Illiberus in Spain is the following: "It is ordered that there be no pictures in church, lest that which we worship and adore be painted on the walls."

It was in the eastern part of the empire that the fight regarding images waxed hottest. In 726 A. D. the Emperor Leo III published an edict against image worship. This was followed by a decree of the Council of Constantinople condemning all worship and use of images, and excommunicating all persons who violated the decree. Thousands of statues and paintings were destroyed; artists were imprisoned, and some of them were drowned or burned. Riot and massacre were common, and occasionally the contest amounted to civil war. The struggle lasted more than a century and finally disrupted the empire.

Many of the early fathers held views of the most extreme character. Clemens Alexandrinus gave it as his opinion that ladies broke the second commandment by using looking-glasses, because they thereby made images of themselves.

But the Church party favoring the use of images finally triumphed. The Pope opposed the iconoclastic movement from the start. In 787 a general council at Nice decided that pictures of Christ, the Virgin Mary, angels and saints, might be set up in churches. This was subsequently confirmed by a synod at Constantinople, and later by the Council of Trent. The practice of placing pictures of sacred objects in the churches was fully established both in eastern and western Europe. This was of great importance to art. The encouragement which Italian artists received by their employment in the decoration of churches was one of the leading factors in the development of painting in Italy.

Some superstitions of the middle ages are curiously illustrated in the history of painting. Many paintings were supposed to have been miraculously produced. Some came down from heaven; others were dug out of the earth; others were capable of reproducing themselves. Some could cure disease; others helped to win battles in war. Many Madonnas were attributed to St. Luke the Evangelist, and a picture of the Saviour was supposed to have been produced by Christ himself. This picture was captured by the Saracens, and was afterward sold to Constantinople for the handsome sum of twelve thousand pounds of silver. Several of the Madonnas by St. Luke are still extant. This evangelist seems to have had a great reputation everywhere as a painter, and he was the patron of many art schools. One of the statutes regulating the corporation of painting at Sienna was headed as follows: "In the name of the Almighty God and of his blessed Mother, the Holy Virgin

Mary, and of all the saints of the Court of Heaven, and especially of the blessed Luke, the evangelist, chief and guide of all painters, who painted and drew the image of the Virgin Mary, Mother of the Son of God."

The ascetic movement among the early Christians had a very unhealthful influence upon art. They regarded the body as a temptation to evil and sought on all occasions to mortify and subdue its passions and desires. To this end they submitted to starvation and all kinds of torture. Christ was believed to have been deformed and one of the ugliest of men. Instead of the healthy, well-rounded, beautiful figures of the Greeks, the early Christian painters produced "melancholy Christs, with large, ill-shaped eyes, looking forth into space and seeing nothing; Madonnas with a deep olive-green complexion, suggesting a bilious temperament; infant Saviours whose attenuated limbs and old-looking faces would seem to speak of the most direful effects of starvation; saints with distorted arms and legs and emaciated to a degree that even St. Simon Stylites might envy."

About the close of the eighth century the Pope issued a bull decreeing that Christ must be represented with all the attributes of the divine that art could lend him; but it was not until the Italian artists commenced the study of classic Greek sculpture that they were able to counteract the influence of an ascetic religion. The Italian art of the middle ages was almost wholly religious. In fact, it was not until the time of Titian and Michel Angelo that it was partially secularized.

In Spain the growth of art was retarded at first by the Mohammedan religion, and in later times by the deep superstition of the people. As late as the sixteenth century many of the artists rivaled the Eastern hermits in their asceticism. One painter, we are told, was in the habit of lying in a coffin several hours a day, contemplating death. Paintings divinely inspired and which were able to work miracles were very common.

The Spanish Inquisition was not content with providing the people with knowledge regarding geography and astronomy, but turned its attention to art as well. Rigid rules were made for painters, and inspectors were appointed to see that the rules were enforced. The sublime assurance of some of these inspectors was only equaled by their zeal. They did not hesitate to criticise Michel Angelo and

Titian. Michel Angelo was especially condemned because in the Last Judgment he pictured "the angels without wings and the saints without clothes."

But the baneful influence of superstition was not confined to southern Europe. In Flanders, as late as the sixteenth century, there was a wholesale destruction of paintings by religious fanatics. And the slow development of art in England was largely due to the influence of religion. On this subject an English historian says: "It is mortifying to reflect that the Reformation, favorable as it was to the exercise of the human intellect and the general cause of human liberty, had in this country at least a very chilling effect upon the state of the fine arts. In the reign of Edward VI images and pictures were not only ejected from the churches, but the people were taught to hold in abhorrence all graphical representations of sacred objects. Queen Elizabeth went further, and issued a decree for obliterating all such delineations on the walls of churches by whitewashing them and inscribing sentences of Holy Writ in the room of these figures. When, about seventy years afterward, the spirit of Puritanism gained the ascendency and broke down all the barriers of the Constitution, civil and ecclesiastic, the ornaments in the churches were among the first objects of spoliation and destruction; the churches were converted into barracks for soldiers and stabling for horses; everything of value was carried off, and men were hired by the governing powers at a daily stipend to tear down crosses and images wherever they could be found, and to break in pieces the beautiful paintings in the church windows; all sacred pictures were commanded to be destroyed by an express ordinance of parliament."

It will thus be seen that the history of art has been intimately associated with that of religion; while at times religion has been the chief opponent of progress in art, on other occasions it has been the chief source of encouragement.

In surveying the history of art, one is forcibly impressed by the fact that in nearly every country the rise of painting has been almost immediately followed by a decline. In some countries these changes have been repeated several times. Some of the causes are easily observed. Prominent among these may be mentioned a decadence of morals, barbaric invasions, civil war, conquest by foreign powers, loss of free institutions, plagues, and famines. Another cause more intimately connected with the practice of painting itself has had a powerful influence in promoting decay. Whenever there has been a general movement away from the observation and truthful representation of nature, and an effort to copy or imitate existing paintings, an immediate decline has always followed. On this point Ruskin says: "So long as Art is steady in the contemplation and exhibition of natural facts, so long she herself lives and grows. But a time has always hitherto come in which, having thus reached a singular perfection, she begins to contemplate that perfection and to imitate it, and to deduce forms and rules from it, and thus to forget her duties and ministry as the discoverer of truth. And in the very instant when this diversion of her purpose and forgetfulness of her function take place—forgetfulness generally coincident with her apparent perfection—in that instant, I say, begins her actual catastrophe."

In the matter of painting, the nineteenth century compares favorably with any other period in the world's history. In some parts of Russia where the Greek Church still tyrannizes over the people, the old Byzantine style still prevails. But outside of the countries under the influence of the Mohammedan or Greek Christian religions the art of painting is at the present time flourishing everywhere in Europe. During no other century have there been so many great painters or so many people who appreciate art.

It is sometimes claimed that the fine arts have a deleterious effect upon morals. Even Ruskin has been quoted in support of this theory. His statement is as follows: "Historically, great success in art is apparently connected with subsequent national degradation. You find, in the first place, that the nations which possessed a refined art were always subdued by those who possessed none; you find the Lydian subdued by the Mede; the Greek by the Roman; the Roman by the Goth; the Burgundian by the Switzer; but you find beyond this that even where no attack by an external power has accelerated the catastrophe of the state, the period in which any given people reach their highest power in art is precisely that in which they appear to sign the warrant of their own ruin; and that from the moment in which a perfect statue appears in Florence, a perfect picture in Venice, or a perfect fresco in Rome, from that hour forward, probity, industry, and courage seemed to be exiled from their walls, and they perish in a sculpturesque paralysis, or a many-colored corruption. But even this is not all. As art seems thus, in its delicate form, to be one of the chief promoters of indolence and sensuality—so I need hardly remind you, it hitherto has appeared only in energetic manifestation, when it was in the service of superstition. The four greatest manifestations of the human intellect which founded the four principal kingdoms of art—Egyptians, Babylonians, Greeks, and Italians—were developed by the strong excitement of active superstition in the worship of Osiris, Belus, Minerva, and the Queen of Heaven. Therefore, to speak briefly, it may appear very difficult to show that art has ever yet existed in a consistent and thoroughly energetic school, unless it was engaged in the propagation of falsehood or the encouragement of vice."

Perhaps we may charitably assume that when Ruskin wrote this he was suffering from an attack of dyspepsia. At least, on another occasion, he took pains to show the fallacy in this argument. He showed that the decline of morals in Greece and Italy was not caused by art, but was merely a concomitant circumstance. The rainbow which is seen at Niagara is not the cause of the cataract.

There is doubtless more reason for saying that a decline in morals has a destructive influence upon art than for saying that a perfect art has an injurious effect upon morals. It is admitted that some paintings, like some books, have a bad influence, but it is also true that paintings, like books, have on the whole done much to promote the advancement of the race, both intellectually and morally.

It will not be denied that the Christian religion has been pre-eminent as a teacher of morals; and yet, before the invention of printing in Europe, painting was one of the chief mediums of instruction in religion.

Unquestionably the fine arts have added to the sum of human happiness, have made the world better. The influence of a beautiful picture is like that of a beautiful flower. It appeals to the better elements in man's nature. It calls him to a higher life than that of sense. In the language of Parry, "Art is truly a divine seed, whose fruit is for the sweetness of man's life."

ABSTRACT OF THE DISCUSSION.

MR. JOHN H. LITTLEFIELD:

As an historical sketch of the development of the art of painting, I find little to criticise in the lecture of the evening. As an artist, however, certain facts connected with the evolution of the technique of this art come to my mind, which may be of supplementary interest. Art is, unquestionably, one of the civilizing influences of the world. Its development has been coincident with that of civilization. The spirit of an epoch gives color and character to its art. While the materialistic spirit predominates to-day in America, and antagonizes the highest development of the art spirit, we may hope that it will ultimately react through the development of liberality among the wealthy until this country shall take its place as the home of art in the future. In regard to the evolution of the technique of the painter's art, it may be noted that in its earliest exercise—as, for example, in the mural paintings of Egypt—its form was the simplest and most homogeneous; the color was applied to flat surfaces, without differences in texture or shading. Figures were represented without background or suggestion of perspective. These elements are of comparatively recent development. Then, following nature, the painter learned to represent shaded parts of his picture by thin applications of pigment, and the lighter and more prominent parts by thicker layers of color. Later we find painters differentiated into different schools according to their style or technique—their methods of imitating nature. We have the impasto school, where the colors are laid in with solidity—in mass, so to speak—and the opposite school, where the tracery is more delicate, and greater attention is paid to the minutiæ of drawing and outline. Other schools have differentiated as the followers of great masters who have impressed their genius and individuality on their art. Their pupils have imitated the work of the master, and perpetuated the peculiarities of his style. The knowledge of chiaroscuro, of the laws of light and shade, of which Leonardo was the first great master, led to a further differentiation of this art. We have historical evidence that there were great painters in Greece as early as the time of Alexander the Great, though their work, being less indestructible than that of the sculptor, has not survived to our day. It is doubtless true, however, that this art has reached its highest evolution in our own time.

Dr. Lewis G. Janes:

If my friend Dr. Dickerman were present, I imagine that he might have a word of criticism upon the remarks of the lecturer concerning the illustrations of the painter's art which we find upon the monuments and tombs of ancient Egypt. Though conventional, the Egyptian painter or sculptor aimed at the production of true portrait-likenesses, and succeeded so well that the portraits of the great kings are always recognizable. It is evident, however, that the art of painting was much more immature in its development in Egypt and Greece than was the art of sculpture. It will be remembered that Prof. Davidson suggested a philosophical reason for this fact in the subordination of the love or emotional element to the more intellectual or mathematical conception of the beautiful. The love or emotional element, which gives warmth and color to art, found freer scope after the advent of Christianity, which has consequently stimulated the higher evolution of the art of painting. Referring to symbolism in art, the speaker said he had often thought that the architect who superintended the decoration of the church in which these meetings are held must have smiled quietly when he introduced so profusely the trefoil, the triple scroll, the three-branched gas-fixtures, and other symbols of the trinitarian idea. These, however, were the conventional forms of church decoration, they were intrinsically appropriate and beautiful, and those of us who are Unitarians, if we are also evolutionists, need not object to this architectural recognition of the relation which we hold to the older faith.

Mr. Lawrence E. Sterner:

I regret that the lecture has been so exclusively historical in its character—that the lecturer has not shown us more clearly the intellectual side of the growth of this art, its relation to the states of culture and civilization in different periods. I should like to have seen the artist traced, as a growing man, from the time of the cave-men to him who is the product of the highest civilization of the present day.

Mr. Rundell, in closing, said that the limitation of time had compelled him to treat only a single phase of the subject. In all its branches it had been treated in a thousand volumes, and could not be rounded into one short lecture. This would explain the deficiencies noted.

THE EVOLUTION OF MUSIC

BY

Z. SIDNEY SAMPSON

AUTHOR OF EVOLUTION OF THEOLOGY, PRIMITIVE MAN, ETC.

COLLATERAL READINGS SUGGESTED:

Pole's The Philosophy of Music; *History of Music*, in English Cyclopædia, Science and Arts Division; Helmholtz's On the Sensations of Tone as a Physiological Basis for the Theory of Music; Hullah's History of Modern Music, and The Transition Period of Musical History; Rockstro's History of Music; Naumann's History of Music; Haweis's Music and Morals; Robert Schumann's Music and Musicians; Hand's Æsthetics of Musical Art; Spencer's *Origin and Function of Music*, in Illustrations of Universal Progress; Blaserna's The Theory of Sound in its Relations to Music.

"*True music is the natural expression of a lofty passion for a right cause. In proportion to the kingliness and force of any personality, the expression either of its joy or suffering becomes measured, chastened, calm, and capable of interpretation only by the majesty of ordered, beautiful, and worded sound. Exactly in proportion to the degree in which we become narrow in the cause and conception of our passions, incontinent in the utterance of them, feeble of perseverance in them, sullied or shameful in the indulgence of them, their expression by musical sound becomes broken, mean, fatuitous, and at last impossible; the measured waves of the air of heaven will not lend themselves to expression of ultimate vice: it must be forever sunk into discordance or silence. And since every work of right art has a tendency to reproduce the ethical state which first developed it, this, which of all the arts is most directly ethical in origin, is also the most direct in power of discipline; the first, the simplest, the most effective of all instruments of moral instruction; while in the failure and betrayal of its functions it becomes the subtlest aid of moral degradation. Music is thus, in her health, the teacher of perfect order, and is the voice of the obedience of angels, and the companion of the course of the spheres of heaven.*"

RUSKIN—Queen of the Air.

THE EVOLUTION OF MUSIC.

By Z. Sidney Sampson.

That the laws of evolution apply to the development of such a purely subjective art as Music we hope to demonstrate in the following lecture. Manifestly, as we progress from studies of external phenomena, as in the domains of biology and sociology, to the more recondite studies in psychological evolution and the growth of mind, the problem becomes increasingly complex. As all phases of art are distinctively phases of mental evolution, the application of the principles of the latter to the history of the former will, if successful, verify the claim of this latest and most imposing of the modern philosophies to be of universal application. In science its position has been secured, owing to the fact that it deals with objective phenomena, wherein analysis and classification are possible; but in respect to mental phenomena, while the laws governing mental progress have been formulated, there is still much work to be done in demonstrating, from the history of the several arts, that these laws are valid. All the arts are forms of purely mental activity, and advance in these, and the improvement of the forms in which they are presented is dependent upon, and conditioned exclusively by, mental progress, and is a certain indication of the latter by reason of the fact that in all art-work the materials given in experience are, through the innate activity of the mind, utilized to body forth the ideals which it has conceived.

The increasing complexity of which we have spoken becomes more apparent as we pass from what we may term the static arts—those which are presented in line and form, viz., sculpture, painting, and architecture—to the dynamic, which produce their effects by succession in presentation—poetry, oratory, and music. The former, being of definite outline, are much more readily studied in the light of evolution principles, and examples of sculpture and architecture remain to us from remote antiquity; whereas of poetry and oratory the remains are extremely limited, and of music we can say that we know nothing which can serve as a basis for a correct history of music in all its departments until several centuries after the Christian era. The causes are not only the destruction of musical manuscripts, but the imperfection in the progress of the art itself. Music is the last of the arts to develop. It did not attain its possibilities of advancement until the eleventh or twelfth centuries as will be shown further on. It is, moreover, pre-eminently the emotional art—the one which most of all appeals to the abstract imaginative faculty, and which relies least for its effects upon external form. It follows that a high civilization only will be capable of producing great artistic, creative musical composition, a civilization higher than that which attained perfection in the plastic arts. The evolution of the higher emotional faculties succeeds and does not precede the development of the higher intellect.

First Period.

Development of Melody.

In the treatment of our subject it may be expected that some discussion should be undertaken as to the remote origins of music. Such arguments as might be adduced would, however, be wholly speculative. We may surmise that imitation of the sounds of nature, or of the cries and calls of animals, was a factor in the case; or we can equally well surmise that it was a development directly due to the consciousness of possessing a faculty of vocalization which led primitive man to his first exceedingly rude attempts at what he might have called music. The invention of musical instruments was quite certainly a merely happy chance. Noticing sounds produced by the wind over some distended substance, or caused by its blowing through some hollow reed or otherwise, man, from motives of curiosity, would have endeavored to reproduce them by his own action, and in the course of ages all our varieties of string and wind instruments would be the result, under the law of evolution. Judging, however, by analogy from existing savage and half-civilized races, he satisfied his earliest musical instincts by mere noise, produced by the rhythmical beating of hard substances together, accompanied with gesticulation, dancing, and clapping of hands, all of which arose from the necessity of giving vent to his emotions in every way which was the most demonstrative. So the barbarous races of to-day are satisfied with the use of instruments of percussion—tom-toms, gongs, cymbals; and even with the civilized Chinese the favorite effects are produced by the beating of copper plates, bells, stones, or wooden tubs. Rhythmical movement as in rude dancing, accompanied with gestures expressive of war and revenge, with shouting and battle cries, all appear together among the universal practices of the earliest tribes of which we have any account; by which, however, the important fact clearly is shown that rhythm answers to some innate necessity in physical expression. The most effective and stately cadences in modern music have for their prototype the barbaric yellings and fantastic dancing of our savage ancestors. Nay, if we follow Darwin and the evolution school into their speculations upon the nebulous past of the race, we must allow that even some of the lowest forms of animal life show marked sensitiveness to musical tones. Even some crustaceans, says Darwin, possess certain auditory hairs which have been seen to vibrate when the proper musical notes are struck. All animals have their well-known peculiar cries. "The gibbon," says Darwin, "further has an extremely loud but musical voice," and he quotes Prof. Waterhouse as stating that "it appeared to me that, in ascending and descending the scale, the intervals were always exactly half-tones, and I am sure that the highest note was an exact octave to the lowest." Instances of musical instinct in animals are too numerous to call for remark.

But if the precise origin of the musical faculty is unknown, so also, as we have said, are the beginnings of what we call music. History does not go back to the time when we do not find the earliest nations in the use of rude musical instruments, and with some capacity of rude vocalization. Assyrians, Egyptians, Hindoos, the Chinese, Japanese, and especially the Hebrews, have already when we first know of them accomplished a very considerable advance over savagery in the musical art. Stringed instruments appear to have made the greatest advance among the East Indians. Of Hebrew music, grand as it undoubtedly was, even in the early temple services, we know but little, except that it was certainly antiphonal. It is claimed, however, that a very few of the ancient Hebrew chants are still sung in some of the synagogues in Europe. We have no space to go into any of these debated topics nor into the uncertain questions regarding ancient musical scales and notation, which perplex the ablest critics.

In music, as in all the arts, a consecutive historical discussion of the subject must begin with the Greeks. That the Greeks, being of Indo-European stock, were indebted to the East for the rudiments of their music is beyond question. But it was a surpassing excellence of the facile and flexible Greek mind that it transformed and amplified whatever it inherited or acquired. In Greece music was exalted, from the earliest legendary era, from the condition of a mere pastime, the accompaniment of sensuous indolence, to rank with poetry and the highest aspirations of philosophy Of this the beautiful legends of Apollo Citharædus, of Apollo and Marsyas, of Amphion, Arion, Bacchus, Orpheus and the Sirens, the latter the originals of the Melusine and Loreley of Teutonic mythology, are ample proof; and still more the fact that instruction in music from the earliest times was made a necessary part of the education of the young, becoming thus inseparable to the Greek from the experiences of daily life and the never-failing inspiration to martial and religious fervor.

Yet music among the Greeks, so far as we can discover, never attained to the dignity of an independent art, but was uniformly associated with the choral dances, with choral declamation in Greek tragedy, or with poetical recitation and rhapsodizing, and as an accompaniment only, having no significance as an art outside of these. For composition in pure tone they seem to have been deficient in faculty or interest, though it is not safe to judge by the fact merely that no specimens remain to us. The rhapsodizing consisted in the recitation of epic or lyric poems, in a monotonous chant of rising and falling tones. The accompanying music was of the kind called accented—i. e., note against syllable—which forbade the carrying of a single tone over several syllables. Such enchaining of notes to syllables was destructive to the working out of melodic ideas in tone to their full extent, and yet that melodic form existed to some degree seems a necessary inference from the variety of stringed and wind instruments in use. Prof. Neumann, in his History of Music, gives an ode of Pindar set to accented music, the genuineness of which is vouched for by Prof. Böckh. But the question must remain largely speculative.

The Romans borrowed their music, as they did their philosophy, from the Greeks, adding nothing of consequence to existing forms or to musical theory, though they advanced somewhat the development of melodic form. The temperament of the Romans was uncongenial to art-sentiment, and such as they possessed was overshadowed by the stronger motives of worldly prudence and aggressive conquest. We pass over several centuries before there emerges a school of music informed with true musical ideas and based upon a correct and satisfactory tonality. We remark, however, that Boëthius, the celebrated author of the Consolations of Philosophy, published his Institutions of Music, in which he showed a lamentable ignorance of the basis of Greek musical theory and scales, but whose misleading text-book was adopted as an authority in the English universities, and whose fundamental errors were thus perpetuated for centuries.

Two distinguished names appear during the early middle ages in connection with ecclesiastical music—St. Ambrose, Bishop of Milan (A. D. 384), and St. Gregory, or Gregory the Great, Bishop of Rome (A. D. 590). Both drew up rituals for the service of the Church, known, respectively, as the Ambrosian and Gregorian, or "Milan" and "Roman." Ambrose is said to have introduced the practice of antiphonal singing, but good authorities deny that the musical forms and systems of notation called Ambrosian and Gregorian are to be ascribed to them, and assert that these appeared long after. None of the so-called Ambrosian music now exists, though it seems certain that it was founded upon the Greek system. The tones called Gregorian are still familiar to us in Catholic and Episcopal services. If not the invention of Gregory, they are still of a remote age which can not be definitely fixed. There was this difference (of importance to the future of musical development) between the two systems: In the Ambrosian the music was accented, as among the Greeks—a note against each syllable. In the Gregorian a series of notes might be carried against one syllable. This so far relieved music from its bondage to the text, and this partial flexibility invited further experiment in free melodic invention.

The extreme of ugliness in music was reached in the subsequent organum, or system of harmony, of Hucbald. This writer allowed progression in consecutive fifths, and asserted it to be a fundamental law of harmony. Musicians will appreciate the barbarity of this. It was so offensive even to the musically educated of his own time that one writer remarks that Hucbald's organum was probably intended as a "penance for the ear," inasmuch as at this period all sensuous beauty, and therefore all musical euphony, was supposed to be a device of the evil one.

With the establishment of the ecclesiastical modes we reach the close of our first period in the evolution of music, reaching from the unknown beginnings of music to about the twelfth century. During this period we find the tonal art confined to successions of single notes, with partly developed melodic form, subordinated as an accompaniment for the voice in recitation, or in the choral odes, or in the hymnology of the early Christians, or the rituals of the Church. Music was now to enter upon a new era and achieve independence in both form and sentiment, and become an art the most completely expressive of the emotional nature. But the advance was painfully slow. From the distressing discords of Hucbald's cacophony to the rich and glowing harmonies of a Beethoven symphony was a journey from darkness into light; and that the journey should have been made is one of the marvels in the history of mental evolution.

Second Period.

Development of Harmony and Polyphony.

The renovation of music came from the peoples of northern Europe. While ecclesiastics were droning their ancient and monotonous chants, the former, exercising an unrestrained and natural tendency to free melodic and harmonic expression, had developed the volk-songs, or people's songs. These, being sung in parts for different voices, and hence called also part songs, were the fruitful origin of all the subsequent wonderful acquisitions in harmonic and polyphonic composition. These songs, in their earliest form, consisted of a melody, with accompaniment by other voices. The influence of the ecclesiastical modes is found in many, but by far the larger part are based upon a musical scale closely allied to the modern system, such as is naturally followed by the voice in free singing. So devotedly attached were the common people to their volk-songs that, in order to increase attendance upon church services, hymns were adapted to volk-song music. The primitive harmonic forms to which this music gave rise were the *faux bourdon*, or falso-bordone—i. e., the holding of a single note in the bass, a droning, like that of a bagpipe, with the performance of other parts in the upper scale; and the descant, or discantus (dis-cantus, something apart from the song), in which the parts which accompanied the principal melody were extemporized, though according to fixed rules. The leading subject, or motive, thus became known, and is still known in polyphonic composition, as the "cantus firmus," and was also styled the "tenor," from the Latin "teneo," to hold, since it was usually taken by the upper voice. The English "plain song" has the same signification. Following closely the above forms, and partly contemporary with them, were the canons and rounds, or catches. The latter were of more formal and technical construction, but were an advance, harmonically, upon the former, in that there was a simultaneous progression of all the parts, the theme being taken up successively by different voices. This was the germ of the immensely varied and differentiated music of the following centuries, for these led directly to the invention of counterpoint and fugue, through which the utmost possibilities in music were finally demonstrated and practically applied. Counterpoint, single and double, was directly an outcome of the discantus, the progression of the accompanying voices being committed to notation, instead of being left to uncertain extemporization. As counterpoint was born of the descant and motet, so fugue was born of canon and counterpoint. A fugue, as the word *fuga*, its Latin original, implies, is, as it were, a flying of the different subjects or themes after each other; these, known as subject, counter-subject, return, etc., being taken up in succession in the different parts and woven into an elaborate polyphonic movement, but subordinate to correct harmonic progression and interdependence. The fugue is the most highly evolved and complex form which music has attained or can attain, and is the final stage of polyphonic differentiation, though not final in what constitutes the highest and truest function of music—viz., artistic, melodic, and harmonic ideas, expressive of a well-defined musical thought, such as are characteristic of what we here call the third period—that of the melodic-polyphonic school.

In compositions of this second period England took a leading part, for the earliest vocal part composition yet discovered is the celebrated "Sumer is icumen in," for six voices, and assigned to the early part of the thirteenth century. John of Dunstable (about 1460) was one of many who wrought in this school. But the precedence, if such it really was, passed in the fifteenth century from England to the Netherlands. In the history of its subsequent development we find, as in the decadence of Greek music, that spontaneity of idea and expression were gradually sacrificed to intricacy of form, artificiality, and ingenious device, though we must allow that, in the long run, this artificial devising was prolific in resources for later music. We have space merely to mention the names of some of the leaders of the Netherland and Gallo-Belgic school: Franco of Cologne, Dufay, Okeghem, Josquin des Près, Adrian Willaert, Tinctoris, Orlandus Lassus, Goudimel. But it must be remembered that these were the Bachs and Beethovens of their time, and what Browning calls their "mountainous fugues" were the mines from which later musical science and art have extracted material wherewith to build the grand tone creations of our own day. Many of these masters, attracted by the great importance given to music in the service of the Catholic Church, wrought mostly in Italy. The first musical conservatory in Naples was founded by Tinctoris, and in Venice by Willaert. Lassus was a most prolific composer, a writer of independent and creative faculty, and not a few of his works hold their place in the estimation of the musical world at the present day.

Something, however, more than the mere mention of a name is due to the work and genius of the great Palestrina (1528–1594). We have noted above that it became a common practice for the composers of church music to take for the principal theme of their masses some well-known popular melody. So general was this practice that their compositions became known by the name of the song thus adapted, such as the mass of the "Armed Man," of the "Lament of the Rose," etc. Ecclesiastical music lost the worthiness of its religious office not only by this intrusion of secular song, but also by the invention of meaningless and florid *fiorituri*, which completely obscured the text of the service. A powerful opposition was provoked among the clergy. For not so valid a reason, Pope John XXII, in 1322, had objected strenuously to the use of counterpoint, the harmonies of thirds and sixths were declared too "voluptuous," and the Ionian mode (our scale of C major) was stigmatized as "lascivious." At the Council of Trent the prevailing style was condemned without reserve. Not long before this, Palestrina's music had become prominent, and to him the Council assigned the duty of preparing a new, more simple, and reverential service. This he accomplished to the satisfaction of church dignitaries and of art as well—perhaps the only instance on record where music was successfully composed to order. His Missa Papæ Marcelli, or Mass of the Pope Marcellus, his patron, was hailed with delight, and conformity to its style was made imperative upon all church composers. Palestrina excels in uniting great effectiveness, breadth, and grace of harmony to noble yet simple melodic thought. Character and individuality, which had been lost in the multiplicity of contrapuntal figures, were restored. Much of his music rises to a grandeur not surpassed by that of any subsequent composer, and the "mode Palestrina" has become established as a distinct form of musical art.

For reasons not wholly discoverable, but dependent upon fluctuations in the art-temperament of different periods among different nations, polyphonic writing ceased almost wholly in Italy, and Germany succeeded to, and has never since lost, that pre-eminence in harmonic invention and profound musical thought and culture which makes her to-day first in the massive forms of symphony and oratorio. We should rather say that it returned to the North, since it had been the Netherland school which had so long held sway in Italy. In entering upon this new phase of German art, we enter upon a period which was perfected on its polyphonic side in Bach and Händel and their illustrious successors.

Not only during this second period was music enlarged by progress in harmonic and melodic invention, through the working out of counterpoint and fugue and the allied forms of the glee and madrigal, but much more by the new methods of representation which were found for it in the Troubadour music, in oratorio, and in opera. The era of the Troubadour, and his brother of northern France, the Trouvere, forms a distinct period in musical art. The influence of their compositions differs from that of the volk-song. The latter was a spontaneous emanation from the popular instinct; the former, though free in its development, yet held closely to the requisites of form, even though wholly dedicated to the highly emotional sentiments of love, honor, and arms, and to the winning of the applause of the fairest in courtly contests, in which the universe of nature and the imagination was ransacked and exhausted for metaphors and conceits. Troubadour music, as it was thus exclusive and personal, decayed with the rise of the feudal system. The nobility and chivalry withdrew to their castles in isolated pride. Local and petty warfares and jealousies were fatal to art culture, and the protection and furtherance of musical art passed from the aristocracy to the free cities. For the permanence of art there must exist a well-organized society to foster and maintain art-sentiment. What the nobility lost, the burghers of the free cities secured. In the North the Troubadours had their brethren of song and poetry in the Minnesingers, the greatest names among whom were Wilhelm Stade, Wolfram von Eschenbach, and Walther von der Vogelweide. Both were indebted to the epoch of the tumultuous influences of the Crusades for their incentive, and to contact with Oriental poetry and fancy. But here once more spontaneity yielded to formalism. The Minnesingers gave place to the Meistersingers, and eloquence was lost in grammar. Under the pedantic technics of the schools of the Meistersingers free art was stifled. The Meistersinger was he who could compose new music to his own new poem. Should he either borrow or imitate, he was a "tone thief," and was banished in disgrace at the public competitions were he "outsung and outdone" by the commission of any one of the manifold sins against poetry and composition which the masters had invented.

Oratorio (or the germ of oratorio) dates from the sixteenth century. In 1556 San Filippo Neri engaged a distinguished musician of his time, Animuccia, to write short hymns to be performed at intervals during the discourses which Neri was accustomed to deliver in the oratory of his church. Hence the name oratorio. The hymns, in course of time, were lengthened, and the discourse itself was replaced by passages of music, or the words of the discourse were themselves adapted to music, resulting in the form of the oratorio substantially as we have it now. Concurrently with the use of sacred oratorio was that of dramatic oratorio, in which, as in our modern opera, interest is centered upon dramatic action, and music and action were accompanied with scenery and stage effects. This was simply setting the older miracle and mystery plays to music. The first of its class was Cavalieri's composition, the Representation of the Soul and the Body (1600). Dramatic oratorio passed ultimately into the *opera seria.* The perfection in oratorio was due to Germany. It was more in sympathy with German seriousness, and their advancing school of polyphonic composition was alone fitted to highly develop that form of art. The Protestant spirit gave it increasing influence and effect, and its grandest results were achieved in the Passion Music of Bach and the incomparable works of Händel.

Vincenzo Galilei, at the beginning of the seventeenth century, was one of a band of nobles and gentry who devised for music-lovers of his day that form of free musical declamation known as the recitativo. It was the era of the Renaissance, which extolled everything Grecian, and the new departure was an attempt at a revival of the Greek practice of rhapsodizing with musical accompaniment. In a line with this was Galilei's endeavor to resuscitate the ancient Pythagorean doctrine of the scales. It was an attempt to mediatize between the strictly rhythmical and oft-repeated stanzas of the volk-song and the cumbersome phrases of contrapuntal and fugal music. Such was the so-called "musica parlante," or spoken music, the direct precursor of modern opera. Two operas—The Combat of Apollo and the Serpent, and The Satyr—were represented in 1590. Caccini and Peri produced Daphne in about 1594, and Eurydice in 1600. The new style was hailed with great enthusiasm. It had a strong fascination for all classes, which the severe forms of oratorio could not possess, and it appealed both to the imagination and to history and personal experience as well. It was greatly advanced by Monteverde, who produced his Arianna and Orpheus in 1607–1608. Monteverde anticipated Gluck and Wagner in his theory that musical form should yield to textual expression, and not be allowed to disfigure it with vocal gymnastics. With the recitativo came to be interspersed in time regular melodic subjects, corresponding to the arias of our modern opera. Cardinal Mazarin introduced the new music into France, where, in the seventeenth century, Lully gave it the permanent form of the French lyrical drama. Schütz furthered its adoption into Germany. In England, Purcell was the most prolific composer of his time. In Italy, Scarlatti (1659–1725) put forth no less than one hundred and fifteen operas and invented the overture. Furthermore, the adoption of the recitativo form in shorter compositions like the cantata by Carissimi and Stradella gave wide prevalence to the new idea.

Gluck, as is well known, labored to restore opera to its original significance, as the appropriate exponent, in music, of worthy dramatic subjects, which with him were wholly classical, and he attempted to do this by dispensing with all meretricious embellishments. The valuable results of his work were largely obscured by Rossini and his successors, Donizetti, Bellini, Mercadante, and others, who aimed at florid vocalization, and overwhelmed, for a considerable period, the true aims of the operatic drama, though these were nobly sustained by the operas of Weber and in Beethoven's Fidelio. Against this flimsy school Wagner raised the standard of revolt. Upon the epics of German mythology, and by uniting, as accessories, all the arts to aid in representation, and by eschewing completely the trivialities of the Italian school, he has enriched the musical drama with creations of extraordinary range and beauty. Whether, indeed, Wagner's peculiar theory of continuous dramatic recitation, and the doing away with all sustained and fully developed melodic and choral forms, as illustrated in his later works, will command the assent of the future of musical art, is a question which sharply divides present opinion, and which it is not pertinent here to discuss.

Third Period.

The Melodic-Polyphonic School.

Bach and Händel open the third period in the history of the evolution of music. Bearing in mind our law of differentiation, of development by specialization—first of the arts from each other, giving to each an independent life and history, and then the specializations in each art—we have seen that in Greece music was subservient to recitation and the choral dances, and its form was melodic and not harmonic, so far as we can judge. Such was its history until the eleventh or twelfth century, when harmony grew up under the inspiration of the free harmonic forms of the people's songs; counterpoint and fugue succeeded. The religious and dramatic oratorio and the varied forms of opera materially enlarged the possibilities of music. At the beginning of the eighteenth century these forms were fully developed, and upon the labors of all previous composers who had wrought in these various forms the great composers of that century entered. Our third period shows the application of these forms, under the genius of masters in the art, to the highest artistic and emotional expression and sentiment, which had themselves been evolved by advance in civilization, and thereby to more just æsthetic conceptions. In Bach and Händel were focused whatever past ages had achieved for music culture, and from them the future of music received its grand impulse toward what it has since attained. They stand like two pillars at the vestibule of the temple of modern musical history. Indebted for much to their predecessors already mentioned, and also to the great organists Buxtehude, Pachelbel, Paumann, and others, yet, even as Shakespeare wrought upon history, narrative, and legend, and as Milton, with all his fervor of poetic instinct, drew from the classics his most exalted imagery, so these masters so concentrated and amplified what they received that their work bears the clearest impress of individuality.

In what we have called the melodic-polyphonic period high and worthy melodic conceptions were united with, and enforced by, rich and ample harmonic forms, through which they were intensified and illustrated. For melody is, and must ever be, the soul of music. It is what form is to the statue and painting, and proportion in architecture, or thought in poetry and oratory. With Händel was born the highest form yet attained of dramatic melody and choral effects. Bach was the musician's composer. His Well-tempered Clavichord has been said to be to the musician what the breviary is to the priest. With Haydn appears what may be called the melodic-artistic school—i. e., melody developed in pure tone form, though he was not the equal of Händel in breadth of style. But in finished melodic and in melodic-harmonic works Haydn marks an advance. He is furthermore entitled to the lasting credit of having established for all subsequent time the symphonic form, as we now have it, and thus in having delivered orchestral music from the bondage of mechanical fugal treatment, and in having thus made possible the achievements of subsequent composers. With Mozart the pure melodic art attained its most perfect and finished exposition. Mozart united to Haydn's grace of form the highest musical thought, and thereby surpassed the latter's too formal composition. Von Weber founded the romantic school, and finally in Beethoven the melodic-harmonic style received its complete development. Beethoven satisfies all the requisites of the most consummate musical art—i. e., simplicity of idea, unity in conception, and extraordinary power of tonal development and harmonic coloring.

Beethoven closed the direct line of evolution of the new school—in other words, we can clearly trace the rise of this school in Bach and Händel, and its growth up to the Beethoven period, through well-marked phases. Since Beethoven's time music has become, as we might say, diffracted, and specialized into conflicting theories and modes.

Mendelssohn and Schumann were contemporary—but Mendelssohn, with his adherence to correctness in form and harmonic rules, is not for a moment to be placed in the same school of composers who follow Schumann's subjective romantic style. Later compositions show, with a few notable exceptions—such as those of Chopin, Rubinstein, and Brahms—a tendency to break loose from all authority of form and indulge in a vague idealism which bears no good promise for a revival of sustained melodic-harmonic compositions, to which music must, however, return if it is to accomplish any definite progress. As there has arisen in these later days, in the art of painting, the school of "impressionists" who would accomplish their effects by contrasts of strong combinations in color, regardless, to a great extent, of correct drawing, so many later composers seek to produce unity of effect by strongly contrasted masses of tone with slight regard for the necessity of grouping these around some central and worthy musical thought. As Prof. Macfarren has justly said, "The development of plan or design in musical composition has been the fruition of the last two centuries, and, in spite of all dispute as to its paramount necessity, hope points to it as the everlasting standard of genuineness in art."

One reason for the divergence of schools of music since the Beethoven period may be found in the fact of the influence of his wonderful personality, working just at the time when there was a universal ferment in literature and art, led by Goethe and Schiller in Germany, and by the Romanticists, typified by Hugo and Gautier, in France. Beethoven's great art-forms thrown into the midst of this new enthusiasm were prolific in diversity, and the last and greatest result of this movement was Richard Wagner, who is a direct consequence of the working of the musical spirit of the age.

The history of the invention of musical notation, which is the sign-language of music, clearly demonstrates the operation of the evolutionary law of differentiation. It advances from rude attempts to a complete system, but through an exceedingly slow development. From what we can learn of the notation of Greek music, and that of the early middle ages, it was alphabetical—namely, letters above the words indicated the tone or intonation. Musical critics are now generally agreed that the invention of line and space notation is not to be ascribed, as it had uniformly been, to Guido of Arezzo. Hucbald, mentioned above, was likewise the originator of a peculiar space notation. In the tenth century we meet for the first time the beginning of line notation—one line only—the position of the marks relatively to the line indicating the tone to be taken. In the eleventh century three more lines were added, and through various intermediate steps, among which was the use of colored lines to indicate variety of tone, was wrought out the notation invented or at least perfected by Franco, of Cologne, which was the immediate precursor of our modern system. Not until his day do we find any indication of the respective length of notes, or division into bars. Such had not really been necessary. Great latitude was allowed in the declamatory recitation of music, and not much more was needed than indication simply for the rising and falling of the voice; but with the advent of part-singing and the movement together of several voices, length of tone had to be clearly marked. In all this the law of evolution was clearly apparent, from alphabet to space-writing, from space- to line-writing, and this progressed contemporaneously with the immense extension of the polyphonic school of composition.

Those who will compare a modern fugue with the simple note-succession of Greek and middle-age music can not fail to be impressed with the wonderful demonstration which our law of evolution receives in the practically unlimited number of tone combinations of which music has been shown to be susceptible, and which, in combination with fertility of melodic invention, has developed musical art to its present results. Concurrently with this increasing complexity in harmony, notation, and instrumentation has been the distinct operation of the correlative law of Integration; that principle of evolution whereby cosmic, biological, sociological, and art growth tend to a unity in variety, and to structural completeness. Compare the unrelated tone successions of ancient and mediæval music, having in themselves no art significance, with the modern oratorio or symphony, with their centrality of idea, though demanding all the resources of musical invention for their complete exposition. A modern musical composition is comparable to an organism—in fact, is such. The principle underlying the growth of an organism is interdependence of essential parts to the life of the whole. Thus elaborate compositions demand such a close relation in the concerted movement of different parts that no one part can be taken away without destroying the unity of presentation; and the composer of highest merit is he who can bring to his service the most varied resources, and yet subordinate the whole to the working out of his subject without giving undue prominence to special effects, a conclusion to which we were previously led from other considerations.

If music is not the first of the arts, it is yet "primus inter pares." It is pre-eminently the emotional art, and yet, for that reason, more likely to be misrepresented in its true function by a weak sentimentalism. All true lovers of music should rejoice that music and musical criticism are coming to be placed upon the same basis of legitimate, rational, and philosophical study with the other arts; that it is steadily rising in the appreciation of the public as an art, not as an amusement; and they should be thankful for that intellectual and emotional expansion of our later civilization which will enable us more and more to reap the full benefit of the highest modern musical culture.

ABSTRACT OF THE DISCUSSION.

Mr. Lawrence E. Sterner:

To music can not be attributed exclusively either a sensuous or a spiritual origin. Sensuous and spiritual music are distinct and have separate histories. Sensuous music has its embryo and development in the seed-sensuous; spiritual music in the seed-spiritual.

The development of instrumental music has been divided into the drum stage (which includes all percussion instruments), the pipe stage (which includes all wind instruments), and the lyre stage (which includes all string instruments). These correspond to the theological, metaphysical, and positive stages of the Comtist, the stone, bronze, and iron ages of the archæologist. The order of development has never varied. The drum is the only musical instrument found alone. Wherever the pipe is in use there also is the drum; wherever string instruments are found there also will be found wind and percussion instruments.

That Sebastian Bach (whose works have been termed "the musician's Bible") was the founder of the "Well-tempered Clavichord," which is our present system of scales (since proved, so far as we may know, to be scientifically correct), is a fact the weight of which should be fully impressed on all minds, as before his time no such scale was known or used, except in a very unpractical manner, and in consequence all music was limited melodically and harmonically.

Everything that was possible to the ancients was accomplished by them. Their musical perception was not so much wanting as the material (harmonic scale) with which to work.

Something of the future of music may be known by retrospection. Percussion and wind instruments, mainly used but two centuries past, have gradually given place to the delicate strings, and it is probable that in their more severe and boisterous forms they will disappear entirely and instruments of even greater delicacy than the violin come into use. As the human heart and understanding mount to greater sensitiveness and culture, the soul seeks, through the arts, to express itself with greater delicacy and refinement.

Mr. August Walther, Jr.:

I doubt whether there is any other city in the world where so much money is spent on musical instruction as in New York. Elevating as this may seem—for what is more elevating to the progressive mind than a tangible proof of the interest taken in the study and advancement of art?—a closer scrutiny of the present state of musical culture will bring us face to face with a fact not very pleasant to contemplate, namely, that our musical education is carried on in a very one-sided and superficial manner, and that the amount of money spent on it bears no comparison to the results achieved. A correct and clear insight into music can be obtained only by a correct and clear understanding of the development of music. This understanding obtained, much that seems obscure, even incomprehensible, will become elucidated. The spirit of many works which were alien to us will appear in a new, clear light; much that seemed insignificant and uninteresting will become of great importance. Unfortunately, this side of our musical education is very much neglected, hence the prevalent ignorance upon matters of the greatest importance.

Mr. Sampson's exposition of the evolution of music was excellent and very interesting, and of infinitely more value to those who wish to *understand* something about music than the incessant thumping and screeching to which our ears are treated daily. I regret that Mr. Sampson did not deliver a cycle of lectures on his subject—his *one* lecture contains sufficient material for such a cycle—for this would have enabled him to make clear much that is still obscure to the minds of some of his audience. Still, his effort must be greeted with rejoicing.

Mr. William Potts:

All we may say of the origin of music, as of language, seems to me to be pure speculation. The growth of the power of perceiving sound was so gradual that we can never get at its origin. The perception of sound still varies greatly in individuals, some perceiving no difference in tones an octave apart. In the development of the scale the science has been loaded with a large amount of unnecessary material, especially so far as vocal music is concerned. We are buried under an avalanche of notation. Music is not notation, but sound and the perception of harmonic sounds. The Tonic Sol Fa system has for the singer the advantage that it indicates a single thing by a single sign, and does not perplex the mind with unnecessary complexities of notation.

Mr. Sampson regretted that his time had been so limited that he could not even allude to some of the most important branches of the topic, such as the rise of the German chorale and Protestant church music and psalmody, the great English school of composers, the peculiarities of Mohammedan and other Eastern music, the considerable results already attained by American composers, and particularly, as bearing on the general topic most directly, the influence of temperament and environment upon the development of different national types of musical composition.

LIFE AS A FINE ART

BY

LEWIS G. JANES

AUTHOR OF A STUDY OF PRIMITIVE CHRISTIANITY, THE EVOLUTION OF MORALS, THE SCOPE AND PRINCIPLES OF THE EVOLUTION PHILOSOPHY, ETC.

COLLATERAL READINGS SUGGESTED:

Spencer's Education, Data of Ethics, and Justice; Sir John Lubbock's The Pleasures of Life; Hamerton's The Intellectual Life; Ruskin's *The Mystery of Life*, in Sesame and Lilies; Emerson's Nature, and Essays; Carlyle's Sartor Resartus; Graham's The Creed of Science; Ferdinand Papillon's Nature and Life; Hinton's Life in Nature, and Man and his Dwelling-Place; Symonds's Essays, Speculative and Suggestive; Taine's Philosophy of Art; Schurman's The Belief in God.

Faithfully yours,
Lewis G. Janes.

LIFE AS A FINE ART.*

By Lewis G. Janes.

" *The Art of Life—the greatest of all arts.*"—Thomas Carlyle.

" *The art of living rightly is like all arts: the capacity only is born with us; it must be learned, and practiced with incessant care.*—Goethe, *in Wilhelm Meister.*

Among the gems of thought which may be gathered by diligent seeking from that wonderful store-house of Hebrew tradition, the Talmud, is this wise precept of Rabbi Hillel, prophetic of the later teaching of the New Testament: "Energetically seize Life." . . . "If we cling to the letter of holy writ, all morality will be lost. Whether anything be written or not, the life decides."

"The life decides," reiterates the modern thinker, the philosophical evolutionist. The object of life is life itself—fullness of life, the free, temperate, and harmonious exercise of every natural faculty in the service of the Good, the True, and the Beautiful. This rule, made universal, should be the ideal end toward which all human activities are directed—the criterion of choice in our vocations, the mentor of our bodily appetites, the educator of conscience, the final test of the morality of actions. What a paltry query is that, whether life is worth living! Life is infinite opportunity. Its worth for us depends largely on our own volition. Our vision of the universe is tinged by the hue of our subjective limitations. What the world is for us depends upon what we are ourselves. Life is never stale, flat, and unprofitable, save as it reflects the dullness of our own torpor and our neglected opportunities. What interest, what zest there is in life for the man who is thoroughly alive—whose faculties are all alert and active, striving for the best possible attainments! How vastly suggestive and inspiring is the untried future with its limitless outlook! The haze and shadow of unsearchable mystery which encompass the span of life at either end, and recede before us as we vainly strive to pene-

* Delivered before the Ohio State University, at Columbus, March 22, 1891; before the Brooklyn Ethical Association, May 24, 1891.

trate its veil, like the mist on yon far horizon, near the ocean's outermost verge, crown the finite realm of the seen with a halo of infinite suggestion, and beckon us on to a limitless voyage of discovery.

Life is, indeed, for each individual largely what he chooses to make it. Granting the limitations of environment, of inheritance, of finite imperfection, it is within the power of each and every one of us to find in these very limitations the spur to noble endeavor, the promise of progressive attainment, the hope for that which at the instant is far beyond the reach of our finite powers. This realization of life's opportunities, I say, is within the reach of all: but whether the potency shall become achievement; whether in maturity of years the promises of earlier life shall find fulfillment; whether we shall retain the hope and zest and enthusiasm of youth, depends mainly on the character of our ideals—on the prevailing attitude of the individual soul toward life and the problems suggested by its daily experiences. In speaking of Life as a Fine Art, therefore, I aim to hold up an ideal, not impossible of realization, of what it should be; not merely to portray its present actualities, which are too often far removed from a standard of ideal excellence. We should always remember, with Mr. Spencer, that "that which the best human nature is capable of is within the reach of human nature at large."

Man, as we find him and as he is revealed to us in history, regards life in one of three possible ways, which we may roughly classify as the empirical, the scientific or legal, and the artistic or philosophical. If we would know what life really is, we must grasp its essential characteristics in each of these several stages of man's mental evolution, for, as Prof. Schurman has well remarked, "the full nature of any reality reveals itself only in the totality of its development."* Primitive man, using this term inclusively, as descriptive of a degree of culture rather than of an era of time—for there are many survivals of the earliest phase of intellectual development at the present day—primitive man is naturally imitative, lacking in originality and individuality of character, impersonal, empirical. That life, for the prehistoric ancestors of the race, was clothed in somewhat somber hues, we can well believe; yet we may easily picture its shadows too deeply by judging of their conditions of existence from our own advanced subjective standpoint. If

* The Belief in God.

their pathway was not cheered by great hopes and high ideals, neither was it darkened by our customary forebodings of future evils, real or imaginary. The day's experience was sufficient unto itself. It brought its little conventional round of joys and sorrows. Its problems were comparatively simple, and belonged to the immediate present. Each one was solved, as well as might be when it arose, on a purely empirical basis. Primitive man viewed the world by piecemeal. His sense of the causal correlation of events was undeveloped by experience. He had little comprehension of the relations between phenomena, and no conception of an underlying or indwelling unity. For him the thought of

"One God, one law, one element"

was impossible. His apprehensions of impending evils dominated his beliefs. His deities were as numerous as his fears, and his temples were rather pandemoniums than pantheons. Of natural law he had no knowledge. His morals, like his conduct in general, were based upon the egoistic data of a narrow personal experience or the authority of arbitrary mandates—the "thou shalt" and "thou shalt not" of an irresponsible, autocratic hierarchy.

As man grew in intelligence, the world gradually assumed for him a different aspect. Beneath its vast, orderly, and manifold activities, at first dimly and afterward more clearly, he apprehended the reality of the one permanent Being which is the nexus of all fleeting and transient phenomena, and whose constant methods of operation, symbolized in the steadily moving order of these phenomena, he interpreted subjectively and described as the laws of Nature. With the development of the historical sense due to a truer conception of the time-element in its relation to the life of the individual and of society, he became conscious of the dramatic tendency thus revealed in the progressive life of the world. A perception of the unity of the Kosmos—the divine order and beauty manifested in the processes of Nature—grew upon him. With the deepening consciousness of his relationship to the past of the race came co-ordinately an intenser outlook toward the future. New hopes, new desires, awakened within his mind The vague fears of impending evil, which filled the soul of primitive man with dread, developed into a calmer and more philosophic sense of awe and reverence, and lent more powerful sanctions to the mandates of conscience—a profounder insight into those uniformities of conduct which were revealed to his clearer vision in the commanding features of the Moral Law. Herein lay the germ of a wiser foresight, a true prophetic outlook, and of a more orderly and progressive individual and social life.

Scarcely can we exaggerate the importance and significance of this step in human evolution. By it, how many irrational fears of the childhood of the race were dissipated; how much larger and grander became the universe; what increase of courage and cheer entered into individual lives; how much more lively and profound became man's sense of responsibility for his actions! In the new conception of the universality and imperative nature of law lay the germs of all the sciences, of more intimate human relationships, of a deepening sense of moral obligation, of an advancing and triumphant civilization. In this and in the allied conception of an indwelling and all-comprehensive unity of force and being lay the possibilities of a new theology, spiritual, universal, monotheistic, which must of necessity become a solvent of national antipathies and a beneficent impulse toward the solidarity and brotherhood of the race.

It is easy to understand, however, that man had not yet taken his final step in intellectual progress. Implied in the new thought were certain dangers and limitations as well as inspirations. It is evident that it might become the source of an intellectual bondage scarcely less oppressive than that of the ignorant empiricism of superstition which it had measurably superseded. Man might easily picture himself in the grasp of inexorable and unmoral forces. Law might, to his spiritual nature, become a weary burden rather than an uplifting helper. His conception of the one Absolute Being would naturally retain a strong residuum of the primitive anthropomorphism, and his God would come to be regarded as the stern lawgiver, the arbitrary and unyielding autocrat of the universe. A sterile monotheism, as under the cultus of Islam, might deliver man over to the rule of an iron and unyielding fate. In philosophy a harsh realism might easily degenerate into a crude materialism, as empty of inspiration toward ideal excellence in character and achievement as it is full of the delusions of intellectual conceit. Under the unopposed and uncounteracted sway of such an intellectual impulse, life would become an habitual round of commonplaces. Religious observances would degenerate into formal conventionalisms. The sense of sin for law-violation and of the hopelessness of escape therefrom by personal effort would be unduly intensified in individual souls. Human nature, held in the grasp of inexorable law, would lose its feeling of dignity and true responsibility. Life, robbed of its natural buoyancy and spontaneity, would become a dull and spiritless routine. In the effort to escape from this bondage of legalism, old superstitions would be revived, and sweep like baleful epidemics through communities. Aspiring souls would eagerly clutch at any wild expedient which seemed to promise an escape from the bondage of legalism and fatalism to the freedom of the spirit.

To the human mind as normally constituted, two things are absolutely essential: a substratum of reality, a *pou sto*, a fulcrum for the leverage of the intellectual and moral as well as of the physical activities of man; and an ideal outlook, a belief in an infinite opportunity for improvement, which would become an incentive to hope, conquest, faith in the essential beneficence of life. The mind of man is not satisfied to rest in a fairyland of conjecture and imagination; it must seek its permanent dwelling-place in a region of solid facts and substantial realities. Neither is it willing to accept the imperfection of present attainments, however real and substantial, as a finality. It must push on to new discoveries of truth, and seek for new applications of such discoveries to the practical problems of life. Its thirst for the ideal is no less normal and imperative than its hunger for the real. Its faith is firm that—

> "There are things whose strong reality
> Outshines our fairyland; in shapes and hues
> More beautiful than our fantastic sky,
> And the strange constellations which the Muse
> O'er her wild universe is skillful to diffuse."

So the art-impulse—spontaneous, vital, creative—breaks through the guerdon of constraining legalism, and, while appropriating all that is helpful and beneficent in science and in the conception of the universality of law, emancipates this conception from its fettering limitations and restores the soul to freedom.

What I conceive to be the essential characteristics of this art-impulse will incidentally appear in the subsequent discussion. Suffice it to say, by way of preliminary definition, that it is that perfected form or mode of mental activity which arises from an approximately complete psychical adaptation to the conditions of the environment—social, intellectual, and physical—out of which it has been evolved; which, no longer conscious of meeting resistance in its efforts at intellectual apprehension, acts, as it were, spontaneously, and conceives of its own activities under the form of freedom; which appears, therefore, to the conscious individual as a self-creative impulse, not as the mechanically constrained resultant of external determinative forces. It is, nevertheless, no supernaturally intruded new creation in man's psychic nature, but a natural evolution out of previously existent modes of psychical activity, having a recognized correspondence with parallel stages of development in every field and phase of the evolutionary process. This may perhaps be rendered clear by an illustration drawn from certain familiar biological phenomena.

Before studying more in detail the characteristics of life as inspired and molded by the art-impulse, let us therefore pause a moment to note that the process of evolution which we have briefly traced in the actuating motives of human thought and endeavor is but a repetition of similar tendencies that are observable throughout all the processes of growing life. In its earlier stages, organic evolution appears to be almost wholly empirical in its method, depending upon accidental juxtapositions and variations, or those which seem accidental, for the conditions under which life is sustained and the operation of the law of natural selection—the chief factor in progressive development—is rendered possible. When more complex organisms are thus finally brought into being, the processes whereby life is preserved and organic changes are initiated involve an exercise of effort which we would naturally infer to be volitional—the strife for definite ends, the overcoming of opposing tendencies and forces, and consequent stress, wear, and pain resulting from the friction of opposition. But the processes which preserve life in highly organized beings have become relatively unconscious and automatic. The subjective accompaniment of their perfect operation is no longer a sense of painful or thwarted effort, but simply a general feeling of well-being and satisfaction. With man it is a consciousness of ability to think, to work, to grapple with the problems of life freely and without friction, sustained by an abundance of stored-up energy.

The earlier efforts of organic growth, which we have characterized as empirical, may be illustrated by the action of the simple unicellular organism when it stretches out its pseudopodia in search for nourishment, obedient to transient and accidental stimuli. The second stage, which we have denominated orderly or scientific, is represented by the action of more highly organized beings when they make repeated conscious efforts, along established lines of least resistance, to seek for and to appropriate nourishment, to initiate growth and variation, to become what they are not; to adapt themselves more perfectly, in short, to an ever-changing environment. Finally, the organism reaches its highest perfection in the production of those spontaneous and automatic impulses which, subjectively regarded, may properly be termed artistic. Such impulses appear to flow from the possession of a surplus of vital energy, and represent and attest the fullness of perfect adaptation. Their character as art-impulses clearly appears in such processes as those involved in the recrescence or renewal of mutilated or destroyed organs. Herein Nature seems to be definitely striving, by sheer excess of productive energy, to fulfill an ideal already constituted—to be working toward an end held definitely in view and prophetically outlined and prefigured. Similar, also, is the principle involved in those processes so familiar in their outcome, yet so mysterious in their rationale, whereby each seed produces an organism after its own kind, imperatively demanding and securing the desired materials in proper proportions and of suitable characters and potencies from the environing soil, air, cellular tissue, or blood-plasma.

Thus the processes of perfected life—being directed, as it were, by an imperative impulse toward an ideal end—may rightly be regarded as art-processes, and Nature in her highest moods is seen to be a divine artist and not a mere mechanical artificer. As to the true artist the technique of his work has become automatic, so it is in these processes of Nature. In all conscious artistic efforts, inner impulse commands the efforts of the artist. He works because he must—from inspiration, as we say—and not by rule or measure; and so it appears to be in these higher processes of organic life.

If we now further contemplate the nature of art, and of all really artistic work, we may be able better to understand the application of the art-principle to the ordering of human life.

The true artist does not imitate: he creates. He does not copy Nature: he studies her varying moods and aspects, he catches her finest spirit, he sees her unity and perfection and ignores her defects, thus portraying her not as she actually is in severest detail, but according to that ideal of perfection toward which she constantly strives. His work thus becomes in truth original and creative. "It is the object of art," says Taine, "to manifest the essence of things." Imitation in art should only be applied "to the relationships and mutual dependence of parts," not to the specific features of the object to be portrayed.* The artist takes the street beggar, perhaps, for his model, but into his dull eyes he puts dignity, animation, and nobility of spirit; his shock of unkempt hair grows radiant under the creative magic of his pencil, and becomes a fit crown for the noblest ideal manhood; the head is raised from its habitual attitude of stolid humiliation and given a regal pose: behold now Moses or one of the inspired prophets! So life, if we would make the most of it, should not be merely imitative, even of the loftiest examples. I am convinced that we do best honor the founder of Christianity, not by his imitation, but by participation in his spirit of original insight, spontaneity, and personal independence; by the effort nobly to live our own lives, to perfect our own personality after its kind and according to its opportunities, even as he developed and perfected his.

The true artistic life is characterized by freedom and spontaneity, not by conformity and compulsion. Its law is graven on the heart, not on tablets of stone or rolls of vellum. The artist does not work by rule and compass, but by the free hand, trained, it is true, by long and patient practice, but obedient to no necessity save that of the instant inspiration of his divine ideal. Art, therefore, does not antagonize science: it assimilates it. The hand must be trained by repeated efforts to a perfect and spontaneous control, the eye to an instinctive perception of color, perspective and the relation of parts. He who paints human figures must understand the human anatomy; but if he possesses no other talent than this scientific knowledge of the structure of the body, no skill in drawing will enable him to

* The Philosophy of Art.

produce artistic effects. Michelangelo bent night after night over the dissecting-table to obtain this accurate knowledge of the human form. How many have done likewise, and how few have become great artists! The true artist studies from life rather than from skeletons and lay-figures. He must catch the play of emotions, the change of feature, in person or in landscape; he must transfer the fleeting but characteristic quality of his subject to the canvas; if he works toward an ideal end, he must strive for an ideal beauty; he must combine qualities on his canvas or in the clay which are nowhere combined in nature, or he fails in his attempt.

So in life, it is the *beauty* of holiness, not holiness by rule and measure, that we must seek. In morality, as in artistic delineation, symmetry and spontaneity indicate the highest type of character and accomplishment. And no matter how rude the material with which we labor, if it so be that we work faithfully and intelligently, the imprisoned god or goddess shall at last step forth, obedient to the command of the master. Whatever may be man's daily occupation, his true vocation is the development of his own manhood, that so he may best serve the world. "Each one of us," says Thoreau, "is the builder of a temple called his body; nor can he get off by hammering marble instead." There is no body so misshapen, there are no features so rugged and ill-formed, that they can not be ennobled and rendered attractive by constant striving for the highest ideals in life and character; nor is any countenance so beautiful, any symmetry of form and feature so perfect, that they may not be fatally smirched and marred by sordid aims and unworthy thoughts. And what is true of the body is true in a yet deeper sense of the life and character. Profound indeed is the truth that "as a man thinketh in his heart, so is he." "Know ye not," says Carlyle, "that Thought is stronger than artillery-parks, molding the world like soft clay?"* Even so it molds the individual character, and directs its physical expression.

All truly artistic productions concentrate attention and command applause, not so much by rigid perfection of detail as by their evident unity of plan and conception. "It is the object of a work of art," says Taine, "to manifest some essential character, and to employ as a means of expression an aggregate of connected parts the relations of

* The French Revolution.

which the artist combines and modifies." And so it is in life: no life can be truly great and worthy which is not in this sense artistic. It must be steadily devoted to consistent and worthy ends, and exhibit a wise symmetry and proportion in its movements. However accurately one may follow set rules of conduct, or obey established codes of conventional ethics, if his life lacks unity, spontaneity, and nobility of purpose, it will fall short of an ideal excellence.

The true artist does not strive primarily for material reward; he desires, above all else, the intrinsic satisfaction which comes from successful accomplishment. His work, aspiring toward an ideal perfection, reaches out toward the infinite, and does not too closely note the effect of each day's effort. "Man," says Goethe, "exists . . . not for what he can accomplish, but for what can be accomplished in him." The artist's work is judged by its intrinsic quality rather than by its quantity: so character, the finished product of the life of man, is a truer measure of his worth than his achievements. "Man, symbol of eternity, imprisoned in time," says Carlyle, "it is not thy works, which are all mortal, infinitely little, and the greatest no greater than the least, but only the spirit thou workest in, that can have worth or continuance." * Many an humble life which the world, perhaps, pronounces a failure, is, from this higher standpoint, an assured and triumphant success.

True art is never parsimonious of time or materials. It keeps its ideal steadily in view, and does not too closely count the cost involved in its pursuit. The exclusive rule of science, unrestrained by ideal considerations, leads to trivial paucities and economies in life. Everything must be weighed and measured and judged by its apparent limitations. Nature and art, on the contrary, are affluent. Their resources are abundant—seemingly illimitable. They strive for fullness of life, and their apparent prodigalities turn out to be in fact the truest economies. As in sculpture the finished statue bears but a small quantitative proportion to the refuse clay and chips and discarded models which have been the necessary accompaniments of its production, so it is in life. Superficially regarded by the quantitative standards of science, activities seem vastly disproportionate to accomplishments. But the philosophical mind does not therefore idly

* Sartor Resartus.

repine, or indulge in useless compunctions and regrets over wasted time: it knows that power only comes by use; that life grows by what it gives; that no energy is wasted which adds to the store of energy, and is wisely devoted to worthy ends, however remote the ideal may seem from instant attainment.

The attempt to order human life in accordance with the principles of the Manchester school of political economy must prove a lamentable failure. Living nature will not conform to the small, egoistic parsimonies of an *a priori* logic. Futile efforts at unwise economies in the vital activities result in confining the energies to a few narrow channels, in the formation of fixed and unyielding habits, in stereotyped modes of thought and action, which are fatal to fullness of life and destructive of its highest utilities. Running in ruts, in the end, is the poorest kind of economy, for the ruts cut deep into the vital parts of our nature, and curtail life not only in its breadth and intensiveness but also in its duration.

"The modern doctrine of evolution," says John Addington Symonds, "infuses life into every matter of inquiry." * Especially in its higher implications—in philosophy, religion, and social affairs—does it come with the benediction of a new light thrown upon the obscure problems of thought and life. Hitherto, in our efforts to solve these problems, we have hardly risen above the empirical plane. A man's religious and philosophical creed, his politics, and his attitude toward social problems, have been matters of inheritance, of convention, of natural or acquired bias or predilection, or, worst of all, of a low self-interest, rather than of thoughtful reflection, study, and vital assimilation. Our professional reformers have indeed occasionally risen above empiricism to the scientific or legal plane in the treatment of these subjects. They have worked unselfishly, desiring the world's advantage; but, failing to grasp the natural laws of growth, their efforts have been largely misdirected. They formulate with mathematical exactness of plan and detail on "scientific principles," as they assert, their schemes for individual salvation and social regeneration—anarchistic, socialistic, nationalistic, or what not. They measure society and man by their little two-foot rules, and seek to fit the living organism to their Procrustean beds—how vain-

* Essays, Speculative and Suggestive.

ly, the world sorrowfully knows. Nevertheless, let us give all such honest efforts due meed of honest recognition, not judging them unfairly by their failures to accomplish definite aims. They have stimulated thought; they have created new ideals for worthy activities; they have afforded scope for altruistic efforts in their devotees; they have helped to expose the imperfections of the existing order and to concentrate efforts for its betterment. Let us be thankful for the ideal republics, the Utopias, the Icarias; for formulated creeds, whether religious or socialistic, which are better than no beliefs at all; for all these are incentives to thought and guides to altruistic endeavor. They emphasize the growing importance of social and religious problems, and stimulate wise minds to seek for their true solution. But, seeing that this world is a growing world; that the conditions we have to deal with are not statical but dynamical; that they belong, indeed, both in the individual and in society, to the department of organic dynamics rather than of inorganic—to the super-organic, indeed, involving the added factors of human self-consciousness and volition; seeing that society is no plastic mass of inert material to be molded at will, but an innumerable body of living, seething, struggling, aspiring individual units, no two of which are identical in nature more than in form or feature—the wise student of man will not anticipate the success of any of these definite plans for social regeneration. He will rightly distinguish the method of art from that of artificiality. His effort should be therefore to enrich the soil, to remove obstructions, to give free play to natural forces, to stimulate thought along evolutionary lines, and thus, by a wise opportunism, to adapt his efforts to existing conditions and make the most and the best of the forces instantly operating, without the unnecessary destruction and waste implied in radical deviations from the line of existing social tendencies. He will strive to

> "Know the seasons, when to take
> Occasion by the hand,"

and thus make his work most fruitful in beneficent results. His method, in other words, will be that of evolution instead of revolution, that of biology and sociology rather than of abstract mathematics, that of the artist and philosopher rather than of the empiricist or scientific dreamer—a method which, being practical and conforming spontaneously to the actual needs and conditions of a growing society, will be most speedily and productively effective.

A wise opportunism such as I have attempted to outline does not involve the abatement by one jot or tittle from the ideal end—the true service and betterment of man. "Art is great," says Ruskin, "in exact proportion to the love of beauty shown by the painter, provided that love of beauty forfeit no atom of truth." This is true also of that highest of all arts, the art of right living; it must forfeit no atom of truth; it must not flinch from its high ideal. Fullness of life being the end which the philosophy of evolution and the art-impulse as applied to life alike have in view, it is evident that no course of action which in its final outcome and totality of effect detracts from this end, which produces a surplus of pain rather than of pleasure, can be deemed ideally right. The surgery of revolution may at times be necessary in the social as the surgeon's knife is to the individual organism; but no plea of instant allegiance to an abstract ideal of truth and justice can justify this resort to militant methods, unless it appears with indubitable clearness that only thus can the totality of life in society be finally increased. All surgery involves an atrophy or loss of vital tissue, and is therefore to be avoided except when it becomes absolutely necessary for the salvation of the organism or the prolongation of life. The wise opportunism advocated by the social philosophy of evolution rests upon the doctrine of relativity, which holds good both in morals and in sociology, and is by no means to be confounded with the temporizing expediency of a false conservatism, which adheres to the conventional from a servile fear of change. In recognizing fullness of life in society and the individual as its true object, and in conforming its action to this end, it *is* dedicating itself to the service of ideal truth. And in declining to be led hither and thither by those attractive will-o'-the-wisps, the *a priori* schemes of social reformers, based upon alleged laws of absolute ethics, it is giving evidence at once of its wisdom and of its consistency.

Evolution preaches no gospel of dilettantism—good for the rich and prosperous, but blind to the evils of society, the struggles of the vicious and the poor. For vice and crime this philosophy has indeed no palliation, save that involved in the recognition that they are inheritances from man's brute ancestry; no easy or sovereign remedy to propose; only the slow natural process of amelioration by education, enlightenment, and the gradual transformation of unfavorable environments. But for man, however lowly, however ignorant, however debased, it bears a gospel of infinite hope and cheer.

Vice and crime shut out that infinite outlook, that *nuance* of encouragement and invitation, which is the soul of the art-feeling. To the poor, however, the perception of life as a fine art is not impossible: it is even more possible to them, perhaps, than to the very rich. These *have* their reward Around them is no divine halo of unrealized possibilities. For the poor, however, who is not also depraved, who has something of hope, something of energy, there is an illimitable outlook, a hope and promise of improvement, a trust in progress. Rags and dirt, even, are not inconsistent with this larger life; only vice and crime, which are always the miseries of choice in part, even when they are portions of the individual's inheritance. The true artist sees something of this hopeful, attractive, infinite side of poverty. He paints the hovel rather than the palace; the lusty bootblack or newsboy on the city street, or the peasant in the field or at the brookside—the humble interior with its homelike aspect, and its occupants happy in the joy of simply living—rather than the pomp of regal magnificence. Such pictures touch the heart with quite other feelings than those of despair at the hopelessness of poverty. They suggest the true comfort, the progressive up-lift, the ideal satisfaction, the real meaning of life, far more effectively than does the pictured pomp of courts or the tinsel show of riches. These portray and emphasize the circumstances as superior to the man; the former illustrate the power and habit of the human soul to triumph over its conditions. Wealth, indeed, is not to be despised or unconditionally condemned. On the contrary, it is one of the factors of our modern civilization—an essential condition of the world's spiritual and moral as well as material progress. But what I desire to emphasize is the fact that it is only a condition—a potency for good if rightly used, of inestimable evil if misused. Its value lies wholly in its use, and not at all in any inherent virtue of its own. Rightly used and equitably distributed according to the deserts of its producers, it is an indispensable factor in all efforts for the enlargement and betterment of life.

Hitherto I have treated of this artistic or evolutionary view of life as an ideal—as something to be striven for and attained But it may also be regarded as a means to this attainment. Like life itself, like the source of all life, it is at once end and method of pursuit.

> "They reckon ill who leave me out.
> When me they fly, I am the wings."

The roundabout mental activity enjoined by the art-ideal, conjoined with bodily health, intellectual seriousness, and moral earnestness, is the best of life-preservers. When the mind runs in ruts, it is steadily sowing therein the seeds of insanities and premature decay; but he who views the world at large, takes an active interest in its affairs, seeks the ethical solution of its problems of individual and social obligation, cultivates pleasurable avocations as well as a useful and honorable vocation, lifts his life out of the ruts, and preserves his faculties intact with lengthening years. How shortsighted is this prevalent tendency to empiricism in the care for the health! By abuse and carelessness we permit special ailments to develop, and then go to the physician for vicarious help. Or, if we have risen to the scientific plane of thought, if we recognize that hygiene has its laws no less imperative than the other laws of Nature, we make our life conform to an unyielding *régime*, we live by rule and measure, rise at a certain hour irrespective of our vital necessities, partake of just so many pounds of solid and liquid food, give so many hours to study, so many to rest, so many to work and recreation, and make life miserable to ourselves and others when any untoward event interferes with this mechanical routine.

Is there not yet a better way—the way of the artistic impulse; which obeys law, indeed, but not under a sense of compulsion; which seeks health not through a rigidly imposed *régime*, but naturally and freely; which avoids that mental dyspepsia—that morbid dwelling upon bodily conditions and ailments—which is a worse affliction than the pangs of physical pain? Over and above the law of routine and stated regularities of habit there is a higher law—not that of wayward, ungovernable impulse, but of healthful spontaneity and diversity—which keeps both mind and body from decay and rust. If the springs of life are sweet, its waters pure and abundant, its courses clear of contamination or obstruction, both body and mind healthfully active, with sufficient diversity of occupation, we shall find life deepening with added years—its best wine saved for the final draught.

Apart from this daily attitude toward the affairs of life—or, more correctly, as a part of it—there is no better life-preserver than an inspiring philosophy, and the consolation of a rational and satisfying religious faith. But it is necessary for us to distinguish between that mode of thought which is properly termed religious and that which is merely theological. The theological mind, resting in the scientific or legal phase of intellectual activity, would define the Infinite by verbal formulas, number and label its attributes like geological specimens, posit a clear-cut, final, and all-comprehensive creed, and make the temple of religion a sort of theological museum of venerable antiquities. A higher philosophy, however, perceives that we can not put God into the crucible of our finite thought—we can not weigh and measure the Infinite with our little rules and scales. With Spinoza, whom Novalis called "a God-intoxicated man," so profound was his sense of the indwelling Unity, it says: "To define God is to deny him." It stands in awe before the mystery and wonder of the universe. Recognizing all Nature as a revelation of the One—all truth, whether secular or sacred, in science and philosophy as well as in Scripture or in creed, as a symbol of his eternal verity, religion can place no bounds in thought to his infinite perfection. As interpreted by the art-impulse, religion becomes an attitude of the soul toward life itself rather than formal observance or dogmatic statement. It reverently recognizes behind the veil of the known, underlying the fleeting phenomena of life, a Power whose universal method is order, and whose steadily progressive order in all the processes of evolution is best symbolized in language as the index of intelligence; who, if not personal, must be super-personal rather than impersonal, since the noblest thoughts, the finest feelings, the tenderest loves which are the endowments of man's personality, spring naturally from its abounding life and maintain toward it a constant and vital relation of dependence.

Unknowable in its essential being because of the finite nature of our faculties, this Power, this Intelligence, this Super-personality, is well known in all of its relations to us, whether symbolized in the phenomena of mind or of external Nature. To the high philosophy of the art-life and of evolution, sin, suffering, and imperfection constitute the necessary background of man's progressive nature, the dark shadows against which the beautiful outlines of his noblest qualities are limned.

In the attitude of the individual soul toward the problems of life this doctrine is nothing else than a restatement in the terms of modern philosophic thought of the Christian law of liberty as opposed to Hebraic legalism.

Infinite in the variety of its manifestations, life never palls to the mind which "accepts the universe," and dwells in this higher region of philosophic thought. It recognizes with Goethe that "Nature's play is ever new, since she ever creates new spectators. Life is her finest invention, and death is her artifice to get more life." With the same great thinker, it adjures man to "live resolutely in the Whole, in the Good, and in the Beautiful"*—a trinity in unity which embodies the ideals of the Art-Spirit. Nothing so deepens and energizes the individual life as moral earnestness, conjoined with a hopeful and optimistic spirit. In the rhythmic play of all natural forces or phenomena; the alternation of day and night, of work and rest, of reflection and executive activity; the varied sequence of the seasons, the pulsing of the blood, the never-ceasing antithesis of good and evil in the soul—the awakened mind of man perceives what Curtis has well termed "the systole and diastole of the visible heart of beauty."

This, then, is the final word of counsel which the philosophy that makes of life the finest, the noblest of all the arts, has for all men, and especially for the young.

Think. Do not let your mind lie fallow. Satan finds mischief for idle minds no less than for idle hands. Think high and noble thoughts, wide-reaching and beneficent; thoughts which memory can not recall without arousing a thrill of thankfulness and satisfaction. Remember that memory is built up of daily experiences, and contains the material of future joy or pain. There is no more terrible retribution than the memory of unworthy thoughts and evil deeds. Seek, then, for the highest truths, each one for himself. Keep an open mind; do not be content to take truth at second hand. Ideas which your mind has not assimilated are stolen property; they are not truly yours. Creeds conventionally professed, formulas mechanically repeated, "ossify the organs of intelligence." Do not avoid considering the graver problems of life; regard them not

* "Im Ganzen, Guten, Schönen, resolut zu leben."

superficially, but profoundly; think through them to their solution. Do not stop short in the mire of pessimism or repose on the flowery banks of fatalism. Take in the lights as well as the shadows of the great world-picture; strive to see the necessary relation of light and shadow, the unity and harmony of the whole. So shall your thoughts, indeed, transform the world and recognize the Reality behind the pageant. As a recent writer has truly said: "We are what we are through thought; and we may reasonably infer that this is not limited to our condition, but that mind penetrates and animates all existence, forming (an) essential part of that which was, and is, and is to be." *

And again the Art-Spirit saith, *Act.* Act nobly and opportunely. Stand on the summit of your moment, and make the most of the fleeting hours. Do not be a shirk. Strive to make the world—your little world, at least—a better and happier world, a more finished and artistic picture. Do not be afraid of dirt and grime, if it so be that your straight way leads through them. View them microscopically; you will find them full of beauty. Remember that out of the blackest mire grows the white lily, *Nymphæa odorata*, symbol of purity, drawing from its murky bed the elements essential to its nourishment. If your path leads over rough places, push on. Stout hearts are born of effort. The ruggedest steeps develop manly strength. Seen in their proper perspective, as we look back along the traveled road, their harsh lines soften into harmony.

Once more the spirit of this new philosophy exhorteth us, *Be sympathetic.* It is only by sympathetic appreciation of his object that the artist can perfectly portray it. No merely intellectual comprehension of form and color and proportion will suffice. How much more is this true of life! When Confucius was questioned about true knowledge, he said: "It is to know men. When you can not serve men, how can you serve the spirits? When you do not know life, how can you know about death?" Know, then, thy brother man. Know him *by heart*, not merely through sight and intellect. Enter into his joys. Participate in his sorrows. Do not let prosperity separate you from your less fortunate fellows, nor adversity chill the fountain of your human sympathies.

* John Addington Symonds, in The Philosophy of Evolution. (Essays, Speculative and Suggestive.)

"No man liveth for himself alone." Helpfully serve others less favored than yourself, not by unwise charity but by inspiration to self-help. Give wisely of your abundance if you will, but, above all, *give yourself*. Remember that wise word of Herbert Spencer: "No one can be perfectly free till all are free; no one can be perfectly moral till all are moral; no one can be perfectly happy till all are happy." It is a noble saying of the Buddhist scripture, worthy of universal repetition: "Never will I seek private, individual salvation; never will I enter Eternal Peace alone."

The Art-Spirit also commandeth us, *Love books*. They are embodied thoughts. They bring to your mind the wisdom of the past, the companionship of master minds. Make good books your companions and friends. But choose wisely: shut the door to those which belittle life or dissipate its golden opportunities. Do not become a mere book-worm or encyclopædia of undigested facts. Be something more than a copyist of the style or thought of other men. "Read only to start your own team," Mr. Emerson said to his student friend. Good advice, if it be interpreted to mean the team of independent and original thought. If it be taken as an invitation to authorship, receive it *cum grano salis*. It is a pity to spoil a good farmer, mechanic, or doctor to make a poor hack writer. Do not live exclusively on books. Mingle also with the living world. Cultivate the *love* of learning; this, says Sir John Lubbock, "is better than learning itself."

In your reading do not neglect history; but see that it is *real* history, the true story of man upon the earth, not a mere string of dates, the annals of princes and dynasties. These are the accidents of history, not its vital incidents. Learn something of the past of the human race; for, as the works of the artist can only be truly known as they are related to his temporal environment, to the tendencies, modes, habits, religion of his time, so we can not master the nobler art of life apart from its environment; we can not know society to-day without keeping step with our father, Man, in his majestic march through the centuries. As art degenerated in the early Christian period through neglect of the living model, so will the art of life be lost if we neglect the living man—the man of to-day and the man who was the life of history.

And again the Spirit of this high philosophy saith, *Love Nature* She is our bountiful mother. But do not view her too much at close quarters. Seek for the right perspective. Cultivate that form of observation that sees more in the object looked at than its mere outlines and limitations, or the details of its structural imperfections. Apprehend the halo of the infinite which crowns and transfigures every finite object. The perception of beauty in Nature is an acquired faculty. Primitive man had it not. There is little note of it in the earlier literatures. Many even of our own time have but a vague appreciation of it. It deepens in the individual soul with the growing life. It takes the hue and color of our thought. What we see in Nature is not herself alone, but herself plus our own awakened sensibilities, moral and spiritual no less than physical and intellectual. The Persian aphorism is hardly less true of man than of Deity: "God maketh of every atom of the universe a mirror, and fronteth each with his perfect face." If the unyielding laws of Nature—the savagery and struggle of the past—her harshness and severity, oppress us; if we incline to pronounce her not only unmoral but immoral; if we see in her no promise for man, the fault is probably in our own mental deficiencies. "When the archer fails to hit the mark," says Confucius, "he turns around and looks for the cause of his failure—in himself." Nature, viewed rightly, holds up a mirror to the soul. All the imaginary pictures of the New Jerusalem, from that of the Apocalypse to those of Swedenborg or the modern spiritualist, how mechanical, how wooden they are! How infinitely inferior in beauty and attractiveness to our own abused and despised little world!

Finally the Art-Spirit counseleth us, *Love life.* Drink deep from its crystal spring. Do not fear to prize life too highly. What it lacks for you now, put into it by your own wise activities. Life has much for you by nature—by inheritance. It may be much more to you under the influence of the art-spirit. Here, if anywhere, in our perception of the infinite value of life—of human life as the final product on this earth of the long travail of Nature—we must find the rational basis of an immortal hope. That which is the supreme product of Nature's long evolutionary travail—the self-conscious individuality of a moral being—she may find means to continue beyond the boundaries of our present existence. Boundless are the possibilities of the Kosmos, which the mind of man has not fathomed: equally boundless may be our rational hope.

Art and Nature, as applied to life, are not antithetical, but supplementary. Art crowns the definite actualities of Nature with the halo of infinite hope, and this impels man to higher realizations. "The art that you say adds to Nature is an art that Nature makes." Art is a higher and a truer nature. "If you take a man as he is made by Nature," says Plato, "and compare him with another who is perfected by art, the work of Nature will always appear less beautiful, because art is more accurate than Nature."

If life seems to you an insoluble problem, cultivate this spirit of rational philosophy and high hope. View life through the artist's eyes. Put behind you the darkness of pessimism and waning hope. Let your philosophy of life be synthetic rather than analytical. Seek for the good in things evil—for the truth in creeds antagonistic. Cultivate a large charity for the thoughts of others, while firmly adhering to your own convictions of truth. Man's beliefs, too, are products of evolution—growths, not manufactures. Under all seeming antagonisms lies some germinal form of truth—as in a similar semblance of antithesis, Nature finds its most perfect manifestation in art, and liberty its complete fulfillment under law.

So in ethics: the compulsion of conscience ultimates in the freedom of the spirit; the sense of obligation is but a step toward the extinction of obligation in willing obedience. The stern mandates of the Ought are not definitive of the last and highest stage in the evolution of conduct. Duty is a school-master, whose control, doubtless, we all yet need, but only as a preparation for the higher university of life wherein natural spontaneity of right action will supersede compulsion—wherein we shall serve the right for love of the right, and find in such faithful and willing service our supremest joy.

As the wise Goethe hath said:

> Art from Nature's rudeness ever seems to fly,
>   Yet, before we think it, they are one again;
> My distrust of Nature, too, has passed away:
>   Art and Nature draw me by a single chain.
> Faithful work—this only—helps the growing life.
>   When in love we labor, serving noble Art,
> Life's horizon broadens—deepens with the strife:
>   Freely then may Nature glow within the heart.

Thus, by consecration is our culture wrought:
  Vainly unreined spirits hasten toward the goal—
  Vainly strive to conquer yon far-seeing height.
He who wills the Great must serve the stringent Ought.
  Only such obedience proves the Master-Soul:
  Law alone assures us Freedom's conquering might.

ABSTRACT OF THE DISCUSSION.

Prof. Almon G. Merwin:

Mr. Merwin said, in substance:

It need hardly be said that I heartily appreciate the fine spirit and the suggestive thought which are illustrated in the lecture of the evening. It is perhaps unfortunate that in these criticisms we make little remark of the greatness of the truth which is set forth by the speaker, while, by selecting and commenting chiefly upon those points which seem to us open to objection, we unduly magnify what appear to us to be his errors. In these remarks, therefore, I by no means wish to be understood as undervaluing the excellence of thought and the fine literary form of Dr. Janes's lecture. It seems to me, however, that in some of his phraseology, and perhaps also in some of his conclusions, he has departed from the strictly scientific mode of treatment which should characterize these discussions. He has given us poetry instead of scientific evolution. He has made frequent use of the word "infinite," for example; but what does the scientific evolutionist know about the infinite? He has said that "the art-impulse, spontaneous, vital, creative, breaks through the bondage of constraining legalism, and restores the soul to freedom." What does he mean by this "art-impulse"? Is it some higher power, some new creation, which revolutionizes the nature of man? He has spoken of this impulse as "automatic." Does this expression truly describe the higher mental activities? This is not, as I understand it, the teaching of psychological science or of evolution. The lower organisms possess a greater number of automatic or instinctive functions than does man. How can this fact be reconciled with the lecturer's theory that functions become automatic as they become more perfect? The lecturer speaks of "the ideal" as something which governs the action of the artist. This is true. But what of it? What is an ideal? Psychologically, this statement only means that the artist's work, like all other voluntary operations, exists in thought before it is realized or objectified. The man who makes a wheelbarrow first conceives of the wheelbarrow in his mind. In other words, he first creates an ideal. The artist only does the same thing. He exercises no new power; the same faculty which governs his conduct, in some degree governs that of all other men. The lecturer, it seems to me, has drawn distinctions which are not justified by a true psychology. He has given us poetry and rhetoric in the place of cold facts and scientific deductions therefrom.

Mr. William Potts:

I am not a psychologist, but it requires no knowledge of psychology to enable me to realize that there are many things in the life of man which have become automatic besides digestion and the vital functions. If we had to think out all our actions for the day, we could not possibly accomplish the work which we do. All things which we do habitually, or after long practice, become to some degree automatic; and it appears to me that Dr. Janes is right in regarding this quality as characteristic of our higher or perfected activities. The performance of the trained musician is largely automatic, and so of all high forms of artistic work. The same principle holds good in every department of our life—from the training of the infant to walk and use his hands up to the exercise of our highest mental faculties. Things which at first need to be thought out and wrought out with foresight and plodding labor, by practice become intuitive or automatic.

Dr. Janes:

I think no higher compliment can be paid to a lecturer than that of an intelligent criticism. Such a criticism I have learned always to expect from Prof. Merwin, and I thank him for it. As he proceeded, however, it appeared to me that his remarks indicated a more intimate acquaintance with text-books of systematic psychology than with works bearing upon the higher phases of the doctrine of evolution. No one who reads Spencer, for example, can fairly object to my use of the word "infinite." This great master teaches us that the apprehension of the infinite is as normal to the human mind as is our comprehension of any of the laws or phenomena of either mental or material things. It is fundamental to all our thought, the condition precedent to all other knowledge. My critic thinks there is some poetry in my essay. This I shall not deny, though I make no pretense to be a poet. But I object decidedly to the inference, "The more poetry, the less truth." Poetry is one of the modes of expressing truth. The poet sometimes arrives at truth—even scientific truth—in advance of the apostle of the scientific method; as did Goethe and our own Emerson in regard to this very doctrine of evolution. Prof. Merwin thinks that the fact that the lower organisms possess a greater number of automatic functions than man somehow discredits my theory. Not at all. This is simply the order of Nature. The lower grade of functions is first perfected—first becomes automatic. The higher are developed and perfected later. Man, though the highest of all the animals in the scale of intelligence, for that very reason has a smaller proportion of automatic functions—though absolutely his instincts are doubtless more numerous than those of the lower animals. My phraseology may doubtless at some points be open to criticism; I have aimed to give my thought popular and unconventional expression. But the essential thought I hold to be strictly in harmony with scientific truth and the doctrine of evolution. I agree with my critic that the Art-Spirit as applied to life is not the gift of a favored few: it is possible in some measure to all. But for that fact this lecture would not have been written. If Prof. Merwin will carefully read his Data of Ethics —particularly the chapter entitled The Psychological View—he will find the exact principles set forth in my lecture enunciated, as applied to man's moral development, in the wonderfully clear and convincing language of Mr. Spencer. In biology, he will find them also illustrated in the works of Cope, Powell, and other writers. I rest my case on the substantial harmony of the views set forth in this lecture with those of the masters of evolutionary thought, claiming no exclusive novelty or patent right for myself.

I thank the audience sincerely for its kind reception of my lecture.

THE DOCTRINE OF EVOLUTION

ITS SCOPE AND INFLUENCE

BY

JOHN FISKE

AUTHOR OF OUTLINES OF COSMIC PHILOSOPHY, THE IDEA OF GOD, THE DESTINY OF MAN, ETC.

COLLATERAL READINGS SUGGESTED:

Spencer's First Principles, Principles of Biology, Principles of Psychology, Principles of Sociology, Data of Ethics, and Justice; Fiske's Cosmic Philosophy, Idea of God, and Destiny of Man.

THE DOCTRINE OF EVOLUTION: ITS SCOPE AND INFLUENCE.*

By John Fiske.

If you take up almost any manual or compendium of history written before the middle of the present century, you will generally find it to be a lifeless catalogue of events, and more likely than not an undiscriminating catalogue in which important and trivial events are jumbled together in utter obliviousness of any such thing as historical perspective. Of great and admirable books of history there were indeed many by illustrious writers of ancient and modern times, in which the men, the measures, and the social features of particular epochs were portrayed with life-like reality and often illustrated and criticised with a wealth of practical wisdom. But the insight into the underlying causes and the general drift of the endlessly complicated mass of human affairs was dim and uncertain, and of the essential unity of history, the solidarity in the multifarious career of mankind, there was hardly a suspicion. Three great books in narrative form, which reached out toward a presentation of the unity of history, may be cited in illustration of the difficulty under which all such attempts necessarily labored in the absence of such broad scientific conceptions as have been gained only within recent times. Bossuet's Discourse on Universal History was a work of noble design; but, being necessarily limited by the narrow theology of the time, it could only see the vast importance of the work of the Hebrew race, and, seeing no further, could not properly estimate even this; while as for any appreciation of natural causes, its perpetual appeal to the miraculous made anything of the sort quite impossible. In Voltaire's Essay on the Manners and Morals of Nations there is a strong foreshadowing of the unity of history, but very slight practical recognition of the differences between one stage of civilization and another, and the philosophy of the book is quite too much that of a sermon on the evils of priestcraft. In the

* Address before the Brooklyn Ethical Association, May 31, 1891. Reprinted from the Popular Science Monthly, September, 1891, by permission of D. Appleton & Co. Revised by the author.

colossal work of Gibbon there is a dramatic unity of design and a sense of historical perspective that from an artistic point of view can not be praised too highly. It is, no doubt, an immortal book, one of the classics for all ages; but as an interpretation of events it goes but little way. The period of twelve hundred years which it covers was crowded with facts of decisive import for all future time which failed to arrest the author's attention. There is no consciousness that this period, which witnessed the decline and overthrow of a certain phase of political organization, was in the main a period of lusty growth and wholesome progress rather than a period of stagnation or decline. Nor, indeed, is there any explanation of the great conspicuous fact of the decline and fall of the Roman imperial organization; we are told *what* events happened, and often *how* they happened, but we are seldom made to understand *why* they happened. The grasp upon the underlying causes is extremely feeble, as one can not but feel in a moment if, after laying down Gibbon, one picks up a volume of Mommsen, or Freeman, or Sir Henry Maine.

Most of the shortcomings of the old method of historical writing resulted from the fact that the world was looked at from a statical point of view, or as if a picture of the world were a series of detached pictures of things at rest. The human race and its terrestrial habitat were tacitly assumed to have been always very much the same as at present. One age was treated much like another, and when comparisons were made it was after a manner as different from the modern comparative method as alchemy was different from chemistry. As men's studies had not yet been turned in such a direction as to enable them to appreciate the immensity of the results that are wrought by the cumulative action of minute causes, they were disposed to attach too much importance to the catastrophic and marvelous; and the agency of powerful individuals—which upon any sound theory must be regarded as of great importance—they not only magnified unduly but rendered it unintelligible when they sought to transform human heroes into demi-gods.

It thus appears that the way in which our forefathers treated history was part and parcel of the way in which they regarded the world. Whether in history or in the physical sciences, they found themselves confronted by a seemingly chaotic mass of facts with which they could deal only in a vague and groping manner and in small detached groups.

Until geology had made some headway, men had no means of knowing that the state of things upon the earth's surface was once utterly different from anything that human tradition can remember, and it was accordingly quite natural that they should suppose that things have always been about as they are. The human mind can not transcend experience. The man who has always lived in a comparatively unchanged environment will, of course, never believe in a different state of things until taught by some fresh experience. How long it was before it was brought home to men that the testimony of the unaided senses needs to be corrected by systematic observation and reasoning! From this point of view, as indeed from some others also, the revolution in astronomical theory effected by Copernicus was one of the greatest events in human history. Its philosophic consequences were profound. In teaching men the necessity of going back of superficial appearances, and subjecting their crude opinions to some kind of critical test, it was an object-lesson of unsurpassed value. Along with this abrupt shifting of man's apparent position in the universe, came the astonishing results of oceanic discovery, enlarging fourfold the dimensions of the known world and bringing the mind into contact with organic and inorganic nature in various new and unsuspected forms. Then came the Newtonian astronomy, in which a generalization from terrestrial physics was extended into the celestial spaces and quantitatively verified. There was an immense enlargement of the mental horizon, and the problems immediately connected with it were enough to occupy the attention of all the foremost mathematical minds for more than a century. It made man a denizen of the solar system as well as of his own particular planet; and in these latter days, since the law of gravitation has been extended to the sidereal heavens and spectrum analysis has begun to deal with nebulæ, there is abundant proof that properties of matter and processes with which we are familiar on this earth are to be found in some of the remotest bodies which the telescope can reach, and it is thus forcibly impressed upon us that all are parts of one stupendous whole.

This enlargement of the mental horizon, from Newton to Kirchhoff, had reference to space. A similar enlargement with reference to time was an indispensable preliminary to any correct understanding of how the world is made and what is going on in it. But, before much headway could be made in geology, it was necessary that physics and chemistry, the sciences which generalize the properties of matter, in the mass and in the molecule, should be to some extent apprehended; and it is almost startling to think how modern all this is—scarcely more than a hundred years since Priestley discovered oxygen, since it became possible to tell what goes on when you burn a log of wood on the hearth! and not so very much longer since Black discovered latent heat and gave us a clew to what happens when water freezes and melts or when it is turned into steam! It is only within fifty years that physics and chemistry have begun to assume the form of coherent bodies of scientific truth. Evidently geology could not be expected to take scientific shape until late in the eighteenth century, or to make any notable conquests before the nineteenth. But when geology did win its first great triumph, about sixty years ago, it was in some ways the most remarkable moment in the history of thought since the promulgation of the Newtonian astronomy. Newton proved that the forces which keep the planets in their orbits are not strange or supernatural forces, but just such forces as we are familiar with on this earth every moment of our lives. Geologists before Lyell had been led to the conclusion that the general aspect of the earth's surface with which we are familiar is by no means its primitive or its permanent aspect, but that there has been a succession of ages in which the relations of land and water, of mountain and plain have varied to a very considerable extent, in which soils and climates have undergone most complicated vicissitudes, and in which the earth's vegetable products and its animal populations have again and again assumed new forms while the old forms have passed away. In order to account for such wholesale changes, geologists were at first disposed to imagine violent catastrophes brought about by strange agencies—agencies which were perhaps not exactly supernatural, but in some unspecified way different from the agencies that are now at work in the visible and familiar order of Nature. But Lyell proved that the very same kind of physical processes which are now going on about us would suffice during a long period of time to produce the changes in the inorganic world which distinguish one geological period from another. Here, in Lyell's geological investigations, there was for the first time due attention paid to the immense importance of the prolonged and cumulative action of slight and unobtrusive causes. The continual dropping that wears away stones might have served as a text for the whole series of beautiful researches of which he first summed up the results in 1830. As astronomy was steadily advancing toward the proof that in the remotest abysses of space the physical forces at work are the same as terrestrial forces; so now geology, in carrying us back to enormously remote periods of time, began to teach that the forces at work have all along been the same forces that are at work now. In that early stage when the earth's crust was in process of formation, when the temperature was excessively high, there were, of course, phenomena such as can not now be witnessed here, but to find a parallel to which we must look to certain other planets—such as violent atmospheric disturbances, and such as the dissociation of chemical elements which we are accustomed to find in close combination. But since the cooling of the earth to a point at which its solid crust acquired stability, since the ancestors of the amphioxus began to swim in the seas and worms to crawl in the ground, if you could at almost any time have visited the earth, you would doubtless have found things going on at measured pace very much as at present—here and there earthquake and avalanche, fire and flood, but generally rain falling, sunshine quickening, herbage sprouting, creatures browsing, all as quiet and peaceful as a daisied field in June, without the slightest presage of the continuous series of secular changes that were gradually to transform the Carboniferous world into what was by and by to be a Jurassic world, and that again into what was after a while to be an Eocene world, and so on until the aspect of the world which we know should quietly emerge.

The influence of the new geology upon men's habits of thought and upon the drift of philosophic speculation was profound. It was proved beyond question that the world was not created in the form in which we find it to-day, but has gone through many phases of which the latter are very different in aspect from the earlier; and it was shown that, at any rate so far as the inorganic world is concerned, its changes can be much more satisfactorily explained by a refence to the ceaseless, all-pervading activity of gentle, unobtrusive causes such as we know, than by an appeal to imaginary catastrophes such as we have no means of verifying. It began to appear, also, that the facts which form the subject-matter of different departments of science are not detached and independent groups of facts, but that all are intimately related one with another, and that all may be brought under contribution in illustrating the history of cosmical events. Thus, in one way and another, about the time when Mr. Darwin set out on his memorable voyage around the world, men were beginning to arrive at a vague general conception of evolution as an orderly succession of phases of nature, in which any given phase is produced from an antecedent phase through the agency of causes which are like those now in operation, and which must therefore admit of definite scientific study and explanation.

The time had at length arrived when the facts of organic life could be brought under this general conception. As long as it was supposed that each geologic period was separated from the periods immediately before and after it by Titanic convulsions which revolutionized the face of the globe, it was possible for men to acquiesce in the supposition that these convulsions wrought an abrupt and wholesale destruction of organic life, and that the lost forms were replaced by an equally abrupt and wholesale supernatural creation of new forms at the beginning of each new period. But as people ceased to believe in the convulsions, such an explanation began to seem very improbable, and it was completely discredited by the fact that many kinds of plants and animals have persisted with little or no change during several successive periods, side by side with other kinds in which there has been extensive variation and extinction. It was further observed that between the forms of successive periods in the same geographical regions there was a manifest family likeness, indicating that the later were connected with the earlier through the ordinary bonds of physical descent. A host of facts from comparative morphology and embryology went to confirm this inference; and so, when after nearly twenty years of incubation Mr. Darwin was ready to plant the seeds of his remarkable theory, he found the soil very thoroughly prepared and fertilized in which to plant them. All that men were waiting for was the discovery of a *vera causa*. All that was wanted was to be able to point to some one agency, similar to agencies now in operation and therefore intelligible, which could be proved to be capable of making specific changes in plants and animals. Mr. Darwin's solution of the problem was so beautiful, it has become so generally accepted and so deeply interfused into all the thinking of our time, it seems now so natural and so inevitable, that we may be in danger of forgetting that the problem was really one of the most complicated and abstruse that the scientific mind has ever grappled with. Starting from the known experiences of breeders of domestic animals and cultivated plants, and duly considering the remarkable and sometimes wonderful changes that are wrought by the simple process of selection, the problem before Mr. Darwin was to detect among the multifarious phenomena of organic nature any agency capable of accomplishing what man thus accomplishes by selection. In detecting the agency of *natural selection*, working perpetually through the preservation of favored individuals and races in the struggle for existence, Mr. Darwin found the *vera causa* for which men were waiting. With infinite patience and caution he applied his method of explanation to one group of organic phenomena after another, meeting in every quarter with fresh and often unexpected verification. He had the satisfaction of living to see pretty much the whole contemporary world of zoölogists, botanists, and palæontologists pursuing the lines of investigation which he had laid down and in general agreement as to the fundamental principle. There was a general acquiescence in natural selection as an agency capable of working specific changes, while further speculation and investigation in all directions were employed in ascertaining the precise character of its work and determining the limits of its efficacy. That all the phenomena of the organic world can be accounted for by natural selection, Mr. Darwin never at any time supposed; nor was he ever so silly as to suppose that all difficulties had been removed by himself or were likely to be removed within a single generation by the collective work of the whole scientific world. The present generation has witnessed a tendency toward restricting the probable limits of the efficacy of natural selection, followed by an equally marked tendency toward enlarging them—a tendency likely to be furthered by Mr. Wallace's recent book, pointing out the great extent of variation that normally goes on within the limits of one and the same species. Such minor fluctuations in scientific theory occur in all departments of inquiry, but no one doubts the essential soundness of the Darwinian theory, and as for the doctrine of special creations which it superseded, we shall probably go back to it when we go back to stone arrow-heads and the primitive Aryan ox-cart, and not before.

It has more than once been observed that, when a new discovery in science is announced to the world, people at first scout it as ridiculous or frown upon it as impious, but afterward, when it is no longer possible to gainsay it, they suddenly find that everybody knew all about it long ago. This habit is probably due to an exaggerated regard for consistency and a failure to realize that the thoughts of men are, and ought to be, widened with the process of the suns. About the origin and history of the doctrine of evolution there is in the popular mind a great confusion of ideas; and this, as we now begin to see, is because the conception of evolution is itself something which has grown up gradually. It is an end toward which the whole momentum of scientific thought since Newton's day has been tending, yet which has been clearly and fully recognized only of late years. As regards Mr. Darwin's contribution to the general result, it admits of precise definition. The doctrine of natural selection, which Mr. Spencer afterward called "the survival of the fittest," belongs to Mr. Darwin and to Mr. Wallace as much as the differential calculus belongs to Newton and Leibnitz. The same problem was solved in the same way, first by Mr. Darwin, and then a dozen years later by Mr. Wallace in complete ignorance of what Mr. Darwin had done. "Darwinism" is the doctrine which maintains that many different forms of animal and vegetable life have a common ancestry, and which defines and describes natural selection as the chief agent in bringing about divergencies. Its distinctive feature—that which constitutes its value and its grandeur as a scientific doctrine—is the discovery and demonstration of the agency of natural selection. No one anticipated Mr. Darwin in that.

But the doctrine of natural selection is one thing, and the doctrine of evolution is quite another thing. It covers much more ground, and a good deal of it is ground with which Mr. Darwin had little or nothing to do. Vague notions of evolution were in the air long before Darwin. When Emerson speaks of the worm mounting through the various spires of form, we are sometimes told that in this and other similar remarks he anticipated Darwin. But such language is misleading. Great writers might have gone on until the present moment expressing a conviction that higher forms of life have been evolved from lower forms, but all that would have been of small avail as scientific doctrine until somebody could show how it has been done. The belief in an evolution of higher from lower organisms was held by a few eminent men of science for a great part of the century preceding Mr. Darwin's discovery. It is a belief that could not fail to be strongly suggested to minds of a certain philosophic cast as soon as the classification of plants and animals had begun to be conducted upon scientific principles. It is not for nothing that a table of classes, orders, families, genera, and species, when graphically laid out, resembles a family tree. It was not long after Linnæus that believers in some sort of a development theory, often fantastic enough, began to appear. Palæontology gave further suggestions in the same direction. When Cuvier brought palæontology into alliance with systematic zoölogy, and effected his grand classification of animals in space and time, he prepared the way most thoroughly for a theory of evolution, though he always resisted any such inference from his work. He builded better than he knew. A general belief in development, as opposed to special creations, was held by Mr. Darwin's distinguished grandfather in England, by Lamarck and Geoffroy Saint-Hilaire in France, and by Oken and Goethe in Germany. In the present age it was maintained in print by Herbert Spencer in 1852, before Darwin had published anything on the subject.

During the early part of the present century applications of the comparative method in various directions were rapidly educating the minds of the younger generation of students into a vague perception of development as something characteristic of all sorts of phenomena. The first two great triumphs of the comparative method were achieved contemporaneously in two fields of inquiry very remote from one another: the one was the work of Cuvier just mentioned, the other was the founding of the comparative philology of the Aryan languages by Franz Bopp in 1816. The work of Bopp exerted as powerful an influence throughout all the historical fields of study as Cuvier exerted in biology. The young men whose minds were receiving their formative impulses between 1825 and 1840, under the various influences of Cuvier and Saint-Hilaire, Lyell, Goethe, Bopp, and other such great leaders, began themselves to come to the foreground as leaders of thought about 1860—on the one hand, such men as Darwin, Gray, Huxley, and Wallace; on the other hand, such as Kuhn and Schleicher, Maine, Maurer, Mommsen, Freeman, and Tylor. The point of the comparative method, in whatever field it may be applied, is that it brings before us a great number of objects so nearly alike that we are bound to assume for them an origin and general history in common, while at the same time they present such differences in detail as to suggest that some have advanced further than others in the direction in which all are traveling; some, again, have been abruptly arrested, others perhaps even turned aside from the path. In the attempt to classify such phenomena, whether in the historical or in the physical sciences, the conception of development is presented to the student with irresistible force. In the case of the Aryan languages no one would think of doubting their descent from a common original; just side by side is the parallel case of one subgroup of the Aryan languages, namely, the seven Romance languages which we know to have been developed out of Latin since the Christian era. In these cases we can study the process of change resulting in forms that are more or less divergent from their originals. In one quarter a form is retained with little modification, in another it is completely blurred, as the Latin *metipsissimus* becomes *medesimo* in Italian, but *mismo* in Spanish, while in modern French there is nothing left of it but *même*. So in Sanskrit and in Lithuanian we find a most ingenious and elaborate system of conjugation and declension, which in such languages as Greek and Latin is more or less curtailed and altered, and which in English is almost completely lost. Yet in Old English there are quite enough vestiges of the system to enable us to identify it with the Lithuanian and Sanskrit.

So the student who applies the comparative method to the study of human customs and institutions is continually finding usages, beliefs, or laws existing in one part of the world that have long since ceased to exist in another part; yet where they have ceased to exist they have often left unmistakable traces of their former existence. In Australasia we find types of savagery ignorant of the bow and arrow; in aboriginal North America, a type of barbarism familiar with the art of pottery, but ignorant of domestic animals or of the use of metals; among the earliest Romans, a higher type of barbarism, familiar with iron and cattle, but ignorant of the alphabet. Along with such gradations in material culture we find associated gradations in ideas, in social structure, and in deep-seated customs. Thus, some kind of fetichism is apt to prevail in the lower stages of barbarism, and some form of polytheism in the higher stages. The units of composition in savage and barbarous societies are always the clan, the phratry, and the tribe. In the lower stages of barbarism we see such confederacies as those of the Iroquois; in the highest stage, at the dawn of civilization, we begin to find nations imperfectly formed by conquest without incorporation, like aboriginal Peru or ancient Assyria. In the lower stages we see captives tortured to death, then at a later stage sacrificed to the tutelar deities, then later on enslaved and compelled to till the soil. Through the earlier stages of culture, as in Australasia and aboriginal America, we find the marriage tie so loose and paternity so uncertain that kinship is reckoned only through the mother. But in the highest stage of barbarism, as among the earliest Greeks, Romans, and Jews, the more definite patriarchal family is developed and kinship begins to be reckoned through the father. It is only after that stage is reached that inheritance of property becomes fully developed, with the substitution of individual ownership for clan ownership, and so on to the development of testamentary succession, individual responsibility for delict and crime, and the substitution of contract for status. In all such instances, and countless others might be cited, we see the marks of an intelligible progression, a line of development which human ideas and institutions have followed. But in the most advanced societies we find numerous traces of such states of things as now exist only among savage or barbarous societies. Our own ancestors were once polytheists, with plenty of traces of fetichism. They were organized in clans, phratries, and tribes. There was a time when they used none but stone tools and weapons, when there was no private property in land, and no political structure higher than the tribe. Among the forefathers of the present civilized inhabitants of Europe are unmistakable traces of human sacrifices and of the reckoning of kinship through the mother only. When we have come to survey large groups of facts of this sort, the conclusion is irresistibly driven home to us that the more advanced societies have gone through various stages now represented here and there by less advanced societies; that there is a general path of social development, along which, owing to special circumstances, some peoples have advanced a great way, some a less way, some but a very little way; and that, by studying existing savages and barbarians, we get a valuable clew to the interpretation of prehistoric times. All these things are today commonplaces among students of history and archæology: sixty years ago they would have been scouted as idle vagaries. Yet to this change is entirely due the superior power of modern historical methods. Formerly the historian told anecdotes or discussed particular lines of policy; now he can do that as much as ever, but he can also study nation-building and discern some features of the general drift of events from the earliest to the most recent times.

If we leave the earth and its inhabitants and turn our attention to the starry heavens, we find plenty of subjects for comparison indicating that there is a general process going on, and that this process has advanced much further in some places than in others. The general process may be roughly described as concentration of cosmical matter, with dissipation of heat. Along with this go sundry attendant or derivative chemical changes. We find gaseous nebulæ; stars ranked in different classes by their colors, perhaps indicating different stages of progress toward consolidation; then planets, first huge ones, like Saturn and Jupiter, with small density, tremendous atmospherical disturbances, and probably some remains of self-luminosity; then such as Mars, Earth, and Venus, with cool, vapor-laden atmospheres and conditions favorable to organic life; then smaller, quickly cooled and solidified globes like our barren moon; then cosmic rubbish like the asteroids, and cosmic dust like the meteors. All, of course, are losing heat. Some have cooled too quickly to allow the development of life upon their surfaces; others are still too hot, but while in this stage can perhaps supply radiant heat and actinism for the support of life upon their neighbors. Obviously the gaseous nebula, being a body in an earlier stage of consolidation and containing a maximum of internal motion, is to be regarded as something like what suns and their planets were in a former stage of development.

Long before all these fruits of modern astronomical observation had been gathered, the contemplation of our sun as a consolidating and radiating body had suggested to one of the most profound thinkers that ever lived the famous nebular hypothesis as an account of the mode of development of our planetary system. The nebular hypothesis, set forth by Immanuel Kant in 1755, was the first constructive work toward a definite doctrine of evolution. The theory was restated in 1796 by Laplace, whose line of argument was very similar to Kant's. Within recent years it has received emendations and qualifications, but the fundamental conception of the nebulous mass acquiring spheroidal shape through rotation, and increasing in oblateness until at some stage in its shrinkage a portion of the equatorial surface is detached as a ring of fragments which ultimately coalesce into a satellite globe—this fundamental conception still remains as a good working hypothesis.

As we now look back over the illustrations here cited—and they are, of course, scanty enough in comparison with what might be adduced—it appears that about half a century ago the foremost minds of the world, with whatever group of phenomena they were occupied, had fallen and were more and more falling into a habit of regarding things not as having originated in the shape in which we now find them, but as having been slowly metamorphosed from some other shape through the agency of forces similar in nature to forces now at work. Whether planets, or mountains, or mollusks, or subjunctive moods, or tribal confederacies were the things studied, the scholars who studied them most deeply and most fruitfully were those who studied them as phases in a process of development. The work of such scholars has formed the strong current of thought in our time, while the work of those who did not catch these new methods has been dropped by the way and forgotten. And as we look back to Newton's time we can see that ever since then the drift of scientific thought has been setting in this direction, and with increasing steadiness and force.

Now, what does all this drift of scientific opinion during more than two centuries mean? It can, of course, have but one meaning. It means that the world *is* in a process of development, and that gradually, as advancing knowledge has enabled us to take a sufficiently wide view of the world, we have come to see that it is so. The old statical conception of a world created all at once in its present shape was the result of very narrow experience; it was entertained when we knew only an extremely small segment of the world. Now that our experience has widened, it is outgrown and set aside forever; it is replaced by the dynamical conception of a world in a perpetual process of evolution from one state into another state. This dynamical conception has come to stay with us. Our theories as to what the process of evolution is may be more or less wrong and are confessedly tentative, as scientific theories should be. But the dynamical conception, which is not the work of any one man, be he Darwin or Spencer or any one else, but the result of the cumulative experience of the last two centuries, this is a permanent acquisition. We can no more revert to the statical conception than we can turn back the sun in his course. Whatever else the philosophy of future generations may be, it must be some kind of a philosophy of evolution.

It was not strange that among the younger men whose opinions were molded between 1830 and 1840 there should have been one of organizing genius, with a mind inexhaustibly fertile in suggestions, who should undertake to elaborate a general doctrine of evolution, to embrace in one grand coherent system of generalizations all the minor generalizations which workers in different departments of science were establishing. It is this prodigious work of construction that we owe to Herbert Spencer. He is the originator and author of what we know to-day as the doctrine of evolution, the doctrine which undertakes to formulate and put into scientific shape the conception of evolution toward which scientific investigation had so long been tending. In the mind of the general public there seems to be dire confusion with regard to Mr. Spencer and his relations to evolution and to Darwinism. Sometimes, I believe, he is even supposed to be chiefly a follower and expounder of Mr. Darwin! No doubt this is because so many people mix up Darwinism with the doctrine of evolution, and have but the vaguest and haziest notions as to what it is all about. As I explained above, Mr. Darwin's great work was the discovery of natural selection and the demonstration of its agency in effecting specific changes in plants and animals; and in that work he was completely original. But plants and animals are only a part of the universe, though an important part, and with regard to universal evolution or any universal formula for evolution Darwinism had nothing to say. Such problems were beyond its scope.

The discovery of a universal formula for evolution, and the application of this formula to many diverse groups of phenomena, have been the great work of Mr. Spencer, and in this he has had no predecessor. His wealth of originality is immense, and it is unquestionable. But as the most original thinker must take his start from the general stock of ideas accumulated at his epoch, and more often than not begins by following a clew given him by somebody else, so it was with Mr. Spencer when about forty years ago he was working out his doctrine of evolution. The clew was not given him by Mr. Darwin. Darwinism was not yet born. Mr. Spencer's theory was worked out in all its parts, and many parts of it had been expounded in various published volumes and essays before the publication of The Origin of Species.

The clew which Mr. Spencer followed was given him by the great German embryologist Von Baer, and an adumbration of it may perhaps be traced back through Kaspar Friedrich Wolf to Linnæus. Hints of it may be found, too, in Goethe and in Schelling. The advance from simplicity to complexity in the development of an egg is too obvious to be overlooked by any one, and was remarked upon, I believe, by Harvey; but the analysis of what that advance consists in was a wonderfully suggestive piece of work. Von Baer's great book was published in 1829, just at the time when so many stimulating ideas were being enunciated, and its significant title was *Entwickelungsgeschichte*, or History of Evolution. It was well known that, so far as the senses can tell us, one ovum is indistinguishable from another, whether it be that of a man, a fish, or a parrot. The ovum is a structureless bit of organic matter, and in acquiring structure along with its growth in volume and mass, it proceeds through a series of differentiations, and the result is a change from homogeneity to heterogeneity. Such was Von Baer's conclusion, to which scanty justice is done by such a brief statement. As all know, his work marked an epoch in the study of embryology, for to mark the successive differentiations in the embryos of a thousand animals was to write a thousand life-histories upon correct principles.

Here it was that Mr. Spencer started. As a young man he was chiefly interested in the study of political government and in history so far as it helps the study of politics. A philosophical student of such subjects must naturally seek for a theory of evolution. If I may cite my own experience, it was largely the absorbing and overmastering passion for the study of history that first led me to study evolution in order to obtain a correct method. When one has frequent occasion to refer to the political and social *progress* of the human race, one likes to know what one is talking about. Mr. Spencer needed a theory of progress. He could see that the civilized part of mankind has undergone some change from a bestial, unsocial, perpetually fighting stage of savagery into a partially peaceful and comparatively humane and social stage, and that we may reasonably hope that the change in this direction will go on. He could see, too, that along with this change there has been a building up of tribes into nations, a division of labor, a differentiation of governmental functions, a series of changes in the relations of the individual to the community. To see so much as this is to whet one's craving for enlarged resources wherewith to study human progress. Mr. Spencer had a wide general acquaintance with botany, zoölogy, and allied studies. The question naturally occurred to him, Where do we find the process of development most completely exemplified from beginning to end, so that we can follow and exhaustively describe its consecutive phases? Obviously in the development of the ovum. There and only there do we get the whole process under our eyes from the first segmentation of the yolk to the death of the matured individual. In other groups of phenomena we can only see a small part of what is going on; they are too vast for us, as in astronomy, or too complicated, as in sociology. Elsewhere our evidences of development are more or less piecemeal and scattered, but in embryology we do get, at any rate, a connected story.

So Mr. Spencer took up Von Baer's problem and carried the solution of it much further than the great German naturalist. He showed that in the development of the ovum the change from homogeneity to heterogeneity is accompanied by a change from indefiniteness to definiteness; there are segregations of similarly differentiated units resulting in the formation of definite organs. He further showed that there is a parallel and equally important change from incoherence to coherence; along with the division of labor among the units there is an organization of labor; at first among the homogeneous units there is no subordination—to subtract one would not alter the general aspect; but at last among the heterogeneous organs there is such subordination and interdependence that to subtract any one is liable to undo the whole process and destroy the organism. In other words, integration is as much a feature of development as differentiation; the change is not simply from a structureless whole into parts, but it is from a structureless whole into an organized whole with a consensus of different functions—and that is what we call an organism. So where Von Baer said that the evolution of the chick is a change from homogeneity to heterogeneity through successive differentiations, Mr. Spencer said that the evolution of the chick is a continuous change from indefinite incoherent homogeneity to definite coherent heterogeneity through successive differentiations and integrations.

But Mr. Spencer had now done something more than

describe exhaustively the evolution of an individual organism. He had got a standard of high and low degrees of organization; and the next thing in order was to apply this standard to the whole hierarchy of animals and plants according to their classified relationships and their succession in geological time. This was done with most brilliant success. From the earliest records in the rocks the general advance in types of organization has been an advance in definiteness, coherence, and heterogeneity. The method of evolution in the life-history of the animal and vegetal kingdoms has been like the method of evolution in the life-history of the individual.

To go into the inorganic world with such a formula might seem rash. But as the growth of organization is essentially a particular kind of redistribution of matter and motion, and as redistribution of matter and motion is going on universally in the inorganic world, it is interesting to inquire whether in such simple approaches toward organization as we find there is any approach toward the characteristics of organic evolution as above described. It was easy for Mr. Spencer to show that the change from a nebula into a planetary system conforms to the definition of evolution in a way that is most striking and suggestive. But in studying the inorganic world Mr. Spencer was led to modify his formula in a way that vastly increased its scope. He came to see that the primary feature of evolution is an integration of matter and concomitant dissipation of motion. According to circumstances this process may or not be attended with extensive internal rearrangements and development of organization. The continuous internal rearrangement implied in the development of organization is possible only where there is a medium degree of mobility among the particles, a plasticity such as is secured only by those peculiar chemical combinations which make up what we call organic matter. In the inorganic world, where there is an approach to organization there is an adumbration of the law as realized in the organic world. But in the former what strikes us most is the concentration of the mass with the retention of but little internal mobility; in the latter what strikes us most is the wonderful complication of the transformations wrought by the immense amount of internal mobility retained. These transformations are to us the mark, the distinguishing feature of life.

Having thus got the nature of the differences between the

organic and inorganic worlds into a series of suggestive formulas, the next thing to be done was to inquire into the applicability of the law of evolution to the higher manifestations of vital activity—in other words, to psychical and social life. Here it was easy to point out analogies between the development of society and the development of an organism. Between a savage state of society and a civilized state it is easy to see the contrasts in complexity of life, in division of labor, in interdependence and coherence of operations and of interests. The difference resembles that between a vertebrate animal and a worm.

Such analogies are instructive, because at the bottom of the phenomena there is a certain amount of real identity. But Mr. Spencer did not stop with analogies; he pursued his problem into much deeper regions. There is one manifest distinction between a society and an organism. In the organism the conscious life, the psychical life, is not in the parts but in the whole; but in a society there is no such thing as corporate consciousness: the psychical life is all in the individual men and women. The highest development of this psychical life is the end for which the world exists. The object of social life is the highest spiritual welfare of the individual members of society. The individual human soul thus comes to be as much the center of the Spencerian world as it was the center of the world of mediæval theology; and the history of the evolution of conscious intelligence becomes a theme of surpassing interest.

This is the part of his subject which Mr. Spencer has handled in the most masterly manner. Nothing in the literature of psychology is more remarkable than the long-sustained analysis in which he starts with complicated acts of quantitative reasoning and resolves them into their elementary processes, and then goes on to simpler acts of judgment and perception, and then down to sensation, and so on resolving and resolving, until he gets down to the simple homogeneous psychical shocks or pulses in the manifold compounding and recompounding of which all mental action consists. Then, starting from that conception of life as the continuous adjustment of inner relations within the organism to outer relations in the environment—a conception of which he made such brilliant use in his Principles of Biology—he shows how the psychical life gradually becomes specialized in certain classes of adjustments or correspondences, and how the development of psychical life consists in a progressive differentiation and integration of such correspondences. Intellectual life is shown to have arisen by slow gradations, and the special interpretations of reflex action, instinct, memory, reason, emotion, and will are such as to make the Principles of Psychology indubitably the most suggestive book upon mental phenomena that was ever written.

Toward the end of the first edition of the Origin of Species, published in 1859, Mr. Darwin looked forward to a distant future when the conception of gradual development might be applied to the phenomena of intelligence. But the first edition of the Principles of Psychology, in which this was so successfully done, had already been published four years before—in 1855—so that Mr. Darwin in later editions was obliged to modify his statement and confess that, instead of looking so far forward, he had better have looked about him. I remember hearing Mr. Darwin laugh merrily over this at his own expense.

This extension of the doctrine of evolution to psychical phenomena was what made it a universal doctrine, an account of the way in which the world, as we know it, has come to be. There is no subject great or small that has not come to be affected by the doctrine, and, whether men realize it or not, there is no nook or corner in speculative science where they can get away from the sweep of Mr. Spencer's thought.

This extension of the doctrine to psychical phenomena is by many people misunderstood. The Principles of Psychology is a marvel of straightforward and lucid statement; but, from its immense reach and from the abstruseness of the subject, it is not easy reading. It requires a sustained attention such as few people can command except on subjects with which they are already familiar. Hence few people read it in comparison with the number who have somehow got it into their heads that Mr. Spencer tries to explain mind as evolved out of matter, and is therefore a materialist. How many worthy critics have been heard to object to the doctrine of evolution that you can not deduce mind from the primeval nebula, unless the germs of mind were present already! But that is just what Mr. Spencer says himself. I have heard him say it more than once, and his books contain many passages of equivalent import.* He

* See, for example, Principles of Psychology, second edition, 1870-'72, vol. ii, pp. 145-162.

never misses an opportunity for attacking the doctrine that mind can be explained as evolved from matter. But, in spite of this, a great many people suppose that the gradual evolution of mind *must* mean its evolution out of matter, and are deaf to arguments of which they do not perceive the bearing. Hence Mr. Spencer is so commonly accredited with the doctrine which he so earnestly repudiates.

But there is another reason why people are apt to suppose the doctrine of evolution to be materialistic in its implications. There are able writers who have done good service in illustrating portions of the general doctrine, and are at the same time avowed materialists. One may be a materialist, whatever his scientific theory of things; and to such a person the materialism naturally seems to be a logical consequence from the scientific theory. We have received this evening a communication from Prof. Ernst Haeckel, of Jena, in which he lays down five theses regarding the doctrine of evolution:

1. "The general doctrine appears to be already unassailably founded.

2. "Thereby every supernatural creation is completely excluded.

3. "Transformism and the theory of descent are inseparable constituent parts of the doctrine of evolution.

4. "The necessary consequence of this last conclusion is the descent of man from a series of vertebrates."

So far, very good; we are within the limits of scientific competence, where Prof. Haeckel is strong. But now, in his fifth thesis, he enters the region of metaphysics—the transcendental region, which science has no competent methods of exploring—and commits himself to a dogmatic assertion:

5 "The belief in an 'immortal soul' and in 'a personal God' are therewith" (i. e., with the four preceding statements) "completely ununitable (*vōllig unvereinbar*)."

Now, if Prof. Haeckel had contented himself with asserting that these two beliefs are not susceptible of scientific demonstration; if he had simply said that they are beliefs concerning which a scientific man, in his scientific capacity, ought to refrain from making assertions because Science knows nothing whatever about the subject—he would have occupied an impregnable position. His fifth thesis would have been as indisputable as his first four. But Prof. Haeckel does not stop here. He declares virtually that, if an evolutionist is found entertaining the beliefs in a personal God and an immortal soul, nevertheless these beliefs are not philosophically reconcilable with his scientific theory of things, but are mere remnants of an old-fashioned superstition from which he has not succeeded in freeing himself.

Here one must pause to inquire what Prof. Haeckel means by "a personal God." If he refers to the Latin conception of a God remote from the world of phenomena and manifested only through occasional interference—the conception that has until lately prevailed in the Western world since the time of St. Augustine—then we may agree with him; the practical effect of the doctrine of evolution is to abolish such a conception. But with regard to the Greek conception entertained by St. Athanasius; the conception of God as immanent in the world of phenomena and manifested in every throb of its mighty rhythmical life; the deity that Richard Hooker, prince of English churchmen, had in mind when he wrote of Natural Law that "her seat is the bosom of God and her voice the harmony of the world"—with regard to this conception the practical effect of the doctrine of evolution is not to abolish but to strengthen and confirm it. For, into whatever province of Nature we carry our researches, the more deeply we penetrate into its laws and methods of action, the more clearly do we see that all provinces of Nature are parts of an organic whole animated by a single principle of life that is infinite and eternal. I have no doubt Prof. Haeckel would not only admit this, but would scout any other view as inconsistent with the monism which he professes. But he would say that this infinite and eternal principle of life is not psychical, and therefore can not be called in any sense "a personal God." In an ultimate analysis, I suspect Prof. Haeckel's ubiquitous monistic principle would turn out to be neither more nor less than Dr. Büchner's mechanical force (*Kraft*). On the other hand, I have sought to show—in my little book The Idea of God—that the Infinite and Eternal Power that animates the universe must be psychical in its nature, that any attempt to reduce it to mechanical force must end in absurdity, and that the only kind of monism which will stand the test of an ultimate analysis is monotheism. While in the chapter on Anthropomorphic Theism, in my Cosmic Philosophy, I have taken great pains to point out the difficulties in which (as finite thinkers) we are involved when we try to conceive the Infinite and Eternal Power as psychical in His nature, I have, in the chapter on Matter and Spirit, in that same book, taken equal pains to show that we are logically compelled thus to conceive Him.

One's attitude toward such problems is likely to be determined by one's fundamental conception of psychical life. To a materialist the ultimate power is mechanical force, and psychical life is nothing but the temporary and local result of fleeting collocations of material elements in the shape of nervous systems. Into the endless circuit of transformations of molecular motion, says the materialist, there enter certain phases which we call feelings and thoughts; they are part of the circuit, they arise out of motions of material molecules, and disappear by being retransformed into such motions; hence, with the death of the organism in which such motions have been temporarily gathered into a kind of unity, all psychical activity and all personality are *ipso facto* abolished. Such is the materialistic doctrine, and such, I presume, is what Prof. Haeckel has in mind when he asserts that the belief in an immortal soul is incompatible with the doctrine of evolution. The theory commonly called that of the correlation of forces, and which might equally well or better be called the theory of the metamorphosis of motions, is indispensable to the doctrine of evolution. But for the theory that light, heat, electricity, and nerve-action are different modes of undulatory motion transformable one into another, and that similar modes of motion are liberated by the chemical processes going on within the animal or vegetal organism, Mr. Spencer's work could never have been done. That theory of correlation and transformation is now generally accepted, and is often appealed to by materialists. A century ago Cabanis said that the brain secretes thought as the liver secretes bile. If he were alive to-day, he would doubtless smile at this old form of expression as crude, and would adopt a more subtle phrase; he would say that "thought is transformed motion."

Against this interpretation I have maintained that the theory of correlation not only fails to support it, but actually overthrows it. The arguments may be found in the chapter on Matter and Spirit in my Cosmic Philosophy, published in 1874, and in the essay entitled A Crumb for the Modern Symposium, written in 1877 and reprinted in

Darwinism and other Essays.* Their purport is, that in tracing the correlation of motions into the organism through the nervous system, and out again, we are bound to get an account of each step in terms of motion. Unless we can show that every unit of motion that disappears is transformed into an exact quantitative equivalent, our theory of correlation breaks down; but when we have shown this we shall have given a complete account of the whole affair without taking any heed whatever of thought, feeling, or consciousness. In other words, these psychical activities do not enter into the circuit, but stand outside of it, as a segment of a circle may stand outside a portion of an entire circumference with which it is concentric. Motion is never transformed into thought, but only into some other form of measurable (in fact, or, at any rate, in theory measurable) motion that takes place in nerve-threads and ganglia. *It is not the thought, but the nerve-action that accompanies the thought, that is really "transformed motion."* I say that, if we are going to verify the theory of correlation, it must be done (actually or theoretically) by measurement; quantitative equivalence must be proved at every step; and hence we must not change our unit of measurement; from first to last it must be a unit of motion: if we change it for a moment, our theory of correlation that moment collapses. I say, therefore, that the theory of correlation and equivalence of forces lends no support whatever to materialism. On the contrary, its manifest implication is that psychical life can not be a mere product of temporary collocations of matter.

The argument here set forth is my own. When I first used it I had never met with it anywhere in books or conversation. Whether it has since been employed by other writers I do not know, for during the past fifteen years I have read very few books on such subjects. At all events, it is an argument for which I am ready to bear the full responsibility. Some doubt has recently been expressed whether Mr. Spencer would admit the force of this argument. It has been urged by Mr. S. H. Wilder, in two able papers published in the New York Daily Tribune, June 13 and July 4, 1890, that the use of this argument marks a radical divergence on my part from Mr. Spencer's own position.

It is true that in several passages of First Principles

* See also Excursions of an Evolutionist, 1883, pp. 274-282.

there are statements which either imply or distinctly assert that motion can be transformed into feeling and thought—e. g., "Those modes of the Unknowable which we call heat, light, chemical affinity, etc., are alike transformable into each other, and into those modes of the Unknowable which we distinguish as sensation, emotion, thought; these, in their turns, being directly or indirectly retransformable into the original shapes" (First Principles, second edition, 1867, p. 217); and again it is said "to be a necessary deduction from the law of correlation, that what exists in consciousness under the form of feeling is transformable into an equivalent of mechanical motion," etc. (First Principles, second edition, p. 558). Now, if this, as literally interpreted, be Mr. Spencer's deliberate opinion, I entirely dissent from it. To speak of quantitative equivalence between a unit of feeling and a unit of motion seems to me to be talking nonsense—to be combining terms which severally possess a meaning into a phrase which has no meaning. I am, therefore, inclined to think that the above sentences, literally interpreted, do not really convey Mr. Spencer's opinion. They appear manifestly inconsistent, moreover, with other passages in which he has taken much more pains to explain his position (e. g., Principles of Psychology, vol. i, pp. 158–161, 616–627). In the sentence from p. 558 of First Principles, Mr. Spencer appears to me to mean that the nerve-action, which is the objective concomitant of what is subjectively known as feeling, is transformable into an equivalent of mechanical motion. When he wrote that sentence perhaps he had not shaped the case quite so distinctly in his own mind as he had a few years later, when he made the more elaborate statements in the second edition of the Psychology. Though in these more elaborate statements he does not assert the doctrine I have here maintained, yet they seem consistent with it. When I was finishing the chapter on Matter and Spirit, in my room in London one afternoon in February, 1874, Mr. Spencer came in, and I read to him nearly the whole chapter, including my argument from correlation above mentioned. He expressed warm approval of the chapter, without making any specific qualifications. In the course of the chapter I had occasion to quote a passage from the Psychology (vol. i, p. 158; cf. Cosmic Philosophy, vol. ii, p. 444), in which Mr. Spencer twice inadvertently used the phrase "nervous shock" where he meant "psychical shock." As his object was to keep the psychical phenomena and their cerebral concomitants distinct in his argument, this colloquial use of the word "nervous" was liable to puzzle the reader, and give querulous critics a chance to charge Mr. Spencer with the materialistic implications which it was his express purpose to avoid. Accordingly, in my quotation I changed the word "nervous" to "psychical," using brackets and explaining my reasons. On showing all this to Mr. Spencer, he desired me to add in a foot-note that he thoroughly approved the emendation.

I mention this incident because our common, every-day speech abounds in expressions that have a materialistic flavor; and sometimes in serious writing an author's sheer intentness upon his main argument may lead him to overlook some familiar form of expression which, when thrown into a precise and formal context, will strike the reader in a very different way from what the author intended. I am inclined to explain in this way the passages in First Principles which are perhaps chiefly responsible for the charge of materialism that has so often and so wrongly been brought up against the doctrine of evolution.

As regards the theological implications of the doctrine of evolution, I have never undertaken to speak for Mr. Spencer; on such transcendental subjects it is quite enough if one speaks for one's self. It is told of Diogenes that, on listening one day to a sophistical argument against the possibility of motion, he grimly got up out of his tub and walked across the street. Whether his adversaries were convinced or not, we are not told. Probably not; it is but seldom that adversaries are convinced. So, when Prof. Haeckel declares that belief in a "personal God" and an "immortal soul" are incompatible with acceptance of the doctrine of evolution, I can only say, for myself—however much or little the personal experience may be worth—I find that the beliefs in the psychical nature of God and in the immortality of the human soul seem to harmonize infinitely better with my general system of cosmic philosophy than the negation of these beliefs. If Prof. Haeckel, or any other writer, prefers a materialistic interpretation, very well. I neither quarrel with him nor seek to convert him; but I do not agree with him. I do not pretend that my opinion on these matters is susceptible of scientific demonstration. Neither is his. I say, then, that his fifth thesis has no business in a series of scientific generalizations about the doctrine of evolution.

Far beyond the limits of what scientific methods, based

upon our brief terrestrial experience, can demonstrate, there lies on every side a region with regard to which Science can only suggest questions. As Goethe so profoundly says:

> "Willst du ins Unendliche streiten,
> Geh' nur im Endlichen nach allen Seiten." *

It is of surpassing interest that the particular generalization which has been extended into a universal formula of evolution should have been the generalization of the development of an ovum. In enlarging the sphere of life in such wise as to make the whole universe seem actuated by a single principle of life, we are introduced to regions of sublime speculation. The doctrine of evolution, which affects our thought about all things, brings before us with vividness the conception of an ever-present God—not an absentee God who once manufactured a cosmic machine capable of running itself except for a little jog or poke here and there in the shape of a special providence. The doctrine of evolution destroys the conception of the world as a machine. It makes God our constant refuge and support, and Nature his true revelation; and when all its religious implications shall have been set forth, it will be seen to be the most potent ally that Christianity has ever had in elevating mankind.

* [" If thou wouldst press into the infinite, go but to all parts of the finite."]

ABSTRACT OF THE DISCUSSION.

Mr. Starr Hoyt Nichols:

In opening the discussion of the able lecture of Prof. Fiske, permit me to express the great delight with which I have listened to his clear and cogent exposition of the principles of the evolutionary philosophy, and of the triumph of those principles, now thoroughly assured, within a marvelously brief space of time. No intelligent person, I think, now doubts the facts upon which the doctrine of evolution is based in the physical world and in biology. No one doubts that the world has had a natural beginning; has been evolved out of pre-existing material by the action of laws that are still operating; that it has reached its present state of relative perfection by the operation of similar natural laws; that in a like manner all forms of vegetable and animal life have come into being, have developed and differentiated into diverse species, obedient to discovered and discoverable laws. Few doubt at the present day that man has had a similar natural origin and life-history. It is only when we come to discuss the origin and history of the mind that we find doubters—whose doubts, it appears to me, are not solved by the introduction of the philosophical theory of the unknowable. We should not forget that the doctrine of evolution is itself in process of evolution. We have yet much to learn about it, to discover many new applications of its principles. So wonderful has been our progress in knowledge, following this clew which Darwin and others have placed in our hands, that it seems to me imprudent to say of any of the problems which reason proposes to the human mind: "Their answer is insolvable; they belong to the realm of the unknowable." Herein, perhaps, I should differ with Mr. Spencer, and with the lecturer of the evening, whose works I have read with much profit and delight.

Dr. Robert G. Eccles:

I do not agree with the last speaker in his expectation that we can ever get along without the unknowable. The expression of such an expectation seems to me to be an evidence of a failure to comprehend the philosophic basis on which the doctrine rests. As long as the human mind is finite, as its attributes are limited, real existence, external to itself, must forever be unknowable in its essential character. It can only be known symbolically, as conditioned by the limitation of our knowing faculties. It is impossible to conceive mind as evolved from any mode of motion. Motion can only beget motion; it is not transformable into thought. The psychic force must exist fundamentally, coextensive with what we term matter. It can not be conceived that at any particular stage of material evolution mind steps in. The two are obverse sides of one unknowable reality. For every motion there must be a corresponding psychical process. The two can not be divorced. The unknowable and the knowable are each infinite and parallel aspects of the universal life.

MR. THADDEUS B. WAKEMAN (condensed):

We all wish to express in words the hearty applause which closed this admirable lecture. It is one of the author's happiest descriptions of the origin and progress of the great modern rising of human thought which we name in the now sacred word *Evolution.*

For two thirds of this lecture, hearty thanks! For the latter third, thanks—with leave to dissent from the agnostic position taken as to the consciousness, mind, soul, etc. Such dissent would surely come from all phases of the positive and monistic schools of thought, and it deserves earnest attention.

The lecturer quoted some words from Goethe, but the words from that great monist which his lecture recalled to me were those of the grand confession in Faust:

"Nun ist die Luft von solchem *Spuk* so voll,"
[Now fills the air so many a haunting spook,]

and ending:

"Wenn Geister spuken, Geh' er seinen Gang."
[When ghosts spook, let man go straight on his way.]

Now, the trouble is that our distinguished lecturer, instead of following this sound advice of Goethe and getting us clearly out of the old spookdom, has left the air as black as night with it. Certainly the best use that can be made of ten minutes now is to indicate, if possible, some way out of this night of the "unknowable" into the clearer day of "reason's brightness."

Fortunately, our lecturer has just dropped the clew to guide our way out in those other precious monistic lines from Goethe's *Sprüche,* which he and we can never quote too often:

"Willst du ins Unendliche streiten?
Geh' nur im Endlichen nach allen Seiten."
[Into the infinite wouldst thou stride?
Go into the finite *only* on every side.]

These lines give no quarter to agnosticism. They are the essence of monistic positivism. They say that the infinite world is but the continuation of the knowable correlations of the finite, and that there is no conceivable way out of that unending circle of "eternal brazen laws" of cause and effect; that there is no "thing in itself," or outside itself, but that every transaction is a fact and a reality all the way and forever! Prof. Haeckel in his letter read here to-night says that such is the verdict of evolution.

Our agnostic friends seem unable or unwilling to have this great "mystery" of the nature of mind explained. They keep telling us that if feeling is not a space-motion-force correlate it must be some indescribable kind of power, entity, or spook. But the monist says: No; it is not such at all, but simply the fact-side of nervous changes noted by the organism. The continued repetition of such notation is a process, called awareness, feeling, consciousness, etc. This new fact of awareness is simply the time correlation of the mechanical and chemical force correlations, for facts are only measurable in and by time, by which some of them are distinguished from others. This fact of awareness of the changes in and about the nervous system is simply feeling-time, for time at bottom is only feeling. That is the fact made by one change contrasted with others, as before, after, or together with them. The comparative easiness of repeated processes gives rise to memory and forms, which are the foundations of intellectual life, and finally reason and the whole data of psychology result. But all these facts of feeling are simply the event-side of the nerve-changes, and no mystery unless we wish to make them so. If we are simply scientists we may be positivists or monists, but not materialists, or atheists, or agnostics, or spookists. If we bottom on the *fact*, as Goethe says in the opening of Faust (line 880), not on the *Word*, or the *Thought*, or the *Power*, but the *Fact*, we shall have a sure bottom to our mental and all other philosophy.

We have banished the spook from every other of the sciences. Now let us get it out of our own heads; that is to say, out of the science of modern psychology.

This subjective time-process-correlation will sustain Religion, God, The Christ, Immortality, and Ethics far better than the old illusions. How, I have said in the Haeckel lecture, and need not repeat. But also remember that Prof. Haeckel in his letter read to-night only refers to the nothingness of the old spook forms of a "personal God and immortality" as wholly incompatible with evolution. The modern monistic scientific realities, which underlie and make true those fundamental words of all religion, he would doubtless assert and defend as bravely as any one in proper time and place.

We must learn, however, to courageously translate the old entical and illusory into the new and scientific conceptions of the soul. "There is no wisdom save in Truth."

Dr. Lewis G. Janes:

In listening to remarks like those of Mr. Wakeman, and especially in reading the letter of Prof. Haeckel, it is strongly impressed upon me that one may be admirably qualified to discuss the physical and biological processes involved in the doctrine of evolution, and yet, by reason of want of training in the science of psychology, may wholly fail to grasp the logic of its higher problems. The question of the nature of knowledge is fundamentally one of psychology. Is the human mind unlimited in its scope and powers, or are its functions conditioned by inherent limitations? Is thought identical with things, or are mental and physical processes essentially disparate? Mental science re-enforces the teachings of common sense by assuring us that our human faculties are finite and limited; that the external reality is not directly presented in the mind, but symbolically represented. Such is the necessary inference from the facts involved in the process of mental evolution—such the only logical and scientific conclusion from the study of the nature of sense-perception and knowledge. It follows, therefore, by an inexorable logic, that we know the universe only as it is related to our finite faculties. Our knowledge of the world is conditioned by our psychical nature and its limitations. Both matter and mind are thus known to us as symbols—as phenomena of an unknowable reality of the existence of which we are assured by a fundamental necessity of thought. The conception of this reality constitutes the only logical basis of philosophical Monism. consistent with the concepts and facts of psychological science. The symbols are knowable, whether they be mental or physical. Mr. Wakeman erroneously assumes that the agnostic regards mind as unknowable. There is no "mystery" in regard to the nature of mind which is not equally affirmable of the nature of matter. The reality underlying both is unknowable in its essential nature; as phenomenal processes both are equally knowable. This is the Spencerian doctrine of the unknowable, so often and needlessly befogged and misunderstood. This is what is meant by the relativity of our knowledge. Another necessity of thought compels the belief that this supreme reality, the nature of which transcends our finite capacity of comprehension, must be infinitely greater and not less than our human personality. It can not be material in its nature, since matter is subordinate to our finite mental faculties. It must be not only supermaterial but superpersonal—a mode of being which, as Mr. Spencer declares, "transcends human personality as much as that transcends a plant's functions." These convictions are forced upon us by logical necessities of thought. They are the common property of all who have completely thought out the problems involved in this discussion. Their inference from the admitted facts of psychological science follows by an inexorable law. The philosophy of evolution as expounded by Mr. Spencer and Mr. Fiske can have no quarrel with dogmatic materialism, or the *soi-disant* objective monism of our friend Wakemau, since they can not meet upon a mutual plane of thought. The one rests on the proved and admitted facts of psychological science as interpreted by strictly logical inferences. The other ignores both the facts and the logic, making its ultimate appeal to the crude, uncorrected data of immediate sense-impressions. If any one can derive any consistent and rational idea from Mr. Wakeman's talk about "feeling-time," and feeling being "the fact- or event-side of nervous changes"—as if these changes were not themselves "facts" or "events"—he is more fortunate than myself. Our friend should take his own advice and "bottom on *fact*"—not on "words, words, words," which have a learned sound, but convey no intelligible meaning.

MR. S. H. WILDER:

May I be permitted to ask a question?

THE PRESIDENT:

Certainly; you may ask the lecturer any question you desire—only please state it briefly.

MR. WILDER (to Mr. Fiske):

Is not the doctrine of the passages which you have quoted from First Principles, and which you have stated to be, if literally interpreted, "untrue, and, in fact, nonsense," the doctrine taught by Mr. Spencer throughout two thirds of that book, and which you have denominated materialism?

MR. FISKE:

There may doubtless be other passages besides those which I have quoted which, literally interpreted, would imply materialistic ideas. For reasons which I have already given, however, I do not think that these passages, so interpreted, express Mr. Spencer's matured opinion. When he wrote these passages he probably had not thought out the questions involved as thoroughly as he did subsequently, and, using language in a somewhat free and popular way, he did not see what inferences might be drawn from such modes of expression.

MR. WILDER:

If you remove these passages, based as they are on the doctrine of the persistence of force, or change their phraseology, what becomes of Mr. Spencer's system of philosophy?

MR. FISKE:

I think the synthetic philosophy would thereby be strengthened and, in fact, rendered impregnable by removing its only vulnerable feature.

LETTER FROM HERBERT SPENCER.

Besides the letter from Prof. Haeckel, the substance of which is quoted in Prof. Fiske's lecture, the following, from Mr. Spencer, was read by the President:

LONDON, N. W., *May* 4, 1891.

DEAR DR. JANES: In old times persecuting priesthoods were content if a so-called heretic would recant and say he agreed with them. Whether he did at heart accept their belief was a matter of indifference so long as he outwardly conformed and professed the belief. These tactics have in our days been inverted. Defenders of the established creed, no longer able now to produce apparent agreement by force, exaggerate as much as they can the disagreement, so as to make their antagonists hateful. Persistently ascribing to them views they do not hold, they thus furnish themselves with weapons of offense; and they find the weapons so convenient and effective that no proof that they are false weapons will make them desist from using them.

I have had to rebut the charge of materialism times too numerous to remember, and I have now given the matter up. It is impossible to give more emphatic denial or assign more conclusive proof than I have repeatedly done, as you know. My antagonists must continue to vilify me as they please; I can not prevent them. Practically they say: "It is convenient to us to call you a materialist, and you shall be a materialist whether you like it or not."

In my earlier days I constantly made the foolish supposition that conclusive proofs would change beliefs. But experience has long since dissipated my faith in men's rationality.

Sincerely yours,

HERBERT SPENCER.

INDEX.

INDEX.

Herbert Spencer's Synthetic Philosophy.

(1.)—FIRST PRINCIPLES.

Part I. The Unknowable. | Part II. The Knowable.

1 vol., 12mo, $2.00.

(2.)—THE PRINCIPLES OF BIOLOGY.

Vol. I.

Part I. The Data of Biology.
" II. The Inductions of Biology.
" III. The Evolution of Life.

Vol. II.

Part IV. Morphological Development.
" V. Physiological Development.
" VI. Laws of Multiplication.

2 vols., 12mo, $4.00.

(3.)—THE PRINCIPLES OF PSYCHOLOGY.

Vol. I.

Part I. The Data of Psychology.
" II. The Inductions of Psychology
" III. General Synthesis.
" IV. Special Synthesis.

Vol. II.

Part V. Physical Synthesis.
" VI. Special Analysis.
" VII. General Analysis.
" VIII. Corollaries.

2 vols., 12mo, $4.00.

(4.)—THE PRINCIPLES OF SOCIOLOGY.

Vol. I. $2.00.

Part I. The Data of Sociology.
" II. The Inductions of Sociology.
" III. The Domestic Relations.

Vol. II. $2.00.

Part IV. Ceremonial Institutions.
" V. Political Institutions.
" VI. Ecclesiastical Institutions.

Vol. III. (Parts VII and VIII.) (*In preparation.*)

(5.)—THE PRINCIPLES OF MORALITY.

Vol. I.

Part I. The Data of Ethics.......$1.25
Cheap edition, paper..... 50
" II. The Inductions of Ethics. (*In preparation.*)
" III. The Ethics of Individual Life. (*In preparation.*)

Part IV. The Ethics of Social Life: Justice..................$ 1.25
" V. The Ethics of Social Life: Negative Beneficence. (*In preparation.*)
" VI. The Ethics of Social Life: Positive Beneficence. (*In preparation.*)

Vol. II. (*In preparation.*)

New York: D. APPLETON & CO., 1, 3, & 5 Bond Street.

ERNST HAECKEL'S WORKS.

THE HISTORY OF CREATION; OR, THE DEVELOPMENT OF THE EARTH AND ITS INHABITANTS BY THE ACTION OF NATURAL CAUSES. A Popular Exposition of the Doctrine of Evolution in general, and of that of Darwin, Goethe, and Lamarck in particular. From the German of ERNST HAECKEL, Professor in the University of Jena. The translation revised by Professor E. Ray Lankester, M. A., F. R. S., Fellow of Exeter College, Oxford. Illustrated with Lithographic Plates. In two vols., 12mo. Cloth, $5.00.

THE EVOLUTION OF MAN. A Popular Exposition of the Principal Points of Human Ontogeny and Phylogeny. From the German of ERNST HAECKEL, Professor in the University of Jena, author of "The History of Creation," etc. With numerous Illustrations. In two vols., 12mo. Cloth. Price, $5.00.

"In this excellent translation of Professor Haeckel's work, the English reader has access to the latest doctrines of the Continental school of evolution, in its application to the history of man. It is in Germany, beyond any other European country, that the impulse given by Darwin twenty years ago to the theory of evolution has influenced the whole tenor of philosophical opinion. There may be, and are, differences in the degree to which the doctrine may be held capable of extension into the domain of mind and morals; but there is no denying, in scientific circles at least, that as regards the physical history of organic nature much has been done toward making good a continuous scheme of being."—*London Saturday Review.*

FREEDOM IN SCIENCE AND TEACHING. From the German of ERNST HAECKEL. With a Prefatory Note by T. H. HUXLEY, F. R. S. 12mo. $1.00.

New York: D. APPLETON & CO., 1, 3, & 5 Bond Street.

www.ingramcontent.com/pod-product-compliance
Lightning Source LLC
Chambersburg PA
CBHW021841290326
41932CB00064B/346

* 9 7 8 3 7 4 4 6 7 5 4 5 1 *